UNITED
STATES
DIPLOMACY
IN
CHINA,
1844-60

UNITED

STATES

DIPLOMACY

IN

CHINA,

1844-60

By Te-kong Tong

UNIVERSITY OF WASHINGTON PRESS   SEATTLE   1964

The map on page 152 is copied from John K. Fairbank's *Trade and Diplomacy on the China Coast* (Harvard University Press, 1951).

This book is dedicated to the memory of
AUSTIN P. EVANS (1883-1962)

PREFACE

SINO-AMERICAN diplomatic relations during the sixteen-year period beginning with the signing of the Treaty of Wanghia and ending with Commissioner John E. Ward's resignation in 1860 laid the foundation for future relationships between the two countries, yet this period has never received the exhaustive treatment that it merits. The mission of Caleb Cushing and the signing of the Treaty of Wanghia at the beginning of this era have been studied in detail by a number of scholars, but the subsequent relations between the United States and China have not hitherto been fully explored by historians. Many writers, both Western and Chinese, have briefly covered the events between 1844 and 1860 in their general studies of American diplomacy in the East or of China's diplomatic relations with the West. Though some of their books are excellent, they need to be revised in the light of recently discovered source materials. Moreover, the events that occurred during the Sino-American diplomatic relations of this period usually have been studied as a series of sporadic and independent incidents. Few historians have showed an interest in establishing a general trend in the formulation of foreign policy on either the Chinese or the American side. In other words, the sequence of history, to borrow a term from Henry Adams, has been generally neglected.

I have based the present study of this neglected period primarily upon official materials released by the Chinese and American governments, but I have also explored the published English and French diplomatic documents and the personal papers of numerous American statesmen, diplomats, merchants, missionaries, naval officers, and other contemporary observers. I have tried to view the history of this period not as a chronology of successive, isolated historical events but as the gradual, hesitant evolution of a basic pattern in Sino-American diplomacy. Unfortunately the comprehensiveness of my analysis has been limited by my inability to consult the masses of documents and private papers preserved by public and private owners in mainland China, for these sources, which are not available at present, may well shed new light on the whole problem. However, using the materials now available to me, I have tried to show the importance of a neglected era in Chinese-American diplomatic history.

TE-KONG TONG

Columbia University

ACKNOWLEDGMENTS

NEARLY ten years of preparation have finally brought this study to book form. In recalling those years, I feel most indebted to a beloved teacher, Dr. Austin P. Evans (1883-1962), formerly head of the History Department of Columbia University, to whose memory this book is dedicated. His guidance and help have enabled me to essay a language other than my mother tongue. Dr. Evans' moral guidance, which reflected not only the best part of the Christian tradition but also the teachings of Confucius, has influenced me far beyond the academic field. It will certainly remain with me throughout my life.

By their unusual scholarship as outstanding historians and their personal encouragement to me as teachers, Professors John A. Krout, Henry F. Graff, Henry Steel Commager, Allan Nevins, Richard B. Morris, William E. Leuchtenburg, and David Donald, presently or formerly of Columbia University, have disciplined me in the field of American history. But it was Professor Donald who actually guided my research and helped bring the manuscript to the present stage.

Professor C. Martin Wilbur, Director of the East Asian Institute at Columbia, and Professor Kuo Ting-yee, Director of the Institute of Modern History, Academia Sinica, both of whom had directed my scholarly work in earlier years, continued their help in the present work.

My deep appreciation goes also to Professor Earl Swisher of Colorado University, Professor John King Fairbank of Harvard, and Professor James W. Morley, my colleague in the East Asian Institute. All have read the whole manuscript or a part of it before publication and offered invaluable suggestions. The personal encouragement and help extended to me by Professor Karl A. Wittfogel and Professor

George E. Taylor of the Far Eastern and Russian Institute of the University of Washington, and by Professor Franklin L. Ho and Mr. Mark L. Peisch, formerly Foreign Student Adviser and now Director of Admissions, both at Columbia, have been indispensable.

Mrs. Ruth Ricard, Mrs. Marjorie Roberts, and Mrs. Jane Vos have all helped in editing or typing the manuscript. The Columbia University Libraries under the direction of Dr. Richard H. Logsdon, particularly the East Asian Library under the direction of Mr. Howard Linton, have provided me with most of the source materials used in this book. I have spent many weeks in the Manuscript Division of the Library of Congress reading through thousands of pieces of its most invaluable collection of manuscripts. The John Hay Whitney Foundation has helped my research with a fellowship. The Bancroft Project at Columbia, formerly under the direction of Dr. Nevins, has facilitated my research with many special purchases. To all of these I express my thanks.

My wife has shared the laborious work with me throughout the preparatory stage. Her optimism, encouragement, and, particularly, her assistance in the preparation of the Chinese bibliography were indispensable in bringing this book to final shape. We both can hardly forget the period after the birth of our first child when for months I was able to work in our small apartment from dusk to dawn without interruption and when often she would get up after midnight to keep me company with a crying baby in her arms.

CONTENTS

ILLUSTRATIONS

MAPS

UNITED
STATES
DIPLOMACY
IN
CHINA,
1844-60

CHINA
PROVINCES AND SEAPORTS 1844-1860

SHERM

1

SETTING THE STAGE

I

THE Wanghia Treaty initiated official diplomatic relations between the United States and China. It was a natural sequence of the growing Chinese policy of appeasement that followed the Opium War. During that period, and even before the American envoy, Caleb Cushing,[1] left the United States for China, merchants were admitted to trade in the Five Ports, (Canton, Amoy, Foochow, Ningpo, Shanghai) on the same terms as the British. "By the time he arrived in 1844," said Professor Fairbank,[2] referring to Cushing, "his primary objective had already been realized." The negotiations, conducted by Ch'i-ying[3] and Cushing during the summer of 1844, which led to the signing of the Treaty of Wanghia on July 3, were merely "an exhibition of shadow boxing."[4]

Generally speaking, the Wanghia Treaty was merely a gross copy of Sino-British treaties that had been signed previously. By this new treaty American citizens were formally permitted to trade in the five ports of Canton, Amoy, Foochow, Ningpo, and Shanghai. All the commercial privileges and extraterritorial grants which the British

---

[1] Caleb Cushing (1800-1879) was born in Massachusetts. After having served in different branches of the American government for many years, he was sent to China in 1844 as the first envoy from Washington to negotiate a Sino-American treaty. Concerning his life and his mission to China see Claude Moore Fuess, *The Life of Caleb Cushing* (New York: Harcourt, Brace and Co., 1923).

[2] John King Fairbank, *Trade and Diplomacy on the China Coast* (Cambridge, Mass.: Harvard University Press, 1951), I, 196.

[3] Ch'i-ying, a Manchu statesman, known in contemporary Western writings as Tsiying, Kiying, or Keying, was the most prominent individual in Chinese foreign relations until 1850. In the summer of 1844 he signed the Treaty of Wanghia with Caleb Cushing, the first treaty between the United States and China. For more information about him see chap. 3.

[4] Fairbank, *Trade and Diplomacy,* I, 196.

had secured through a bloody conflict were to be extended, without
reservation, to American citizens.[5] In addition, Cushing succeeded in
securing more extensive privileges than the British had obtained.[6] It
is of particular interest to note that Article 34 of the Treaty of Wanghia specified that the treaty should be revised after twelve years.[7]
This arrangement, which the British had failed to obtain, but later
secured through the most-favored-nation clause, became, as we shall
see in the following chapters, the source of trouble in the 1850's. It
gradually developed into a treaty-revision movement, eventually leading to the second Anglo-Chinese war.

Soon after the treaty was signed, the American diplomats put extraterritoriality into practice; it was maintained for a solid century. On
June 16, 1844, while the Wanghia negotiation was in progress, a clash
between a group of Chinese and a few armed Americans took place in
front of the American consulate at Canton. During this incident, Hsü
Ya-man, a Chinese citizen, was shot to death. Immediately, the
Chinese authorities requested that the American legation punish the
guilty American. This request, however, was refused by Cushing, who
instead ordered the American consul, Paul S. Forbes, to summon a
jury of six American residents of Canton on July 11. The jury subsequently delivered a verdict of acquittal on the grounds of self-
defense.[8] In the meantime, Cushing brought up an old case in which
an American citizen named Sherry had been killed by Chinese soldiers
at Whampoa in May, 1841, while the Opium War was at its height.
Sherry was killed in a boat which the Chinese mistook as belonging to
the British. "Upon your excellency's own view of the law of homi-
cide," said Cushing to Ch'i-ying, "the rule of life for life does not
apply to the case of firing at and killing the wrong person by mistake;
which, upon the facts alleged by your excellency, is as truly the case
of Sue Aman [Hsü Ya-man] as that of Sherry."[9] Since Hsü was a

---

[5] For a comparative study of both the original texts and the English and Chinese
versions of the American and British treaties with China consult *Treaties, Conventions, etc., between China and Foreign States* (Shanghai: Published at the Statistical
Department of the Inspectorate General of Customs, 1908), I, 159-210, 473-508.

[6] According to Cushing's report to the Department of State, there were five
important items specifically concerning the transit duties and tonnage dues contained
in the Treaty of Wanghia that were not secured by the Treaty of Nanking. See
House Report, No. 596, 30 Cong., 1 sess., May 4, 1848, p. 3.

[7] *Treaties, Conventions, etc.*, I, 486.

[8] *Chinese Repository* (a monthly magazine published in English at Canton from
May, 1832, to December, 1851, edited by Elijah Coleman Bridgman), XIV, No. 11
(Nov., 1845), 526-30.

[9] Cushing to Ch'i-ying, Macao, August 20, 1844, *Chinese Repository*, XIV, No. 11
(Nov., 1845), 537.

stranger at Canton, without a strong family to demand redress, Ch'i-ying, who was already tired of the Cantonese chauvinist action[10] and realized his lack of power to reverse the American decision, agreed to drop the case in order to avoid further diplomatic complications. This settlement released Cushing from possible embarrassment because he (like his successors until 1848) possessed no constitutional power to try any American citizen.

Having completed a remarkably successful mission, Cushing left Macao on the *Perry* on August 27, 1844, to report back to Washington.[11] In spite of considerable loss of their country's sovereignty through the new treaty, the Chinese diplomats, particularly Ch'i-ying, felt satisfied by the new agreement. On September 9, two weeks after Cushing had sailed, Ch'i-ying sent two letters to him—one official and one informal—notifying him that the Emperor had ratified the treaty. In his official letter Ch'i-ying said that to each article of the treaty negotiated at Wanghia, the Court at Peking had replied "let it be granted." He said he now held the copy of the treaty, ratified by the Emperor, and that he would hold it until the arrival of the one ratified by the government of the United States, at which time they would be exchanged.[12] Two weeks later, the Imperial Commissioner also forwarded to his American friend a portrait of himself in Manchu costume together with his warm good wishes.[13] This portrait still hangs in the Museum of Fine Arts at Boston.

Upon Cushing's departure from the China coast, Commodore Foxhall A. Parker, naval commander on the East India station, and Dr. Peter Parker, the Chinese interpreter for the American legation during the negotiation of the Wanghia Treaty, were put in charge of the

---

[10] In many memorials submitted to the Emperor as well as in personal memoirs, the Chinese officials at Canton had repeatedly complained against the unruly action of the Cantonese. For example see *Ch'ing tai ch'ou pan i wu shih mo* (The Management of Barbarian Affairs of the Ch'ing Dynasty from Beginning to End; Peiping: Palace Museum, 1930; hereafter cited as *IWSM* with *TK* to indicate the period of Tao-kuang, and *HF* for that of Hsien-feng), LXXV, 11 ff.; also see Huang En-t'ung, "Fu-yuan chi-lioh" (A brief record of pacifying [the men] from afar), *Ya-p'ien chan-cheng* (The Opium War; Shanghai: Shen-chou kuo-kuang she, 1954), V, 419. The "Fu-yuan chi-lioh" was a rare pamphlet originally written by Huang En-t'ung, right-hand man of Ch'i-ying during all his negotiations, as a part of his personal memoir. It has been reprinted and included in the *Opium War* series published in Communist China by the Communist Chinese Historical Society.

[11] Cushing to Calhoun, No. 95, Macao, August 27, 1844, Diplomatic Despatches, microfilmed by the U.S. National Archives Service, Microfilm No. 92, Roll No. 3 (hereafter cited as *DD-USNA*, 92:3).

[12] Ch'i-ying to Cushing, Canton, Sept. 9, 1844, *DD-USNA*, 92:3.

[13] Fuess, *Life of Caleb Cushing*, p. 444.

Portrait of Ch'i-ying

American legation at Canton. But Commodore Parker soon left the Chinese waters, and Peter Parker then became a *de facto* chargé d'affaires at Canton.

Born in Framingham, Massachusetts, in 1804, Peter Parker received an M.D. at Yale University thirty years later. Before entering Yale, however, he had thought of becoming a foreign missionary. Consequently, he applied, in 1831, to the American Board of Commissioners for Foreign Missions for an appointment. He was accepted and assigned to China.

Following his graduation from Yale in June, 1834, Parker left New York for a trip to Canton, where he arrived four months later.[14] After a brief stay at Canton, Parker realized that overcoming the language barrier was a prerequisite for any missionary work among the Chinese. At the advice of a friend, Parker went to Singapore, which, until 1842, was the center of American missionary work in the Far East.[15] The Chinese community there was quite friendly toward Western missionaries and gave Parker ample opportunity to learn the Chinese language, particularly the dialect of Fukien, the province he planned to be his final destination. He reached Singapore in December, 1834, and after ten months of intensive study[16] returned to Canton, speaking a workable, though not fluent, Cantonese.

On November 4, 1835, he opened the famous Ophthalmic Hospital at Canton. Because of his work there he later became known as the founder of medical missions in China. The hospital proved successful and its founder earned an enviable reputation with his Chinese patients, among whom were the famous Imperial Commissioners, Lin Tse-hsü and Ch'i-ying. In February, 1838, with the cooperation of his fellow missionary friends, Parker founded the Medical Missionary Society in China.[17]

He returned to the United States in 1840, while the Opium War was in progress. On March 29, 1841, he married Harriet Webster, a relative of Daniel Webster, then the Secretary of State. During this

[14] Concerning Parker's early life and his early mission to China see George B. Stevens, *The Life, Letters, and Journals of the Rev. and Hon. Peter Parker, M.D.* (Boston: Congregational Sunday-school and Publishing Society, 1896), pp. 53-79. For a brief biographical sketch of Peter Parker see Allen Johnson and Dumas Malone, eds., *Dictionary of American Biography* (New York: Charles Scribner's Sons, 1931), XIV, 234-35.

[15] Samuel Wells Williams, *The Middle Kingdom* (New York: Wiley and Putnam, 1848), II, 325-80.

[16] Stevens, *Life . . . of Peter Parker,* pp. 115 ff.

[17] D. MacGillivray, *A Century of Protestant Missions in China* (Shanghai: The American Presbyterian Mission Press, 1907), p. 653.

period he obtained many interviews with Presidents Van Buren, Harrison, and Tyler and their Secretaries of State, all of whom were then watching the Opium War with some interest. In June, 1842, he returned to Canton with his young wife to resume his medical mission.

When Cushing arrived at Macao in February, 1844, he found Parker to be the only competent American citizen who could serve him as both secretary and Chinese interpreter. In a formal letter, signed on February 25, 1844, he appointed Parker his Chinese secretary to the mission with a compensation of fifteen hundred dollars per annum.[18] The following summer Parker became indispensable during the negotiations at Wanghia. The details of the treaty were conducted chiefly by Huang En-t'ung,[19] a veteran Chinese diplomat in the Nanking negotiations of 1842 and now provincial treasurer at Canton, and the "barbarian physician" Parker, who was to become a leading and most influential figure in the American legation.

Before Cushing left Canton for the United States, he requested Parker to accept a formal appointment from the American government. This request was agreed to by Parker on condition that his missionary work should not be interrupted by official appointment. Cushing agreed to this stipulation and promised to forward his opinion to Washington.[20] Therefore, after the departure of Cushing for the United States, Parker was at the wheel, and Sino-American diplomatic relations at Canton went on smoothly.

II

While Cushing was still on his way home, the original copy of the Wanghia Treaty was rushed to Washington. On December 10, 1844, it was read to the Senate at a secret session. It was approved by a unanimous vote on January 16, 1845, and the President signed it the following morning.[21] A week later President Tyler sent a message to Congress recommending that Congress make suitable provision for the establishment of diplomatic relations with China.[22]

First of all, he suggested, "a permanent minister or commissioner with diplomatic functions, as in the case of certain of the Moham-

---

18 Stevens, *Life ... of Peter Parker*, p. 250.

19 Concerning Huang's career as a diplomat and his official activities at Canton see following chapter.

20 Parker to James Buchanan, Canton, January 22, 1846, *DD-USNA*, 92:4.

21 *Senate Documents*, No. 58, 28 Cong., 2 sess., pp. 1-14; *House Exec. Doc.*, No. 69, 1-15.

22 *Sen. Doc.*, No. 58, 28 Cong. 2 sess., pp. 1-2. For general reference see Tyler Dennett, *Americans in Eastern Asia* (New York: The Macmillan Co., 1922), pp. 145 ff.

medan states" should be sent to China "for the preservation and culti-
vation of the subsisting relations of amity between the United States
and Chinese government."[23] He further requested that the present commercial consulates in China be abolished and as a substitute, some
representation by a higher authority should be established, especially
inasmuch as both the British and the French already had "paid
consuls" for all the Five Ports, one of whom had the title and exercised the functions of consul general.[24] In conclusion, the President
demanded that Congress should make some provision, written into
law, to cope with the special position in which the Treaty of Wanghia
placed American citizens residing or doing business in China. The
twenty-first and twenty-fifth articles of the treaty stipulated that citizens of the United States in China were wholly exempted, both in
criminal and in civil matters, from the local jurisdiction of the Chinese
government, and were amenable to the laws and subject to the jurisdiction of the appropriate authorities of the United States alone.[25]

On March 13, 1845, Alexander Hill Everett of Massachusetts was
appointed commissioner to China.[26] In the meantime, Dr. Peter
Parker's commission as secretary and interpreter to the United States
legation to China was formally issued.[27] The remainder of Tyler's
recommendations, however, remained in abeyance for many years.
The required law giving judicial power to the consuls was not made
until 1848; the merchant-consul system remained on the China coast
for another decade.

The new commissioner, Alexander Hill Everett, was born in 1790
and was a graduate of Harvard in 1806. He had accompanied John
Quincy Adams as his private secretary when the latter was appointed
minister to Russia in 1809. Everett remained in Russia for two years;
then he was appointed secretary of the American legation at The
Hague in 1815 for a year. Coming back to the States to marry in
1816, he returned to The Hague in 1818 as chargé d'affaires until

[23] *House Exec. Doc.*, No. 69, 28 Cong., 2 sess., pp. 1-2.

[24] *Ibid.;* for general reference on the United States consular service at the time
consult U.S. Department of State, *The United States Consular System: Manual for
Consuls and also for Merchants* (Washington, D.C.: Taylor and Maury, 1856),
pp. 5-24; for the shortcomings of United States consular service in China see Eldon
Griffin, *Clippers and Consuls* (Ann Arbor, Mich.: Edwards Brothers, 1938), p. 48.

[25] *Sen. Doc.*, No. 58, 28 Cong., 2 sess., pp. 1-2.

[26] Buchanan to Everett, No. 1, Washington, D.C., April 15, 1845, Diplomatic Instructions, microfilmed by the National Archives Service, microfilm No. 77, Roll No.
38 (cited hereafter as *DI-USNA, 77*:38), pp. 24-27.

[27] Buchanan to Peter Parker, Washington, D.C., April 16, 1845, *DI-USNA, 77*:38,
pp. 35-36.

1824; then he was appointed by President John Quincy Adams as minister to Spain for four years. During the Jacksonian administration Everett joined the Democratic party.[28]

As the first United States commissioner to China under the new treaty, Everett was instructed by the Secretary of State, James Buchanan, "to cultivate the good will of the Chinese Government and the people," and was charged with "a general superintedence in the spirit of the Treaty."[29] However, he was given no actual authority to exercise judicial or executive functions under the extraterritorial grant. As none of the United States consuls at the Five Ports could try and punish an American citizen for murder, or any other crime, the Secretary of State warned Everett that he would, on certain occasions, be "embarrassed." "What is then to be done? Shall a citizen guilty of murder or high crime pass unpunished?" No, Buchanan's directive went on, the President had directed the accused party be sent home for trial.[30]

On a new mission to a strange empire, Everett sailed from New York on June 1, 1845, aboard the U.S.S. *Columbus* of the East Indian squadron under the command of Commodore James Biddle, who was also assigned by the Navy Department for a new mission to the Far East.[31] Two months later, on July 30, the *Columbus* reached Rio de Janeiro. No longer a well man, Everett suffered ill health and discomfort during the hot and lengthy sea voyage. Upon his arrival in Rio de Janeiro, the fleet surgeon, Dr. B. Ficknor, advised him to abandon his trip to China and Commodore Biddle consented to detach a special ship, the frigate *Brandywine*, to convey Everett home. Everett chose to ignore the physician's advice and decided to proceed. Continued bad health forced him to reverse his decision, however, and eventually he boarded a merchant ship bound for New York.

Before leaving Rio de Janeiro, Everett authorized Commodore Biddle to act as "Temporary Commissioner"; Biddle was to proceed to China and exchange the ratifications of the Treaty of Wanghia because the deadline was approaching.[32] In a report to the State

[28] For a good biographical sketch of Everett see Johnson and Malone, eds., *Dictionary of American Biography*, VI, 220-21.
[29] Buchanan to Everett, No. 2, Washington, D.C., April 15, 1845, *DI-USNA* 77:38, pp. 28, 33.
[30] *Ibid.*, pp. 29-30.
[31] Everett to Buchanan, Washington, D.C., April 21, 1845; New York, April 28, 1845, *DD-USNA*, 92:4.
[32] Everett to Biddle, on board the U.S.S. *Columbus*, August 8, 1845, *DD-USNA*, 92:4.

Department, Everett stated that he did not wish the President to think he was resigning. He assumed that his health would soon be restored and that he would be able to reach China before the Commodore's return.[33]

III

Delegated by Mr. Everett, with "full power" to exchange the ratifications of the Wanghia Treaty with the Chinese authorities, Commodore Biddle proceeded to the China coast as acting commissioner from the United States. The Commodore, at this time, was one of the oldest and most distinguished officers in the United States Navy. His name was the seventh on the navy list in 1845. He was a nephew of Captain Nicholas Biddle, who lost his life during the Revolutionary War. Young James had entered the Navy in 1800. During the war with Tripoli he had served as a midshipman on board the *Philadelphia* and was imprisoned at Tripoli when that vessel was captured. He later served in the War of 1812 and received a gold medal from Congress. Some years later he served as one of his government's representatives in negotiating the United States' first treaty with Turkey.[34]

Biddle arrived at the Bogue on December 26, 1845. He immediately notified the Chinese authorities and requested an appointment. After a short exchange of correspondence between the two parties the ratifications of the Wanghia Treaty were exchanged on December 31, 1845, just a few days before the deadline set up by the treaty.[35] The exchange took place at the country residence of P'an Shih-ch'eng, a noted hong merchant at Canton, who had played an important role in the negotiation of Wanghia.[36]

[33] Everett to Buchanan, Rio de Janeiro, September 28, 1845, *ibid.*

[34] Charles Oscar Paullin, *Diplomatic Negotiations of American Naval Officers, 1778-1883* (Baltimore, Md.: The Johns Hopkins Press, 1912), pp. 223-25.

[35] Biddle to Buchanan, No. 1, Canton, Dec. 31, 1845, *DD-USNA*, 92:4.

[36] P'an Shih-ch'eng was a descendant of the wealthy hong merchant Puankhequa (in Mandarin pronounced P'an Ch'i-kuan, the business name of P'an Chen-ch'eng). He had become well acquainted with the American merchants and was greatly respected by them. As a "barbarian expert," he has been credited with being the first pioneer to urge the modernization of the art of war, particularly stressing the need for a modern navy in China. He had participated in all Sino-foreign negotiations at Canton in the early 1840's and had become one of Ch'i-ying's most indispensable aides during that period.

Both Chinese and Western historians are in disagreement as to P'an's status of a hong merchant. According to the Ch'ing government documents, he was frequently referred to as "hong merchant P'an Shih-ch'eng," but private sources, preserved both in England and China, indicate that he was not a hong merchant. According to these sources, Puankhequa's business was inherited by a certain P'an T'ing-kuan, a different person entirely. Chinese historians, however, failed to identify definitely who P'an T'ing-kuan was; some of P'an Shih-cheng's direct descendants also dis-

As soon as the ratifications were exchanged, P'an Shih-ch'eng, at the direction of Ch'i-ying, the Chinese Imperial Commissioner, called upon Dr. Parker and requested an interview with Acting Commissioner Biddle. In this interview, P'an asked Biddle's advice about existing difficulties with Sir John Davis, the British envoy and chief superintendent of British trade in China.[37]

By the Treaty of Nanking, signed in 1842, China stipulated that she would pay twenty-one million dollars to Great Britain in certain specified installments. These payments were made promptly, according to schedule. The last installment, consisting of two million dollars, was to become payable on December 31, 1845. The treaty provided that upon payment of the final installment the British forces would be withdrawn from the islands of Chusan, outside the port of Ningpo. However, when payment of the last installment was approaching, the British envoy, instead of applying for that payment, demanded as the condition of the withdrawal of the British troops from the islands a guarantee that the government of China would not transfer these islands to any foreign power. "... it is the general belief here," Biddle stated in a subsequent report to Washington, "that it is not intended to restore the islands as the treaty stipulates." In the interview, Biddle told P'an:

. . . this demand was offensive to the national pride of China, and would, among the Western States, be deemed highly insulting; that it was impossible the British could seriously entertain any suspicion of an intention on the part of China of transferring these islands to a foreign power, and that therefore the demand of a guarantee must be a mere pretext for retaining possession of the islands.[38]

Consequently, he advised the Chinese to send the last installment to Sir John Davis and to require that upon its payment, the British troops should be withdrawn in fulfillment of the treaty.[39]

claim his status as a hong merchant and claim he was a salt-tea merchant. In the United States National Archives, P'an Shih-ch'eng is frequently mentioned as Pun Tingqua, Pun Ting Kwa, or Pwan Tingkwa, the Cantonese pronunciation of P'an T'ing-kuan. Thus it would seem that P'an Shih-ch'eng and P'an T'ing-kuan were actually the same person, which would settle P'an Shih-ch'eng's status as a hong merchant.

[37] Biddle to Buchanan, No. 2, Canton, Jan. 8, 1846, *DD-USNA*, 92:4. Ch'i-ying also was ready to seek French help, but the French minister precipitantly left China to avoid involvement. See Fairbank, *Trade and Diplomacy*, I, 271. Ch'i-ying's approach to the French for help was reported by the British consul at Canton to the authorities at London, but P'an's conversation with Biddle seemed not to have been known to the British.

[38] Biddle to Buchanan, No. 2, Canton, Jan. 8, 1846, *DD-USNA*, 92:4.

[39] *Ibid.*

In a subsequent report to the State Department, Biddle stated that the refusal to withdraw these troops from Chusan was a clear violation of the Treaty of Nanking. This violation of a treaty stipulation, by the first Western nation with which China concluded a treaty, said Biddle, might prove injurious to all the Western nations. The Chinese would now tend to cling more and more to their ancient policy of remaining isolated from the rest of the world.[40]

The Anglo-Chinese dispute, fortunately, was settled without incident, and the P'an-Biddle interview has passed unnoticed. However, this minor episode clearly reflected the general trend of the development of the Sino-American diplomatic relations at the time. Enriched by their experience in governing their colonies, the British were pursuing a rather high-handed China policy at the time. The United States, on the other hand, showed a different face to the Chinese. With the memory of colonial revolution fresh in their minds, the American diplomats were not impressed by the Machiavellian methods that the European politicians adopted in playing contemporary international politics. Thus, individual American envoys to China, from Caleb Cushing and James Biddle on, as we shall see in later chapters, were, with few exceptions, more or less hostile to the British for their abuse of China. Their sympathy with the plight of the Chinese naturally encouraged the Chinese to seek them out and to ask their advice. This American understanding of the humiliated Chinese Empire went far to create an era of good feeling between these two countries, covering almost the whole Tao-kuang regime, with the diplomats on both sides being enlightened and liberal-minded.

IV

Another problem that embarrassed Acting Commissioner Biddle was a judicial case. The Acting Commissioner really had no power to solve it, but he could not escape from it as Cushing had done in the Hsü Ya-man case nearly two years before. Early in February, 1846, a Chinese merchant, named Shing Ho, submitted a complaint to Biddle against an American merchant, Samuel Wetmore of Wetmore and Company, who had refused to pay a valid bill to the Chinese merchant. Wetmore, moreover, took back the bill from the Chinese, while the latter was demanding the payment. In a desperate attempt to receive the money due him, Shing Ho submitted a petition to Biddle, appeal-

---

[40] Biddle to Buchanan, No. 5, Canton, Feb. 21, 1846, *ibid*.

ing for justice and saying:[41] "If our house consequently are to lose both the money and the bill, then truly it is beyond the common sense of mankind." The petition went on to say:

We have long looked up to your Honorable nation whose (good) faith and justice are instructive and what is straight and what is crooked, certainly it can clearly investigate. We beg that the original bill (or certificate) may be returned and we shall be grateful for the unbounded favor. We repair before the bench of H. E. James Biddle, Minister and Commissioner of the United States of America requesting that he will devise means that this may be granted to be done.

According to Dr. Parker, Shing Ho was "a very respectable man." In his report to Washington Biddle said

a clearer case of injustice and impropriety than Mr. Wetmore's conduct on this occasion could not well happen. . . . Had I refused or neglected to bring it before the public officers of the two nations, the American name and credit in this country would have been affected most injuriously. The necessity of bringing an American merchant before the tribunal of the two nations charged with such violent and palpable injustice toward a Chinese is greatly to be regretted.[42]

Biddle had no real power to force Wetmore to make payment on the bill, but sent Dr. Parker to "exhibit" the case to a member of the house of Wetmore and Company. But Parker's mission failed. Subsequently, Biddle asked Parker to get one of Wetmore's friends to speak to him on the subject, but he found out that none of Wetmore's countrymen at Canton were on intimate terms with him.

After a lengthy correspondence between the Commissioner and Wetmore, the latter frankly told Biddle that he continued to reply "only for courtesy's sake." Then he began to question the constitutional basis of the Acting Commissioner's interference in a civil case, saying:[43]

Against these irregular proceedings we beg you to notice our earnest protest and we caution you against any verbal or written expression of opinion unfavorable to our commercial reputation, as for all such we hold you responsible.
We are disposed to deny your right to decide in this matter officially either under any general powers, or under any special authority that may

---

[41] Shing Ho's petition to Acting Commissioner Biddle included in Biddle's report to the State Department, No. 7, Canton, Feb. 28, 1846, *DD-USNA*, 92:4.
[42] *Ibid.*
[43] Wetmore to Biddle, Canton, Feb. 17, 1846, attached to Biddle's report No. 7, *DD-USNA*, 92:4.

have been delegated to you for we know of no sufficient powers that can be in your possession in accordance with the Constitution of the United States and any others we are quite ready to contest. We would submit, of course, to the award of a Judicatory [sic] of the United States, if one were here established, and there were no laws placing us under its jurisdiction: but we add, that not now, or at any time hereafter, will we receive as a final decision of our right the judgement of any one individual in China. However greatly we may value your opinions on general subjects, we will not respect your own decision in this case.

At a later meeting, the Commodore was still trying to settle this case justly. He sent Dr. Parker with Shing Ho to the Wetmore's house, hoping for a reasonable settlement. "When all were assembled," Parker recollected later, "Mr. Wetmore asked in what capacity he was to regard me. 'A friend to both parties' was the reply."[44]

Though this case was at last settled through the persuasion of the American envoy, it could by no means have been considered settled by any process of law. During this controversy, Wetmore was not particularly to be blamed. To trade with China in those days was a risky business. The Western merchants residing in China were, as one of them frankly confessed, "money-making, practical men." "Our business is to make money, as much and as fast as we can:" he said, "—and for this end all modes or means are good which the law permits."[45] Consequently, they felt that to take advantage of a legal vacuum in attempting to make some profits was far better and more moral than to engage in illegal activities such as opium smuggling, which was popular among the British as well as many American merchants.

This dispute between Shing Ho and Wetmore was the first civil case to occur under the Treaty of Wanghia. Naturally the American envoy was terribly "embarrassed" by his lack of judicial power to make a just settlement, as the authorities at Washington had predicted. It furnished good examples of how Chinese foreign trade was conducted during the early period of the post-treaty days and also of how the Western merchants succeeded in taking advantage of the Chinese extraterritorial grants and made use of the shortcomings in the legal system of their home governments while trying to make quick money in China. Biddle's report to Washington on these matters urged President Polk and Secretary Buchanan to request Congress

[44] Parker to Biddle, Canton, Feb. 29, 1846, ibid.
[45] Rutherford Alcock, *The Capital of the Tycoon* (New York: Harper and Brothers, 1863), I, 38.

to establish consular courts and to readjust the American consular system throughout the world.

In short, the two problems that Acting Commissioner Biddle encountered during his mission to China, namely the American position during an Anglo-Chinese dispute and the readjustment of the United States diplomatic and consular service so as to ensure a more extensive and suitable exercise of extraterritorial rights in China, were really the two major problems confronting all the American commissioners to China dealt with in this study. Both of these major problems occurred almost simultaneously during the mission of Acting Commissioner Biddle and not long after the official inception of Sino-American diplomatic relations.

While Biddle was busily occupied with miscellaneous diplomatic and judicial affairs at Canton, Mr. Everett was rapidly regaining his health at home and making arrangements to sail for China.[46] The news of his recovery reached the China coast in March, 1846.[47] Americans at Canton expected that he might reach China before Commodore Biddle's departure from the Chinese waters. The Commodore, however, pressed by his assigned naval duties to the north and to Japan, could not remain long enough to meet Everett. After notifying the Chinese authorities[48] and transferring his duty to Dr. Peter Parker, whom he had appointed chargé d'affaires of the United States ad interim,[49] he left Canton on April 15, 1846.[50] In the next months Biddle visited three of the four northern ports along the China coast. On July 7, 1846, he left the Chusan Islands and sailed for Yedo, Japan.[51]

---

[46] Everett to the Department of State, Washington, D.C., April 24, 1846, *DD-USNA*, 92:4. This document bears no number.

[47] *The Chinese Repository*, XV, No. 3 (March 3, 1846), 158.

[48] Stevens, *Life . . . of Peter Parker*, p. 273; Biddle to Ch'i-ying, Canton, April 15, 1846, attached to Biddle's report to Washington, No. 11, *DD-USNA*, 92:4. This notice was immediately acknowledged by the Chinese authority, see Ch'i-ying to Biddle, Canton, April 22, 1846, attached to Parker's dispatches to Washington, No. 1, *DD-USNA*, 92:4.

[49] Biddle to Parker, Canton, April 15, 1846, attached to Parker's dispatches, No. 1, *DD-USNA*, 92:4. This appointment was later approved by the Department of State. In his Instruction No. 9, issued on January 28, 1847, to Everett, Buchanan wrote: "The appointment made by Commodore Biddle, on the 15th April last, of Dr. Peter Parker, as Chargé d'affaires of the United States, *ad interim*, was quite satisfactory to the Department." *DI-USNA*, 77:38, p. 51.

[50] Paullin, *Diplomatic Negotiations*, p. 224; Biddle to Buchanan, No. 11, on board the U.S.S. *Vincennes*, April 18, 1846, *DD-USNA*, 92:4.

[51] Paullin, *Diplomatic Negotiations*, p. 224.

2

THE AMERICAN SCENE

I

In the first years after the signing of the Wanghia Treaty, the United States had no China policy, nor had the American envoy to China, Acting Commissioner Biddle, been given any clear instructions as to how to proceed. Since he possessed no power to solve any problem that was raised by the new treaty, Biddle solved the miscellaneous diplomatic and judicial problems that arose as his common sense dictated. He acted only on problems for which the treaty obliged him to seek a solution.

Generally speaking, the Wanghia Treaty was not a necessity either for the Chinese or the Americans. To the Chinese the signing of the Treaty at Wanghia was merely the signing of an unnecessary document; to the Americans it was a political luxury which the United States actually did not deserve at the time. There is a Chinese saying: "A family has to be rich for three generations before it is able to enjoy its wealth." This was true of the United States in the 1840's; the young country had much to learn before it could enjoy such an unexpected luxury.

First of all, the Wanghia Treaty was not welcomed by the American merchants in the China trade, which had been successfully carried on for sixty years without a treaty. In these sixty years Sino-American trade had, of course, undergone several ups and downs, but ever since Major Samuel Shaw's first trip to China on the *Empress of China* in 1784, it had progressed quite profitably and without serious setbacks.[1] In spite of strong restrictions such as the *co-hong* sys-

---

[1] For a general survey of the American China trade during the pretreaty days see Kenneth Scott Latourette, "The History of Early Relations between the United States and China, 1784-1844," *Transactions of the Connecticut Academy of Arts and Science*, XXII (1917), 17.

tem set up by the Chinese government to govern the foreign trade at Canton, the American merchants were fairly content and had no serious complaints.[2]

In the early years immediately after Major Shaw's first trip, the American China trade had not been very prosperous, but it was soon promoted by the European wars following the French Revolution in 1789. During the war years the United States became the common carrier of Europe. Large portions of the continent and of the West Indies were thrown open to American goods. This resulted in a wider market for tea, the major export from China; and it provided American merchants with specie and with goods needed for their cargoes to Canton.[3] In addition to the impetus given by the European wars, the Americans began to carry to Canton such new commodities as furs and sealskins from the northwest coast of North America, and products of the South Seas, which also found a ready market in China.[4]

The result of the European wars and the opening of new avenues of trade was the building of an efficient merchant marine and a phenomenal growth in American commerce with China. In the trading seasons preceding the War of 1812, about thirty to forty American ships entered the port of Canton.[5] The average value of imports to Canton in these years was between three and five million dollars, that is about 5 per cent of the whole export business of the United States.[6] This prosperous American trade with China suffered some setbacks during the War of 1812. Here, as in other branches of commerce, fear of capture by the British kept American ships at home. The total commerce from 1812 to 1815 was barely half that of the years before the war.[7] This recession, however, soon disappeared after the war was over. From 1815 on there was a growing home

[2] Many books deal with the life and trade of Western merchants at Canton during the pretreaty days. For brief but interesting firsthand descriptions consult the following books: Samuel Shaw, *The Journals of Major Samuel Shaw, the First American Consul at Canton* (Boston: Wm. Crosby and H. P. Nichols, 1847), pp. 163-200, 290-316; William C. Hunter, *The "Fan Kwae" at Canton* (Shanghai: Kelly and Walsh, 1911); Robert B. Forbes, *Personal Reminiscences* (Boston: Little, Brown and Co., 1882), pp. 333 ff.; C. Toogood Bowning, *The Stranger in China* (2 vols.; Philadelphia: Leo and Blanchard, 1838).

[3] Timothy Pitkin, *A Statistical View of the Commerce of the United States of America* (New Haven, Conn.: Durrie and Peck, 1835), pp. 246-47.

[4] Latourette, "The History of Early Relations," pp. 64-74.

[5] *Sen. Doc.*, No. 31, 19 Cong., 1 sess.

[6] *American State Papers, Class IV, Commerce and Navigation* (Washington, D.C.: Gales and Seaton, 1858), I, 927-28.

[7] *Sen. Doc.*, No. 31, 19 Cong., 1 sess., pp. 1-3, 9, Table G.

market in the United States for Chinese goods. In March, 1822, the House Committee on Commerce took official notice in its report of the importance of the American trade in China, declaring: "It is inferior to that of no nation, Great Britain excepted."[8]

Over a period of several decades, the character of American investors in the China trade underwent periodic changes. Until the War of 1812, the commerce had been in the hands of a comparatively large number of small firms and individuals, located in nearly all the seaports of the North Atlantic states. About the time of the war, trade began to decline in the smaller ports, such as New Haven, Norwich, and later even in Providence and Salem; it was confined to the larger cities, New York, Boston and Philadelphia, where it was gradually concentrated in the hands of large firms.[9]

The period after the War of 1812 was also marked by obvious changes in the nature of the goods carried in the China clippers; these changes were no less noticeable than those in the nature of the organizations engaged in the China trade. After the war, the fur-sealing trade declined rapidly, and the imports to China consisted chiefly of specie.[10] Next in importance were cotton, rice, copper, lead, steel, ginseng (only in small quantity), rattans, pepper, nutmegs, tin, cochineal, corals, British manufactures, and opium.[11]

Tea remained the chief export from China to the United States until the thirties.[12] In the fifteen years after 1820, silk was of great importance, amounting on occasion to more than one-third the total imports of the United States from China, but it declined before the outbreak of the Opium War.[13] Nankeens, a kind of Chinese cotton goods, had the same fluctuations as silk. Other Chinese goods, such as cassia, chinaware, fire screens, firecrackers, camphor, rhubarb, fans, and sugar candy, were exported in small quantities.[14]

There were, however, occasional periods when trade declined. Sometimes, optimistic merchants imported too largely on credit; too many inexperienced men were drawn into the trade, and the market

---

[8] *American State Papers, Class IV*, II, 637.
[9] For a brief but brilliant description of the gradual shift see Latourette, "The History of Early Relations," pp. 64-74; also consult Samuel Eliot Morison, *The Maritime History of Massachusetts 1783-1860* (New York: Houghton Mifflin Co., 1922), pp. 64-78, 273-85.
[10] Latourette, "The History of Early Relations," p. 40.
[11] *Ibid.*, pp. 71-74.
[12] "Commerce of the United States with China," *Hunt's Merchant Magazine*, II, 55.
[13] Pitkin, *A Statistical View*, p. 301.
[14] Latourette, "The History of Early Relations," p. 80.

became overstocked. These were followed by commercial failures, the most serious of which occurred in 1826. It was not until the early thirties that the China trade fully recovered. During this period of depression the small ports and the small investors suffered the most. Thus the general tendency to concentrate the business in a few large firms in Boston, New York, and Philadelphia was hastened.[15]

The volume of Chinese foreign trade during the decade of the Opium War varied from a few million dollars to about ten million. During these years, the American China trade was, of course, interrupted, but it was not seriously jeopardized. It recovered soon after the war, as the figures in the following table show:

THE FOREIGN TRADE BETWEEN THE UNITED STATES AND CHINA[16]

Year	Exports from China	Imports into China
1836	$7,324,816	$1,194,264
1837	8,965,337	630,591
1838	4,764,536	1,516,602
1839	3,678,509	1,533,601
1840	6,640,829	1,009,966
1841	3,985,388	1,200,816
1842	4,934,645	1,444,397
1843	4,385,566	2,418,958

Among the merchants who engaged in the China trade in Boston, New York, and Philadelphia, those in Boston played a leading role both in business and politics. John Quincy Adams, their spokesman at the Capitol, for instance, was the first American statesman to advocate a strong China policy.[17] The merchants themselves were equally influential in Sino-American diplomatic affairs as in domestic politics connected with the China trade. As Latourette points out, the Oregon Territory was probably preserved on their behalf:[18] "It can safely be said, however, that the Oregon Country was preserved to the United States because of the importance it was felt to have in the Canton commerce, and because of the claims to it which the early fur trade had established . . . ."

It should be noted that the early fur trade, as well as the early northwest coast trade as a whole, was controlled by a few large firms,

---

[15] *Ibid.*, p. 70.

[16] J. Smith Homans, ed., *A Cyclopedia of Commerce and Commercial Navigation* (New York: Harper and Brothers, Publishers, 1858), pp. 1912-13.

[17] A. Whitney Griswold, *The Far Eastern Policy of the United States* (New York: Harcourt, Brace and Company, c. 1938), p. 173; *Chinese Repository*, XII, 145.

[18] Latourette, "The History of Early Relations," p. 57.

such as Dorr and Sons, and by a few Boston families such as the Lymans, Sturgis, Perkins, Lambs, and Coolidges.[19] The Forbes family of Russell and Company had dominated the American consulate at Canton for nearly a generation. At home they were also frequently consulted by the Secretaries of State concerning a proper China policy. When planning Cushing's mission to China in 1843, Secretary of State Daniel Webster wrote to the merchants in the China trade asking for suggestions. John M. Forbes was among the first to respond.[20] In 1854 when the American government was moving for a treaty revision in China, Secretary of State Marcy asked Robert B. Forbes for suggestions; Forbes' reply was later forwarded to Commissioner McLane for reference.[21]

Another important aspect of early Sino-American commerce was the opium trade. The importation of this drug into China was first strictly regulated in 1729,[22] but for a century it had been smuggled in in ever-increasing quantities, despite being completely outlawed in 1796. Most of the drug came from India through British channels, but Americans also had a remarkable share in the opium trade.

As soon as Major Samuel Shaw arrived in China he found out that a "handsome profit" could be made on opium and that a "good market" existed for it in China, where it could be "smuggled with the utmost security."[23] However, the Americans did not join in the smuggling to any great degree until twenty years later. Taking advantage of the policies adopted by the British East India Company, which prohibited private English ships from carrying trade between Europe and China and forbade its own company's ships to carry opium, the American traders began to carry Turkish opium from Smyrna to Canton in 1805. The first shipment was reported to have contained 102 piculs (about 500 silver dollars per picul). From that point on, the trade developed steadily and profitably. The traffic in Turkish opium soon became an American monopoly.[24] Sporadic Chinese attempts to interfere with the opium trade, in addition to added risks in smuggling, gave chances to the wealthier American houses, such as the re-

---

[19] *Ibid.*, p. 35.

[20] John M. Forbes, *Letters and Recollections of J. M. Forbes*, I, 115.

[21] See chap. 13.

[22] For a survey of early opium policy see Kuo T'ing-i, *Chin-tai Chung-kuo shih* (Modern History of China) (Hong Kong: Commercial Press, 1940), II, 35 ff.

[23] Samuel Shaw, *The Journals of Major Samuel Shaw, the First American Consul at Canton* (Boston: Wm. Crosby and H. P. Nichols, 1847), pp. 238, 265.

[24] Charles C. Stelle, "American Trade in Opium to China in the Nineteenth Century," *The Pacific Historical Review*, IX (December, 1940), 444.

spectable J. and T. H. Perkins of Boston under the direction of John P. Cushing, to dominate the trade.

In 1830, the great Canton house of Perkins and Company was dissolved. Its business in opium smuggling was continued by the respectable Russell and Company under the direction of Thomas Tunno Forbes, John Forbes, and later by Robert Bennet Forbes— all related to Cushing. Since 1818 the American traders had kept a "receiving ship" mooring near one or another of the islands below the mouth of the Pearl River, most frequently at Lintin. Here American vessels carrying opium could make their delivery before they proceeded to Whampoa with their other cargo. By operating this receiving ship, alone, Robert Bennet Forbes was able to collect thirty thousand dollars per annum.[25] The unusual profits from the opium trade had led the Boston merchants gradually to extend their business from the Turkish opium to Indian opium to compete seriously with the British opium smugglers. On the eve of the Opium War, Russell and Company had expanded to the third greatest agency for Indian opium.

Despite the increase of profits, American opium traders were handicapped by the expiration of the East India Company's China privileges in 1834, which coincidentally terminated the American monopoly over the traffic in Turkish opium. Thus American capital no longer played a dominant role in providing opium for American consignment, and American vessels were still barred from carrying opium between India and China. The decline of the American opium trade in the late 1830's coincided with an increase of tension over the opium problem between the Chinese and the British. This mere coincidence exempted the Americans from being seriously involved in the first Anglo-Chinese war.[26]

After the outbreak of the Opium War, a number of swift and comparatively light ships were built for carrying opium. They were owned

[25] Stelle, "American Trade," X (March, 1941), 70. Tyler Dennett stated that John P. Cushing had discontinued dealing in opium after 1821, perhaps influenced to do this by his friend Houqua. This is a mistaken statement. In fact Cushing continued dealing in opium until 1828. See Baker Memorial, Perkins & Co. Letterbooks, Perkins & Co. to Byers, June 25, 1821; Massachusetts Historical Society, Perkins, MSS, Extracts from Letterbooks, J. & T. H. Perkins to J. P. Sturgis, May 22, 1819, quoted in *ibid.*, p. 63.

[26] *Ibid.*, p. 74. For additional reference on opium trade in China in the pretreaty days see Michael Greenberg, *British Trade and the Opening of China, 1800-1842* (London: Cambridge University Press, 1951), chap. v, pp. 104-43. Dr. Stelle's essay was based upon a thorough research of the letterbooks of the Boston merchants, whereas the fifth chapter of Greenberg's book was based on a study of the *Jardine Matheson Archives* kept in Cambridge University Library.

by John M. Forbes and Russell and Company.[27] After the signing of
the Treaty of Nanking, when the British government was bound by
the treaty to outlaw British ships that carried opium, the American
ships enjoyed a legal vacuum; they monopolized the transportation
of the illegal drug and became a deadly competitor to the British carrying trade in the East.[28] This revived the American opium trade,
though in a different way.

From the beginning of the China trade, the American merchants
engaged in it had been content with the old trading system at Canton.[29]
During the Opium War they were hostile to the British and considered
the war "one of the most unjust wars that one nation ever waged
against another."[30] However, in the chaotic atmosphere of wartime
China, the American merchants at Canton, as well as John Quincy
Adams at home, had asked the federal government to readjust the
system of Sino-American diplomatic relations to be like that of the
British, who were soon to sign a treaty with China.[31] As soon as the
war was over and the American merchants were formally admitted to
the Five Ports on an equal footing with the British, this view changed
rapidly in favor of retaining the diplomatic status quo. As a matter
of fact, the official diplomatic relations between China and the United
States, which were finally established through the signing of the Treaty
of Wanghia, were opposed by the resident merchants in China.[32]

---

[27] Latourette, "The History of Early Relations," p. 71.

[28] See chap. 4.

[29] The opinion of the American merchants at Canton during the pretreaty period
is well reflected in Hunter's, *The "Fan Kwae" at Canton,* and Robert Forbes's,
Personal Reminiscences. The last part of Forbes's reminiscences deals with his life in
China.

[30] Hunter, *The "Fan Kwae" at Canton,* p. 154.

[31] For the merchants' opinion consult *House Doc.,* No. 40, 26 Cong., 1 sess., p. 3.
For general reference about Adams' activities in Chinese affairs consult Tyler
Dennett, *Americans in Eastern Asia* (New York: The Macmillan Co., 1925),
pp. 106-8.

[32] While Cushing was on his way to China, Edward King, an American resident merchant in Canton, who also served as the United States consular agent
in China, wrote to the Secretary of State at Washington saying: "Our countrymen have now all the privileges granted to the British and the feelings of the government and people of China continue to be favorably disposed toward Americans.
I have been careful in my proceedings to avoid prejudicing any action that a new
agent of the Government may wish to adopt, and hope that what has been done
may be satisfactory." See Edward King to the Secretary of State, Canton, September 20, 1843, *CD-USNA,* 101:3. Even after Cushing had arrived at Macao in 1844,
one of the China merchants wrote strongly against his negotiation with the Chinese government because the American merchants were "now on very best terms
possible with the Chinese." "He *cannot* make us better off," wrote the merchant,
"—and a very few of his important airs will make us hated by the Chinese, and
then we lose all the advantages we now have over the English." See *Niles' National
Register,* LXVII, No. 1721 (September 21, 1844), 36.

In the years after the signing of the Wanghia Treaty, the American merchants enjoyed a postwar boom in the China trade. They welcomed an independent and peaceful China in which a profitable foreign trade could be carried on without incidents. To them the territorial integrity and sovereignty of China must be kept inviolate lest the economic interest of the United States in China be jeopardized.[33] This desire of the merchants to maintain the commercial interest of the United States in China later formed the basis of the famous Open Door policy.

II

Next to the merchants, missionaries formed the second most important American interest group in Chinese affairs. The American missionary service in China was begun by the American Board of Commissioners for Foreign Missions in the 1830's. The Board, which was originally interdenominational, was first organized in 1810. Later, with the withdrawal of other groups, it became the organ of the Congregational churches, and other churches set up separate mission boards. It was the first Protestant organization in the United States to send missionaries to China. During this early period, lasting into the 1850's, there were more than a dozen different Christian organizations participating in the work in China.

Like the merchants in the China trade, the first American missionaries came from the big cities of the North Atlantic states. Among the eight Christian institutions that sent missionaries to China before 1850, two had their headquarters in Boston, four in New York, one in Richmond, Virginia, and another in Nashville, Tennessee.[34] Most of the

---

[33] For an excellent treatment on this subject consult Earl Swisher, "The Character of American Trade with China, 1844-1860," *University of Colorado Studies,* Ser. C (Studies in the Social Sciences), I, No. 2 (1941), 165-80. The author, however, seems to have overlooked the fact that the traditional attitude of the merchants at Boston changed a great deal in the late 1850's. For further information on this subject see chap. 13.

[34] For early missionary work in China consult K. S. Latourette, *A History of Christian Missions in China* (New York: The Macmillan Co., 1932), pp. 207 ff. Also see David Abeel, *Journal of a Residence in China* (New York: J. Abeel Williamson, 1836) pp. 4-60. The distribution of early missions to China is as follows: the two missions from Boston were American Board of Commissioners for Foreign Missions (entered China in 1830) and American Baptist Missionary Union (entered China in 1842); the four from New York were the American Protestant Episcopal Church (1835), The Reformed (Dutch) Church in America, (Northern) Presbyterian Church in the U.S.A. (1843), and Methodist Episcopal Church (1847); the one from Nashville, Tennessee was (Southern) Methodist Episcopal Church (1848); the one from Richmond, Virginia was Southern Baptist Convention (1836).

missionaries were born in the North Atlantic states.[35] Unlike the China trade in the United States, which was gradually concentrated in a few large firms in the big seaports, support for the China missions gradually came from all over the country.

Their role in Sino-American relations was entirely different from that of the merchants. Unlike the latter, the missionaries were very much troubled before the Opium War when Christianity was forbidden in China. Thus when the war broke out they wholeheartedly desired a British victory; and after the war was over, they were eager for a treaty with China so that their work among the Chinese could be protected by extraterritorial privileges. But after the Treaty of Wanghia was signed, they soon became discontented again.[36] The reason for this discontent is easily understandable. Their final goal was the conversion of the Chinese nation of four hundred million souls to Christianity. The rejection that they encountered in trying to introduce their new religion into an old culture was too strong for them to withstand. They felt that there was too much work to be done and too little that they could achieve. Therefore, they were never satisfied by any temporary success. It was quite natural that the more enthusiastic they were, the more difficulties they had to encounter. Hence they ran into trouble not only with the Chinese but also with their own merchants and government. Their untiring efforts, however, caused them to play two important but contradictory roles in the future development of China for more than a century.

First of all, they were a sort of progressive force in China in the modernization movement that reshaped her three-thousand-year-old civilization and brought her into the family of nations. For the convenience of preaching to the Chinese, the missionaries introduced into China different kinds of modern institutions and much "useful knowledge"[37] that helped the Chinese to modernize their country. As a matter of fact, to no one does China owe so much for assistance in her modernization movement than she does to the Western missionaries.

See D. MacGillivray, *A Century of Protestant Missions in China* (1807-1907) (Shanghai: The American Presbyterian Mission Press, 1907), pp. 251, 297, 332, 366, 379, 411, 429, 313.

[35] New York, for instance, was the native state of many of the leading missionaries in the early days, such as David Abeel, E. C. Bridgman, Peter Parker, Samuel Wells Williams, etc.

[36] See chap. 5.

[37] The Society for the Diffusion of Useful Knowledge was established in 1834 at Canton by a joint effort of American and British missionaries. See *The China Mission Handbook* (Shanghai: American Presbyterian Missionary Press, 1896), p. 180.

Chinese cartoonist's view of Western missionaries preaching in the street

The missionaries from America were different from the American merchants in many ways. They were more highly educated; and unlike the latter, who did not like to stay in China longer than their business required, the missionaries lived in China for decades, for life, or even for generations. They stayed there to teach as well as to learn. Consequently they became the first group of modern teachers in China; they taught science and other "useful knowledge" to the Chinese in addition to Christian doctrines. In the same way, they also became the first Sinologists in America. The first thing they acquired from the Chinese was, of course, the Chinese language; an efficient use of this not only enabled them to become good missionary workers but also to control the most important branch of the United States consular and diplomatic services in China. For many decades after the signing of the Treaty of Wanghia, it was the American missionaries who interpreted and translated for the American foreign services in China; this work gave them a chance to influence American diplomacy in China.

There was a second role that the Western missionaries played in the development of modern China, but which the missionaries themselves would find it hard to admit. For the sake of rapid penetration into China, the missionaries occasionally, though unintentionally, supported the British in their encroachment on the already weakened Celestial Empire. It was very natural for the missionaries to want to penetrate to the remotest corners of the empire and to get in touch with the Chinese masses. In fact they would be pleased if the anti-Christian government were weakened so that they could obtain more protection from the Western countries for their proselytizing. This protection was also what the British traders, particularly the opium smugglers wanted.[38] In this way the interests of the British and the American missionaries in China were parallel.

Long before the outbreak of the Opium War, the missionaries had traveled on the opium smugglers' ships in order to visit the otherwise inaccessible ports. They also occasionally served as interpreters.[39] This practice was continued in the postwar days. Therefore for many years after the Opium War, the American Christian missionaries unintentionally allied themselves with the British traders and became a

---

[38] For general reference on the opium trade in China see Fairbank, *Trade and Diplomacy on the China Coast* (Cambridge, Mass.: Harvard University Press, 1951), I, 285-364.

[39] Hunter, *The "Fan Kwae,"* p. 70.

strong pro-British force within the American diplomatic service, although for humanitarian reasons, they too opposed the opium trade.

III

In addition to the merchants and missionaries, there was a third group in the United States interested in Chinese affairs: the professional politicians on Capitol Hill. Their interest in China resulted in the United States' navy operation in the Far East in the early treaty days. In 1819, the United States frigate *Congress* was sent to Canton. It was the first of the American naval ships to visit that port.[40] In 1830 the *Vincennes*, the first American naval ship to circumnavigate the globe, called at Macao; two years later the frigate *Potomac* also visited Canton.[41] In 1832, Edmund Roberts, a special agent of the United States government, was sent with two ships, the *Peacock* and the schooner *Boxer*, to secure treaties with the Eastern powers and to protect the interests of American seamen. This expedition visited Manila, Canton, Cochin China, Siam, and Muscat, and secured treaties with the last two. Roberts visited Canton briefly in November, 1832.[42] Four years later Roberts returned to the Far East in the *Peacock* to exchange ratifications. Again he stopped at Macao but was ordered to leave by the Chinese government.[43] The Roberts expedition was a sign of an awakening interest on the part of the government of the United States. President Jackson was himself interested in the China trade, which he mentioned in his annual message of December, 1831.[44] Moreover, the search for more commodities for the United States trade in China was one of the basic reasons, in addition to scientific research and territorial exploration, that had led the government to send several special naval expeditions to the South Seas during the period.[45]

After the Opium War had started, the American merchants at Canton requested naval protection; the East India squadron, under the

---

[40] Charles Oscar Paullin, *Diplomatic Negotiations of American Naval Officers, 1778-1883* (Baltimore, Md.: The Johns Hopkins Press, 1912), pp. 168-81.

[41] Jeremiah N. Reynolds, *Voyage of the U.S. Frigate Potomac* (New York: Harper and Bros., 1835), pp. 343-44.

[42] Edmund Roberts, *Embassy to the Eastern Courts of Cochin China, Siam and Muscat in the Sloop of War Peacock, 1832-1834* (New York: Harper and Bros., 1837), p. 124.

[43] William Samuel Waithman Ruschenberger, *A Voyage Round the World* (London: R. Bebtley, 1838), p. 374.

[44] James Daniel Richardson, ed., *A Compilation of the Messages and Papers of the Presidents* (New York: Bureau of National Literature, 1917), II, 551.

[45] Charles Wilkes, *Narrative of the United States Exploring Expedition during the Years 1838, ' 39, '40, '41, '42* (Philadelphia: Lea and Blanchard, 1845), I, 175.

command of Commodore Lawrence Kearny, was dispatched to China. With two ships—the *Constellation* and the *Boston*—Kearny reached Macao early in 1842.[46] On October 6, 1842, after the Sino-British Treaty of Nanking had already been concluded, the Commodore addressed a letter to the Chinese governor, Ch'i-kung, at Canton asking for the most-favored-nation-treatment for American citizens in China.[47]

During this period some leading statesmen in Washington had the idea of signing a treaty with China. Their leader, John Quincy Adams, chairman of the House Committee on Foreign Relations, favored a positive China policy, but most of the politicians at the Capitol were somewhat indifferent because their attention was focused on territorial and land problems, the Mexican problem, the Oregon problem, and the slavery problem.[48] Both Houses of Congress were preoccupied with these questions; there was not sufficient time for discussions on Chinese affairs. To the average politician a diplomatic mission to China was unnecessary, if not a nuisance.

Early in 1843 when President Tyler's message urging the establishment of a mission to China was brought up in Congress, it met with opposition from members of both Houses. Senator Thomas H. Benton's opinion, for instance, reflected the average politician's misunderstanding of the situation in China at that time, even though the "Old Bullion," a Democrat, was an opposition leader against the Tyler administration. Concerning a mission to China, Benton said:[49]

... That there was no necessity for a treaty with China, was proved by the fact that our trade with that country had been going well without one for half a century and was now growing and increasing constantly.... All things are going on well between us and the Chinese. Our relations are purely commercial, conducted on the simplest principles of trade, and unconnected with political views....

The crucial point of Benton's argument was that China was "not within the system, or circle, of American policy." "She can have no designs upon us, or views in relation to us," Benton stressed, "and we have no need of a minister to watch and observe her conduct." As

---

[46] For a detailed description of the preparation of the Kearny mission see Carroll Storrs Alden, *Lawrence Kearny, Sailor Diplomat* (Princeton, N.J.: Princeton University Press, 1936), pp. 109-87.

[47] *Sen. Doc.*, No. 139, 29 Cong., 1 sess.; also see *IWSM-TK* LXIII, 17.

[48] For a good survey see Dennett, *Americans in Eastern Asia*, pp. 102-8; also see Samuel Flagg Bemis, *The American Secretaries of State and Their Diplomacy* (New York: Pageant Book Company, 1958), III, 170 ff.

[49] *Congressional Globe*, XII, No. 25, 27 Cong., 3 sess. (March 8, 1843), 391.

Benton understood, the mission was politically, commercially, and religiously useless, "especially as she [China] had expressed a desire to extend to this country the benefits of trade upon equal terms with Great Britain."[50] He thought that the mission to China was only an excuse to enable a gentleman who loved to travel to go to Europe and Asia "at the expense of the United States, and to write a book."[51]

Early in 1844 when the Cushing mission was already on its way to China, the House Committee on Foreign Affairs still tried to hold it back. On one occasion, it stated: "The missions to China ... the Committee considers useless; all the good they do may be done better otherwise...."[52] Regardless of the opposition at home, however, Cushing's mission to China proved to be a great success for American diplomacy in the Far East, and resulted in the signing of the Treaty of Wanghia in July, 1844. Since this subject has been well covered by both Chinese and Western historians, it requires little description here.[53]

IV

After the Wanghia Treaty was ratified, the federal government failed to take further measures (other than the appointment of a commissioner to China for the exchange of ratifications) to put it into practice and to formulate a proper policy for the commissioner to follow. For nearly a decade after the signing of the treaty, the American diplomatic and consular services in China were constantly embarrassed by the lack of suitable congressional legislation that might enable them to function properly.

The American diplomatic and consular service in China, however, was not the only part of the United States foreign service that was limited by a lack of adequate power. The system of foreign service as a whole was in an unhealthy condition. And even the State Department was not effectively operated.

The Department of State had been established in 1789. Its organizational system remained unchanged until 1833, when Louis McLane was head of the Department and made some minor improvements.[54]

---

[50] *Ibid.*, p. 392.   [51] *Ibid.*, p. 391.

[52] *House Report*, No. 166, 28 Cong., 1 sess., February 15, 1844, p. 4.

[53] For detailed descriptions about the negotiation and signing of the Treaty of Wanghia the following accounts may be consulted: Ping-chia Kuo, "Caleb Cushing and the Treaty of Wanghia, 1844," *Journal of Modern History*, V, No. 1 (March, 1933), 34-54; Dennett, *Americans in Eastern Asia*, pp. 145 ff.; Claude Fuess, *The Life of Caleb Cushing* (New York: Harcourt, Brace and Co., 1932) I, 397 ff.

[54] Graham H. Stuart, *The Department of State, a History of Its Organization, Procedure, and Personnel* (New York: The Macmillan Company, 1949), p. 77.

When the Treaty of Wanghia was signed, the Department contained seven bureaus (i.e., diplomatic; consular; home; archives, laws, and commissions; pardons, remissions, copyrights, and library; disbursing and superintending; translating and miscellaneous). Chinese affairs were placed under the charge of the second of the three clerks assigned to the diplomatic bureau.[55]

The State Department at this time was very understaffed. Early in 1843, Secretary of State Daniel Webster reported that the Department had only fifteen regular clerks and two messengers. Extra business was handled by employees on temporary basis for periods ranging from four days to nine months.[56] When John C. Calhoun became the head of the Department, he reported in February, 1845, to the Chairman of the Ways and Means Committee that during the years 1818 to 1845, a period of twenty-seven years, only four regular clerks had been added to the Department, and only one of these during the last eighteen years.[57] When James Buchanan became the Secretary of State in March, 1845, he also complained that the United States diplomatic correspondence with all the nations of the world was carried on by three regular clerks, assisted by two copying clerks, while the consular section was even worse off, with only two clerks. And of all the persons belonging to the Department, the Secretary was the only one with authority to sign a single paper or to decide on any question, however trivial it might be.[58]

In 1849 Secretary John M. Clayton reported that the State Department had twenty-four clerks, one regular and two assistant messengers, two extra clerks, seven packers, and a laborer.[59] During William L. Marcy's term as Secretary of State, the Department was again reorganized in August, 1856, to include a total of fifty-seven persons.[60] Thus the Department of State was smaller than a first-class United States consulate at the present time.

The American diplomatic and consular establishments overseas were in an even worse condition. When the Wanghia Treaty was signed, the United States had nine ministers extraordinary and plenipotentiary (including the China mission) and twelve chargés d'affaires.[61]

---

55 *Ibid.* p. 78.
56 *House Doc.,* No. 84, 27 Cong., 3 sess., Jan. 25, 1843, pp. 1-3.
57 Stuart, *Department of State,* p. 101.
58 *Ibid.* p. 104.
59 *House Ex. Doc.,* No. 43, 31 Cong., 1 sess., Feb. 21, 1850, p. 2.
60 *House Ex. Doc.,* No. 30, 34 Cong., 3 sess., Jan. 5, 1857, pp. 1-3.
61 Stuart, *Department of State,* p. 108.

With the exception of the United States minister to England, who received a salary of $9,000 per annum,[62] the United States ministers and commissioners to other countries were generally underpaid, and their legations poorly staffed.

In the 1840's, the American consular establishments throughout the world still remained in the stage of a merchant-consul system. Out of 170 consuls appointed to foreign ports, only a few were paid by the government. As late as 1853, there were but ten salaried consuls; the remainder derived their salaries from consular fees.[63]

Worst of all was the United States diplomatic and consular service in China. When Everett was appointed the United States commissioner to China, he was given an annual salary of only $5,000,[64] a little more than half of the amount received by the United States minister to England. He was given a few assistants but no official residence, although his Chinese counterpart, the Imperial Commissioner or governor-general, had an annual allowance ranging from three to six times as much as he, plus an army of servants and a magnificent palace.[65]

For nearly a decade after Cushing's mission, the American legation was located at Macao. The whole legation consisted of a few poorly paid officials. In addition to the commissioner and the secretary, there were one or two clerks and a Chinese "teacher." At that time, the Chinese language was used for official diplomatic correspondence in China. In the American legation, Dr. Parker had served as the official interpreter and translator for more than a decade. But strictly speaking, Parker's Chinese was very poor and hardly suitable for official use, as Commissioner Humphrey Marshall wrote in 1853:[66]

Doctor Parker cannot write a despatch of mine into the Chinese court

---

[62] *Ibid.,* p. 98.

[63] U.S. Department of State, *The United States Consular System: Manual for Consuls and also for Merchants, Shipowners and Masters* (Washington, D.C.: Taylor and Maury, 1856), pp. 5-24; or see Eldon Griffin, *Clippers and Consuls* (Ann Arbor, Mich.: Edwards Brothers, 1938), p. 48.

[64] Buchanan to Everett, No. 1, Washington, D.C., April 15, 1845, *DI-USNA,* 77:38. The annual salary of the U.S. commissioners to China was periodically raised after 1848.

[65] See chap. 3.

[66] Humphrey Marshall to State Department, No. 16, Shanghai, May 26, 1853, *House Document,* No. 123, 33 Cong., 1 sess., p. 140. All of Commissioner Marshall's official reports to the Department of State together with other official correspondence attached to them were published by Congress as *House Document,* No. 123, which will be cited hereafter as *Marshall's Correspondence.*

language with any confidence in the correctness of the translation, *if at all*. Hence he employs an assistant, called teacher, to do this part of the business. This teacher is a Chinese, who does not understand one word of the English language. The interpreter takes up my despatch and translates it verbally into Chinese, as *he speaks the language;* the teacher catches an idea of the original, and according to *his* finding thereof writes it in the character used at court.

Besides these technical handicaps, the American legation was not furnished with sufficient means for the daily routine work. For many years after its establishment, the legation did not have even an American flag, nor were there sufficient legal reference books for research on legal cases.[67]

The United States consular service in mainland China was in an even worse shape. Major Samuel Shaw, who had been appointed to the position of a consul at Canton in the 1780's, was succeeded by unpaid volunteers, mostly merchants. This practice was not changed by the signing of the Treaty of Wanghia, although the number of American consuls in China was increased. The work in the different consulates after the opening of the Five Ports was unbelievably confusing. In those days, the State Department at Washington did not know how many consuls it had appointed abroad, where they were, and how they were working.[68] One of the most amusing cases occurred in August, 1853, when Commissioner Marshall reported to the State Department:[69]

Letters constantly arrive here from the Department of State, and addressed to "Dwight Webb, Esq., United States Consul at Fuhchowfoo." I have to say to you that no person has ever filled the consulate at Fuhchowfoo, and there never has been, and is not now in China, such a person as Mr. Dwight Webb.

Moreover, the American consulates in the Five Ports throughout the period covered by this study were understaffed; usually there was only one official in the consulate—the consul himself. Thus compared with their English counterparts, the American consuls were very much embarrassed by their inferior position. In 1849, for instance, Charles William Bradley was appointed United States consul at Amoy. Upon his arrival at Amoy, he found himself in a poor situation as compared

---

[67] *Ibid.,* p. 169; John W. Davis to Secretary of State, No. 11, Jan. 27, 1849, *DD-USNA,* 92:6; see also chap. 8.

[68] Chester Lloyd Jones, *The Consular Service of the United States, Its History and Activities* (Philadelphia: The John C. Winston Co., 1906), p. 23.

[69] *Marshall's Correspondence,* p. 233.

with the British consular settlement there which, as Bradley saw, consisted of "a Consul, Vice Consul, First Assistant, Second Assistant, Interpreter, Assistant Interpreter, Medical Attendant, Chinese Writer, Linguist, and many minor servants . . . and of a vessel of war from that government being constantly stationed in the harbor. . . ."[70] Embarrassed, Bradley comforted himself by appointing his son, Charles W. Bradley, Jr., to the position of vice-consul.[71]

In addition to this inadequacy in organization and maintenance, the work and authority of the individual officials and institutions overlapped. The commissioner, the secretary of the legation, and the different consuls all worked and reported independently to the Department of State. Thus as time passed, conflicts over power as well as over ideas increased among them and among the missionaries and the merchants who wanted to influence the functions of the legation. Moreover, since the mail to, and the reply from, the United States took more than a year, these conflicts (which usually were appealed to the State Department for proper solution) could hardly be settled within two years; and the commissioners and consuls rarely served longer than that.

This kind of confusion gave most of the officers a free hand to do whatever they wanted. In the late 1850's at Foochow, the United States consul, Samuel L. Gouverneur, once forced an American merchant from Boston by the name of Dexter to pay some extra fees for consular service. When the merchant remonstrated against such an improper charge, the consul replied that Dexter could not help himself but must pay it. Dexter answered that he could complain to the government, to which the consul replied rather humorously:[72]

Well what will you get; it will take six months for a reply, the Government will then call upon me to explain the Charge, I will not answer for a long time, and will not then give a very lucid explanation. I will then receive sharp reply stating that my answer is not satisfactory. I will answer that I have no other explanation to give; and they will then remove me. All this will take two years and that is as long as I care to stay in this damned country.

The consul's reply is as realistic as it is amusing. As a result of this

---

[70] William L. Bradley to John M. Clayton, No. 7, Amoy, July 1, 1850, Consular Dispatches from Amoy as microfilmed by the National Archives Service, microfilm number 100, Roll No. 2, hereafter to be cited as CD-USNA, Amoy, 100:2.

[71] Ibid., No. 2, Amoy, November 26, 1849.

[72] John E. Ward to Lewis Cass, No. 27, Hong Kong, November 29, 1860, DD-USNA, 92:20.

kind of confusion and the lack of information in general, the authorities in the cabinet as well as the politicians in Congress could not understand what was going on in China, particularly when a controversial event, such as the Taiping Rebellion, occurred.

Moreover, since the compensation of a commission to China was too low to attract any particular attention of any interest group, even in a spoils system,[73] the American legation to China was exempt from being a prey to the position-hungry politicians. The general result was that United States diplomacy in China was completely independent of American domestic politics. Even had the diplomats been shifted with every administration, it would have made no serious difference, for neither major political party favored any particular policy toward China.

V

Owing to the general negligence in the United States toward Chinese affairs and to the poor organization of the diplomatic and consular service, Washington lost its initiative in directing the United States diplomatic and consular services in China. Unlike the British government, which always took self-initiated aggressive action in the East, the United States government was compelled to move ahead reluctantly. Driven by the accumulated problems deriving from extraterritoriality, Congress passed a bill in August, 1848, four years after the Treaty of Wanghia, for the creation of consular courts.[74] Because of the confusion caused by the personal conflicts among diplomatic and consular officers, the State Department gradually moved to regulate the diplomatic and consular services in China. In 1853 the consulates were ordered to be subject to the direction of the commissioner, and "all correspondence between the Secretary of Legation and the Department of State, should be transmitted through the Commissioner."[75]

Among these readjustments, most important of all was the making of a proper China policy by Washington. Prior to the end of the Pierce administration, many of the capable Secretaries of State, such as Daniel Webster and John C. Calhoun, were completely taken up with domestic politics, European and Latin American problems, as

---

[73] As a matter of fact, two appointees for the commissionership to China declined the appointments because of its low compensation. See *DI-USNA*, 77:38, pp. 71, 73.

[74] See chap. 7.

[75] William L. Marcy to Robert M. McLane, No. 3, November 16, 1853, *DI-USNA*, 77:38, p. 96.

well as personal presidential ambitions. Chinese affairs were not important enough to attract their specific attention. They took no initiative action but let the diplomatic service in China go its own way. Therefore, for nearly a decade after the signing of the Treaty of Wanghia, the American commissioners to China were given no specific instructions. They were allowed to make their own decisions as they saw fit. Consequently, the United States commissioners to China were vested with "large discretionary powers."[76] They were actually the policy-makers, although their decisions were subject to final approval from Washington.

Therefore, in the early period—from Acting Commissioner Biddle to the early 1850's—each American commissioner, as we shall see in following chapters, had specific proposals regarding the formation of a proper China policy. Since commissioners to China had comparatively short terms, most of them had no chance to put their policy into practice. Thus their suggestions had no definite influence upon Washington. They were usually shelved as soon as the commissioners left China.

Regardless of the fact that their proposals varied in method and outlook, their basic principle remained consistent. It is interesting indeed for historians to see that the dispatches submitted by the different commissioners were coincidentally based upon one common principle, which, in later years, was known as the "Open Door" doctrine—that is, the territorial integrity of China and equal commercial privileges for all Western powers. Thus, any power that aimed to dominate China alone was to be opposed by the United States. This common principle, which was intermittently put into practice by the different commissioners, formed a general trend of United States policy toward China in the early period.

Counterbalancing this general policy, however, was a contrary policy adopted by Peter Parker, who was given six interim appointments as chargé d'affaires until he himself became commissioner to China in 1855. The combined length of Parker's service as chargé d'affaires and commissioner was longer than all the terms of different commissioners put together. Unlike the other commissioners, Parker favored a policy similar to that of the British; he was willing to adopt force-

---

[76] In Secretary Marcy's second instruction to Commissioner McLane on November 9, 1853, for instance, the Secretary wrote: "The accounts do not furnish satisfactory information of its present condition or enable us to conjecture, with any degree of certainty, what will be its result; it is therefore necessary that you should be vested with large discretionary powers." *DI-USNA,* 77:38, p. 90.

ful means to compel the Chinese to accept Western terms. Thus during his long service in the legation, Parker formulated a pro-British policy contrary to the general line of "Open Door." These two lines of American policy were put into practice intermittently and alternately for more than a decade after the signing of the Treaty of Wanghia.

The former policy reached its climax when Humphrey Marshall was commissioner to China in 1852. He was recalled early in 1854 because his opposition to the British and to the Taiping Rebellion (which was then considered by the American public as a Christian revolution in China) had raised serious objection within the United States.

After the recall of Marshall, American policy toward China gradually swung in another direction. It was fixed by the appointment of Peter Parker to the commissionership in 1855. Parker's policy of collaboration with the British reached its peak after the "Arrow War" in the winter of 1856.[77] During that crisis, the United States government was confronted with the alternatives of either cooperating with Britain in order to have a share in defeated China or of helping China in order to bring the British encroachment on China to a halt. The urgent situation in China forced the Washington authorities to make an immediate choice. The traditional practice of consulting the merchants or missionaries before making a decision,[78] or of letting the commissioner himself judge according to the circumstances, was no longer applicable to the new situation. It was now the State Department that had to make the final decision.

The crisis coincided with the election of James Buchanan to the

---

[77] See chap. 13.

[78] In 1843 when Congress had approved the proposal of a China mission and before it was known who would be the commissioner, Daniel Webster, the Secretary of State, sent a circular letter to most of the American merchants resident in Boston, Salem, New York, and elsewhere, engaged in the China trade, inviting suggestions. This letter received wide attention from the American merchants in the China trade. See Dennett, *Americans in Eastern Asia,* p. 135. This practice was later continued by Webster's successors. In the spring of 1854 when the United States diplomatic functions in China reached another turning point because of the British appeal for close Anglo-American cooperation in China, Secretary of State William L. Marcy also consulted the Boston merchants for information and suggestions. Their opinion, which obviously influenced Marcy's new policy toward China, was forwarded to Commissioner Robert M. McLane as important reference for his diplomatic functions in China. See R. B. Forbes to Caleb Cushing, Boston, February 11, 1857, Cushing MSS., Library of Congress. For Marcy's comment on these suggestions see Marcy to McLane, No. 7, Washington, D.C., May 8, 1854, *DI-USNA,* 77:38, p. 99.

White House in 1856. Having served as Secretary of State for four years, Buchanan was, comparatively speaking, well acquainted with the United States diplomatic service in China. When the State Department decided to recall Parker it reversed its former practice and took the diplomatic service into its own hands. The lengthy instruction that Secretary Lewis Cass issued to Commissioner William Reed (Parker's successor as commissioner to China) on May 30, 1857, was the longest and most itemized specific document that a Secretary of State had ever issued to a commissioner to China. "But on your side these efforts [for the negotiation of a new treaty with China] must be confined to firm representations, appealing to the justice and policy of the Chinese authorities," stressed Cass, "and leaving to your own Government to determine upon the course to be adopted, should your representation be fruitless."[79] Only after this period did Washington begin to exercise even a remote control over its diplomats in China, who were no longer to enjoy such "large discretionary powers." The authorities in Washington had taken more than ten years to establish a policy and to realize the importance of the "Open Door" doctrine, which had been first laid down by Everett in 1847 and which was to be continued for a whole century thereafter.

[79] Cass to Reed, No. 2, Washington, D.C., May 30, 1857, *CI-USNA,* 77:38, p. 159.

3

PROBLEMS OF READJUSTMENT

IN CHINA

I

THE foreign treaties that China signed with the Western powers after
the Opium War gradually reshaped the old Chinese political and economic system, a great part of which could trace its origin back thousands of years. During the postwar period, however, the Ch'ing officialdom did not change in form so much as in function. There was no
special office in charge of the Empire's foreign affairs until 1860. Up
to that date, Chinese foreign affairs were assigned to the local authorities under whose jurisdiction the Five Ports were located. In order to
understand how Chinese policy was carried out during this period, it
is necessary to make a brief review of the contemporary Chinese political and economic system.

In imperial China, the Emperor was the fountainhead of all governmental power. Nominally his will was the law of the land, though not
without some constitutional checks.[1] Under him the central government was organized into two councils—the *Nei-ko* (or Cabinet) and
Chun-chi ch'u (or Grand Council)—under which there were six boards
(or *Pu*)—Civil Appointments, Revenue, Rites, War, Criminal Affairs,
and Public Works—and many minor bureaus. The Cabinet was an old
institution inherited from the Ming dynasty. It contained six members
called *ta-hsueh-shih* (or grand secretaries) of whom three were Manchu and three Chinese. Originally, these six members formed a col-

---

[1] For a general description of the officialdom in the Ch'ing period see Hsiao I-shan,
Ch'ing-tai t'ung-shih (A General History of the Ch'ing Period) (Shanghai: Com-
mercial Press, 1927), I, 453-563; or *Ch'ing shih kao* (Draft History of the Ch'ing)
(Peiping, 1828), book 33, "Chih-kuan chih." For reference in English see Pao
Chao Hsieh, *The Government of China (1644-1911)* (Baltimore, Md.: The Johns
Hopkins Press, 1925). For brief summary in English see Samuel Wells Williams,
The Middle Kingdom (New York: Wiley and Putnam, 1848), I, 296-353; or Hosea
Ballou Morse, *The International Relations of the Chinese Empire* (London: Long-
mans, Green and Co., 1910), I, 1-25. For a special discussion on the Emperor see
Hsieh, pp. 24-44.

lective leadership functioning as a secretariat in the Court, but its power gradually was shifted to the Grand Council (literally means "the board of military strategists"), which was a later institution established for military campaigns by Emperor Yung-cheng in the early years of the eighteenth century. The membership of these two councils usually overlapped; as the Grand Council became more extensively organized, it gradually took over the power previously enjoyed by the Cabinet. During and after the Opium War, it was the Grand Council, over which Mu-chang-a presided, that had actually assisted the Emperor to write edicts and to forward to him the memorials submitted by the local authorities.[2]

The local administrative unit in the Ch'ing Empire was the province, which occupied a semiautonomous position vis-a-vis the imperial government at Peking. The highest official in charge of provincial administration was the governor-general (or *tsung-tu*), who had jurisdiction usually over one to three provinces. He had the right to exercise all governmental power: the political, judicial, and, in part, the military.[3] Under the governor-general, there was a governor in each province. In theory, the governor was under the over-all supervision of the governor-general, but, in practice, the governor-general had no power to hold the governor in check. On the contrary, the governor usually served as a check upon the governor-general. In places where a governor-general and a governor resided together, such as in the city of Canton, there was usually a struggle between them, which often resulted in the withdrawal of the less powerful, less clever, or less favored one from the province.[4]

To supervise or to assist the governor-general or the governor in public administration on a special occasion, an Imperial Commissioner was usually appointed. This appointment, however, was temporary,

---

[2] For a biographical sketch of Mu-chang-a see Arthur W. Hummel, ed., *Eminent Chinese of the Ch'ing Period* (Washington, D.C.: Government Printing Office, 1943), I, 582-83.

[3] Nominally both the governor-general and the governor were also military officers included in the list of the Department of War. But of the two kinds of troops camped within their jurisdiction the chief administrators had command over only the "Green Battalions," which were recruited from the Chinese population. The "Banner Garrisons," which were mostly recruited from the Manchu, were under a Tartar general. Of all the troops in the provinces, a governor-general directly commanded his vice-regal brigades, and a governor, his governor's brigades, each amounting to a few thousand men, though nominally a governor-general was the supreme military commander of the whole area under his jurisdiction. See Hsiao, *Ch'ing-tai t'ung-shih,* I, 513-27; Hsieh, *The Government of China (1644-1911),* p. 298.

[4] Hsieh, *The Government of China (1644-1911),* p. 293.

established only for certain particular events, such as for opium suppression or dike repair, and the like, or during an emergency, such as the Nanking negotiation of 1842. The Imperial Commissioner usually possessed a high, if not the highest, civil or military rank in the Empire, with many actual as well as honorary titles. He was either sent out alone for special missions or was assigned to some local position, such as that of governor-general.[5]

Under the supervision of the governor-general and the governor, the provincial government was organized into many departments and bureaus, among which the most important ones were those of the provincial treasurer and the provincial judge. The provincial treasurer or *pu-cheng-shih-ssu* (commonly called *fan-t'ai*) was in charge of the civil service of each province and of supervising the collection and remittance of taxes within the province.[6] He was directly appointed by the Emperor and was responsible in financial matters to the Board of Revenue at Peking.

The provincial judge or *an-ch'a-shih-ssu* (commonly called *nieh-t'ai*) was in charge of supervising criminal cases in the province. Like the provincial treasurer, he was directly appointed by the Emperor and independent of the control of the governor-general and the governor. The *fan-t'ai* and *nieh-t'ai* also served as checks and balances in the local government. In addition to these two offices, there were salt comptroller or *yen-yun-shih-ssu* (in some provinces also called *yen-yun-tao* or circuit of salt distribution), grain intendent or *liang-tao* and many others in charge of different kinds of local administration.[7]

The administrative system within the province was divided into three levels, namely, *tao*,[8] *fu* or *chou*, and *hsien* or *t'ing*, headed re-

---

[5] During the Wanghia negotiation, for instance, Imperial Commissioner Ch'i-ying's full title was as follows: Ch'i-ying of the Imperial House, Minister and Commissioner Extraordinary, Vice Guardian of the Heir Apparent, Governor-General of the Two Kuangs, Superintendent-General of the Trade and Foreign Intercourse of the Five Ports. See the introductory paragraph of the Wanghia Treaty in *Treaties, Conventions, etc., between China and Foreign States* (Shanghai: Statistical Department of the Inspectoral General of Customs, 1908), p. 473.

[6] Each province ordinarily had only one provincial treasurer, but the province of Kiangsu was an exception. It had two provincial treasurers, one with its office at Soochow, and another at Nanking. See *Ch'in ting Ta'-ch'ing hui-tien shih-li* (Annotated Collected Institutes of the Ch'ing) (Shanghai: Commercial Press, 1909), *chüan* 24, 5b; *chüan* 361, 2a.

[7] Hsiao, *Ch'ing-tai t'ung-shih*, I, 493-94; Hsieh, *The Government of China (1644-1911)*, pp. 289-320.

[8] The *tao* was not an ordinary administrative unit with a fixed area. It was originally designed for the administration of certain specific governmental undertakings, such as salt control (*yen-yun tao*), and the like. In its later development, however, the *tao* system had a dual purpose. In the middle of the Ch'ing period, the

spectively by a *taot'ai*,[9] *chih-fu* or *chih-chou*, and *hsien-chih-shih* of the *hsien* or *t'ung-chih* of the *t'ing*. After the Five Ports were formally opened for foreign trade, the foreign consuls had to get in touch with the *taotais* of Shanghai, Ningpo, and Amoy. Conditions in Canton and Foochow, where the provincial capitals were located, however, were different since it was possible for the foreign consuls there to communicate more easily with the higher Chinese authorities. There the *taotai's* power in "barbarian administration" was narrowly limited.

The military system in the middle of the Ch'ing period is also worth noting. Before the Taiping Rebellion the regular Ch'ing army was divided into two categories—the Eight Banners and the Green Battalions. The former was recruited primarily from the victorious Manchus, the latter from the conquered Chinese. After the Manchu conquest of China in 1644, these Eight Banners were sent out as Tartar garrisons to different strategic posts throughout the Empire; each was commanded by a high ranking Tartar general. The Green Battalions, which were treated only as a supplementary force, played no important role in the military campaigns previous to the Taiping Rebellion. In the Opium War, therefore, it was these Manchu troops who were badly defeated by the British invaders; but it was from their commanders that most of the first "barbarian experts," notably Ch'i-ying and Ilipu, who negotiated the first Sino-Western treaties, were drawn.[10]

The Ch'ing customs service was another peculiar institution strange to contemporary Western observers as well as to modern historians. Prior to the Opium War in China, no great distinction existed, from the official Chinese viewpoint, between overseas and domestic trade, both

---

ordinary *tao* had under its jurisdiction several districts possessing many kinds of governmental power, such as the command of local militia and the supervision of local judicial cases. This kind of *tao*, therefore, was an administrative unit between the prefectures and the province. But the other kind of *tao*, such as *liang tao* and *yen-yun tao*, preserved the old form, with jurisdiction over certain governmental undertakings rather than over certain fixed areas. These two kinds of official functions, however, were sometimes combined into one office. The customs service of Shanghai, for instance, was under the supervision of the *taotai* of the Su-Sung-T'ai *tao* whose jurisdiction covered an area of two *fu* (Su-chou and Sung-chiang) and one *chou* (T'ai-ts'ang) in which the port of Shanghai was located. For a general description of the *tao* system see Hsiao, *Ch'ing-tai t'ung-shih*, I, 493-94; or *Ch'in ting Ta-Ch'ing hui-tien shih-li*, *chüan* 25, 1-6.

[9] The term *taot'ai* has been commonly used as *taotai*, which I have used throughout this essay.

[10] Ilipu was appointed in April, 1842, acting assistant military lieutenant-general at Cha-p'u, and later that year Tartar general at Canton. Ch'i-ying was the Tartar general at Sheng-ching (Mukden), 1838-1842, and at Canton and Hangchow during the later part of 1842. See Hummel, *Eminent Chinese of the Ch'ing Period*, I, 130-34, 387-88.

of which were usually conducted by Chinese merchants; nor did the government rely upon such trade for its major revenue. During the middle of the nineteenth century, there were twenty-nine customs stations located mainly on the routes of China's domestic trade;[11] the "maritime customs collectorates" (*hai-kuan*) of the southern coastal provinces (at Canton, Foochow, Cheng-hai, and Shanghai) were included among the twenty-nine.[12]

Five of these customs stations were under the Board of Public Works; duties collected were used to support different kinds of public works. The other twenty-four stations were under the Board of Revenue. Each customhouse had an annual quota to fulfill.[13] The one with the largest quota was, of course, the Yueh-hai-kuan (or the Customhouse of Kwangtung province). Its chief, the Yueh-hai-kuan *chien-tu*, commonly known as the Hoppo in Western writings, was appointed directly from Peking with an annual salary and allowance of nearly 3,000 taels.[14] His office was completely independent of all local authorities, and the duties he collected were used for the expenditures of the Manchu palace at Peking. In the pretreaty days, however, the Hoppo at Canton had never collected the payments directly from foreign traders. He collected the customs through the monopolistic or-

---

[11] *Ta-Ch'ing hui-tien* (Collected Institutes of the Ch'ing) (Shanghai: Shanghai Bookstore, 1899), *chüan* 17, 7b-8a.

[12] John K. Fairbank, *Trade and Diplomacy on the China Coast* (Cambridge, Mass: Harvard University Press, 1953), p. 255.

[13] *Ta-Ch'ing hui-tien, chüan* 17, 7b-8a.

[14] Mr. Stanley F. Wright, the most authoritative author on the Chinese customs service, seems to have made a mistake in his invaluable book, *Hart and the Chinese Customs* (Belfast: Wm. Mullan and Son, 1950). Concerning the Hoppo's annual compensation, he stated: "His salary of tls. 25,000 (say £8,000) a year was, from the Western point of view, a substantial one . . ." (p. 69). As this writer understands, the highest pay ever received by a Ch'ing customs officer was that of the superintendent of the Kiukiang Customs House, who had an annual allowance of ts. 11,000. See *Ch'in ting Ta-Ch'ing hui-tien shih-li, chüan* 263, 1a. The ordinary compensation received by a Ch'ing official was, as a rule, divided into two items—his fixed salary with some food rations according to his rank and an annual allowance varying according to the location of his office; the latter was usually ten times as much as the former. According to the *shih li* mentioned above, the annual allowance of the Hoppo at Canton was tls. 2,500. Hence his total compensation for a year might not exceed tls. 3,000. According to the same Chinese source, the annual allowance of the governor-general of the two Kwang provinces, the highest paid official at Canton, was only tls. 15,000. The Hoppo, who occupied a much inferior position in that area, could never receive an official compensation of tls. 25,000 per annum.

[15] As a well-known historical institution, *co-hong* has been discussed by numerous writers both in Chinese and in Western languages. For detailed reference see Liang Chia-ping, *Kuang-tung shih-san-hang k'ao* (A Study of the Thirteen Foreign Factories in Canton) (Shanghai: Commercial Press, 1937).

ganization of the Chinese security merchants, the well-known *co-hong* system.[15]

After the Opium War, however, the monopolistic *co-hong* was abolished. According to the Treaty of Nanking, the Hoppo had to meet the foreign traders in Canton face to face. The customhouse in Foochow, which had been under the supervision of the Tartar general there,[16] was now under the direction of the provincial treasurer of Fukien province; the customhouses in other ports were under the supervision of the *taotai* of their respective localities.[17]

II

Since the Manchu government had created no centralized institution to supervise the foreign trade in the Five Ports, the ordinary local officials at the different ports—that is, the governor and the *taotai*, appointed in the traditional way—were incompetent both in training and in experience to bear the new responsibilities suddenly thrust upon them. Under the new circumstances, therefore, the service of a new group of trained-on-the-job "barbarian experts" became indispensable. Among them, Ch'i-ying was the most eminent figure and acted as the *de facto* foreign minister of China for seven years after the Opium War. His intelligence and experience guided the Chinese foreign policy during those critical postwar years.[18]

Ch'i-ying, known in Western writings as Tsiying, Kiying, or Keying, was an imperial clansman, a Manchu noble, who began his career in the Imperial Clan Court at the beginning of the nineteenth century. In 1815 he became the superintendent of customs at Shanhaikuan; the experience gained here in the Chinese customs service was apparently helpful in his later diplomatic negotiations. Having been promoted to the vice-presidency and presidency of different boards at Peking in the mid-1830's, he was appointed in June 1838 as the Tartar general of Sheng-ching, residing at Mukden. In March, 1842, when the Opium War was at its climax, he was transferred to Canton as the Tartar general in that city. But on the way to Canton, he was detained to act

---

[16] Hsiao, *Ch'ing-tai t'ung-shih*, I, 513-27; Hsieh, *The Government of China (1644-1911)*, pp. 255 ff.

[17] *IWSM-TK*, LXX, 20-21.

[18] For a biographical sketch of Ch'i-ying see Hummel, I, 130-34. Some historians have claimed that Mu-chang-a, rather than Ch'i-ying, actually guided China's foreign policy after the signing of the Treaty of Nanking. But Mu-chang-a knew comparatively little about the "barbarian affairs," although he was a major supporter of Ch'i-ying. During the postwar years most of Emperor Tao-kuang's edicts concerning foreign affairs were based upon Ch'i-ying's memorials.

as the Tartar general of Hangchow. Later he was given the title of Imperial Commissioner to negotiate with the British invaders at Nanking. Consequently, he signed the Treaty of Nanking, together with two other colleagues, Ilipu and Niu Ch'ien, on August 29, 1842; later, on October 8, 1843, he also signed the famous Supplementary Treaty of the Bogue (Hu-men-chai) with Sir Henry Pottinger, head of the British delegation. It was through this treaty that the Chinese granted consular jurisdiction and other extraterritorial rights to the British, including the most-favored-nation treatment.[19] These treaty privileges were soon extended by the Chinese government to all other Western countries.[20]

During his four years at Canton (1844-48), Ch'i-ying organized a well-staffed headquarters and signed successively three treaties with four Western powers in addition to Great Britain: one with the United States, the Treaty of Wanghia on July 3, 1844; one with France on October 24, 1844; and another with Sweden and Norway on November 20, 1847.[21] These treaties were drawn up along lines that Ch'i-ying had long contemplated.

Though shrewd, the Manchu, being handicapped by his lack of modern training, had constantly been out-maneuvered by the "barbarians" who, taking advantage of the most-favored-nation treatment, had so increased their demands that eventually the "appeasement policy" set up by Ch'i-ying had to be abandoned and the Chinese were forced to return to their old way of "barbarian management."

It is popular among both Chinese and Western writers to assert that Ch'i-ying's policy was a policy of appeasement and friendship and was bitterly opposed by the so-called war party in the Court. This assertion is only partly true. During the initial stage of the Opium War, it seemed that all mandarins in Peking, including the Emperor himself, were eager to fight. The atmosphere in Peking was completely changed, however, after Chinkiang had been lost to the "barbarian invaders," when in the summer of 1842 Nanking was in danger of falling, and particularly when the high-ranking officials at Peking were preparing to move their families out of the city in their fear of a possible British attack.

It may be noted that during the thousands of years of her experience, China had been conquered many times by frontier barbarian tribes whose military power was superior to hers. When the Opium

---

[19] *Treaties, Conventions, etc., between China and Foreign States,* pp. 198-207.
[20] *IWSM-TK,* LXVIII, 40b.

War extended to the Yangtze valley, the Chinese seemed to believe that history was to repeat itself once more. The new conquerors might eventually build up a dynasty in China to substitute for the Manchu rulers who had come to power only two centuries before.[22] To their surprise, however, the British forces withdrew peaceably after merely signing a commercial treaty at Nanking. It had cost the Manchus so little to avoid so big a danger. Such a miracle had never before happened in Chinese history! Therefore, after the successful conclusion of the Nanking truce the war party in Peking completely disappeared. There was no war talk even in the tea shops.[23] The whole mandarin class awakened to the realization that the Western barbarians were neither ordinary frontier rebels, who could be easily suppressed by the Celestial forces, nor real conquerors who might intend to build up a new dynasty in China. All they wanted was a profitable commercial settlement—a rather reasonable demand. Hence the whole Court, particularly the Emperor himself and the "premier," Mu-chang-a of the Grand Council, began to favor a policy of appeasement, and Ch'i-ying naturally became their spokesman.

After the Nanking negotiations, therefore, Ch'i-ying was fully convinced by the popular reasoning that "there is no other way to pacify the barbarians but to conduct commercial affairs [with them]."[24] All that the foreigners wanted was merely commercial profit; such demands could be successfully and reasonably settled by peaceful means. This idea was also shared by the Emperor, who thought that the "barbarian" demands were derived from the desire of getting "more taels of silver" from him.[25]

----

[21] For general reference, see Morse, *The International Relations of the Chinese Empire*, I, 331, 332.

[22] During the initial stage of Nanking negotiations in August, 1842, when Chang Hsi, the first Chinese messenger aboard the British warship, was told by the British interpreter, Robert Morrison, that the British forces would eventually conquer all parts of China, including Peking, he replied that even if the English were capable of doing so, the Chinese people still would not be willing "to accept you English barbarians as the new rulers of China." Chang's reply well expressed the public opinion and fear of the Chinese people on the street at that time. See Chang Hsi, *Fu-i jih-chi* (A Diary on the Appeasement of Barbarians) (Peiping: Wen-hua-k'o, 1935), p. 27.

[23] "Juan-ch'en szu-i" (Private Discussions on the Soft Dusts), *Ya-p'ien chancheng*, V, 529. The "Private Discussions" was written by an unknown author at Peking during the Opium War period. It contains many invaluable inside stories of the contemporary Court.

[24] *IWSM-TK*, LXXII, 450.

[25] When Emperor Tao-kuang heard that the British were demanding the return of the prisoners of war whom the Chinese had captured and already slain in 1841, he said: "These fellows are only trying to get more taels of silver from me." See "Juan-ch'en szu-i," p. 529.

But Ch'i-ying was no fool. He never conceded to the foreigners anything that he considered really harmful to his country. He was, however, not a student of modern international law; he had no idea about the purely Western conception of so-called sovereign rights. China granted extraterritoriality because this grant seemed to be a convenient procedure for "barbarian management" in the Five Ports. Ch'i-ying was probably the first Chinese high-ranking mandarin to realize that the Western "barbarians" were also highly civilized peoples with whom he could make friends.[26] The "barbarian officials," so it seemed to him, were as respectable, reasonable, and just as the mandarins themselves; if they were treated in the right way, they usually appeared very reasonable, extremely respectful, and obedient.[27] Was it not convenient to let these barbarian officials punish their own criminals in the trading ports? The same line of reasoning was followed in granting separate settlements for foreign residents in the Five Ports. Why should not the Chinese authority permit the barbarian merchants to live together in a separate section? The Manchu had lived in the separate Tartar cities for centuries. By this convenient arrangement, it was apparent that less trouble had occurred than if they had mingled with the ordinary Chinese.

As to the arrangement of a fixed tariff rate set up by the treaties, Ch'i-ying never considered it a settlement harmful to the Chinese nation. On the contrary, this new arrangement, according to the original Chinese program, might increase the annual revenue three times.[28] This assumption was proved true soon after foreign trade at Canton was resumed.[29] Ch'i-ying's original program was aimed at raising the

---

[26] For a good summary of Ch'i-ying's personality and his attitude toward the Western people see Fairbank, *Trade and Diplomacy,* I, 104-13; or Earl Swisher, *China's Management of the American Barbarians* (New Haven, Conn.: Far Eastern Publications, Yale University, 1953), pp. 18-19.

[27] See Ch'i-ying's memorial concerning his interview with Paul S. Forbes, the United States consul at Canton, *IWSM-TK,* LXIX, 34b-37; for an English translation of the same memorial see Swisher, *China's Management,* pp. 132-35.

[28] *IWSM-TK,* LXIX, 15-16; Huang En-t'ung, "Fu yuan chi lioh," p. 419.

[29] In a memorial submitted about a month after the foreign trade was resumed at Canton, Ch'i-ying stated: "Now from July 27 [1843], the date of opening of the customs according to the new regulations, up to September 3, altogether fifty-three English and American merchant ships entered port, all consigned to the ten-odd generally trusted hong merchants. They exchanged their goods and paid duties. Customs collections amounted to more than 128,900 taels. Compared with the amount collected last year from August 6 to September 14, this is an increase rather than a decrease." See *IWSM-TK,* LXVIII, 28a ff. English translation is taken from Swisher, *China's Management,* p. 125. Huang En-t'ung, who had negotiated the new tariff schedule both with Great Britain and with the United States, basing his figures on a report submitted by the Hoppo at Canton in 1845, roughly calculated as follows:

tariff duties on the large items, such as cotton, tea, silk, and some
Western textile products, and to reduce the duties on small items, such
as clocks, watches, ginseng, and the like. Then the duties collected
from those items whose rates were raised, as he assumed, would be a
hundred times more than the amount lost by reduced rates.[30] Although
the total raised was much higher than the old imperial and customary
local charges combined, still it was less than the total (including different kinds of extra fees paid merely to satisfy the corrupt officials)
that the British and American merchants at the time estimated to have
been actually levied under the previous spoils system.[31] Thus, the so-
called fixed tariff, which was so bitterly hated by the patriots in the
later years, appeared to the old Chinese diplomats to be very reasonable and convenient. It might be profitable to the "barbarian merchants," yet it was by no means harmful to the Chinese nation. Moreover, these new arrangements, as Ch'i-ying understood, must be extended to all Western nations. This idea was another aspect of Ch'i-
ying's policy: the principle of equal treatment of all Western nations.

However, why China voluntarily extended her equal commercial
privileges to nations other than the British after the Treaty of Nanking
has since been a subject of long dispute among the Chinese, British,
and American writers, each of whom has given the credit to his own
statesmen.[32] The latest and most authoritative author in this field,

---

"Before the new regulations were put into practice, the annual collection from the
Customs House at Canton was about 1,300,000 taels. Even in the best years, it had
never exceeded 1,600,000 taels; and in the bad years sometimes fell under 1,000,000
taels. After the new tariff schedule was published, however, the annual collection was
between 2,000,000 and 2,300,000 taels, excluding the amount collected in Shanghai
and other ports. As compared to pre-treaty days, it has exceeded the former quota
about one million taels annually." See Huang En-t'ung, "Fu-yuan chi lioh," p 422.

[30] The American tariff duties fixed by and made a part of the Treaty of Wanghia
(see *Treaties, Conventions, etc., between China and Foreign States,* pp. 487-94) were
based upon the agreement signed between China and Great Britain in July, 1843, on
the tariff of duties on the foreign trade with China *(ibid.,* pp. 167-76). The duty on tea
was raised from tls. 1.3 per picul to tls. 2.5 per picul. The duty on cotton was raised
from tls. 0.15 to tls. 0.4 per picul. See Huang En-t'ung, "Fu yuan chi lioh," p. 422.

[31] Under the old system, the merchants paid more irregular fees and taxes than
official custom duties. For a general survey see Fairbank, *Trade and Diplomacy,*
p. 252.

[32] The British claim was based upon Lord Aberdeen's instructions to Sir Henry
Pottinger, No. 30, F.O., London, Nov. 4, 1841. See Morse, *The International Relations of the Chinese Empire,* I, Appendix M, 662-63; or see Cushing's correspondence
in *Sen. Ex. Doc.,* No. 67, 28 Cong., 2 sess., pp. 100-2. For the American claims see
Thomas Kearny, "The Tsiang Documents, Elipoo, Keying, Pottinger and Kearny and
the Most Favored Nation and Open Door Policy in China in 1842-1844: An American Viewpoint," *The Chinese Social and Political Science Review,* XVI, No. 1 (April,
1932), 77-104; John Watson Foster, *American Diplomacy in the Orient* (New York:
Houghton, Mifflin and Co., 1903), pp. 77 ff.; John Holladay Latane, *A History of*

Professor John King Fairbank, nevertheless accepted the Chinese idea that the Western claims were not well founded, "for the ancient idea of equal treatment of all barbarians was applied by the Manchu negotiators of 1842-44 of their own accord." "Since the Emperor was accustomed to viewing all men from afar with equal compassion," stressed Fairbank, "his ministers almost instinctively decided to extend the British treaty terms to the Americans. Their aim was to prevent the British themselves admitting the Americans to these privileges and so winning for Britain the gratitude which ought really to be felt by the Americans towards the emperor."[33]

As a matter of fact, however, Emperor Tao-kuang at the time had never thought of the "ancient idea." In many edicts issued after the Treaty of Nanking had already been signed, he still expressed his wish to confine the nations other than the British to the old port of Canton.[34] But the Emperor after receiving two memorials submitted respectively by Ilipu and Ch'i-ying on this subject suddenly changed his attitude. These two memorials on the same subject were similar even in wording and were apparently written by the end of 1843; they reached Peking on January 17 and 19, 1844.[35] "In August [1842]," said Ch'i-ying, "while I was negotiating with the English [at Nanking], I already thought of the possibility of all barbarians demanding the same privileges." How this thought came into his mind is a very interesting question. Was it due to his remembrance of an "ancient idea" or due to some outside pressure? To this writer, it seems that the French warships that sailed into the Yangtze River during the Opium War played an important role in the making of this Chinese decision.

During the Sino-British negotiation at Nanking in the summer of 1842, two French warships, which according to the contemporary Chinese reports were larger than the English ships, dropped their anchors outside the city of Nanking. On August 29, 1842, through the recommendation of the English, the French commander Cecille met Ch'i-ying and Ilipu aboard a British ship.[36] On September 2, 1842, only

---

American Foreign Policy (New York: The Odyssey Press, 1940), pp. 323 ff.; Willis Fletcher Johnson, *American Foreign Relations* (New York: The Century Company, 1916), I, 464, and many other books. For the Chinese claims see Tsiang Ting-fu, "The Extension of Equal Commercial Privileges to other Nations than the British after the Treaty of Nanking," *The Chinese Social and Political Science Review*, XV, No. 3 (October, 1941), 425.

[33] Fairbank, *Trade and Diplomacy on the China Coast*, I, 195-96.
[34] *IWSM-TK*, LXIII, 29; LXIV, 3 ff.
[35] *Ibid.* LXIV, 37-47.
[36] *Ibid.*, LIX, 42.

three days after this interview, there was a rumor spread among the staff members of the Chinese delegation that the French also were asking for additional ports for trade. Subsequently, as one of the staff noted in his diary "all the high ranking officers [i.e. Ch'i-ying, Ilipu, and Niu Chien] were deeply grieved."[37] We still do not have any evidence to prove that the French had really requested equal treatment with the English. However, even if it was just a rumor, it brought the question of equal treatment to the serious consideration of Ch'i-ying and Ilipu as early as August, 1842. Therefore, even while the Nanking negotiations were still in progress, Ch'i-ying had already made inquiries of the English concerning the extension of equal treatment to other Western nations.[38] It was because Ch'i-ying was so anxious to extend the equal treatment to other nations, that he was outmaneuvered by the British politicians, who, as a counter request, wrote the most-favored-nation clause into the Treaty of Bogue signed in October, 1843.[39]

Moreover, in the later negotiations, Ch'i-ying was further outmaneuvered by the American and French diplomats. During the Sino-American negotiations at Wanghia, the problem of equal treatment showed up in a different way. The American envoy demanded the privileges of renting land and constructing churches and cemeteries at the treaty ports. Ch'i-ying refused at first but agreed eventually, because, as he reported to the Emperor later:

... the said barbarian envoy replied that both the Europeans at Macao and the British at Hongkong could build churches for worship and select land for cemeteries, thus enabling the living to pray for blessings and the dead to find burial; that the number of his countrymen coming to China to trade is not great, nor have they dared to ask for any grant of territory, and if they were not allowed to rent land for construction they would really be in a quandary.[40]

But once this request was granted, it was automatically extended to the British according to the most-favored-nation clause.

During the Sino-French negotiations at Whampoa in October, 1844, the arguments turned out to be more interesting. The French envoy argued that the French had had very little commerce with China. If he, the honorable commissioner from a great Western empire, succeeded only in concluding a commercial treaty, which actually meant noth-

---

[37] Chang Hsi, *Fu-i jih-chi*, pp. 74-75.
[38] *IWSM-TK*, LXIV, 43.
[39] *Treaties, Conventions, etc.*, pp. 201 ff.
[40] *IWSM-TK*, LXXII, 15b ff.; English translation taken from Swisher, *China's Management*, p. 163.

ing to France, his long trip was obviously a waste. Hence, he would have "no face to report to his own emperor." Thus, he requested the Chinese Emperor to issue an imperial rescript for the toleration of Catholicism in China.[41] This request, as stated in Ch'i-ying's memorial, sounded very reasonable to the Emperor and was granted. Accordingly, Catholicism was tolerated through an imperial rescript issued on December 28, 1844; so consequently were all Christian missionaries to China.[42]

Thus, with foreign demands increased, Ch'i-ying's prediction of a once-for-all settlement could not materialize. Through the most-favored-nation clause, the "barbarian demands" snowballed. Gradually these demands led to a treaty revision movement that caused the Second Anglo-Chinese War in which Ch'i-ying lost his life in 1858.[43]

III

Ch'i-ying and his colleagues were, beyond doubt, the first group of modern diplomats in China. Their successful negotiation with the "barbarians" had actually brought China's traditional "barbarian management," for the first time in its history, to the threshold of modern diplomacy. These diplomats, however, were all self-educated through practical negotiations with the Westerners and lacked sufficient training to play international politics in a modern world. Thus in every negotiation they were badly out-maneuvered by the shrewd Western, particularly British, diplomats; but the Chinese officials were still not conscious of having been tricked.

Another reason that eventually led Ch'i-ying's policy to break down and was an even more serious handicap to the Chinese diplomats than their lack of modern training, was the fact that China was militarily unprepared to resist foreign encroachments effectively. Lack of sufficient defensive power had made her an easy prey for growing European imperialism. No matter how skillful China's diplomats might have been, therefore, it was inevitable that she was to suffer more humiliation and defeat. Unfortunately, Ch'i-ying became the scapegoat for this unavoidably declining Celestial Empire.

Not fully realizing these handicaps, however, Ch'i-ying and his group conducted the "barbarian affairs" with too much self-confidence, which

---

[41] *IWSM-TK,* LXXII, 46.

[42] For an English version of the imperial rescript granting toleration to Christianity, see Morse, *The International Relations of the Chinese Empire,* I, Appendix W, 691.

[43] See chap. 14.

was obviously derived from oversimplified assumptions in their understanding of contemporary international affairs. First of all, it was their belief that "there was no way to pacify the barbarians but to conduct commerce." They sincerely believed that the foreign trade at the Five Ports must be supervised by experienced hands from their own group, lest the well-managed "barbarian affairs" be jeopardized by green hands. Soon after the British treaties were signed, therefore, Ch'i-ying presented to the Emperor a complete list of recommendations for the important positions in the Five Ports. This group of appointees, to quote from a modern writer, formed the privileged "Ch'i-ying's staff."[44] They all received, through the recommendation of Ch'i-ying, special favors from the Emperor and held the most desirable posts in the corrupt officialdom of the Ch'ing dynasty. The easy fortune enjoyed by these men naturally attracted jealous eyes from all circles.

The second oversimplified assumption they shared (which was also shared by many of their countrymen) was that these "barbarian treaties" were permanent settlements. They were frequently cited by the Chinese officials as "peace treaties for ten thousand years." To the Chinese diplomats in the 1840's the "barbarians" seemed to have been satisfied by these new arrangements. The "barbarian nature," however, they thought, was very temperamental. The only way to keep them under control was to treat them with justice. It would deprive them of any possible pretext to raise more demands. Few Chinese then could understand the diplomatic functions of the Western nations. The "national foreign policy" of the Western countries was at that time completely unknown to the Chinese; the only thing that attracted their attention was the personal behavior of the individual "barbarian officers." Thus their capability as "barbarian experts" was also judged

---

[44] For general reference to "Ch'i-ying's staff," see Fairbank, *Trade and Diplomacy on the China Coast,* I, 186 ff. Fairbank's treatment of this subject is no doubt the best account to date. However, there are some minor errors. In his reference to Shu Kung-shou, for instance, the author mistook him as "the former Ningpo prefect." Actually Shu had never been a prefect at Ningpo. According to Ch'i-ying's memorial submitted in August, 1843, Shu had served as a district magistrate under the jurisdiction of the prefecture of Ningpo before the Opium War. During the British invasion of Chusan in 1841, Shu was the acting subprefect of Ting-hai *t'ing* (in other memorials he was mentioned as subprefect of Shih-p'u), which he lost to the British invaders, and was subsequently sentenced to a suspended death punishment that was later reduced to exile to Sinkiang. See *IWSM-TK,* LXX, 6b; LXXIII, 25-26; LIX, 31; LXXII, 44b; LXXVI, 11b. Also see Liang T'ing-nan, *I fen chi wen* (Contemporary Account of the Barbarian Trouble) (Shanghai: Commercial Press, 1937), p. 87. For more information about Ch'i-ying and his staff see Huang, "Fu yuan chi lioh," pp. 419-33; Swisher, *China's Management,* chap. ii, pp. 17-38; Ch'en Kung-lu, *Chung-kuo chin-tai shih,* pp. 70-96.

by the extent to which they could get these individual "barbarian officers" under their control.

Moreover, Ch'i-ying also clearly realized that China was incapable of carrying on an effective resistance against a "foreign" invasion. Therefore, in the post-Opium War years he did all he could to make the "barbarians" satisfied in order to keep the "barbarian management" in *status quo*. In doing so, the local incidents occurring between Chinese and foreigners had to be reduced to the minimum lest they serve the "barbarians" as pretexts. Thus, in many local incidents Ch'i-ying always meted out more serious punishment to the Chinese party than the law required, although he was completely incapable of inquiring into the misdeeds of the foreign party. Sometimes his judgments were made even at the expense of the traditional pride of the boastful local populace, the stubborn Cantonese. To the Cantonese people, therefore, Ch'i-ying appeared like a bloody despot in his treatment of his own countrymen, but when dealing with the Westerners he was definitely a devil-fearing coward.[45]

In fact, the Chinese people and especially the Cantonese, who later instigated the anti-Manchu revolution in China, never really accepted the defeat they received in the Opium War. To them it was the corrupt "barbarian" Manchu government that was defeated by the British, yet the Western "barbarians" were actually afraid of the Chinese people, who in turn were oppressed by the Manchu officers. Thus an unfortunate cycle was formed: the "barbarians" were afraid of the Chinese people; the Chinese people were afraid of the officers of the Manchu government; and the Manchu officers were afraid of the Western "barbarians."

Unfortunately, like most of the Manchu nobles in the Ch'ing period, Ch'i-ying paid almost no attention to the public opinion of the Chinese society at Canton. Thus his popularity among the Chinese declined as rapidly as the influence of his enemies increased. Therefore, the only support upon which Ch'i-ying and his men could rely was the imperial confidence. In the early 1840's this was in their favor; but as time passed and the memory of the dreadful defeat in the Opium War faded away, while the "barbarian" accidents and demands increased from day to day, the Emperor began to think that the Western "barbarians" were rather spoiled by Ch'i-ying's soft policy.[46]

---

[45] For further information about the "barbarian accidents" at Canton and Ch'i-ying's unpopular method of settlements, see chap. 6.

[46] *Ibid.*

When Ch'i-ying was recalled from foreign service in 1848, his Chinese successors simply reversed his unpopular policy in order to win public support from the populace at Canton and elsewhere in China. By doing this they also succeeded in winning new favor from the Emperor, who was looking for a change of his "barbarian policy."

IV

For further understanding of commercial and diplomatic developments in China during the later period, some aspects of the life and commerce in the various trading ports need more explanation. Before the Opium War the foreign trade at Canton was not a blessing to the Chinese people in that city, nor was it an indispensable economic source to the nation as a whole. The Manchu government never relied upon it as a major source of state revenue. For the convenience of administration and for the sake of the monopolists who usually had their supporters at Peking, the foreign trade at Canton before the Opium War was controlled by a handful of fabulously rich merchants, who formed a monopolistic guild, the *co-hong*. Howqua, one of the leading members, for instance, had a family fortune, according to an estimate in 1834, of $26,000,000.[47]

Among the early Western visitors to China, however, there was no one who was not struck by the poverty of the Cantonese masses, and few who were not impressed by the wealth of the hong merchants, the gold mine for corrupt government officials. Thus, the foreign trade in old Canton was a nuisance that helped to corrupt the government. In the early days the corrupt officials at Canton and the royal family at Peking derived money for their expenditures from it. They looked to the "barbarian trade" at Canton as a blessing. The local populace, particularly the local literate class, was hostile to it. To the ordinary Cantonese people and the literate class, the Western "barbarians," who usually associated with the groups they hated and despised, were men whose moral standards were low and whose desire for profits was almost unquenchable. This common misunderstanding regarding the Westerner also helps to explain why the Cantonese people were more "anti-

---

[47] "Assuming the purchasing power of money at that time as being but twice greater than at the present day [1881]," said a contemporary American merchant, "it would now represent a sum of $52,000,000." Hunter, *The "Fan Kwae" at Canton before Treaty Days, 1825-1844* (Shanghai: Kelly, 1911), p. 48. For the nature of the *co-hong* consult Hosea Ballou Morse, *The Gilds of China, with an account of the Gild Merchant or Co-hong of Canton* (London: Longmans, Green and Co., 1932), pp. 65 ff.

foreign" than the people in other ports. After the Opium War, while the economic and social conditions in China were fast changing as a result of the opening of new ports and the abolishment of the *co-hong* system, this militant Cantonese tradition was continued.

These changes, however, were not fully recognized by the authorities at Peking, particularly the militant young Emperor, Hsien-feng, who came to power in 1850. To him, the foreign trade in the Five Ports, which was the shadow of a foreign threat to the security of the royal family rather than a financial resource, was a nuisance. He wanted to limit the foreign trade and the activities of the Western "barbarians" in the Five Ports as strictly as possible. His anxiety to keep the foreigners away developed to such an extent that after the signing of the Treaty of Tientsin in 1858, he even intended to free China of tariffs so that he could persuade foreign ministers to abandon their privileges of traveling in interior China and of residing in Peking in exchange. Also, even as late as 1858, the Manchus still did not consider the dreadful Taiping Rebellion to be as serious as a supposed invasion of the Western foreigners. Thus he repeatedly refused Western offers of assistance for the suppression of domestic foes or foreign invaders.[48]

But with foreign settlement rapidly developing in the Five Ports, particularly at Shanghai, China was fast drawn into the family of nations, economically and politically. Her political institutions and national economy, therefore, gradually took a modern form. As a result of these changes, there came into being a commercial class that became the seed of the so-called compradore class in the later years. In the same way, with the rapid expansion of foreign trade, custom duties gradually became an indispensable part of China's revenue.[49] Most important of all, foreign influence began to play a decisive role in the development of domestic politics in China.

While the Emperor and his conservative subjects at Peking were still ignorant of these changes, the "barbarian experts" dealing with the foreigners at different ports gradually became aware of them. They learned many important new lessons, which their predecessors—the "barbarian experts" in the Tao-kuang period—had no chance to ac-

---

[48] See chap. 15. Also consult Ch'en Kung-lu, "Ssu-kuo T'ien-ching t'iao-yueh chih ching-kuo," *Chin-ling Hsueh-pao,* I (1931), 407-22.

[49] In the late 1850's the tariff duties collected by the Shanghai customshouse were an indispensable financial source in the Imperialist military campaign against the rebels (both the Taipings and the Triads), although Emperor Hsien-feng was not aware of it. See chap. 15.

quire. Therefore, in the later period the young Emperor's edicts were occasionally, but skillfully, ignored by his "barbarian experts" through collective action. They recognized that the custom duties collected at Shanghai were necessary to the military campaign against the Taipings. They also realized that Western military power was irresistible but that, through skillful management, the Westerners could be used in the Chinese civil war. This new method later proved efficient and successful not only in the campaign against the Taipings, but also in all later civil wars in China.

When the second group of "barbarian experts" were about to be graduated from their apprenticeship in modern diplomacy in the late 1850's, the conservative force at Peking, including the young Emperor, was crushed by a new foreign war. As soon as the war was over, the idea of Chinese seclusion vanished like the smoke from the burnt summer palace. In 1861 a modern Chinese foreign office, the Tsung-li ya-men, was established, and foreign ministers were allowed to reside at Peking. Then a modern Chinese diplomacy began.

As has been mentioned before, Sino-American diplomatic relations in the early period of the era covered by this study were "definitely commercial."[50] As time passed, however, the relations of the two countries were gradually extended to all other fields of modern diplomacy. It is rather amusing to note that these two nations were reluctantly drawn closer only by an outside force—the British.

---

[50] Tyler Dennett, "How Old Is American Policy in the Far East?" *The Pacific Review,* II, No. 3 (December, 1921), 463 ff.; Eldon Griffin, *Clippers and Consuls* (Ann Arbor, Mich.: Edwards Brothers, 1938), p. 33.

4

AMERICAN COMMERCIAL

AND CONSULAR SETTLEMENTS

IN THE FIVE PORTS

I

No SOONER had the new treaty ports been opened for foreign settlement than the Americans began to move in. In 1842 there were forty-nine adult male Americans, some of whom had families, residing in Canton, Macao, and Hong Kong, in eleven firms and several missionary societies.[1] In the first years after the opening of the new ports, however, Canton remained the center of foreign trade in China. It was there that the American merchants and merchant consuls had made their headquarters in the pretreaty days; and from there they now began to extend their commercial and consular settlements to other ports.

Until the end of the Opium War, the United States had only one consulate in China, that is, at Canton. The first American consul appointed to that port was Major Samuel Shaw, supercargo of the *Empress of China*, the first American ship to sail into a Chinese harbor; it arrived at Canton in 1784. During his second visit to Canton in 1786, Shaw was "elected" United States consul to China by Congress "without being entitled to receive any salary, fees, or emoluments."[2] After that, American consuls at Canton were recruited in the same way from among the American merchants residing there. This was the merchant-consul system that was continued into the postwar days. Under this system, the consuls were primarily merchants but were appointed by the United States government to act as consuls in the ports in which they traded. They received no compensation for their service except a few consular fees, nor had they regular tenures. They did

---

[1] Hosea Ballou Morse, *The International Relations of the Chinese Empire* (New York: Longmans, Green and Co., 1910), I, 346.

[2] Samuel Shaw, *The Journals of Major Samuel Shaw, the First American Consul at Canton* (Boston: Wm. Crosby and H. P. Nichols, 1847), p. 114.

not have special offices, nor was their work specified by detailed government regulations. A merchant consul might travel from time to time and from place to place as his business required. His first concern was his own business, not his consular duties. During his absence from a port for which he was appointed consul he could appoint whomever he saw fit as vice-consul or commercial agent to replace him and then had to wait for approval from the authorities at Washington, which usually took more than a year. In the postwar years, when the Americans were given the privilege of extraterritoriality, the American consuls did not until 1848 have legal power to exercise it. The whole merchant-consul system was not to be superseded until 1855.[3] When the new treaty ports were opened, therefore, it was these American merchant-consuls who were appointed either by the home government or by the American consul at Canton to establish their official organizations in the different ports.

During the Opium War, P. W. Snow was the American consul at Canton. The only American consul then in China, he had received his appointment from the State Department in 1835. Early in 1843, Snow left Canton for a trip home because of ill health. Upon his departure he appointed a fellow merchant, Edward King, consular agent at Canton, to take charge of the United States consulate at that port.[4] Ch'i-ying sent a notice to King formally informing him that Canton was re-opened for trade on July 27, 1843, and that Americans were also admitted to other new ports trading under the regulations just issued by the Chinese government.[5] "It becomes us to inquire," Ch'i-ying wrote,

---

[3] For further information about the evolution of the American consular system see Eli T. Sheppard, *American Consular Service*, in *The University Chronicle*, IV, No. 6 (Berkeley: University of California, December, 1901), 412, 414-17; for American consular service in the Far East see Eldon Griffin, *Clippers and Consuls, American Consular and Commercial Relations with Eastern Asia, 1845-1860* (Ann Arbor, Mich.: Edwards Brothers, 1938), pp. 48-52; for a historical survey of the system see United States Department of State, *Manual for Consuls* (Washington, D. C.: Taylor and Maury, 1856), pp. 1-24.

[4] Snow to Daniel Webster, New York, April 24, 1843, Consular Despatches, Canton, microfilmed by the U.S. National Archives Service, Microfilm No. 101, Roll No. 3. Pages are not numbered. Hereafter to be cited as *CD-USNA*, Canton, 101:3.

[5] An English copy of the *Public Notice* issued by the Chinese government was included in the Consular Despatches from Canton. See Paul S. Forbes to the Secretary of State, Canton, October 7, 1843, *ibid*. The official dates of opening of the four northern ports were: for Amoy, November 2, and Shanghai, November 17, 1843; for Ningpo, January 1, and Foochow, June, 1844. See John King Fairbank, *Trade and Diplomacy on the China Coast, the Opening of the Treaty Ports, 1842-1854* (Cambridge, Mass.: Harvard University Press, 1953), I, 155. The opening of Foochow was delayed because the British had failed to find a suitable consul for that port; the opening of Ningpo was delayed by the lack of a suitable Chinese administrator. See *IWSM-TK*, LXX, 21a; LXIX, 15-16a.

"whether the American nation will or will not appoint consular officers to proceed to each port to make arrangements."[6] To this inquiry King replied that "the High Commissioner from the United States" would arrange for consuls for the new ports when he arrived. Until such consuls were appointed, the supercargoes and captains of American vessels resorting to the new ports would conform to the regulations and be responsible to the Chinese government for the duties on vessel and cargo and for the good conduct of the seamen.[7]

Since he was unable to return to China, Consul Snow resigned his position at Canton early in April, 1843; Paul S. Forbes, a member of Russell and Company then at Canton, was appointed in his place.[8] The new consul presented his credentials to Ch'i-ying, the Imperial Commissioner, on October 2, 1843, in a ceremony that put the officials of the two nations on an equal basis.[9]

The first American consulate in these newly opened treaty-ports was set up at Shanghai by Henry G. Wolcott, a merchant from Russell and Company. Wolcott went to Shanghai as soon as the port was officially opened to foreign trade in November, 1843. He obviously had intended to take up his residence at Shanghai upon his arrival. He went to the *taotai*, Kung Mu-chiu, desiring to lease a house, but was informed that the Chinese government had already entered into an agreement with the British consul whereby all land within certain boundaries was to be leased only through the agency of the British consul. Wolcott then addressed himself to George Balfour, the first British consul at Shanghai, and was given permission to secure the lodging he desired.[10]

In the meantime, Wolcott also made a short visit to the neighboring port, Ningpo.[11] When the news reached Canton that Wolcott was at Ningpo, Consul Forbes appointed him United States vice-consul of that port on March 22, 1844.[12] Wolcott seems not to have accepted his

---

[6] Ch'i-ying to King, Canton, August 1, 1843, *CD-USNA*, 101:3.

[7] King to Ch'i-ying, Canton, August 3, 1843, *ibid.*

[8] Paul S. Forbes to the Secretary of State, Canton, October 7, 1843, *ibid.* It seems that Snow had formally resigned before he reached New York on April 23, 1843. Edward King resigned his position as consular agent on September 20, two days before Forbes's acceptance of his new appointment.

[9] *Ibid.*

[10] *House Doc.*, 123, 33 Cong., 1 sess., pp. 210-23. A comprehensive study of the conflicts between the American merchants and the British consuls in the early period is to be found in the correspondence submitted by Commissioner Humphrey Marshall in 1853. For a good summary see also Tyler Dennett, *Americans in Eastern Asia* (New York: The Macmillan Co., 1922), pp. 194-205.

[11] Griffin, *Clippers and Consuls*, p. 258.

[12] Reporting this appointment to the Department of State, Forbes stated that "this

Ningpo appointment; instead he acted as United States consul at Shanghai upon his return there from a brief southern visit.

Not long after his return to Shanghai, Wolcott found that the American trade in that port was constantly increasing.[13] He himself was engaged with the Japanese at Nagasaki in an indirect cotton trade, which was reported to be very prosperous.[14] This prosperous outlook obviously made Wolcott eager for a long-range program. In December, 1845, Wolcott went to Canton for a short visit. On March 17, 1846, he addressed a letter to Acting Commissioner Biddle, who was in Canton for the exchange of ratifications of the Wanghia Treaty, asking for a formal appointment as United States consul at Shanghai.[15] This was promptly given to him together with the necessary equipment for the establishment of a United States consulate at that port.[16]

On his return to Shanghai as acting consul of the United States, Wolcott immediately erected a flagstaff and proceeded to fly the American flag. This show of color, however, was promptly protested by the British consul, who had taken over the area in which the American consulate was located—outside the northern gate of the district city of Shanghai along the bank of the Huang-p'u River—as a "British Concession," for which he had issued some "Regulations," with the approval of the Chinese authorities, to govern the residents of all nationalities.[17] At this protest the American flag was pulled down. It was not raised again until the arrival of J. Alsop Griswold, the regularly appointed American consul at Shanghai, in the fall of 1848,[18] when the number of American residents at the port had greatly increased.

The formal establishment of American consulates in other newly opened ports was delayed for many years. Amoy was officially opened by the Chinese two weeks before Shanghai, but there was no American

---

appointment was rendered necessary by the absence of any person to represent the Government of the United States and enter American ships at the Custom House." See Forbes to the Secretary of State, No. 21, Canton, July 1, 1844, *CD-USNA*, 101:3. The regulations issued by the Department of State permitted U.S. consuls to appoint consular agents as well as vice-consuls within their districts, but these appointments had no status as "consular officers" until 1856. See Chester Lloyd Jones, *The Consular Service of the United States* (Philadelphia: The University of Philadelphia, 1906), p. 23.

[13] Wolcott to James Biddle, Canton, March 17, 1846, *DD-USNA*, 92:4.

[14] Biddle to the Navy Department, No. 17, on board the *Columbus* off the coast of Japan, July 31, 1846, *DD-USNA*, 92:4.

[15] See footnote 13, above.

[16] Biddle to Wolcott, Canton, March 30, 1846, *DD-USNA*, 92:4.

[17] *House Doc.*, No. 123, 33 Cong., 1 sess., pp. 210 ff.

[18] See chap. 10.

consular establishment in that port until the arrival of Charles W. Bradley in August, 1849.[19] This port was first entered by two American missionaries, David Abeel and Willion J. Boone, who early in 1842 had set up a missionary station on the island of Kulangsu, which was under British occupation until 1846.[20]

Amoy was an important Chinese seaport. American vessels had for a long time been using that port, even before it was formally opened for trade. American opium smugglers had frequented Amoy before the Opium War.[21] Commodore Lawrence Kearny of the United States East India squadron had visited Amoy in 1843 before leaving China for home. This made Amoy "the first port north of Canton to be visited by an American warship."[22] In the Consular Despatches there is a letter written to the President on October 29, 1844, by a certain Th. G. Peachy of Williamsburg, Virginia, begging to resign his commission as consul at Amoy in China.[23] There is no record of his appointment or that of a successor. In 1846, Commodore Biddle also visited that port; he found no American consul or resident merchant there.[24] Regular American cargo ships, however, arrived in Amoy soon after it was opened, though few records of the returns of American

---

[19] Bradley to John W. Clayton, Amoy, August 14, 1849, *CD-USNA,* Amoy, 100:1.

[20] It was said that David Abeel "was the *first* United States Consul appointed at *any* port north of Canton, being commissioned to Amoy." See William C. Hunter, *The "Fan Kwae" in Canton before Treaty Days, 1825-1844* (Shanghai: Kelly, 1911), p. 19. But this statement is not proved by any source, including Abeel's personal memoir. The possibility of his appointment, however, should not be written off, for in those days even "the department [of State] was sometimes without the knowledge of even the names of our representatives at certain points" (see Jones, *The Consular Service of the United States,* p. 23). He might have accepted some appointment by the United States consul at Canton right after the Opium War, but failed to do anything about it. For more information about the missionaries at Amoy see the following chapter.

[21] A few Americans at Canton had long found the opium trade highly profitable and did not consider this traffic disreputable. Many of them at one time or another were connected with it. William C. Hunter, the agent of the highly respectable Russell and Company of Boston and the famous author of two invaluable books, had once "availed" himself "of a suggestion from the house to take a run [of opium smuggling] to Namoa," an outside opium smuggling station of Amoy. He had a cargo of 300 chests valued at about $300,000. See Hunter, *The "Fan Kwae" at Canton,* p. 66.

[22] Charles Oscar Paullin, *Diplomatic Negotiations of American Naval Officers 1778-1883* (Baltimore, Md.: The Johns Hopkins Press, 1912), p. 203. For more information about Kearny and his diplomatic activities in Chinese waters in 1842 see C. S. Alden, *Lawrence Kearny, Sailor Diplomat* (Princeton, N.J.: Princeton University Press, 1936), p. 169.

[23] Peachy to President Tyler, Williamsburg, October 29, 1844, *CD-USNA,* Amoy, 100:1.

[24] "East India Squadron Commodore Biddle... (1845-1847)," in Navy Department Archives quoted in Griffin, *Clippers and Consuls,* p. 286.

ships are left.[25] American ships were later also engaged in the coolie trade in that port.

Ningpo was opened on January 1, 1844. With the exception of a short visit by Wolcott, few American merchants stayed at this port until many years later. Unlike the merchants, however, the American missionaries moved into Ningpo in groups. As Wolcott returned to Shanghai after a short visit to Ningpo, he may have delegated his consular duties to a missionary physician, Dr. D. N. McCartee, who had entered the port in 1843 and opened a missionary hospital. It seems that he remained in Ningpo as a consular agent as well as a missionary for many years, but he was not formally appointed acting consul until May 19, 1854, when he was given a commission by Commissioner McLane.[26]

In the fall of 1844, an American naval vessel, the *St. Louis*, commanded by Lieutenant E. G. Tilton, paid a short visit to Ningpo. "She attracted much attention as the natives had never before seen an American ship of war."[27] But few American merchant ships had sailed into the harbor.[28] In 1846, Commodore Biddle paid a similar visit to Ningpo; he found that there was little foreign trade and that all resident Americans were missionaries.[29]

Foochow was not opened until the arrival of the first British consul, in June 1844. Three months after its opening one American merchant vessel (the first foreign ship to enter that port under the treaty) arrived, but she found no customers there. Greatly disappointed, the supercargo proposed selling his cargo of black pepper, rattans, longells, cottons, and other goods "at reduced prices," and left the harbor after a month of unpleasant stay.[30] It was not until November 5, 1852, ten

---

[25] Early American commercial returns of the port of Amoy can only be found in English figures. According to British records, there were two American ships in 1846, six in 1847, and eight in 1848, that entered Amoy. See *ibid.*, Appendix 4C, p. 402; also see *Consular Returns of British Trade with China for the Year 1846, (1847, and 1848)* (Hong Kong: Printed and Published at the Office of the *China Mail* in 1847, 1848, and 1849 respectively).

[26] Griffin, *Clippers and Consuls*, pp. 297 ff.; Magruder to Marcy, Ningpo, June 22, 1855, *CD-USNA*, Ningpo, 111:1.

[27] Paullin, *Diplomatic Negotiations*, p. 210.

[28] One American ship, which has not been identified, arrived in Ningpo in December, 1842; it was ordered by the local Chinese authorities to go back to Canton. *IWSM-TK*, LXIII, 3-10; see also Earl Swisher, *China's Management of the American Barbarians, A Study of Sino-American Relations, 1841-1861, with Documents* (New Haven, Conn.: Yale University Far Eastern Publications, 1951), pp. 103-4.

[29] "Biddle to Bancroft, July 2, 1846," Navy Department Archives quoted in Griffin, *Clippers and Consuls*, p. 298.

[30] *IWSM-TK*, LXXIII, 10-49a; Swisher, *China's Management*, p. 181.

years after the departure of the first American vessel from Foochow, that an American consulate was formally established by Caleb Jones, the first United States consul at Foochow.[31]

Some general characteristics of the American consular service in China during the fifteen years after the signing of the Treaty of Wanghia may be pointed out. As previously stated, American consuls in the Chinese treaty-ports did not have legal power to handle the extraterritorial cases until 1848. The merchant-consul system as a whole remained in China for another seven years. It was natural that the consuls were recruited from the resident merchants. In the ports such as Ningpo, where few merchants resided, missionaries were also occasionally enlisted into the service. During a period of over a decade, however, more than a score of merchants were appointed consuls or commercial agents in the different ports, although missionary appointees were very few.[32]

The geographical origins of the United States consular officers in China were similar to those of the American merchants trading in that country. Massachusetts supplied at least ten, including most of the merchant-consular officers; New York, eight or nine, chiefly men who were neither merchants nor missionaries; Pennsylvania, at least three, including two merchants; California, Connecticut, and Maryland two each, chiefly men who were neither merchants nor missionaries; and Maine, New Hampshire, Ohio, Rhode Island, South Carolina, and Virginia, one each.[33]

In spite of the fact that a few of the several dozen appointees were almost illiterate, the United States consuls in China were generally capable men, "the average of ability equalled and perhaps surpassed that

---

[31] Griffin, *Clippers and Consuls,* pp. 294 ff. The history of the consular arrangements at Foochow is difficult to trace, since they were often made irregularly; sometimes the appointees never took up their assigned duties. An official publication states that the American consulate at Foochow may have been first established in 1842, but the consular archives were lost during a fire (*ibid.*). Jones's first eight reports to the Department of State are missing, No. 9, dated April 5, 1855, from Shanghai was the first to appear in the Consular Despatches. In 1848, Commodore Biddle also remembered that he "saw at the American Consulate [at Canton] a Commission from the President appointing Mr. McIntosh consul for one of the ports of China," but he could not remember which port it was. Since Mr. McIntosh had at that time already returned to the United States, this commission was not delivered. It was because Biddle feared it might be used by some irresponsible person that he called it to the attention of the Department of State. See James Biddle to the Secretary of State, Philadelphia, March 21, 1848, *CD-USNA,* Canton, 101:3. This story indicates that in the early period American consular appointments along the Chinese coast were rather frequent.

[32] Griffin, *Clippers and Consuls,* p. 230.

[33] *Ibid.* Many of the "service consuls" appointed after 1856 were neither merchants nor missionaries.

of diplomatic officers."[34] Moreover, the appointments of these people were comparatively free from the influence of domestic politics. Since there were very few missionary appointees, the United States consuls in China were comparatively free from domination by the missions. From purely commercial considerations, they were frequently Anglophobes,[35] and from time to time clashed with the missionary interest that formed a strong pro-British faction in the United States diplomatic service.

The influence of the merchants in the United States consular service in China, however, was gradually reduced. In the early period, when merchants made up nearly all the population of foreign communities in China, the merchant-consul fitted well into the prevailing scheme. In some cases he was subject to the rivalry and suspicion of his fellows, but he was not a different order of being. As time passed, however, the foreign population in the treaty-ports became diversified. In addition to merchants, there were missionaries, seamen, respectable men of affairs, drifters, law-abiding citizens, lawless ruffians, "doubtful gentry with shadowy claim on American citizenship,"[36] and others. Lines of distinction, therefore, gradually emerged that weakened the influence of merchants and gave consuls new obligations to other Americans. It made the abolition of the merchant-consul system inevitable. In 1855, through a special act of Congress, the merchant-consuls were superseded by the "service" or "political" consuls. The anti-British attitude of the consuls remained unchanged or was perhaps intensified, particularly among the "political" consuls.[37]

II

Parallel with the progress of preliminary consular settlements in the Five Ports, American trade with China started to boom, so that from 1845 to 1860 the total volume of Sino-American trade increased from nine and one-half million dollars to twenty-two and one-half million.[38]

---

[34] "It is not clear how much political considerations affected appointments of merchant consuls [remarked Eldon Griffin]. Merchants served chiefly during the first half of the period. In the entire period the Whigs, who claimed some mercantile support, captured the presidency for only one term, 1849-1853." See *ibid.*, pp. 229-30n.

[35] In 1856, when the anti-British attitude of the American merchants gradually changed, the merchant-consul system was superseded by the "political" consuls.

[36] *Senate Exec. Doc.*, No. 22, 35 Cong., 2 sess., II, 843.

[37] Griffin, *Clippers and Consuls*, p. 231.

[38] For detailed figures before 1856 see S. Smith Homans, Jr., ed., *A Historical and Statistical Account of the Foreign Commerce of the United States* (New York: G. P. Putnam and Co., 1857), p. 181; for figures after 1856 see *Commerce and Navigations of the United States*, published by the Treasury Department since 1856.

During the postwar period, the United States and Great Britain remained the two great competitors in the China trade. In the first years after the signing of the Treaty of Wanghia, however, the balance of trade in China's five ports was greatly in favor of Great Britain. The figures for 1844 are a good example:[39]

THE CHINESE FOREIGN TRADE IN 1844

	United States	Great Britain	Other Countries	Total
Export	$6,686,171	$17,925,360 (exclusive of specie)	$895,899	$25,513,370 (exclusive of specie)
Import	$1,320,170 (merchandise)	$15,929,132	$401,025	$17,843,249
	$1,125,700 (specie)	$20,000,000 (estimated value of opium)		
Balance	$5,591,700 (against U.S.)	$18,003,772 (in favor of G.B.)		

This trend was maintained for a few years after 1844. In 1844, as indicated in the above table, the balance against the United States was $5,591,700 of which $1,125,700 was paid in specie, the rest being paid in bills on London, which also created a balance against the United States there. In the following two years the bills paid on London were of similar amounts.

The American businessmen were not pessimistic over their disadvantageous position vis-à-vis the British for trade with China. As they saw it, British trade was constantly declining while that of the United States was increasing. For instance, in 1846, the Anglo-Chinese trade shows a decline of $6,096,099 from the previous year's total imports into China and a decrease of $11,319,761 in exports from her, while

---

[39] For a detailed statistical study of China's foreign trade in the early years under the new treaties see *Consular Returns of British Trade with China,* in which American figures are also given. For a comparative study of British and American trade in China see *House Report,* No. 596, 30 Cong., 1 sess., May 4, 1848 pp. 3 ff., report submitted by T. Butler King from the Committee on Naval Affairs. The figures in the table are based upon King's report. While a certain amount of opium was also imported by the Americans, no figures are available.

the records exhibit a gradual but steady increase of American imports into China.[40]

According to the contemporary American business observer, T. Butler King, who submitted a report to Congress in 1848, the causes that operated to depress and limit the trade between China and Great Britain did not prevail or exist between the United States and China. The favorable balance of British trade with China in the postwar years, for instance, was founded on an estimated value of the opium that was smuggled into China. The figures on the opium trade, he believed, were unreliable; the trade itself was illegal and undependable. In his opinion, the American trade with China, founded on a more favorable basis, had a very hopeful future, particularly in the cotton trade.

The statistics of the early postwar years show that more than two-thirds the value of the imports into China were of cotton and cotton manufactures. In 1846, for instance, legal imports into Canton alone amounted to $12,390,213, of which cotton and cotton fabrics constituted more than two-thirds the value; $5,095,407 was for raw cotton and $3,684,494 for cotton fabrics. They totaled $8,779,901. According to King's investigation, most of the raw cotton imported to China came from British India and was very inferior to American cotton. In the postwar years (1845-47) the average balance of trade against the United States and in favor of China was $5,347,442, which could be easily overcome by a well-managed American cotton trade. King's report to Congress was submitted during the period when "King Cotton" was growing in power and obviously gave some encouragement to southern statesmen as well as to the "Cotton Whigs" in the North. King also stated that American merchants were engaged to a certain extent in the opium trade and that the returns from this might reverse the trade balance against the United States.[41] The business records of later years have proved that King's analysis and prediction in 1848 were sound, although he had underestimated the British trading potential.

Despite the fact that the international trade at Shanghai rapidly increased, Canton remained the center of China's foreign trade for some years. According to the commercial records preserved by the Canton consulate, the total volume of American trade at Canton during the period from 1844 to 1852 was increasing, although some items in the

---

[40] King's report, *ibid.*
[41] *Ibid.* See following section for the American opium trade in China.

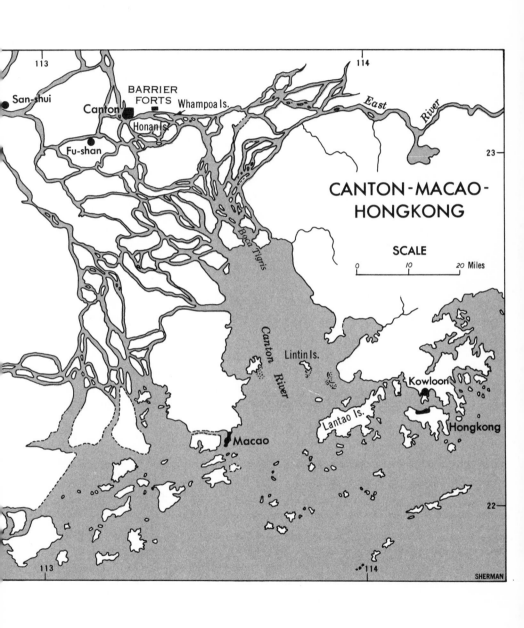

CANTON-MACAO-
HONGKONG

SCALE

0   10   20 Miles

San-shui
113
BARRIER
FORTS   Whampoa Is.
Canton
Honan Is.
Fu-shan

East
River

23

Boca Tigris

Canton River

Lintin Is.

Kowloon

Lantao Is.

Hongkong

Macao

22

113   114

SHERMAN

export business declined.[42] In 1844 sixty American vessels with a total tonnage of 25,877.70 tons entered the port of Canton. In 1852 there were seventy-five incoming American vessels at Canton, but the total tonnage was twice that of 1844, amounting to 57,228.17 tons.[43] While a new source of American revenue was discovered, the import of American silver dollars into Canton was constantly being reduced.[44] An American passenger ship, the steamer *Midas*, started a business along the Chinese coast in 1846; this began a new era in coastal communication in China.[45]

In the early years after the opening of Shanghai, American trade there was more of a coastal business than a direct transoceanic enterprise. The seventeen American commercial vessels that arrived at Shanghai in 1846 were all registered as entering from, as well as sailing for, Hong Kong. Owing to the geographical advantages of Shanghai, however, its commerce developed rapidly, and gradually this port surpassed Canton.[46]

The commerce at Amoy lagged behind considerably. For ten years after its opening, Amoy's trade with the American merchants never exceeded $120,000 annually.[47] Ningpo and Foochow had almost no business at all; this had led the British, in 1850, to propose exchanging these two ports for the three "inland" ports of Hangchow, Suchow, and Chinkiang.[48]

III

In this general survey of the foreign trade in the Five Ports during the postwar years, the opium trade, which was even more active than

---

[42] The export of green teas from Canton, for instance, declined from 13,557,054 pounds in 1844 to 8,113,472 pounds in 1852, but import of American ginseng into Canton was still increasing: (counted by pieces) 3,092 in 1844; 248,412 in 1849; 313,-274 in 1850; 304,812 in 1851; and 209,272 in 1852. See *House Doc.,* No. 123, 33 Cong., 1 sess., pp. 107-8.

[43] *Ibid.* See Griffin, *Clippers and Consuls,* Appendix 4C, p. 399, which gives a complete list of American vessels and their commerce in the Five Ports during the period from 1845 to 1860, but the figures of 1844 are not included. Consul Forbes's semiannual reports on the returns of American vessels arriving at Canton in 1844 give the number as 58 vessels with a total tonnage of 23,751.8/95 tons. See *CD-USNA,* Canton, No. 21, July 1, 1844; No. 29, January 1, 1845.

[44] The import of American silver dollars into Canton was reduced from 462,080 in 1844 and 496,007 in 1845 to 4,027 in 1849, 109,900 in 1850, 58,848 in 1851, and 122,300 in 1852. See *House Doc.,* No. 123, 33 Cong., 1 sess., p. 108.

[45] Biddle to Buchanan, No. 9, *DD-USNA,* 92:4.

[46] For an item by item study of the merchandise imported and exported by the American merchants at these two ports see *House Doc.,* No. 123, pp. 120-22.

[47] *Ibid.* Also see Griffin, *Clippers and Consuls,* Appendix 4C, p. 402.

[48] Morse, *The International Relations of the Chinese Empire,* I, 360.

the legal trade, deserves attention. The total amount of this contraband smuggled into China in the years after the Opium War greatly exceeded the combined total value of other British and American imports into China.[49] Hence during this period more than half of the shipping business along the China coast was conducted by the opium clippers, many of which were built in the United States and sent to China expressly for that purpose. The British opium conveyers, which at first were handicapped by the Opium War and later outlawed, at least nominally, by the British Order-in-Council, were outsailed by the American opium clippers.[50]

Most of the American opium clippers were built at Boston and New York for the sole purpose of opium smuggling. They were capable of outsailing any other ships afloat at the time and were so heavily armed that they could overcome interference from pirates and mandarins alike. In addition to opium distribution, they were also good for conveying passengers—a very prosperous business after the Five Ports were opened and passengers increased in number. Moreover, they could also be used to carry other kinds of cargo in the coastal and international business, such as transporting rice from Manila to Amoy.

The increase in opium smuggling, together with the increase in the carrying trade conducted by American citizens under the protection of the American flag, greatly alarmed both Washington and London in the postwar period. The British were alarmed by the American competition in the carrying trade which, in their opinion, was originally a British monopoly. The Americans were alarmed on commercial and humanitarian grounds. Although many of the United States businessmen were pleased by the increment to the carrying trade, others were disturbed by the increase in opium smuggling, which had already jeopardized the normal import trade in China. Consequently, while the British were fighting to legalize the opium trade, the Americans were trying to suppress it.

In the postwar years American merchants in China seem to have been entirely satisfied with the new commercial arrangements. During the first years after the opening of the Five Ports, there were few complaints against the Chinese from the American merchants who wanted

---

[49] In 1844 the total value of foreign imports into China was $17,843,249, but the total value of opium smuggled into China by the British alone was estimated at about $20,000,000.

[50] For general reference see Dennett, *Americans in Eastern Asia,* pp. 115-27; Fairbank, *Trade and Diplomacy,* pp. 134-35, 285-364.

to keep the commercial *status quo* in China.[51] Any change in commercial arrangements (particularly the legalization of opium trade) would jeopardize their interests in that country. Their desire was unintentionally supported by their government, which, on moral grounds, had repeatedly expressed its attitude toward the illegal opium trade in China. From 1840 on, the federal government repeatedly ordered American diplomats and naval officers to halt American smugglers. Commodore Lawrence Kearny, who arrived in the Chinese waters in April, 1842, arrested one of the opium clippers, the *Ariel,* and gave serious warnings to the others, but he possessed no legal power for further action in suppressing American contraband carriers in foreign waters.[52] The American government, however, never gave up its effort for the suppression of American opium smugglers in Chinese waters, and the American diplomats were constantly under orders to oppose the legalization of the opium trade in China. It is rather amusing to note that the untiring efforts of the American diplomats to oppose the legalization of opium frequently ran into British traps. Thus, the opium trade in China at last was legalized and the legalization lasted for more than half a century.[53]

[51] During the first decade after the signing of the Treaty of Wanghia, the American merchants in China were satisfied with the tariff and other commercial arrangements under the treaty. Even as late as 1858, when the Treaty of Tientsin was signed, the American merchants still felt that "the tariff of 1844 was a fair one, and that little modification was needed." See chap. 16. The merchants were also opposed to the legalization of the opium trade. Many of the law-abiding merchants, such as the American firm of Olyphant and Company, were hostile to opium trade from the very beginning. See *Canton Register,* August 21, 1838; see also Kenneth Scott Latourette, "The History of Early Relations between the United States and China, 1784-1844," *Transactions of the Connecticut Academy of Arts and Science,* XXII (1917), 111.

[52] C. S. Alden, *Lawrence Kearny,* pp. 169 ff.; *Sen. Doc.,* No. 139, 29 Cong., 1 sess., p. 14.

[53] See chap. 15.

5

SPREADING THE "KINGDOM OF GOD"

I

WHILE American merchants and diplomats were busily establishing themselves in the Five Ports, American missionaries worked even more zealously to penetrate the "Celestial Empire" and to spread their "Kingdom of God." This opportunity, which was first given French missionaries through the Sino-French Treaty of 1844, was automatically extended to the Americans through the most-favored-nation clause of the Treaty of Wanghia.[1]

Prior to the signing of the treaties, American missionary activities in China had begun in 1830 with the arrival of the Reverend Elijah C. Bridgman of the American Board of Commissioners for Foreign Missions, and the Reverend David Abeel of the Reformed (Dutch) Church in America.[2] After their arrival, American missionaries went to China in rapidly increasing numbers. Dr. Samuel Wells Williams of the American Board, the famous author of *The Middle Kingdom*,

---

[1] Angelus Francis J. Crosse-Aschoff, *The Negotiations between Ch'i-ying and La-grene, 1844-1846* (St. Bonaventure, N.Y.: Francis Institute, 1950), pp. 90 ff. Through the Sino-French Treaty of 1844, foreign missionaries were formally permitted to reside and to preach in the Five Ports.

[2] David Abeel, *Journal of a Residence in China* (New York: J. Abeel Williamson, 1836), pp. 4-60. The first American missionary service in China is said to have been brought about by D. W. C. Olyphant, a leading China merchant and head of Olyphant and Company at Canton and New York. In a letter to his Christian friends in the United States written on August 6, 1827, from Canton, Olyphant said: "... God, in His inscrutable providence, has seemingly shut up this nation from an approach to the light in any other way ... if any of the Churches are [sic] willing to put their hands to the work I hope I can assure that mine shall not be slack with them ... as tho' the call of Christ was imperative that what I do for Him, (Oh what a mite will it be) I must do in China—i.e. that I must render my talent, whatever it is, subservient to His interests there." This letter is said to have been largely responsible for bringing the first American missionaries to China. See a letter from D. W. C. Olyphant, August 6, 1827, copied by a Chinese typist under the supervision of D. W. Lyon, Shanghai, 1916 (Missionary Research Library, New York).

arrived in China in 1833;[3] Dr. Peter Parker, the well-known "barbarian physician," sent by the same institution, arrived in 1834;[4] the Reverend Issachar J. Roberts of the American Baptist Church, who missed the chance to baptize a Chinese emperor, but later became the yellow-robed imperial patriarch of the newly established Chinese Christian Empire at Nanking, arrived in 1836;[5] the Reverend W. J. Boone of the American Episcopal Board of Foreign Missions, who later became the first Episcopal Bishop in East Asia, arrived in 1837.[6]

There had been many Christian societies organized at Canton before the treaties were signed. The Society for the Diffusion of Useful Knowledge was established in 1834; the Medical Missionary Society was established in 1835, and the Morrison Education Society was organized in 1835[7] in memory of the late Robert Morrision, the first Protestant missionary in China, who had been sent out by the London Missionary Society in 1807 and who died in 1834.

Prior to the signing of the treaties, however, Christianity in China had been forbidden to the Chinese people under penalty of death. Because of these restrictions, most of the American missionaries, after a short stay at Canton or Macao, went to Southeastern Asia, where great Chinese communities flourished, some under Western supervision. These communities provided facilities for learning the Chinese language, the competent use of which was an absolute necessity for future missionary work in China. Consequently, some mission centers were established in Malacca, Java, Batavia, Penang, and Singapore, where many missionaries eagerly awaited a chance to get to the Chinese mainland.[8] It was natural that when the Opium War broke out, the missionaries were even more eager than the British government to open up the Empire. Unlike the American merchants, who viewed the British war with China as "one of the most unjust wars ever waged by one nation against another,"[9] many American mission-

---

[3] Frederick Wells Williams, *The Life and Letters of Samuel Wells Williams, LL.D* (New York: G. P. Putnam's Sons, 1889), p. 54.

[4] See chap. 1, pp. 7-8.

[5] Samuel Wells Williams, *The Middle Kingdom* (New York: Wiley and Putnam, 1848), II, 375. Another source indicates that the Baptists began to work at Canton in 1844. See *The China Mission Handbook* (Shanghai: American Presbyterian Missionary Press, 1896), p. 241.

[6] *Ibid.,* p. 180.

[7] Williams, *The Middle Kingdom,* II, 353-55.

[8] D. MacGillivray, ed., *A Century of Protestant Missions in China, 1807-1907* (Shanghai: The American Presbyterian Mission Press, 1907), pp. 3-4.

[9] William C. Hunter, *The "Fan Kwae" in Canton before Treaty Days, 1825-1844* (Shanghai: Kelly, 1911), p. 154.

aries, if not all, praised the war and demanded that China must "bend or break."[10] They justified their convictions in such terms as: "God has often made use of the strong arm of civil power to prepare the way for his own kingdom."[11]

As soon as the war was over, missionary service at Canton was openly resumed. After an interval of three years, Bridgman and Parker were able to return from Hong Kong and the United States to their old station.[12] In 1844 Roberts also moved his station from Hong Kong back to Canton.[13] They were gradually followed by the missionaries from other churches.

When the excited missionaries returned to Canton after the war, they discovered, however, that the war had not changed the old Canton except to make the people even more hostile to foreigners. At first they were prevented from entering the city of Canton. Later they were confronted with the problem of renting houses for missionary service and for private residence, even outside the walled city of Canton. Irritated by the boycotts of the native people, the missionaries began to appeal to Acting Commissioner Biddle, who was then at Canton for the exchange of ratifications of the Treaty of Wanghia. Biddle, however, did not seem to favor missionary demands very enthusiastically. In reply to their petition concerning the refusal of the local gentry to lease a house, Biddle replied that the local authorities of the two governments should give approval in advance to all contracts between American and Chinese citizens for housing. Since the local authorities had not been consulted at all in this case, it was useless for him to send a protest to the Chinese government. Moreover, Biddle did not join the missionaries in supporting the English, who were then demanding forcible entry into the city of Canton.[14]

After Biddle's departure from Canton, Dr. Parker, who was one of the three signers of the petition, was left in charge of the American legation as chargé d'affaires. Taking advantage of his official position in the American legation, Parker immediately revived the old cases. Throughout his first two terms as chargé d'affaires most, if not all, of

---

[10] *Chinese Repository,* IX, No. 5 (May, 1840), 2.
[11] G. R. Williamson, ed., *Memoir of the Rev. David Abeel, D.D.* (New York: Robert Carter, 1848), p. 215.
[12] George Barker Stevens, *The Life, Letters and Journals of the Rev. and Hon. Peter Parker, M.D.* (Boston: Congregational Sunday-School and Publishing Society, c. 1896), pp. 234 ff.
[13] Williams, *The Middle Kingdom,* II, 361.
[14] Biddle to Bridgman, etc., Canton, January 3, 1846, *DD-USNA,* 92:3.

his correspondence with the Chinese authorities was concerned with the problems raised by the American missionaries, among whom Parker was one of the most active.[15]

II

The first northern port to attract the American missionaries was Amoy. Amoy was first visited by David Abeel and William J. Boone. Abeel had arrived in Canton in 1830, but he soon left China for Southeastern Asia after realizing that conditions at Canton were not favorable for Christian preaching. During his travels he also devoted himself to learning the Chinese language from the overseas Chinese, most of whom had migrated from Fukien province through the port of Amoy.[16] After a few years of untiring study, Abeel was able to converse with the Chinese in the Amoy dialect. Abeel went to Macao at the end of 1841, when he thought a long-waited "new era" was approaching.[17] There he was joined by the Reverend William J. Boone of the American Episcopal Church and his wife, who intended to remove their missionary station from Batavia to a "colder climate."[18] Obtaining a letter from Sir Henry Pottinger, the British sole plenipotentiary, minister-extraordinary, and chief superintendent of trade at China, whose wife was an acquaintance, the two American missionaries took up their residence at Kulangsu in the harbor of Amoy, where the local British commander assigned a big house to them. Both Abeel and Boone were able to converse with the native Chinese in their local dialect. The populace at Kulangsu and Amoy was friendly to them. Backed by British bayonets and welcomed by the Chinese people, the missionary service in Amoy, therefore, was conducted under the most favorable circumstances.[19]

Abeel's efforts at Amoy were quickly reinforced by other mission-

---

[15] On April 15, 1846, Dr. Peter Parker was appointed for the first time chargé d'affaires of the United States, *ad interim*, by Acting Commissioner James Biddle. This appointment lasted until June 22, 1846, when Commissioner Alexander H. Everett arrived in Canton. After the death of Everett on July 27, 1847, Parker became, for the second time, chargé d'affaires of the United States, *ad interim*, until the arrival of Commissioner John W. Davis on August 21, 1848. For his official dispatches to the State Department during these two terms, see *DD-USNA, 92:4; 92:5*.

[16] For an interesting description of his earlier travel in the Far East before 1834, see his *Journal of a Residence in China and the Neighboring Countries* (New York: J. Abeel Williamson, 1836). The whole book is worth a careful reading.

[17] *Memoir of David Abeel*, p. 211.

[18] *The China Mission Handbook* (Shanghai: American Presbyterian Press, 1896), p. 180.

[19] *Memoir of David Abeel*, pp. 215 ff. The author gives a very interesting description of his pioneer life at Amoy. A part of his diary at Amoy was intermittently published in the *Chinese Repository* (Vols. XII and XIV).

aries, particularly the Presbyterians. Despite the favorable conditions at Amoy as a missionary depot, there were serious handicaps. The very damp climate was harmful to the Americans. Mrs. Boone was the first victim; she died early in 1842, a few months after her arrival at Kulangsu. In October, 1844, Boone himself was compelled because of ill health to return to the United States.[20]

Not long after Boone's departure from Amoy, sickness also forced Abeel to leave. He departed in such ill health that he thought he might not survive the trip home.[21] Shortly thereafter the Presbyterians also withdrew from Amoy, leaving the interests and the work of the church they represented to the Reformed (Dutch) Church Mission which, after Abeel's departure,[22] was under the charge of Elihu Doty and William J. Pohlman. In 1857 the Reformed Church resolved to discontinue cooperation with the American Board and placed the Amoy mission under its own newly organized Board of Foreign Missions.[23] The American Reformed Church remained in operation at Amoy until the Chinese Communists took over the Chinese mainland in 1949.

American missionary work at Ningpo was begun by Dr. Daniel J. MacGowan in 1843, who was sent there by the American Baptist Board of Foreign Missions with the cooperation of the Christian Medical Society at Canton.[24] He established a small hospital at Ningpo soon after his arrival. According to the Baptist historians, MacGowan has the honor of having established the first permanent mission work in that port, but he stayed at Ningpo only a few months.[25] His work, however, seems to have been continued by the Reverend Walter M. Lowrie of the Presbyterian Church and by Dr. D. B. McCartee, who later became the first United States consul at that port. They arrived in Ningpo in 1844.[26]

In the early days after their arrival, the American missions seem to have done their work in a Taoist temple within the northern gate of the city until separate quarters were built.[27] In 1845 another Presby-

---

[20] George Smith, *Narrative of an Exploring Visit to Each of the Consular Cities of China and to the Islands of Hong Kong and Chusan in Behalf of the Church Missionary Society in 1844-46* (London: Seeley, Burnside and Seeley, 1847), I, 111.

[21] *Memoir of David Abeel*, pp. 256 ff.

[22] MacGillivray, *A Century of Protestant Missions*, pp. 266-367.

[23] *Ibid.*, pp. 368-69.

[24] *Ibid.*; Lida Scott Ashmore, *The South China Mission of the American Baptist Foreign Mission Society* (Shanghai: Methodist Publishing House, 1920), p. 5.

[25] MacGillivray, *A Century of Protestant Missions*, p. 336.

[26] Kenneth Scott Latourette, *A History of Christian Missions in China* (New York: The Macmillan Co., 1932), p. 240.

[27] George Smith, *Visit to Each of the Consular Cities of China*, p. 144.

terian, Richard Cole, moved to Ningpo with the Mission Press, a missionary publishing house which had been first established at Macao in June of the preceding year under his charge. The Mission Press remained at Ningpo until 1860, when it was moved to Shanghai.[28] The Reverend Josiah Goddard, a Baptist, was transferred from Bangkok to Ningpo in 1848, after eight years of missionary service in Siam.[29] The Goddards worked in Ningpo for three generations until they were expelled, first by the Japanese and later by the Chinese Communists.

In 1850 the Presbyterians were aided by the arrival of Dr. W. A. P. Martin. Martin later joined the diplomatic service and became the Chinese interpreter of the American legation during the negotiation of the Tientsin Treaty of 1858. His remarkable linguistic talent enabled him to extend his interpreting service even among the Chinese, some of whom were unable to communicate among themselves because of the mutual unintelligibility of their dialects. After the Anglo-French-Chinese war of 1860, he moved to Peking, where he later joined the Chinese civil service. His command of the Chinese language and classics were qualifications that assisted him to attain the presidency of T'ung-wen-kuan, the first modern college to be established by the government of China. Among his "disciples" were numerous high-ranking officials who enrolled for short periods of training. Martin stayed at Peking for nearly half a century and played an indispensable role in the modernization movement in China during the Ch'ing period.[30]

The beginning of American missionary service at Shanghai is marked by the arrival of Bishop Boone in 1845. Boone had been the only representative of the American Episcopal Church in China before 1844, but he had been compelled by ill health to leave Amoy for home in October, 1844. The 1844 triennial convention of the American Episcopal Church appointed three missionary bishops, one of whom was assigned to China. Upon his return to the United States, Boone was consecrated and was to go to China with a stipend of $1,500 a year.[31] Early in 1845, with a party of nine, including his small son, he departed. On May 25, 1845, he left Hong Kong for Shanghai on a

[28] MacGillivray, p. 636. See also Gilbert McIntosh, *A Mission Press Sexagenary* (Shanghai: American Presbyterian Mission Press, 1904), pp. 1 ff.

[29] MacGillivray, p. 336; Williams, *Life and Letters,* II, 375.

[30] W. A. P. Martin, *A Cycle of Cathay* (New York: Fleming H. Revell Co., 1900), pp. 51-57, 165-203, 293-327.

[31] *Spirit of Missions,* X, No. 1 (January, 1845), 28; X, No. 8 (August, 1845), 250-51; see also George Smith, *Visit to Each of the Consular Cities of China,* p. 111.

British schooner, an opium smuggler with 750 chests of the drug on board, in the company of a representative of the British Church Missionary Society, George Smith.[32] In Shanghai, Boone built a church and later also established a school for Chinese children. After five years of service he reported that he had twelve converts in his Shanghai Church.[33]

The number of American missionaries at Shanghai increased rapidly after the arrival of Bishop Boone. Different kinds of missionary institutions were established one after the other, and their service was soon extended to interior China. The Baptists, headed by the Reverend and Mrs. Matthew T. Yates, who were sent by the (Northern) American Baptist Missionary Union, began their service at Shanghai in 1847.[34] A year later a Methodist Church was also established by Dr. C. Taylor, who was sent there by the Southern Methodist Episcopal Church.[35] The American Board, although it did send a representative to Shanghai in 1847, did not formally begin its service in that port until 1854.[36]

Foochow was the last of the Five Ports to be exploited by the missionaries. The first Protestant missionary to reach Foochow was Reverend Stephen Johnson, who had labored twelve years among the overseas Chinese in Siam before he was transferred there early in 1847.[37] While Johnson was busily preparing his missionary work at Foochow, the (Northern) American Methodist Episcopal Church also sent a mission there headed by Reverend Judson D. Collins and Reverend Moses C. White. They were heartily welcomed by Johnson, near whose place they succeeded in renting a house as a chapel. Later they were joined by Reverend Henry Hickok and his wife, and Reverend R. S. Maclay. The latter was subsequently credited as the "founder of Methodism in Eastern Asia," but not until ten years after his arrival was a single Chinese converted.[38]

[32] Smith, pp. 110-19.

[33] Spirit of Missions, XVI, 383; Latourette, A History of Christian Missions in China, p. 250.

[34] MacGillivray, A Century of Protestant Missions, p. 317; Charles E. Taylor, The Story of Yates the Missionary (Nashville, Tenn.: Sunday School Board, Southern Baptist Convention, 1898), pp. 41 ff.

[35] James Cannon, History of Southern Methodist Missions (Nashville, Tenn.: Cokesbury Press, 1926), p. 95.

[36] Latourette, A History of Christian Missions in China, p. 248.

[37] S. Johnson, "Notices of Fuchou fu," Chinese Repository, XVI, No. 10 (October, 1847), 483-500; MacGillivray, A Century of Protestant Missions, p. 254.

[38] The China Mission Handbook pp. 218-19; John Morrison Reid, Missions and Missionary Society of the Methodist Episcopal Church (New York: Phillips and Hunt, 1879), I, 411 ff.

III

Immediately after Christianity was legalized in 1844 the Chinese people, except the Cantonese, showed little objection to the new religion. As a matter of fact, on many occasions they welcomed the missionaries cheerfully. It was not only because China was traditionally a secular state, liberally tolerant of all religions, but also because Confucians were opposed to the worship of idols, to which the Christians likewise objected. In the early period after the arrival of the Christian missionaries, the upper-class Chinese even invited the missionaries to their homes to persuade their superstitious wives and daughters to give up idolatry.[39] Therefore, at the opening of the Five Ports, Christian missionaries were comparatively well received except at Canton, where the populace was prejudiced by traditional "barbarian management."

Despite the favorable intellectual atmosphere, however, the Chinese proved to be among the most invincible foes Christianity had ever encountered in its long history. First of all, Christianity appeared to the Chinese as a new social force, both inspired and promoted by the West, rather than merely a religion. But unlike other major religions in China, such as Buddhism and Taoism, which did not seriously question the Confucian way of social and family life, Christianity in the 1840's began to challenge the fundamental principles of the formation of Chinese society.

One of the most serious challenges to the Chinese was the missionaries' denial of the Chinese practice of filial piety. For instance, on one occasion when a young Chinese was converted to Christianity, Dr. Martin wrote:[40] ". . . God gave him grace in this instance to break the bond of filial piety, which in China so often stands in the way of piety to God." The Chinese had considered filial piety the flower of their civilization; it actually possessed social and economic as well as moral significance. Therefore, this single aspect of Christian preaching seemed to have the potential power to break up respectable families and lead a peaceful society into calamity. "For a Chinaman to accept Christianity," wrote an American minister to China in a later period,[41] "involves so complete a surrender of all that belongs to his education, his theory of government, and sociey, his views of nature,

---

[39] W. A. P. Martin, *A Cycle of Cathay, South and North, with Personal Reminiscences*, p. 67.

[40] *Ibid.*, p. 68.

[41] *House Exec. Doc.*, No. 1, Part I, 49 Cong., 1 sess., p. 149.

his ancestral worship, his domestic relations, and his modes of life, that it is a wonder that a convert is made." This astute observation explains the slow progress of the missionary work in China.

Christian, particularly Protestant, missionaries were equally handicapped by their untimely arrival in China. During the Opium War most of the British interpreters were recruited from the British missionaries, who, owing to their long acquaintance with the Chinese, were able to force more difficult conditions on the Chinese negotiators than other "barbarian" staff members.[42] Consequently, they were considered as among the most hated "devils" that the Chinese had fought. It was thus hard for them to convert the educated and patriotic Chinese when they came to China in the bloody path of the invading British army.

Their missionary work was further jeopardized by their association with the opium smugglers. On their way to their new posts most of the missionaries sailed on opium clippers, which in those days provided the most convenient facilities for communication between the different ports. Moreover, it was well known that they frequently relied for postal and banking facilities on the opium smugglers, who in some cases also provided financial support. Some of the British missionaries had even acted as interpreters for the opium smugglers.[43]

The language barrier formed another obstacle to missionary work. At the time of the Opium War, for instance, a Chinese-speaking American physician by the name of Pa-li-li (probably Peter Parker) was once visited by a Chinese tourist at Macao. When the latter noticed a bottle of mysterious drugs on the physician's desk, he asked the doctor if these drugs were *ku*, a poison usually used by Chinese black magi-

---

[42] Such famous British interpreters as Robert Morrison, K. F. A. Gutzlaff, and W. H. Medhurst were all recruited from the British missionary service in China. For instance, Morrison served during the negotiations at Nanking in 1842. His spoken Chinese was so fluent that the Chinese were led to believe that he was originally a *han-chien* (i.e., Chinese traitor) who had been converted to the "barbarian religion" for money.

[43] Hunter, *The "Fan Kwae" at Canton*, p. 70; MS letter of J. I. Shuck, Shanghai, May 7, 1851 (Southern Baptist Archives, Richmond, Va.), quoted in Earl Cranston, "Shanghai in the Taiping Period," *The Pacific Historical Review*, V, No. 2 (1936), 149-60. In some anti-Christian works published in China during the postwar period the most serious "crimes" committed by the Western missionaries and their Chinese converts were their association with the most hated "devils" along the Chinese coast, those who sold opium and other kinds of "immoral foreign drugs." These anti-Christian writers seem to have believed that all Chinese Christians converted in those days were opium dealers who had some connection with the opium clippers. See T'ien-hsia ti-i-shang-hsin-jen, *P'i-hsieh chih-shih* (Abolition of Heresy with Evidence) (n.p., 1861).

cians for immoral purposes. Since *ku* was forbidden under the death penalty by the Chinese law, few people had ever really seen it, but the peculiar look of this Western medicine had provoked this visitor to raise the question. To his surprise, the doctor's answer was a firm "yes." Astonished by Pa-li-li's answer, the tourist asked for further information as to who was the maker. "Both England and France can make it," said Pa-li-li. "Can your country [i.e., the United States] also make it?" "Oh, yes," said Pa-li-li, "but not as good as this one." "Alas!" the visiting Chinese murmured to himself prayerfully, "Why should you, Creator, teach those people to make such murderous drugs to kill other people?"[44] Such misunderstood conversations obviously had turned the Chinese-speaking "ambassador of God" into a murderous black magician. Hence it was not surprising to see that many a Chinese adventurer went to the missionaries to seek the help of their "magic tricks," while others tried to enlist their assistance for rebellion.[45]

Failing to obtain cooperation from the Chinese educated class and handicapped by their own limited ability in handling literary Chinese, the missionaries, with the help of some Chinese of questionable training in literary work, translated "the language of God," the Bible, into Chinese. This work, particularly the New Testament, was published in enormous quantities and distributed to anyone who cared to accept it. These Chinese translations of Christian literature exemplified the poorest version of Chinese ever set in print. "When we start to sing the hymns in Chinese," said Professor Ku Teng-ju, one of the leading Christian scholars in present-day China, "we cannot help trembling while cold perspiration breaks out throughout our body."[46] When it was compared with the highly refined Buddhist literature, the Chinese translation of the Bible appeared to the educated Chinese as no more than an unconvincing collection of poorly written legends.

Unaware of their shortcomings, the missionaries, however, were a group of aggressive evangelists who were anxious for quick results. Since they were actually the first foreign settlers in the newly opened trading ports to mingle with the strange Chinese whom they actually

---

[44] *P'i-hsieh chih-shih*, II, 12 ff. This book is a very poorly written anti-Christian work containing a great many slanders against the Chinese Christians. It has been published twice and seems to have been widely diffused at the time of publication. Most of the stories told in this book are unbelievable; among them, however, the story cited above may not be entirely groundless.

[45] *Chinese Repository*, XIII, No. 5 (May, 1844), 235.

[46] *Tao-feng Christian Journal* (New York, 1953-1954), II, 2.

did not understand, "missionary incidents" were unavoidable and increased as time passed. The first American missionary incident, which occurred at Canton, was the famous Roberts case which formed the center of American claims against China for nearly ten years.[47]

Although the protection of American commercial interests in China was the reason behind the establishment of American diplomatic relations with the Manchu government and the purpose of the first Sino-American treaty, American missionaries were as influential in determining United States policy in China during this period as were the American businessmen.[48]

---

[47] *Senate Exec. Doc.*, No. 30, 36 Cong., 1 sess., p. 105.

[48] Prior to the first decade of this century, no other subject was discussed so voluminously in the diplomatic correspondence of the United States as the protection of missionaries in China. But from the beginning of United States diplomacy in the East, American policy was a nonreligious one. American missionaries in the East enjoyed no more privileges than did other American citizens. For a good survey on this subject see Frank E. Hinckley, *American Consular Jurisdiction in the Orient* (Washington, D.C.: W. H. Lowdermilk and Co., 1906), pp. 108 ff. The missionary influence on United States diplomacy in China was primarily created by the direct participation in the U. S. diplomatic service of individual missionaries. such as Peter Parker and Samuel Wells Williams.

6

ANTIFOREIGN MOVEMENT,

OPEN DOOR PRINCIPLE,

AND IMPERIALISM

I

WITH the growth of trade and missionary work in the Five Ports, administrative problems in the trading ports, particularly in Canton, increased proportionally. As a result of the Opium War, the most pressing problem was the increasing hostility of the Chinese populace at Canton toward foreigners; the Chinese people, particularly the Cantonese, could scarcely accept defeat. They thought it was the corrupt Manchu government that was defeated, not China or the Chinese people.[1]

For more than a thousand years the Cantonese people had treated all foreigners trading in that port as bearers of tribute, submissive to Chinese control. With the exception of a few "barbarian riots" at Canton, the foreigners there also took the Chinese treatment for granted. With the exception of the people serving in the different hongs, few Chinese had any personal contact with Westerners, for they had been carefully segregated.[2] When the Opium War was over, the Western "barbarians" suddenly mingled with the local populace on the street.

Although the Chinese still felt they were superior to the "barbarians," the foreigners felt exactly the opposite because they had just won a decisive victory over China. This feeling on the part of the Chinese, plus a wartime hatred, led the Cantonese people to be more hostile to the Western "barbarians" than before. Their hostility was well reflected in the so-called city question, the Cantonese ban against Western people entering the city of Canton, at a time when the Westerners insisted that the privilege of entry was a treaty right.[3]

---

[1] Hsia Hsueh, *Chung-hsi chi-shih, Chüan* XIII; Hsiao I-shan, *Ch'ing-tai t'ung-shih* (General History of the Ch'ing Period) (Peiping: Pei-p'ing wen-chih hsueh-yuan, n.d.), IIIb, 247 ff.

[2] Kuo T'ing-i, *Chin-tai Chung-kuo shih* (Hong Kong: Commercial Press, 1940), I, 377 ff.

[3] Hosea Ballou Morse, *The International Relations of the Chinese Empire* (New York: Longmans, Green and Co., 1910), I, 367 ff.

It should also be noted that the "city question" was not merely the result of traditional Chinese hostility toward the foreigners. Its causes also lay in some serious disturbances that occurred in the postwar period. In the old days foreign sailors were strictly forbidden to come into Canton, but now, permitted by the treaty and privileged by extraterritoriality, they began to frequent the noisy Chinese streets. Worst of all was their association with Chinese prostitutes, with whom they consorted on the streets during the day. The conservative Cantonese were unaccustomed to such behavior.

This problem started as soon as the Treaty of Nanking was signed. Later, in 1842, Governor Ch'i Kung at Canton began to complain to the British consul that unruly Western sailors were taking commodities away without leaving any payment and that others were carousing with Chinese prostitutes, wandering along the streets in groups, and beating the Chinese people.[4] He then begged the consul to do something to control them. In October, 1845, the *Chinese Repository* also complained that drunken sailors had done great damage in many ways at Canton.[5]

In those days the American sailors who, as Consul Griswold remarked later, were in a "disorganized state" caused serious trouble not only to the Chinese authorities, but also to the consular officers of their own country. Occasionally the American consul even borrowed Chinese soldiers to round up the unruly American sailors. On one occasion fifteen California sailors were confined to a Chinese jail by order of the American consul.[6] Worst of all were the European sailors from countries that had no treaty relations with China. They were exempt from punishment no matter what kind of crimes were committed.[7]

These evils naturally helped to intensify the "city question" at Canton. In other northern ports the problem was comparatively light, since they did not have a tradition of "barbarian exclusion." Moreover, foreigners did not settle there in large numbers until many years later.

---

[4] Liang T'ing-nan, *I-fen chi-wen* (Contemporary Account of the Barbarian Trouble) (Shanghai: Commercial Press, 1937), p. 94.

[5] "During the month [it reported], we have seen them raving mad, like demons, beating themselves, beating one another, and like a Malay 'running amuch,' sauntering through the narrow streets pelting the Chinese, and overturning and smashing whatever they could that came in their way." See *Chinese Repository*, XIV, No. 10 (October, 1845), 494.

[6] Griswold to Daniel Webster, Shanghai, December 1, 1851, *CD-USNA,* Shanghai, 112:1; *Spirit of Missions*, XVII (1852), 203, 446.

[7] *Senate Exec. Doc.*, No. 30, 36 Cong., 1 sess., p. 382; *Marshall's Correspondence*, p. 156.

Chinese cartoonist's view of sailors in a Western bar

Shanghai, where the foreign settlement grew rapidly, was the only exception. In Shanghai, however, the foreigners built practically an entirely new town in a suburb of that city; this self-inflicted segregation also helped to reduce local incidents. Furthermore, the local populace of the northern ports were rather pleased by the arrival of foreigners who brought them new profits that previously had been monopolized by a few rich merchants at Canton.

While the Canton city dwellers were in trouble over the "city question," the villagers in the districts adjacent to Canton were aroused by similar cases. Previously the Western merchants had been forbidden to go hunting in the countryside; but now, privileged by the new treaties, they were free to visit the country at will. Their frequent bird-hunting expeditions to the countryside gradually annoyed the peaceful but ignorant villagers, who did not enjoy seeing a group of bearded "foreign devils" carrying dangerous weapons and wandering around their residence area. To these Cantonese farmers, the Western hunters looked like the sailors who were wandering in the Canton streets. For protection against their supposed immoral purposes, the villagers began to build fences around their villages. When a foreigner of presumably doubtful morality appeared, the farmers would rush their wives and children to shelter behind the fences. The foreigners, driven by curiosity or simply because of carelessness, occasionally stepped into the protected area of the farmers. Owing to the difficulty of mutual communication, quarrels sometimes became unavoidable and occasionally led to fist fights or even bloodshed.[8]

Those local incidents were usually so overexaggerated by the active participants that hostility on both sides increased. As time passed, the Chinese public was aroused by the accumulated "Sino-barbarian" clashes and turned their protests, which were constantly ignored by their government, into large-scale antiforeign as well as anti-Manchu actions.[9] The participants in these mass movements were people of all classes, including a great number of enlightened people as well as the former hong merchants who had previously been very friendly to the Westerners.

On the other side, the Westerners, particularly the British residing

---

[8] For a general survey see Liang T'ing-nan, *I-fen chi-wen*, pp. 97 ff.

[9] On one occasion the magnificent office of the Prefect of Canton was burnt by a mob. This action expressed the vigorous anti-Manchu sentiment of the populace. At another incident even Ch'i-ying was insulted when none of the Cantonese literary talents was willing to draft a "public notice" for him in accordance with what he had dictated. See Liang, *I-fen chi-wen*, pp. 97 ff.

at Canton, were equally irritated by the exaggerated stories spread in the Western societies that dramatized the extent of the local anti-foreign movement. They petitioned their respective governments to take aggressive action to protect their "treaty rights." Actually, these local accidents could have been ironed out gradually by honest and friendly negotiations between the governments involved had the British not been accustomed to using a high-handed policy in treating the peoples and governments of colonial and semicolonial countries.

As a matter of fact, none of the so-called local incidents that occurred at Canton during the postwar years was solved in a way satisfactory to both sides. The British authorities, in dealing with these matters, frequently applied the gunboat policy. On some important occasions, such as the incident of April 1, 1847, their abuse of this policy brought unbearable disgrace to the dignified Manchu Imperial Commissioner, Ch'i-ying, and his enlightened soft-spoken Chinese colleague, Governor Huang En-t'ung. While making repeated concessions to the "barbarians," these two statesmen had constantly neglected public opinion at Canton. Since both of them clearly recognized China's inability to carry on effective resistance against the British, the only thing they could do was to suppress the Cantonese antiforeign activities in order to calm the British.

This method of action, however, achieved only contrary results. Their arrogant suppression of the ever-rising antiforeign movement at Canton irritated the populace even more. In the winter of 1846-47 the mass movement at Canton was already beyond the Manchus' control. Unfortunately, when the masses at Canton had defied Ch'i-ying's authority, the victorious British became equally intolerable. Their action not only destroyed Ch'i-ying's career and his appeasement policy but also brought to an end the new method of China's "barbarian management," which the Emperor himself had sponsored since the close of the Opium War. Thus ended the first phase of China's apprenticeship in modern diplomacy.

II

It was in this chaotic period that Alexander Hill Everett arrived in Canton. On his recovery from a protracted illness, Everett, the first United States commissioner to China under the Treaty of Wanghia, had sailed from New York for China on June 22, 1846. After a trip of nearly four months, he landed at Macao on October 6.[10] Having

---

[10] Everett to Buchanan, No. 13, Canton, November 1, 1846, *DD-USNA*, 92:4.

stayed there for two weeks, he went to Canton and took rooms at the residence of Paul S. Forbes, the United States consul at Canton. On October 27, an interview with the Chinese Imperial Commissioner, Ch'i-ying, was arranged at the same place in which Biddle had exchanged the ratifications of the Treaty of Wanghia with the Imperial Commissioner.[11]

This interview was held after a very simple but friendly ceremony in which Everett presented his credentials. Soon after the interview, Everett retired to Macao, where the American legation was officially located. He did not return to Canton until June. During Everett's stay at Macao, Sino-British relations deteriorated daily. At first the British presented to Ch'i-ying some secret demands requesting the opening of an additional port at Assam in southwestern China. Assam was not a good locality for any kind of large international trade, but it did have a great potential market for the opium trade among the poor masses in southwest China. Ch'i-ying, of course, was intelligent enough to detect the British intention. Before giving any definite answer to the British, he sent P'an Shih-ch'eng for the second time to inform Everett, obviously hoping to enlist the sympathy and assistance of this new United States commissioner. Unfortunately Everett was sick at Macao. Since P'an could not reach him personally, he held an interview with Peter Parker, the secretary of the legation, but the advice he received is not known.[12] The British request regarding Assam was said to have been rejected by Ch'i-ying.[13] P'an's visit to the American legation was the last attempt of the Chinese authorities to consult with the Americans about their disputes with the British.

A few months after Everett retired to Macao, the Sino-British problems led to an open clash. The British made a surprise attack at the Bogue on April 1, 1847, under the pretext that China had voided the Treaty of the Bogue by refusing the British entry to the city of Canton.[14] With the capture of the Bogue, the British forces proceeded to Canton, whose population numbered more than a million, and threatened to bombard it. After a short humiliating negotiation with

---

[11] *Chinese Repository*, XV, No. 12 (December, 1846), 624.

[12] Everett to James Buchanan, No. 26, Macao, February 28, 1847, *DD-USNA*, 92:4.

[13] *Marshall's Correspondence*, pp. 169, 208.

[14] For general reference in English see Morse, *The International Relations of the Chinese Empire*, I, 388-89; for the contemporary writings in Chinese see Liang, *I-fen chi-wen*, pp. 99-100; for an impartial contemporary observation written by the American commissioner see Alexander H. Everett to the Secretary of State, No. 28, Macao, April 10, 1847, *DD-USNA*, 92:4.

the British, Ch'i-ying conceded to the British demand that they might enter the walled city of Canton after a period of two years and allowed their unprovoked attack at the Bogue to pass unprotested.[15]

Contemporary American observers at Canton believed that Great Britain would turn China into a second India. Ch'i-ying's one-sided submission could not stop the British. In his report to Washington in April, 1847, Commissioner Everett wrote:[16]

They [the Chinese mandarins] appear to be aware that Great Britain is determined to get possession of their country—that they have no means of escape, except by obtaining aid from other foreign powers,—and that France, Russia and the United States may be relied upon for sympathy. . . .

Parker also reported:[17]

In conversations with English officers, I have been struck with the coolness with which they remark that "through the force of circumstances the British Government may be compelled to take possession of a portion of South China." . . . Sir John Davis [British Governor of Hong Kong] has been most fully sustained by the home government, and . . . the honor of the British Government may require further demonstration of its power. . . .

The American merchants in China also expected at no distant day to pay duties through a British customhouse in Canton.[18]

In such circumstances, therefore, the American commissioner was confronted with a serious diplomatic problem, namely, what step the United States should take during the coming crisis in China. As this was left blank in his instructions from the State Department in Washington, he himself had to attempt to make a proper China policy for his country.

On April 10, 1847, immediately after the British attack at the Bogue, Commissioner Everett sent a long report to Washington suggesting some principles for formulating a proper United States foreign

---

[15] Liang, *I-fen chi-wen*, pp. 100, 104.

[16] Everett to the Secretary of State, No. 28, Macao, April 10, 1847, *DD-USNA*, 92:4.

[17] Peter Parker to James Buchanan, Confidential, No. 36, September 25, 1847, *DD-USNA*, 92:5.

[18] *Ibid.* The belief of the Americans in a supposed British conquest of China seems to have been inspired merely by the arrogant activities of the British governor of Hong Kong, Sir J. F. Davis, who had reversed completely Sir Henry Pottinger's good-will China policy. Although Ch'i-ying had tried to make Davis an "intimate friend," the new minister preferred gunboats to friendship. For a comparative study of the policies pursued by Pottinger and Davis see Fairbank, *Trade and Diplomacy on the China Coast* (Cambridge, Mass.: Harvard University Press, 1953), I, 268 ff.

policy toward China.[19] "What then," he asked, "in such a state of things would naturally be the conduct of these powers?" If the interest of China alone were at stake, wrote Everett, there would be no motive for other Western powers to attempt to interfere. But when the interests of other nations were also involved, the case was different. What interest did the other Western powers have in China now? According to Everett, it was China's independence. The annexation of China to Great Britain would upset the balance of power among the members of the Christian Commonwealth and "seriously endanger the independence of even the most powerful, including the United States." Thus the three Western powers, Russia, France, and the United States, all had a direct interest "in preventing the Chinese empire from being swallowed up in that of Great Britain; or even from coming more immediately under her influence." Moreover, stressed Everett, "these powers undoubtedly have the right, and are bound in honor and duty, to adopt such measures as they may think best fitted to promote the object."[20]

What preventive moves, then, should be taken by the other Western powers? Everett suggested that "the first step would seem to be the establishment of a full understanding among these powers as to the nature of the crisis and the interest which they all have in its results." "This point being settled," he said, "the measures best fitted to avert impending evils, would naturally suggest themselves, and would probably be agreed upon without much difference of opinion." Everett further reminded the Secretary of State that Russia was in a more favorable position to make close connections with China. Hence she should be the first country to be consulted, and a friendly understanding between her and other foreign powers upon the whole subject should be made. Then Everett went on to suggest:[21]

. . . a temperate, but, at the same time, firm and serious appeal to Great Britain by the several Governments, which have common interest in this subject, acting in concert, might give a better direction to her policy, and induce her to reconsider her projects against the independence of the Celestial Empire.

There is even reason to believe, wrote Everett, "that it might secure the independence of China for an indefinite future period. . . ."

---

[19] Alexander H. Everett, to the Secretary of State, No. 28, Macao, April 10, 1847, *DD-USNA*, 92:4.
[20] *Ibid.*
[21] *Ibid.*

This dispatch is really an "Open Door" note drafted by an American statesman half a century earlier than John Hay's. Unfortunately Everett died at Canton on June 28, 1847,[22] at about the time his report was reaching Washington. His thoughtful policy seems to have attracted no proper attention in Washington. After his death, American diplomacy at Canton under the direction of the chargé d'affaires, Peter Parker, immediately swung in another direction.

Except for Everett's eight-month service, it was Parker who, during the four years after the signing of the Treaty of Wanghia, actually directed American diplomacy at Canton. In the absence of specific instructions from Washington, he was left almost completely free to interpret the treaty at will.

As an eager but unsuccessful missionary, Parker, for the sake of his mission alone, had from the beginning favored a tough policy against China. As an American diplomat at Canton, he, like Everett, felt uneasy watching the British working for the supposed dismemberment of the Celestial Empire; however, he was more sympathetic with the British than with the Chinese. In April, 1847, while Commissioner Everett was drafting his program for united action of the different Western powers against the British threat to Canton, Parker, obviously without consulting the United States commissioner, expressed to the British authorities his "entire concurrence" with the British action.[23] After the death of Everett, he became openly sympathetic with the British. In his report to Washington on September 15, 1847, Parker wrote:[24]

From the tone of the home press my impression is that the next move of the [British] Government will be to place a British Minister at Peking, and there to obtain redress for grievances; (and that they have much to complain of can not be denied) and if this be the only object, the public sentiment of the West will sustain them. . . . The possibility, not to say probability, of this event, at no distant day (perhaps within twelve or eighteen months).

After that, Parker kept himself closely connected with the British envoy at China, formulating a policy entirely opposite to Everett's "Open Door" principle.

---

22 *Ibid.*

23 Morse, *The International Relations of the Chinese Empire,* I, 388.

24 Parker to Buchanan, Confidential, No. 36, Canton, September 25, 1847, *DD-USNA,* 92:5.

III

The outstanding example of Parker's method of action toward the Chinese can be found in the Roberts case, which formed the chief American claim against China for nearly ten years. In the postwar days, the troublesome missionary I. J. Roberts was the most active missionary at Canton, but he was probably not very suitable for such a position. He was described by a contemporary British writer as "intolerant and bigoted to the Baptist dogmas, irritable, peevish, inconsistent, and vacillating—a man singularly illiterate, without stability of character or pleasantness of manner."[25]

After moving back to Canton in 1844, Roberts, "without the consent of the Chinese authorities," and against the advice of Paul S. Forbes, the American consul at Canton, but under "the supposed sanction [of] a high officer [of] the United States," presumably Parker, built a house and a chapel in the "worst section of Canton."[26] Here Roberts hired a few Chinese assistants of doubtful qualifications to help him conduct the religious service, during which small coins were frequently distributed to the audience as compensation for their attendance. Hence Roberts attracted a great crowd of local vagabonds who were interested in the monetary remuneration rather than the preaching. During a service in May, 1847, the money was not equally distributed. A quarrel followed that resulted in a robbery in which a mob of vagabonds participated.[27] Roberts estimated his loss at about $3,000 and appealed to Commissioner Everett, who notified Ch'i-ying. According to the Treaty of Wanghia, it was referred to an impartial commission consisting of one or more individuals from each nation. The commission, as duly organized later, found that the loss was only about tls. 1,000 or $1,400. In the meantime some lost property valued at $400 was recovered. Unfortunately, before the case could be successfully settled, Everett died at Canton. Then Parker, acting as chargé d'affaires of the American legation, took over the case and demanded that the Chinese authority pay for the loss according to Article 19 of the Treaty of Wanghia.[28] This demand seems to have been based upon a forced interpretation of the article.[29]

---

25 Lin-Le (Augustus F. Lindley), *Ti-ping-tien-kwoh, The History of the Ti-ping Revolution* (London: Day and Son, 1866), II, 566.
26 Paul S. Forbes to John W. Davis, Canton, January 27, 1849, *DD-USNA, 92:6.*
27 *Ibid.*
28 For a detailed review of the Roberts claim see Davis to the Secretary of State, No. 9, November 24, 1848, *DD-USNA, 92:6.*
29 Article 19 of the Treaty of Wanghia reads as follows: "All citizens of the United States in China peaceably attending to their affairs, being placed on a

Following his own interpretation of the treaty, Ch'i-ying, therefore, refused to pay Roberts' claim, but he promised that the Chinese government would help in the recovery as the treaty required. Besides, Ch'i-ying said the Chinese local government was financially incapable of being responsible for such burdens.

Parker insisted that the treaty required the payment of Roberts' claim. Avoiding the English version of the treaty, he rested his demand on the Chinese text, which read: [in Cantonese pronunciation] *"Paou Ho Ki Shih Kia Tsuan Gan"* (To provide protection for the security of person and family).[30] The term *Tsuan Gan* (or *ch'uan-an* in Mandarin) means "security," but Parker ungrammatically set the Chinese phrase apart and insisted that it meant "entirely secure." He warned the Department of State:[31] "In the present instance the interest at stake is comparatively trivial but the *principle* may involve tens of thousands, and even millions of dollars." Parker continued, "I could therefore have wished that the discussion of so important a subject with this government, might have been conducted by the superior experience of Mr. Everett before his decease." Since it had happened otherwise, he said, he had to meet it "in the absence of specific instructions" from the State Department.

In a later letter to Ch'i-ying, Parker also warned him: "Your excellency speaks of the inability of the local officers to make indemnity in such cases. The undersigned has never asked this. It is the Government of China alone that he has called upon." He even indulged in such language as: "The undersigned, as in duty bound, once more calls upon your Excellency for the indemnity of 1,000 Taels due Reverend Mr. Roberts, and if payment is long deferred, the Government of the United States, will justly demand interest on the same."[32]

While the Roberts argument was still hot, another case occurred. A Chinese merchant by the name of Wang Chi-hsi was said to have

common footing of amity and goodwill with subjects of China, shall receive and enjoy, for themselves and everything appertaining to them, the special protection of the local authorities of Government, who shall defend them from all insult or injury of any sort on the part of the Chinese.

"If their dwelling or their property be threatened or attacked by mobs, incendiaries, or other violent or lawless persons, the local officers, on requisition of the Consul, will immediately despatch a military force to disperse the rioters, and will apprehend the guilty individuals and punish them with utmost rigour of the law." See *Treaties, Conventions, etc., between China and Foreign States* (Shanghai: Statistical Dept. of the Inspectoral General of Customs, 1908), I, 480.

[30] Parker to Ch'i-ying, August 4, Canton, 1847, *DD-USNA*, 92:5.

[31] Parker to James Buchanan, No. 33, Canton, August 17, 1847, *ibid.* It seemed that Ch'i-ying's refusal was based upon the same kind of reasoning.

[32] Parker to Ch'i-ying, Canton, January 22, 1848, *ibid.*

owed the American firm, Nye Parkin & Co., about nine thousand taels of silver, and refused to pay it back. After a single complaint from Parker, Ch'i-ying immediately ordered Wang arrested, but the case turned out to be more complicated, since Wang was bankrupt and the American party was not the only one to suffer. Parker, however, insisted that if Wang failed to pay, the Chinese government must pay for him. Moved by Wang's pitiful situation, Ch'i-ying asked Parker to re-examine the case. Parker replied with a very impolite letter.[33] As there was no international court to which to appeal, Ch'i-ying tried to persuade Parker through the medium of their personal friendship. In a private letter to the latter, Ch'i-ying wrote:[34]

You and I, Sir, have been mutual friends for these ten years and have never had any disagreement. Now Sir you have been raised to the honor of Chargé d'Affaires. Evidently you are able judiciously to decide this whole business, so as to give satisfaction. I do not presume to believe every word that Wang Tshih-she [i.e., Wang Chi-hsi] says to me is true, and also beg you Sir will not altogether rely upon the truth of what Messrs. Nye Parkin & Co., say to you.

In this correspondence, which was written in Chinese, the terms and styles adopted by both sides were remarkably distinct. Ch'i-ying's letters were written in a very humble style with unusual politeness, while Parker's letters were very demanding and high-handed in tone. It seems that Parker, as a long-time resident at Canton, was familiar with the British style of demanding claims against the Chinese. He seems to have realized that the money could not be recovered from the "penniless vagabonds";[35] he also seems to have learned from past experience that the money could be squeezed from the Imperial Treasury, if he insisted.

Parker had been merely a "barbarian physician" at Canton, serving as a humble clerk in the Wanghia negotiation when Ch'i-ying was sent to Canton as a dignified Imperial Commissioner to negotiate with the high-ranking "barbarian officer," Cushing. Only five years after Wanghia, however, the former American clerk began to treat the Imperial Commissioner arrogantly. Although Parker was still much more moderate than the British, he had definitely helped to humiliate the Imperial Commissioner, who had already lost his popularity among

---

[33] Parker to Ch'i-ying, January 31, 1848, *ibid.;* see also Parker to Ch'i-ying, February 24, 1848, *ibid.*

[34] Ch'i-ying to Parker, undated private letter, *ibid.*

[35] Parker to Ch'i-ying, Canton, August 4, 1847, *DD-USNA,* 92:5.

the Chinese people and his stature among his colleagues. Hence Ch'i-ying was frequently accused by the Chinese of being too kind to the "barbarians."

Commissioner Everett had once complained that the Celestial Empire had placed Great Britain and the United States "upon one and the same footing."[36] It is unlikely that this assertion was correct at the time; as a matter of fact, Ch'i-ying had twice consulted the Americans concerning China's difficulties with Great Britain with the obvious hope of enlisting their assistance and sympathy. It was only after his relations with Parker deteriorated that he began to treat the Americans "upon one and the same footing" with the British. By that time, Ch'i-ying was almost completely isolated on all sides, distrusted by Chinese and foreigners alike. It would have been a miracle if he could have survived such circumstances.

IV

The first sign of Peking's distrust of Ch'i-ying's appeasement policy was the removal of Huang En-t'ung, who had been Ch'i-ying's closest associate since 1842. In January, 1847, Huang was dismissed on the pretext that he had mistakenly recommended to the Emperor an old man for employment in the military service.[37] On hearing of his removal, it was said, Ch'i-ying burst into tears. Commissioner Everett was right when he reported to Washington that he had received "tolerably authentic" information attributing Huang's removal to "his supposed predilection for foreigners." He wrote:

Both he and the Viceroy, Tse-yeng [Ch'i-ying], are, as I have mentioned in former despatches, generally regarded, as among the persons, most friendly to the extension of intercourse with foreigners. It is understood that there is much division of opinion at Court upon this subject: and if the cause here assigned for Wang's [Huang's] removal be the true one, the fact would seem to indicate an increase of power in the party opposed to the formation of more intimate relations with the Christian world.[38]

On the removal of Huang, Hsü Kuang-chin was appointed to replace him as governor of Kuang-tung; Yeh Ming-ch'en was appointed provincial treasurer. Born in Honan province and acquiring a *chin-shih* degree early in life, Hsü was a formidable man of learning, though

---

[36] Everett to James Buchanan, No. 28, Macao, April 10, 1847, *DD-USNA*, 92:4.

[37] Huang En-t'ung, "Fu yuan chi lioh," p. 425.

[38] Everett to Buchanan, No. 26, Macao, February 28, 1847, *DD-USNA*, 92:4.

unfamiliar with "barbarian management."[39] In obvious disagreement with Ch'i-ying, Hsü did not participate in any foreign negotiations until after the recall of Ch'i-ying,[40] when he became governor-general of Liang-kuang and Imperial Commissioner in charge of foreign trade in the Five Ports. Yeh was promoted to the governorship.[41]

Thus after February, 1848, the Hsü-Yeh team completely reversed the Ch'i-ying line of foreign policy. Both Hsü and Yeh, it must be noted, were among the best products of the old Chinese civil examination system. Boastful and dignified, they were men of high principle and literary fame. Unlike Ch'i-ying, who had treated the foreigners with remarkable courtesy, Hsü and Yeh did the opposite. "In reply to foreign requests," as a contemporary Chinese historian wrote, "they simply wrote a few lines if they cared to reply at all."[42]

In June, 1848, Sir George Bonham, the newly appointed British governor of Hong Kong, began to write to Hsü suggesting that preliminary arrangements be made for entry into the city of Canton in 1849, something Ch'i-ying had promised for two years. The British proposal was consistently ignored. At last, when the deadline of the entry into Canton approached, Hsü held an interview with Bonham in February, 1849, and formally rejected the British demand. In the meantime the two Chinese officers frequently conferred with each other on the "city question" and jointly decided that public opinion at Canton, which their predecessors, the Manchu overlord Ch'i-ying and his Chinese associate, Huang En-t'ung, had long neglected, should be respected. As soon as this news was known to the people, the whole populace of the city rose as one man. The gentry and the literati, including the former hong merchant, Howqua, took the lead. Within a few days a militia of more than one hundred thousand men was organized and an anti-British parade was held. It was so vigorous a demonstration that it made the English believe that the populace at

---

[39] For a good biographical sketch of Hsü Kuang-chin in English see Hummel, *Eminent Chinese of the Ch'ing Period (1644-1912)* (Washington, D.C.: Government Printing Office, 1943-44), I, 319.

[40] Ch'i-ying was recalled in February, 1848. He was made a Grand Councilor in the Grand Council, the highest honor and the noblest position a mandarin could expect in the Ch'ing period. As far as foreign affairs were concerned, however, he was only kicked upstairs; "barbarian management" was no longer in his charge, but in that of the newly appointed officials at Canton. However, Ch'i-ying continued to be favored during Emperor Tao-kuang's lifetime.

[41] For Yeh Ming-ch'en see Hummel, *Eminent Chinese of the Ch'ing Period*, II, 940.

[42] Ch'i-hsuan ho-shang tiao-sou, *Ying-chi-li ju-ch'eng shih-mo-chi* (The Story of the English Entry into Canton from Beginning to End), *Ts'ung-shu chi-ch'eng*, No. 3999 (Ch'ang-sha: Commercial Press, 1939), p. 2.

Canton was really out of the control of the Chinese government. Meanwhile, the local gentry and merchants, headed by Howqua and encouraged by the mandarins, held a meeting at which it was decided to put a stop to the foreign trade; the American and French consuls were told that England alone would be responsible for the resulting loss. A public letter was also sent to Bonham. Under these circumstances the British authority yielded and promised to postpone indefinitely the issue of entry into the city.[43]

During this period, the Emperor himself was prepared to let the "barbarians" enter Canton if they insisted;[44] but to his surprise they were scared away by the anti-British outburst, so directly in contrast with the methods that Ch'i-ying had vainly pursued for the past eight years and which the Emperor had long suspected of being too lenient. This "victory" of the Cantonese people was applauded throughout China and Hsü and Yeh were praised as great "barbarian suppressors."[45]

When he heard of this successful demonstration and the British concession, Emperor Tao-kuang was naturally pleased. On May 7, 1849, he therefore issued an edict with his famous vermilion pen to reward all those who had participated in the patriotic demonstration. This statement, which actually sounded the mourning bell for Ch'i-ying's appeasement policy and closed China's first apprenticeship in modern diplomacy, read in part as follows:[46]

It is nearly ten years since the barbarian affairs became a calamity along the coast. Military expenditures were greatly increased and troops were exhaustively recruited. Although comparatively quiet in recent years, yet the rigid and lenient methods for barbarian management were not well balanced and created more problems. I, the Emperor, have restrained my emotions [for years] lest the people in the coastal regions might suffer more from it, but I hoped that great justice would surely prevail after a short endurance of minor injustice. This is the natural law. Recently the English barbarians resumed their request to enter the city of Canton. From successive memorials, I came to know that Hsü Kuang-chin, the Governor-General, was able to handle the request properly as the circumstances required. Today I received another memorial [from them] reporting that the merchants at Canton all understood the great principle [of patriotism] and offered financial contributions to redress the disgrace; the gentry thereof also rendered their assistance to the government that had caused the barbarians to withdraw their request. Now commerce has

43 Liang, I-fen chi-wen, pp. 111-12.
44 IMSM-TK, LXXIX, 39b.
45 Liang, I-fen chi-wen, p. 113.
46 Liang, I-fen chi-wen, p. 112; IMSM-TK, LXXX, 15.

been resumed as usual without the loss of a single soldier nor the shooting of a single arrow. The said Governor-General and the Governor have pacified the barbarians without the slightest compulsion so that peace may be maintained forever. The extent of my pleasure and compliments [to them] can hardly be expressed. Hence their remarkable service must be rewarded accordingly. . . .

Consequently, both Hsü and Yeh were given hereditary titles as well as honorary decorations, very unusual in the officialdom during the Ch'ing period. All gentry and merchants participating in this movement received different kinds of imperial awards, which were given on the very day when the news of the withdrawal of the British demand reached Peking. These prompt awards indicated the disgrace of the former Imperial Commissioner, Ch'i-ying.[47] In the imperial rescript, the terms "rigid" and "lenient" methods of "barbarian management" obviously referred to the rigid policy adopted by former Imperial Commissioner, Lin Tse-hsu, the great opium suppressor, and the lenient appeasement policy practiced by Ch'i-ying in the post-Opium War period. The Emperor thought that both Lin Tse-hsu and Ch'i-ying had overdeveloped their policies in directions that could only lead to more trouble. Thus, this edict really indicated that the Court at Peking was about to shift its "barbarian policy." This shift, as a matter of fact, had been under consideration ever since the recall of Huang En-t'ung, and the victory achieved by Hsü and Yeh at Canton seems to have given definite proof that the new policy was wise.[48]

---

[47] Hsia Hsueh, *Chung-hsi ch'i-shih, chüan* 13, p. 17a.

[48] Soon after the Emperor's edict was issued, some memorialists at Peking began to impeach Ch'i-ying and Huang En-t'ung, charging them with "cowardliness" and "deception." "Had they remained in the positions of Governorship any longer," said one memorialist, "the clash between the people and the barbarians would be endless, and the result would be unthinkable." He then praised the Emperor for having skillfully shifted the "barbarian policy" and achieved a victory. This memorial was favorably accepted by the Emperor. See *IMSM-TK,* LXXX, 18b-20a.

7

THE DAVIS MISSION

AND THE ESTABLISHMENT

OF CONSULAR COURTS

I

ABOUT the time the Chinese Imperial Commissioner, Ch'i-ying, was recalled to Peking, the United States appointed John W. Davis the new commissioner to China. A native of New Holland, in Lancaster County, Pennsylvania, Davis acquired an M.D. degree at the University of Maryland in 1821 and became a professional physician. He was later elected three times to serve as congressman from Indiana, and he became Speaker of the House in 1845. Three years later, on January 28, 1848, he received his appointment to China.[1]

Upon the departure of Davis for his new mission on March 8, 1848, Buchanan, then Secretary of State, issued no specific instructions as to the policy the United States was to follow regarding China. He merely insisted that the American claims for loss of property of American citizens in China should be continued. This item formed the essential part of the first letter of instruction to Davis; it seems to have been based primarily upon Parker's reports.[2]

Although he arrived in Canton on August 21, 1848, Davis was unable to obtain an interview with the Chinese authorities until October 6, when, after much unpleasant correspondence, he was received by the new Imperial Commissioner, Hsü Kuang-chin, and the new governor of Kwangtung, Yeh-Ming-ch'en, in a country house of Howqua, the former hong merchant.[3] "The party was ushered in by Howqua," re-

---

[1] Allen Johnson, ed., *Dictionary of American Biography* (New York: Charles Scribner's Sons, 1943), V, 136-37.

[2] James Buchanan to John W. Davis, No. 1, Washington, January 28, 1848, *DI-USNA*, 77:38.

[3] The meeting was first mistakenly reported by the *Chinese Repository* as taking place in a "warehouse of Howqua." See *ibid.*, XVII, No. 10 (October, 1848), 543-44. This story was followed by Dr. Earl Swisher. See Swisher, *China's Management of the American Barbarians: A Study of Sino-American Relations, 1841-1861, with Documents* (New Haven, Conn.: Yale University Far Eastern Publications, 1951), p. 189n.

ported the *Chinese Repository*, "and the Governor-General and the Governor received the commissioner [Davis] with considerable coldness and formality." "The contrast between the hauteur and ignorance of these two high officers," the report continued, "and the inquisitiveness and affability of their predecessors Kiying [Ch'i-ying] and Hwang [Huang En-t'ung] is very great."[4]

This discourteous interview clearly indicated that Hsü and Yeh disapproved of the politeness of their predecessors, who, it seemed to them, had been abused by the "barbarians." The Americans' request for an interview, as Hsü and Yeh saw it, was no more than a signal for presenting demands. Hsü reported to the Emperor that he was intentionally cool to the American commissioner in order "to break his [Davis'] proud and domineering spirit."[5] "Davis, personally, has been quiet," said Hsü. "Since he made no demands on this occasion, it would seem that hereafter he will not go to the extent of causing unfortunate complications."

Actually, as soon as Davis sat down to work, he resumed the previous claims. It appears that at first he had no real knowledge of these claims. He simply did as he was instructed by the State Department and as he was advised by Dr. Peter Parker. In the meantime, a new instruction from Washington, stating that "the Government is both able and willing to perform the duty which it owes to American citizens by enforcing their just claims under the treaty against the Government of China,"[6] had also hastened his decision to proceed with the claims against China. Realizing the previous difficulty in presenting them, Davis decided first to back his action with warships, which "might be instrumental," as he reported to Washington, "in setting our affairs in a more desirable position with the Government of China."[7]

Subsequently he forwarded some letters to Governor-General Hsü reiterating the previous demands, but Hsü promptly rejected them. In a report to Washington, Davis stated that he could see no good reason for continuing this correspondence with the Chinese without making "some belligerent demonstration" to enforce the American demands.[8] Thus he called the two American gunboats, the *Preble* and the *Plymouth*, to Whampoa to prepare for "belligerent demonstrations." In reporting this action to Washington, however, Davis stated that he was

---

[4] *Ibid.*, XVII, No. 10 (October, 1848), 543.
[5] *IWSM-TK*, LXXIX, 26b.
[6] Davis to Buchanan, No. 5, Canton, September 26, 1848, *DD-USNA*, 92:6.
[7] *Ibid.*
[8] Davis to Buchanan, No. 8, Canton, October 27, 1848, *DD-USNA*, 92:6.

not entirely convinced of the justice of this case, but he had taken the position of his "more experienced predecessor, Peter Parker."[9]

Obviously, Davis was faced with a dilemma. On the one hand, he was directed by the Department of State, as well as pressed by his indispensable "more experienced predecessor," to proceed with the claims against China. On the other hand, after an examination of the case, he began to doubt the justice of the American claim; he thought that Washington was ill-informed and he himself, poorly advised. A month after his previous report he shrewdly explained to the State Department that "most of the cases of difficulty arising from selection of residence for citizens of the United States in Canton have been for those for missionaries from our own country." He added that he was satisfied that these difficulties generally arose from no improper conduct on the part of these gentlemen.[10]

Considering the Roberts incident as a special case, Davis reminded the Department of State that the basis of the claim was dubious. It presented to his mind three questions:[11] (1) Was the government of China bound to indemnify an individual for losses sustained by a mob? The Chinese government did not pay her own citizens for losses sustained in this way. "I am not aware of what may be the law of other nations," reported Davis in puzzlement, "nor can I find any international law touching the question." (2) Was the government of China bound to pay indemnity to any citizen of the United States, under the treaty, for losses sustained by a mob? Davis said that Article 19 of the treaty was the only one bearing directly upon this second point, but he doubted that it had given the American citizens such a right. (3) Was Roberts entitled to indemnity in his particular case? Davis stated that Roberts had violated Article 17 of the Treaty of Wanghia, which provided that citizens of the United States desiring houses or places of business must allow local officers of the two governments to select them. The duty of these officers was to choose appropriate sites, bearing in mind the feelings of the people who lived in that area. In the case of Roberts, stated Davis, these provisions were not complied with. "There is no doubt," said Davis, "Mr. Roberts' location is in one of the most degraded and vicious neighborhoods in the suburbs of Canton."

---

[9] *Ibid.* Davis' request for gunboats was probably made more because of his irritation at Hsü's rude treatment than for the sake of the $1,400 claim.

[10] *Ibid.*, No. 9, Canton, November 24, 1848.

[11] *Ibid.*

The Commissioner, therefore, asked the State Department for specific instructions concerning "this *particular case.*" If the Department should, upon examination of the case, decide to force the collection of the $1,000 from the Chinese, definite measures would have to be taken. "I may be permitted to say," he said, "that according to the diplomatic ethics of the English government (and I must confess I do not admire the authority when I quote it) that sum might be withheld from duties payable by American merchants, or the port of Canton might be blockaded," or other alternatives might be adopted. He reminded the State Department, however, that the Westerners had constantly abused their treaty privileges at Canton, sometimes to an intolerable extent. His report went on to say:[12]

The Chinese authorities inflict the most hideous punishments upon their subjects for no other crime than that of being poor and unable to pay their debts and frequently, if rumor be true, in civil courts foreigners are too much in the habit of forcing collections from insolvent Chinamen knowing that the friends of the debtor rather than see him incarcerated, bambooed, and otherwise punished will step forward and pay the debt for him. . . .

Davis added, however, that, so far as he knew, the American citizens in China had never indulged in such practices. After this report was mailed, Davis forwarded no request to the Chinese authorities with regard to the Roberts claim, which had been a major issue of the American diplomatic service at Canton since the death of Everett in June, 1847.

Davis' apathy in this case may have caused some conflicts among the American personnel in the American legation and in the consular service. On January 27, 1849, he sent another report to Washington in which he also enclosed a letter from Paul S. Forbes, the United States consul at Canton, who sharply attacked both Roberts and Parker for abusing the treaty privileges and causing unnecessary trouble.[13] Forbes said that, against his advice and without the consent of the Chinese authorities, Roberts had built a house and a chapel in the worst locality at Canton and had often expressed himself to an unnecessary degree and was constantly "giving great annoyance to the Authorities, both Chinese and American, without doing the slightest good or advancing the cause of Religion which seems to be his object. . . ." Frequent collision of the missionaries with the people of China, said Forbes, was daily endangering the peace and safety of other members

---

[12] *Ibid.*
[13] Paul S. Forbes to John W. Davis, Canton, January 27, 1849, *DD-USNA,* 92:6.

of the foreign community at Canton. These dangerous missionary activities at Canton, Forbes charged, were under the supposed sanction of the government of the United States. " . . . this feeling has grown out of the fact," he stressed, "that an officer of the Government and one who has at times been its representative [i.e., Parker] is a clergyman and missionary and it is this circumstance which induces greater vigilance on the part of the mandarins in reference to religion and tends to weaken and interfere with the legitimate influence which our Government should have with the Government of China." Thus he urged his government to issue "special instructions" to its officers in China lest the Chinese people and mandarins assume that the United States intended to overturn their religion and their traditional social order.

Forbes's anti-Parker statement seems to have been encouraged, if not requested, by the Commissioner. It was delivered to Davis on January 27, 1849, the same day that Davis sent his long Dispatch No. 11 to Washington, which included the Forbes letter as an additional explanation of the recent difficulties with Roberts. Davis stated with regret that Roberts still continued to have trouble with some vagabond Chinese. He went on to say that the original difficulty between them had been reported to Washington previously. In closing he said that he would let the attached letter from the American consul speak for him concerning Roberts' recent troubles.[14]

Since the texts of both the commissioner's dispatch and the consul's letter were very long and were written on the same day, it seems unlikely that Davis enclosed Forbes's letter in his dispatch by chance and without arrangement with the consul beforehand. Before he introduced Forbes's letter, moreover, Davis also mentioned his previous unfavorable comments about Roberts. All these show that Forbes's letter had the Commissioner's approval.

It was also surprising that while the drafting of these two documents was in progress, Parker was kept completely in the dark. He had no opportunity to know the contents of the letter until a few hours before the mail was closed.[15] A quarrel among the three seems to have followed after the mail was sent, but it was not until February 7, 1849, that Parker was able to write an explanation directly to the Secretary of State.[16]

---

[14] Davis to Buchanan, No. 11, Canton, January 27, 1849, *DD-USNA*, 92:6.
[15] Parker to the Secretary of State, Canton, February 7, 1849, *DD-USNA*, 92:6.
[16] *Ibid.*

The conflict between Parker and Forbes was a reflection of the differences within the American community. As a missionary whose professional interest was parallel to that of the British rather than to that of his own people, Parker from the very beginning had favored close cooperation with the British and had constantly kept in close contact with the British diplomats. Although his opinions and actions were contrary to those of the commissioners', he had not been seriously challenged until 1849, when Forbes, for the first time, expressed his objection to Parker's conduct. Though Forbes was obviously acting with the approval of Davis, the Commissioner himself was by no means a firm man. He did not possess the unusual statesmanship of his predecessor, Everett, nor had he the strong will of his successor, Humphrey Marshall. He made no definite statement concerning a proper policy toward China as did Everett and Marshall; and he provided no strong suggestions to Washington. Thus throughout Davis' term as commissioner to China, Sino-American diplomatic relations were at a standstill: on the one side, the new Chinese authorities at Canton adopted a policy of nonintercourse with the Westerners, and on the other side, the American commissioner stopped pressing the so-called American claims against China. But Davis did not openly abandon the American claims against China; he simply shelved them, leaving their resolution to his successor.

II

Despite Davis' feebleness, he was obliged to undertake one major innovation in Sino-American relations; he was instructed by the Department of State to organize the establishment of American consular courts in China, which had been provided for by the treaty but had been delayed for four years. Before the establishment of the American consular courts in China, civil and criminal cases were usually dealt with by extralegal means, if they were reviewed at all. Prior to August, 1848, American diplomats and consuls possessed no legal power to deal with any judicial case. The case of the murder of Hsü Ya-man in 1844 had been solved through a political compromise between Cushing and Ch'i-ying. The case of *Shing Ho* vs. *Wetmore & Co.*, brought before Acting Commissioner Biddle in 1846, was solved by a "friend of both sides" rather than by a judge.[17] The claims of Roberts against the Chinese government and others were presented by Dr. Peter Parker as diplomatic and political demands rather than as a judicial case.[18]

---

[17] See chap. 1.   [18] See chap 6.

Since the Chinese were then ignorant of the Western legal process, all incidents occurring between Chinese citizens and foreign subjects were usually treated by the mandarins as political and diplomatic conflicts between the two governments. As a rule, even until the 1850's they solved the problem by arbitrary action, mostly at the expense of their own people, in order to avoid further diplomatic complications.

Early in 1847, however, an American merchant in China was about to leave for home without paying a sizable debt to an Englishman named Martin Ford. The creditor addressed a petition to J. F. Davis, the British governor of Hong Kong, who forwarded it to Paul S. Forbes, the United States consul at Canton. Forbes replied that the American consul possessed no legal power to prevent any American citizen from leaving China. Failing to obtain assistance from the powerless consul, Governor Davis wrote to Commissioner Everett for a solution.[19] "I regret extremely," Everett wrote in reply, "that Mr. Ford should have been subjected by the act of a citizen of the United States to the inconvenience of which he complains. I do not see that he had any other remedy but to prosecute his claim in the court of the United States, where he will obtain justice and if the debtor has the means of payment. . . ."[20]

As a counter measure, the British governor of Hong Kong issued orders to his consul at Canton directing him to warn the British subjects in China not to allow any Americans to incur debts. He further suggested that the British consuls refuse to interfere should an American citizen attempt to enlist their aid in collecting a debt from a British subject "until such time as the Government of the United States should have made due provision for the administration of equal justice."[21] This British order naturally alarmed the American residents in China, who hastened to petition Washington to establish consular jurisdiction.

As early as 1845, President Tyler, acting on the recommendation of Caleb Cushing, had requested such legislation, but his request was ignored because Congress was busy with domestic politics and the Chinese issue had attracted comparatively little attention. In the following years other measures were introduced to regulate and define the powers, duties, and compensation of consuls, but they also met much delay in the Senate and finally lapsed because of "want of time and

---

[19] J. F. Davis to Alexander H. Everett, March 8, 1847, *DD-USNA*, 92:4.

[20] Everett to J. F. Davis, Macao, March 10, 1847, *ibid*.

[21] John W. Davis to the Secretary of State, No. 4, Canton, August 24, 1848, *DD-USNA*, 92:6.

the pressure of other important business."[22] At the beginning of 1847, however, Secretary of State Buchanan began to send urgent recommendations[23] to Congress asking for judicial power for American ministers and consuls in China and Turkey. After much consideration, Congress passed the necessary act, which the President signed on August 11, 1848.[24]

By this act, the commissioner and the consuls of the United States in China were vested with judicial authority in both civil and criminal matters, and it became part of their consular duties to exercise the new authority in conformity with the laws of the United States. The act gave these functionaries complete power to hear charges against and to try all citizens of the United States accused of crimes committed in the dominions of China. (In the original act, Macao was also included, but it was later dropped because of protest from Portugal.)[25]

The commissioner was given the power "to hear and to decide all cases criminal and civil" and to punish crime by fine or imprisonment or both. Both murder and insurrection or rebellion with a subversive intention against the Chinese government were classified as capital offenses punishable with death, a sentence that the commissioner was empowered to execute provided that the consul and his associates in the trial (four or more respectable citizens of the United States invited by the consul) all concurred in opinion. The commissioner was also given the power to prescribe the form of all legal processes in the various consular courts and to establish how they should be carried out. These regulations had to be drawn up in writing, however, and submitted for the advice of the consuls or as many of them as could be consulted.[26]

The consul was given the power to issue his warrant for the arrest of any citizen of the United States in China charged with committing an offense against the law of the United States. Any consul, sitting alone for the trial, could decide all criminal cases in which the fine imposed did not exceed one hundred dollars or the term of imprisonment did not exceed sixty days. Generally, no such decision could be ap-

[22] *Congressional Globe*, 30 Cong., 1 sess., April 19, 1848, p. 648. For a general survey of consular legislation in this period see Chester L. Jones, *The Consular Service of the United States, Its History and Activities* (Philadelphia: The John C. Winston Co., 1906), pp. 11-14.

[23] James Buchanan to Alexander H. Everett, No. 9, January 28, 1847, *DI-USNA*, 77:38, p. 43; *House Doc.*, No. 12, 29 Cong., 2 sess., December 15, 1846, pp. 1-10.

[24] *The United States Statutes at Large*, IX, 276-80.

[25] *Ibid.* IX, Sec. 2, 276.

[26] *Ibid.* IX, 276-80, Sections 4, 5, 9, 13, 15, 16, and 23.

pealed. In cases in which the penalty went beyond this limit, the defendant might appeal to the commissioner.[27]

Upon receiving Buchanan's instruction, accompanied by a copy of the act, Davis immediately reprinted it and distributed it to American citizens in China on November 29, 1848. In the meantime, he began to draft the necessary orders and regulations for the establishment of consular courts in the different ports. There were, however, neither sufficient law books nor jurists to consult for the drafting of these regulations. Consequently, he made a trip to Macao, Hong Kong, and Manila in a vain search for help. "I was left solely to my own resources in execution of the task thus assigned to me," Davis reported to President Polk. "Nor was I able to find in all China, Hong Kong, Macao or the Philippine Islands, either an American lawyer or an American law-book to aid, with the exception of the Statutes of the United States and Kent's Commentaries."[28]

As a result, all the necessary regulations for the establishment of consular courts were drafted by John Davis, a professional physician with his "limited knowledge of law."[29] *The Regulations for the Consular Courts of the United States of America in China*, issued by Davis on January 2, 1849, established a consular court for each consulate in China and ordered each consul to appoint a clerk and a marshal.[30]

---

[27] *Ibid.*, Sections 5, 7, 8, 10, and 20. Under this act, the commissioner to China was given $503.33 in addition to his regular salary as compensation for his judicial services. The consuls, acting as judicial officers, were also given some compensation, although their consular service was still left without regular payment. See John M. Clayton to John W. Davis, No. 7, May 5, 1849, *DI-USNA*, 77:38, pp. 61-62.

[28] Davis to the Secretary of State, No. 11, Canton, January 27, 1849, *DD-USNA*, 92:6. Davis probably took this trip as much for pleasure as for the search of legal assistance.

[29] *Ibid.*

[30] *Regulations for the Consular Courts of the United States of America in China: together with the Act of Congress, of August 11th, 1848, and Forms for Blanks in Consular Courts* (Canton: Printed by the Press of S. W. Williams, 1849), microfilmed in *DD-USNA*, 92:6. The fifth section of the law of August 11, 1848, provided that "the Commissioner, with the advice of the several consuls for the five ports named in the said treaty [the Wanghia Treaty], or so many of them as can conveniently assemble, shall prescribe all forms." Since there were only two American consuls in all China, one residing at Canton (Paul S. Forbes) and the other at Shanghai (J. Alsop Griswold), this regulation was countersigned by Forbes alone, and then put into practice.

According to Davis' report, American trade in the other three ports—Amoy, Foochow, and Ningpo—had not justified the appointment of consuls. Davis added, however, that American trade at Amoy was increasing and might require the appointment of a consul. "There have been consuls appointed at some of the above named ports some years back," reported Davis, "but, as far as I am advised, no American has ever made a residence at either of those places in a consular capacity." Thus by the time the necessary regulations and other decrees were published, only one consular court

The first person tried by the consular court at Canton was an American sailor charged with larceny. He was found guilty and was sentenced to one year's imprisonment. But as soon as the sentence was announced another difficulty arose, namely, procuring a proper place of confinement, as there was no American jail that could be used by the consular courts, nor were there enough funds to feed the convict in jail. This criminal was temporarily kept under confinement in the hull of a vessel belonging to an American citizen, who was then appointed marshal of the consular court at Canton, but he housed the prisoner without any means to defray the expenses of his keep. Therefore Davis wrote to the President requesting additional funds, "say, fifteen hundred dollars," to pay the expenses necessarily incurred in organizing these consular courts.[31] This lack of sufficient funds actually prevented the consular courts in China from full operation for many years.[32] Moreover, the decisions reached by the consular courts in China were later declared "unconstitutional" by the Supreme Court of California in 1859. The court charged that Congress, using extraterritorial powers in legislating directly upon the persons and property of American citizens in China, had exceeded its powers under the Constitution of the United States. The authority it conferred upon commissioners to make regulations was a delegation of legislative power, and therefore unconstitutional.[33]

(the consular court at Canton) had been established, and it was put into operation immediately. See Davis to President Polk, Canton, February 18, 1849, *DD-USNA*, 92:6. The delay of the establishment of the consular court at Shanghai and the absence of Griswold's signature of the *Regulations* were probably due to the fact that Griswold was traveling and did not have a permanent office at Shanghai.

[31] Davis to President Polk, Canton, February 18, 1849. *DD-USNA*, 92:6.

[32] As late as 1860 the American consular court at Shanghai still lacked a jail. Convicts thus had to be released before serving their sentences. See William B. Reed to Lewis Cass, No. 23, Shanghai, June 30, 1858, *Reed Correspondence*, p. 335; John E. Ward to Lewis Cass, No. 3, Macao, February 22, 1860, *DD-USNA*, 92:20.

[33] *Forbes* v. *Scannel* (April, 1859), *Reports of Cases of the Supreme Court of the State of California* (San Francisco, Calif.: Sumner Whitney, 1875), pp. 243-91.

8

A DIVIDED EMPIRE

AND THE UNSTABLE AMERICANS

I

AFTER the resignation of Commissioner Davis at the end of May, 1850, the American legation in China was left without a commissioner for nearly three years. During this period the political situation in China underwent a radical change. First, the change of regimes at Peking led the Chinese "barbarian management" into a new phase in which newly recruited Chinese administrators were more hostile to the foreigners and more unsophisticated in the carrying out of their new foreign policy. Second, a rebellion broke out in South China. It became one of the largest civil wars ever fought in one nation, completely upsetting the political, economic, and social orders in that empire for the next fourteen years. As a consequence, these two events reshaped the political outlook of the Celestial Empire during the Hsien-feng period (1850-62), making it entirely different from that of the previous Tao-kuang regime (1821-50). Both events deserve brief review.

Early in 1850 Emperor Tao-kuang died. He was succeeded by Emperor Hsien-feng, a militant young prince who was then in his twenties. The young Emperor was a capable ruler, though he was rather arrogant. Ambitiously, he set out to rebuild the declining empire. Almost immediately he abolished the spoils system, inherited from his father, and instituted a sweeping reorganization of the Grand Council, the core of Ch'ing officialdom.[1]

In the later years of the Tao-kuang period, the Grand Council was headed by Mu-chang-a, a Manchu. He had served in the Council for twenty-three years and had been chief for ten of these. Despite strong

---

[1] For a good survey of the reform movement at the beginning of the Hsien-feng period consult Hsiao I-shan, *Ch'ing-tai t'ung-shih* (General History of the Ch'ing Period) (Peiping: Pei-p'ing wen-chih hsueh-yuan, n.d.), IIIbl, 314-24; see also Chin Chao-feng, *Ch'ing-shih ta-kang* (Shanghai: K'ai-ming Bookstore, 1935), pp. 395 ff.

Emperor Wen-tsung (Hsien-feng) of the Ch'ing dynasty

opposition from his fellow grand councilors, Mu-chang-a had supported Ch'i-ying during the Nanking negotiations in 1842 and during
the signing of treaties with the United States and other Western
powers. By the end of the Tao-kuang period his reputation had declined rapidly; he had come to be regarded by the Chinese populace,
and particularly the literati, as the mainspring of the spoils system.
This system had provoked numerous uprisings throughout the empire
during the Tao-kuang period. Actually, Mu-chang-a could hardly
have been responsible for the widespread corruption during the Tao-
kuang period; rather, it was the natural consequence of the imperial
system. However, as chief minister of the Grand Council, he was the
one most open to blame. His removal was therefore inevitable upon
Emperor Hsien-feng's ascension to the throne; and, since Ch'i-ying was
one of Mu-chang-a's close associates, he too shared the misfortune of his
colleague. Thus, on December 1, 1850, soon after the burial of the
late Emperor, Mu-chang-a and Ch'i-ying were deprived of their respective offices and censured by a special edict issued by the young
ruler.[2]

In his formal edict Hsien-feng denounced the political decadence
that had led to the social and moral decline of his empire. He specifically named Mu-chang-a as the one who had deliberately barred
all competent men from his administration and perpetrated a long list
of other abuses while in office. At the same time, his decree cited Ch'i-
ying as another conspirator, branding him as stupid, a born coward,
and a man who had oppressed the Chinese people in his attempt to
please the "barbarians." The "city question" at Canton was particularly cited as "solid proof" of his cowardliness.[3] Consequently, Mu-
chang-a was stripped of all office, and Ch'i-ying was degraded to a
fifth-rank official, an expectant assistant director in one of the six
boards.[4]

After Mu-chang-a's removal, domestic as well as foreign policies immediately swung in the opposite direction, when the Emperor elevated
Ch'i Chün-tsao to the post of chief councilor. Ch'i, an outstanding
Chinese scholar, had served as a member of the Grand Council for
more than ten years. Ever since the Opium War he had bitterly opposed the policies of Mu-chang-a and Ch'i-ying. At the same time,

---

2 *Shih-lu:HF*, chüan 20, pp. 30 ff.
3 *Ibid.*, p. 30a.
4 *Ibid.*, p. 31a.

the Emperor also appointed Tu Shou-t'ien, his former tutor of Chinese classics, as one of his close advisers. In contrast with the team of Mu-chang-a and Ch'i-ying, which had invoked the sharp criticism of both Chinese and Manchus, the appointment of Ch'i Chün-tsao and Tu Shou-t'ien, both Chinese, was enthusiastically acclaimed throughout the country.

In fact, even during the Tao-kuang period, the Manchu rule in China had begun to decline. The once prominent Manchu administrators and political leaders were now regarded as incompetent in the management of affairs of state. [5] It was widely agreed that important political and state offices should be entrusted mostly to Chinese officials. This view, moreover, had even gained acceptance among the Manchus themselves.[6] After consolidating their own power around the Emperor, Ch'i and Tu persuaded their young master to recall to service those Chinese officials, such as Lin Tse-hsü, the great opium suppressor, who had been degraded by their predecessors.[7] At the same time, they gradually replaced the old-guard "barbarian experts" who had enjoyed unprecedented privileges and imperial favor for more than ten years. In addition to Huang En-t'ung, who had been dismissed by the late Emperor, such "barbarian experts" as Hsü Chi-yü, P'an Shih-ch'eng, Hsien-ling, Wu Chien-chang, Chao Ch'ang-ling, and many others who had been prominent during the "barbarian management" in the early 1840's, were discharged from active service.[8]

In the area of foreign policy the change in personnel proved to be a serious setback in China's relations with the Western countries as well as in her modernization movement. Although the old-guard "barbarian experts," headed by Ch'i-ying, were hardly experts in modern diplomacy, they were nevertheless more experienced than the new school of "barbarian experts," headed by the Emperor himself. Unlike his father, who had entrusted "barbarian affairs" to some of his loyal

---

[5] The decline of the Manchus is treated in John K. Fairbank's, "The Manchu-Chinese Dyarchy in the 1840's and 50's," *Far Eastern Quarterly*, XII, No. 3 (May, 1953), 265-78; also consult Alfred Kuoliang Ho, "The Grand Council in the Ch'ing Dynasty," *Far Eastern Quarterly*, XI, No. 2 (February, 1952), 167-82; Hsiao I-shan, *Ch'ing-tai t'ung-shih*, IIIb2, 314 ff.

[6] Even the leading Manchu statesman Wen-ch'ing, who served as chief councilor in 1856, also openly admitted that the Manchu politicians were incompetent to manage the state affairs and that the Chinese were more capable than their Manchu colleagues. See Hsiao I-shan, *Ch'ing-tai t'ung-shih*, IIIb2, 315.

[7] *Shih-lu:HF, chüan* 9, pp. 19-20a.

[8] For short biographic sketches of these officials consult Earl Swisher, *China's Management of the American Barbarians, A Study of Sino-American Relations, 1841-1861, with Documents* (New Haven, Conn.: Yale University Far Eastern Publications, 1951), pp. 705 ff.

officials, the young monarch took matters directly into his own hands. Unfortunately, the militant young sovereign, as well as his most trusted lieutenants, had not served an apprenticeship under the old-school "barbarian experts" of the Tao-kuang period. Their lack of sufficient knowledge and experience in dealing with the Westerners, therefore, led them into a series of errors similar to, but more serious than, those made by the mandarins on the eve of the Opium War. The bitter lessons learned by the late ruler and his advisers were now wasted.

Unable to develop a positive policy of their own, the new Emperor and his immediate advisers merely laid the blame for "barbarian troubles" on their predecessors, who, they claimed, had pampered and appeased the unreasonable "barbarians." Proud and militant, he sought to regain his lost dignity as the ruler of the human race. Like most of his subjects, he was firmly convinced that the Celestial Empire was far superior to foreign nations in everything, including the techniques of warfare. All the defeats and humiliations that China had suffered during his father's rule were now attributed to the administrative incompetence of its officials. According to this theory an adequate defense program had not been maintained. Because of this laxity in defense preparedness, the sudden outbreak of the Opium War had temporarily paralyzed China. Confident that such military penetration could be prevented in the future, Emperor Hsien-feng reaffirmed his faith in the existing coastal defenses.[9]

The Emperor was convinced, moreover, that the policy of nonintercourse with the foreigners, instituted by Yeh Ming-ch'en, governor-general at Canton, would forestall any foreign entanglements. Unfortunately, among the newly appointed experts, Yeh Ming-ch'en was the only one with any real degree of experience in dealing with the Westerners. He had won, so it appeared to the contemporary Chinese, the only diplomatic "victory" at Canton since the Opium War; he had prevented the British from entering the city, a feat which even the most experienced diplomat, Ch'i-ying, had failed to accomplish. There had been little "barbarian trouble" at Canton since that event. In a memorial submitted in September, 1855, Yeh boasted:[10]

. . . in Canton prior to 1847, incidents arose repeatedly; every month several outbursts occurred and the clamor could not be settled. The more [the foreigners] were conciliated the more intractable they became. But during the eight years since 1848 [i.e., after the recall of Ch'i-ying and

---

[9] *Shih-lu:HF*, chüan 8, p. 18b.
[10] Swisher, *China's Management of the American Barbarians*, p. 304; *IMSM-HF*, XI, 16b-17a.

after his coming into office] the barbarians have not ventured to act out-
rageously, and so the people have so far kept the peace.

Yeh simply neglected the dispatches delivered by the foreign envoys,
regardless of what the results might be. As time passed, his policy of
nonintercourse proved effective in keeping all Westerners, regardless
of origin, at a distance, but it gradually drove all the Western countries into a united action against China. It was only through bitter
experience and a new foreign war that the mandarins of the Hsien-
feng regime gradually acquired a knowledge of modern diplomacy.

Thus from the Opium War (1839-42) to the end of the Anglo-
French Chinese war (1858-60) the foreign policies instituted by the
two Manchu emperors and their officials went through two similar
cycles. The first extended from 1839 until 1850; the second, from
1851 to 1861. The errors made, the lessons learned, and the final
foreign policy adopted by the Chinese during the first were simply
repeated during the second, although with more serious consequences.
The change of regimes in 1850 was the significant turning point from
the first cycle to the second.

In addition to the change of regimes in China, the Taiping Rebellion, which broke out in the same year as the political change-over,
added further difficulties to China's foreign relations. The Taiping
Rebellion was the first and only Christian uprising in the long history
of China, even though it was carried out in the manner of traditional
peasant uprisings. Hung Hsiu-ch'uan, the leader of the Taipings, was
a self-baptized Christian. In the post-Opium War period, he began to
preach Christianity in Kwangsi Province, and organized his converts
into the "Society of the Worshippers of God," with himself as head.
The activities of the society were so successful that in 1846 Hung was
invited to join the Rev. I. J. Roberts in Canton. Roberts, as mentioned before, had a chapel in the "worst section" of the city and had
"4 or 5 salaried Chinese assistants."[11] The invitation to Hung, who
already had an army of converts, caused jealousy among these assistants, who eventually succeeded in persuading Roberts to get rid of
him.[12]

Disappointed by his unsuccessful association with the Western missionaries, Hung returned to his old post at Kwangsi and continued his
preaching. His society's numbers were augmented from day to day

---

[11] Paul S. Forbes to John W. Davis, January 27, 1849, *DD-USNA*, 92:6.
[12] Chien Yu-wen, *T'ai-p'ing-chun shou-i shih* (A History of the Taiping Revolution) (Chungking: Commercial Press, 1944), pp. 129-30.

with members of the lower classes in the Kwangtung and Kwangsi areas and particularly from his own clansmen, the Hakkas. Owing to the misgovernment of the Manchu dynasty, as well as to the traditional clan wars among the hostile native clans, the God worshippers were at last led into an all-out rebellion, which began in the spring of 1850 at Chin-t'ien, Kwangsi. Because the Manchu government troops were unable to suppress them, the rebels were encouraged to start a drive to the north and eventually to set up a dynasty.[13]

Two months after the outbreak of the rebellion, Hung succeeded in taking the large city of Yung-an in Kwangsi Province, just after he had himself crowned the Heavenly King (the *T'ien Wang*) and established his dynasty, the Heavenly Kingdom of Great Peace (or *T'ai P'ing T'ien Kuo*). His armies were commanded by his immediate associates who received the title of *wang* (prince). In March, 1853, after a successful campaign in the Yangtze valley, Hung captured Nanking, where he set up his "Heavenly Capital." It remained in Taiping hands for over ten years.[14]

As soon as Hung had taken Nanking he sent an invitation to the Baptist missionary, I. J. Roberts, asking him to come to Nanking so that "the Gospel may be made plain, baptism (immersion) may be received, and the truth published."[15] Roberts, however, did not reach Nanking until October, 1860.

The Taiping rebels were extremely religious. They held prayer service three times a day in addition to Sunday services. Each unit had its separate chapel. Wherever they found a pagan temple— Buddhist, Confucian, Taoist, or Mohammedan—they burned it. The Confucian classics, so precious to the educated Chinese, were rigidly banned. Thus, at the beginning of the Taiping Rebellion the Westerners were excited by the Christian revolution in China. They soon found themselves in a dilemma: the Catholics were definitely opposed to the new dynasty, which they thought was a Protestant movement, and the Protestant missionaries were equally divided since Taiping beliefs and practices were not entirely in agreement with any of their respective churches. Thus, in the years immediately after the Taipings

---

13 For detailed information about the Taipings consult Lo Erh-kang, *T'ai-p'ing t'ien-kuo shih-kao* (Draft History of the Heavenly Kingdom of Great Peace) (2 vols.; Shanghai: Chunghua shu-ch'u, 1955). These two volumes contain most of the up-to-date historical documents of the Taipings discovered in China and abroad. For reference on the above statement consult Volume I of Lo's book.

14 For further reference consult *ibid.,* Vol. I.

15 I. J. Roberts to Humphrey Marshall, May 30, 1853, *Marshall's Correspondence,* p. 185.

established their "Heavenly Court" at Nanking, both the British and
the Americans were uncertain about how to formulate a proper policy
toward the divided Chinese Empire.[16]

II

At the beginning of the chaotic Hsien-feng period, the United States
did not have a commissioner in China. After the resignation of Commissioner Davis, Dr. Parker was appointed for the fourth time as
chargé d'affaires of the American legation in China. Seeing the
imperial government beset by this new civil war, Dr. Parker, who was
in constant touch with other Western envoys and consuls in China,
considered the moment auspicious to extend Western treaty privileges
in the already weakened Chinese Empire.[17] In April, 1851, Parker
was ready to offer some pratical suggestions to the State Department.

In a confidential report Parker warned of the necessity of joint action
with the British in the impending crisis. He said the Chinese government could not long retain friendly intercourse with the Western
powers with which she had made treaties. "To prevent the necessity
of any *one* of these powers adopting *excessive* measures," Parker suggested, "it is proposed that joint *pacific* steps be taken by *all*."[18]

This proposal seems to have been initiated by the British consul,
John Bowring. In his report to Washington, Parker mentioned that
Bowring had told him about the British intentions in China: if Great
Britain must act alone, that action would be a hostile military campaign; but, if the Western treaty powers should act jointly, their
problems with China could be settled through peaceful negotiations.
Therefore, Parker was convinced that the success of the policy of
extension of treaty privileges through peaceful negotiation depended
on the arrangement among the several powers to act simultaneously
even though independently.

Parker went on to emphasize that this view was attracting attention in the diplomatic circles of Europe, and that the United States
policy toward China as set up by the late commissioner, Alexander H.
Everett, had to be reversed. He specifically called the attention of the
authorities in Washington to a confidential dispatch submitted by
Everett to Buchanan on April 10, 1847—a paper that suggested joint
action of the United States, France, and Russia in opposing Britain's

---

[16] See following chapter.
[17] See Parker to the Secretary of State, No. 15, Confidential, Canton, April 22,
1851, *DD-USNA*, 92:7.
[18] *Ibid*. Italics in the original.

domination of China.[19] Parker suggested "an important modification of . . . that dispatch," namely, inviting "the Government of Great Britain . . . to cooperate *with* those of Russia, France, Spain, and United States, and not the latter to combine *against* her."[20] Parker's proposal, however, seems to have failed to attract proper attention among authorities in Washington, who at this time were having trouble finding a new commissioner to China. A year later, when Parker heard that the United States was sending Commodore M. C. Perry to the East for an expedition to Japan, he once more requested that the naval force be used in the Chinese waters to enforce American claims. "Such a demonstration [of force] is *practicable*," wrote Parker, "and in my opinion, if judiciously and firmly made, will redound to the honor of the United States and promote the *interests of both countries*."[21]

Parker's proposal was again set aside by the Department of State. When it reached Washington a new commissioner, Colonel Humphrey Marshall, had already been appointed and was on his way to China. But Parker's influence on the Department should by no means be underestimated. In the instructions issued by the State Department to Marshall, American claims against China (at that time Roberts' claim of $1,400 remained the largest) were still particularly stressed. Upon Marshall's arrival in China, he worked on the case much more seriously than his predecessor, Davis, had done.[22]

The new commissioner was a native of Kentucky and had graduated from West Point in 1832. He was a professional soldier and a self-educated lawyer. During the Mexican War he had been a colonel; later he was elected to Congress, where he served until his appointment in August, 1852, as commissioner to China.[23]

Marshall has frequently been described by historians as a controversial figure. Tyler Dennett, a noted diplomatic historian once remarked: "He was not admirably fitted for the duties of diplomacy; he was autocratic, dictatorial, pitifully vain, and gifted with singular

---

[19] For Everett's original confidential dispatch, No. 28, see *DD-USNA*, 92:4.

[20] Parker to the Secretary of State, No. 15, Confidential, April 22, 1851, *DD-USNA*, 92:7.

[21] Peter Parker to Daniel Webster, No. 32, Canton, August 19, 1852, *DD-USNA*, 92:8.

[22] Unlike Commissioner Davis, who thought that the justice of the Roberts claim was "subject to doubt," Commissioner Marshall thought it must be enforced or we "may as well tear up the treaty." See Marshall to Marcy, No. 24, Shanghai, July 30, 1853, *Marshall's Correspondence*, p. 223.

[23] Allen Johnson, ed., *Dictionary of American Biography* (New York: Charles Scribner's Sons, 1943), XII, 310-11.

capacities for controversy, yet intellectually he was an able man."[24] This comment is unjust. As a matter of fact, Marshall was the first United States commissioner to China, under the Treaty of Wanghia, who worked seriously as a resident commissioner. His methods of action and the environment in which he was working were different from those of his predecessors in China. Everett, the first commissioner under the treaty, had been a remarkably farsighted diplomat as well as a man of high principles; unfortunately, ill health caused him to die prematurely, before he could put any radical changes into effect. Davis, Marshall's immediate predecessor, was a shrewd politician, who, during his stay in China, never gave serious consideration to formulation of a United States policy; nor did he make any statement without reservation. He relied on the "more experienced" secretary of the legation, Peter Parker, with whom he disagreed but whom he hesitated to challenge openly. In his sixteen months' stay in China he worked out no practical or constructive program.

Marshall's difficulties, therefore, were caused by his conscientiousness in carrying on the work under his charge. The so-called controversies that Dennett mentioned, such as Marshall's open break with the long-experienced Peter Parker, his failure to obtain support from the United States navy, and his anti-British stand,[25] were but the natural outcome of America's unstable diplomacy and her unhealthy diplomatic and consular institutions in China. Had his predecessors worked as seriously as Marshall, they might have faced the same kinds of problems.

When Marshall's appointment was made, Secretary of State Daniel Webster gave him no specific instructions concerning the fundamental principles of United States policy toward China. The conflict of ideas between Everett and Parker and between Parker and Forbes seems to have attracted no attention in the State Department. The first instruction that Webster issued for Marshall, on August 11, 1852, was by and large the same as that received by his predecessors years before. Many sections of the letter were even worded in the same way.[26]

---

[24] Tyler Dennett, *Americans in Eastern Asia* (New York: The Macmillan Co., 1922), p. 206.

[25] *Ibid.* pp. 206-25.

[26] For example, concerning the claims against China which formed the essential part of the instruction for many years, Webster wrote: "During your residence in China you may sometimes be applied to interpose in behalf of American citizens for the purpose of obtaining satisfaction of claims which they may have upon the Chinese Government, or the redress of grievances which they may experience in the course of

Upon his arrival in Canton on January 31, 1853, Marshall immediately dispatched a letter to the Chinese authorities requesting a
personal interview so that he might present his credentials. Unfortunately Governor-General Yeh Ming-ch'en was absent; his official
duties had been temporarily transferred to the then Acting Governor
Pei-kuei, a Manchu of high rank. Considering that Pei was merely
acting governor of Canton and not in a position important enough to
be entrusted with foreign negotiations, Marshall planned to sail
north to Foochow, Nanking, or even Tientsin, "to open a correspondence directly with the central power at Peking."[27] He was, however,
"exceedingly embarrassed" by the withdrawal of all the naval vessels
from Canton by the order of Commodore J. H. Aulick, who, in a
formal letter, stated that "the opinion of the Commissioner alone
would not be sufficient" to obtain a vessel for his service.[28]

Failing to obtain an interview with the Chinese authorities of a
higher rank at Canton and neglected by the naval officers, Marshall
retired to Macao, where he immediately set the legation and all the
consulates in China to work. He issued a circular on March 3, 1853,
addressed to the American consuls in the Five Ports, demanding "an
official statement" from each, listing, year by year since 1844, the
amount of American business in each port, the number of vessels
entered and the number cleared, their tonnage, the duties paid to the
Chinese government annually, their judicial functions, and "other
facts" within their knowledge. Marshall also emphatically requested
detailed information about the coolie trade along the Chinese coast;
his interest was not humanitarian, but rather economic. As a southerner, with the interests of American southern planters at heart, Marshall was acutely aware of the serious competition that would be
created in the cotton trade and other kinds of plantation trade by the
use of the cheap Chinese labor made available to the East Indian
planters by British agencies. Hence, he suggested to the State Depart-

---

their dealings and transactions. In cases of this nature where the intervention of this
Government shall be proper according to the public law, you will afford such official
aid as may appear to you appropriate to the occasion whether you have special instruction from this Department or not." See Daniel Webster to Humphrey Marshall,
No. 1, Washington, August 11, 1852. *DI-USNA*, 77:38, p. 78. The same wording had
been used previously by Secretary John M. Clayton in his instructions to Commissioner Davis. See Clayton to Davis, No. 7, Washington, D.C., May 5, 1849, *ibid.*,
p. 50.

27 *Marshall's Correspondence*, pp. 24-25.

28 J. H. Aulik to Humphrey Marshall, February 5, 1853, *Marshall's Correspondence*, p. 20.

ment that the United States should prevent the use of American shipping for furthering Chinese emigration.[29]

In the meantime, he also suggested to the State Department the building of a permanent residence for the American legation, which he estimated would probably cost $15,000; he preferred Shanghai to Canton for its location. He also suggested that Congress should invest the commissioner to China with judicial powers to hear and determine cases of piracy on the high seas.[30]

While Marshall was busy improving the American legation at Canton, the power of the Taiping rebels reached its peak. Marshall thought that this rebellion gave the United States an excellent opportunity to extend her commerce with the Celestial Empire. Since it was a Christian revolution, led by a liberal force in a mysterious heathen land, it excited most of the foreign residents in China—missionaries, merchants, and diplomats alike. This development, as well as the intensified policy of nonintercourse adopted by Governor-General Yeh Ming-ch'en, at Canton, caused Marshall to sail north for a close personal investigation of the situation.

---

[29] *Marshall's Correspondence*, p. 79.
[30] *Ibid.*, p. 80.

9

THE MARSHALL MISSION

AND ITS FAILURE

I

MARSHALL arrived in Shanghai on March 27, 1853, aboard the United States warship *Susquehanna,* which had been placed at his disposal for the short trip from Hong Kong to Shanghai by the navy commander at Canton.[1] At the time of Marshall's arrival, Shanghai as well as the entire coastal region of southeastern China was in a chaotic state. Nanking had already fallen to the rebels and all the trading ports along the southeastern coast were threatened by a wave of new uprisings directly or indirectly fomented by the Taipings. Until the moment of his arrival, Marshall was still unable to decide on a definite policy. In a report to Washington the day after he reached Shanghai, Marshall said that his "future must be determined by circumstances."[2] After a relatively short time, however, he was able to formulate a course of action.

First of all, Marshall sought to determine the relative situations of the Imperialists and the rebels. Such information was prerequisite to his formulation of an effective China policy. Only when adequate and reliable intelligence reports about both sides were in their hands could the Western powers intervene and try to bring the conflict to an end

---

[1] On March 15, 1853, Marshall wrote to Commander John Kelly, commanding officer of the U.S. naval force in the China seas, requesting the service of the ship *Susquehanna* for conveyance to Nanking. At this time Commodore Aulick had already been replaced by Commodore M. C. Perry as commanding officer of the U.S. Navy in the East and had left China, but Perry had not yet arrived. Kelly responded favorably to Marshall's request and promptly assigned the *Susquehanna* to the Commissioner, who sailed to Shanghai on board the ship a few days later. See *Marshall's Correspondence,* p. 85. Also consult Francis L. Hawks, *Narrative of the Expedition of An American Squadron to the China Seas and Japan performed in the Years 1852, 1853, and 1854, under the Command of Commodore M. C. Perry* (New York: D. Appleton and Co., 1856), p. 157.

[2] Marshall to the Secretary of State, No. 10, Shanghai, March 28, 1853, *Marshall's Correspondence,* p. 97.

through diplomatic pressure.[3] The civil war had already jeopardized American import trade in China. If it was permitted to continue, its effect on trade was bound to worsen. In the absence of foreign intervention, Marshall concluded, the civil war could only lead to "the utter paralysis of trade for years to come."[4] The corrupt Manchu government was unable to suppress the rebellion. "I am convinced that there never has been, in the history of mankind," wrote the American commissioner, "a worse government than that which for some years past has afflicted China." The rebels unfortunately were equally incompetent to take over the reins of government.[5] "It would be very important to the United States, indeed to the world," Marshall suggested to the Department of State, "could western powers unite in sending their diplomatists to Pekin *or to Nankin,* and so, by a timely interference, put an end to this internal strife, which promises nothing half so much as the utter paralysis of trade for years to come." Marshall seems to have understood that the diplomatic pressure of the concerted Western powers could bring a prompt end to the Chinese civil war, since neither side could survive if the Western powers decided to intervene. For these reasons Marshall desired a policy of decisive intervention by the Western treaty powers so that the Chinese civil war might be brought to an end as soon as possible. At the same time, he sought to take advantage of the crisis to force further treaty concessions for the Western powers from the future Chinese government.[6]

Until the proper moment for decisive intervention arrived, however, Marshall thought the Western powers should maintain an "absolute neutrality in good faith,"[7] and carry on their diplomatic relations with the Manchu government as usual. Once additional privileges were obtained by the foreigners from the present dynasty, the rebels would never be able to reverse them, even if they should succeed in overthrowing the Manchu dynasty in China. Nevertheless, these concessions must be obtained through formal negotiations; the Western powers must not violate any treaties that were still in force.

In his attempt to implement this policy, Marshall found himself seriously handicapped. First of all, the United States Navy com-

---

[3] Marshall to Marcy, No. 20, Shanghai, June 21, 1853, *ibid,* p. 184.
[4] *Ibid.*
[5] Marshall to Marcy, No. 16, Shanghai, May 26, 1853, *ibid.,* pp. 140 ff.
[6] Marshall to Marcy, No. 20, Shanghai, June 21, 1853, *ibid.,* p. 184.
[7] In many letters to the American consuls, merchants, and missionaries in different ports, Marshall repeatedly cautioned them that this principle must be maintained. See *ibid.,* pp. 161, 183.

manders refused to lend him any support. Commodore M. C. Perry, eager to launch his expedition against Japan, deprived Marshall of the use of the *Susquehanna* shortly after it arrived at Shanghai.[8] The withdrawal of this vessel from his service denied him his only means of obtaining indispensable firsthand information about the rebellion.[9]

In the meantime, American residents in Ningpo and Foochow had written to the Commissioner asking for naval protection in view of the threat of new outbreaks in these two ports. Lacking the authority to dispatch a warship, Marshall had to ask the assistance of a French steamer to enable the American residents at Ningpo to escape, while those at Foochow he advised to withdraw to safety by whatever means they could devise.[10]

In the middle of May when Shanghai was still under the threat of war, Commodore Perry ordered the last remaining United States naval vessel, the *Plymouth*, to leave Shanghai. This move aroused considerable alarm among the foreign residents of that city, particularly the Americans. Marshall then addressed an appeal to Perry to delay his impending expedition to Japan, because the situation in China was more urgent. His request, however, was completely ignored.[11] On May 18, 1853, the port of Amoy was taken in a fresh uprising of a secret society, leaving the American residents stranded without naval protection from their own country.[12]

----

[8] *Ibid.*, p. 141. Before Commodore Perry left the United States for a new mission to Japan, he had already decided to take the *Susquehanna* as his flagship. However, upon his arrival at Macao early in April, he found the designated flagship "nowhere to be seen." Thus the Commodore immediately dispatched a ship to Shanghai to order the missing warship to await him at that port. Consequently, the *Susquehanna* was taken from the Commissioner after she arrived in Shanghai. See Hawks, *Expedition . . . to China Seas and Japan*, pp. 157 ff; see also Edward M. Barrow, *The Great Commodore, the Exploits of Matthew Calbraith Perry* (New York: The Bobbs-Merrill Co., 1935), p. 342.

The Chinese claimed that the *Susquehanna* with Commissioner Marshall aboard sailed up the Yangtze "to help suppress the rebels," but that she went aground at the mouth of the Huang-pu River and was forced to return to Shanghai. See *IWSM-HF*, VI, 10b, 12, 13, 29-30. These Chinese reports were apparently groundless. When the Taipings captured Nanking, the Chinese authorities at Kiangsu appealed to all foreign consuls at Shanghai for military assistance. But their appeals were turned down. "*If* the mere presence of the *Susquehanna* would raise the siege of Nanking" wrote Marshall on March 28, "the policy of so doing would be very questionable in my opinion." See *Marshall's Correspondence*, p. 97. The *Susquehanna* went aground once at the mouth of the Yangtze, but it happened while the ship was entering the Shanghai harbor. See Hawks, *Expedition . . . to China Seas and Japan*, p. 167.

[9] Humphrey Marshall to M. C. Perry, Shanghai, May 13, 1853, and December 26, 1853 (Confidential), in *Marshall's Correspondence*, pp. 133, 351.

[10] *Ibid.*, pp. 99, 161-62.

[11] *Ibid.*, p. 125.

[12] *Ibid.*, p. 137. Some modern writers have attributed the Navy's refusal to Mar-

Marshall's plan was further hampered by the crude organization of the American legation itself, which up to this time did not even possess an American flag.[13] Far more serious was the lack of an efficient interpreter. Parker had accompanied Marshall to Shanghai, but remained there only for a short period; he then retired to Canton because of financial reasons.[14] After the departure of Parker, Marshall enlisted another missionary, the Rev. M. C. Culbertson, as his official interpreter. Culbertson's facility in Chinese, however, was definitely limited. He spoke only a southern dialect, although Chinese officials in Shanghai all spoke Mandarin. Later, Marshall was able to secure the services of a competent Chinese linguist, but he was soon discharged under orders from Washington, because he was not an American citizen.[15]

Frustrated in all his efforts, Marshall, upon his arrival in Shanghai, seems to have been willing to explore the possibility of cooperating with the British.[16] The British at first appeared to be willing. Early in 1850, however, even before the outbreak of the Taiping Rebellion, Rutherford Alcock, the British consul at Shanghai, had already announced a "gunboat policy" in China in the "true spirit of commercial imperialism."[17] Alcock's policy was then fully supported by Sir George Bonham, the British envoy to China and governor of Hong Kong.[18] As the Taiping Rebellion spread eastward toward Shanghai early in 1853, and began to attract foreign attention, both of them realized that the present crisis in China would afford them an unusual opportunity to consolidate their position still further. Bonham's first

---

shall's discourteous manner in presenting this request. See John K. Fairbank, "The Provisional System at Shanghai in 1853-54," *CSPSR*, XVIII, No. 4 (January, 1935), 480; Fairbank, *Trade and Diplomacy on the China Coast, the Opening of the Treaty Ports, 1842-1854* (Cambridge, Mass.: Harvard University Press, 1953), I, 415. The Navy's negligence was actually the result of the prevailing expansionist spirit for the opening of Japan. It had dominated U.S. naval attention ever since the middle of the 1840's. See Barrows, *The Great Commodore*, pp. 242-43, 298.

[13] Dr. Parker informed Marshall that "none were ever here from the time of Mr. Cushing." See Marshall to the Secretary of State, No. 17, May 30, 1853, *Marshall's Correspondence*, p. 169.

[14] Parker had resigned from the American Board as a medical missionary and became a private physician at Canton. Since the medical practice gave him a remarkable income, he refused Marshall's request to stay at Shanghai, where an eye doctor was not so needed as in Canton.

[15] *Marshall's Correspondence*, pp. 233 ff.

[16] Prior to May 30, 1853, no evidence is found that Marshall was hostile to the British. Even as late as June 21, Marshall still suggested "a timely interference" in the Chinese civil war by "Western Powers." See *Marshall's Correspondence*, p. 184.

[17] Fairbank, *Trade and Diplomacy*, I, 375.

[18] Bonham to Clarendon, No. 46, April 15, 1850, *F.O.*, 17/166 quoted in *ibid.*, I, 376.

thought was to cooperate with the Imperialists, if they should appeal to him for military assistance, since he might thereby gain important advantages for British commerce.[19] He reached Shanghai at about the same time as Marshall, but was forced to relinquish such plans because a quick victory by the rebels now seemed almost certain.[20] Determined to find another solution, Bonham arranged a meeting with the newly arrived American commissioner, who was apparently also willing to see him.

Consequently, the two ministers held a meeting early in April, 1853, and exchanged views about the crisis in China. It is unfortunate that the British kept no records of this conference and that the American records, along with some of Marshall's remarks on the British China-policy, were accidentally lost.[21] At this meeting Marshall apparently encouraged the British minister to sail up the Yangtze to obtain more firsthand information about the rebels, while Marshall himself proposed to seek an interview with the Manchu authorities. The British evidently agreed to the former suggestion, but were opposed to the latter. In a report to London written just after the meeting, Bonham stated: "I much regret this move on the part of the Americans, as I fear it will induce a belief in the rebel mind that foreigners intend to side with the Imperialists."[22] Obviously, at that time the British favored cooperation with the rebels since "more political and commercial advantages were likely to be obtained from the insurrectionist than they could ever obtain from the Imperialists."[23]

After further contact with the rebels, however, the British were again puzzled. For one thing, the rebel chief proclaimed himself ruler of all nations throughout the world and showed no inclination or even willingness to establish direct relations with the Western powers. Moreover, the British could not tolerate the curtailment of opium smoking by the Taipings.[24]

---

[19] Bonham to Malmesbury, March 11, 1853, *F.O.*, 17/200, quoted in William Conrad Costin, *Great Britain and China 1833-1860* (Oxford: The Clarendon Press, 1937) p. 160.

[20] Bonham to Clarendon, August 4, 1853, *F.O.*, 17/204, *ibid.*, p. 161.

[21] Marshall to the Secretary of State, No. 17, Shanghai, May 30, 1853, *Marshall's Correspondence*, pp. 161 ff.

[22] Bonham to Clarendon, No. 4, April 22, 1853, included in "Correspondence Respecting the Civil War in China, March-August, 1853," *British and Foreign State Papers*, XLIV, 497.

[23] Bonham to Clarendon, August 4, 1853, *F.O.*, 17/204, in Costin, *Great Britain and China 1833-1860*, p. 161.

[24] *British and Foreign State Papers*, XLIV, 497 ff; Thomas T. Meadows, *The Chinese and Their Rebellions* (London: Smith, Elder and Co., 1856), pp. 257 ff.

Nevertheless they still felt optimistic about their future relations with the Taipings, whom they were reluctant to spurn. In order to appease the rebels, Bonham deliberately sought to avoid the Imperialists. Hence he did not even want a treaty revision during this period, even if the Imperialists should agree to it. "Treaty revision also must wait," Bonham wrote Clarendon, "since a treaty with the Imperialists would involve active support of them and better terms might eventually be got from the rebels, if they were victorious."[25] In other words, the so-called British neutrality in the Chinese civil war was merely an excuse for waiting for a more propitious moment to cooperate with the rebels.

Before a rebel victory could be assured, however, the British would not give up the opportunity offered by the present crisis for more concessions from the Manchu government. Such concessions could only be obtained by extralegal means[26] rather than legal negotiations, which would involve active support to the Imperialists. These practical considerations determined the British method of action in southeastern China in 1853, and therefore the British were obviously anxious to bring the American commissioner into line.

Unlike the British, the American policy of neutrality adopted by Marshall was primarily due, as he often complained, to the fact that he was "without means to do anything."[27] Unable to make direct contact with the rebels during this critical period, Marshall began seeking means to negotiate with the Imperialist government, which was still officially recognized by the United States. The American Commissioner hoped to take advantage of the crisis to persuade the Imperialists to receive the Western commissioners at Peking and to open China at large for foreign commerce. His efforts to continue negotiations with the Imperialists brought him into conflict with the British, who were afraid that if American assistance were offered to the Manchu government it would "embarrass" the British.[28]

Early in April the British at Shanghai even suspected that the *Susquehanna* was sailing up the Yangtze to aid the Imperialists.[29] But all

---

[25] Fairbank, *Trade and Diplomacy*, I, 414.

[26] See next chapter.

[27] Marshall to the Secretary of State, No. 13, Shanghai, April 28, 1853, *Marshall's Correspondence*, p. 99.

[28] Sir George Bonham to Lord J. Russell, Shanghai, March 28, 1853, *British and Foreign State Papers*, XLIV, 478.

[29] *Ibid.*, p. 501. Also see Bonham to Hammond, April 13, 1853, *F.O.*, 17/200, quoted in Costin, *Great Britain and China*, p. 182.

the British documents were based upon the same Chinese bulletin issued by the prefect of Ch'ang-chou. This bulletin advised the inhabitants along the Yangtze River not to be alarmed by the sailing up the river of a fleet of about ten steamers of "barbarian volunteers," who would help the government to suppress the rebels. In this bulletin the prefect of Ch'ang-chou said that he had been notified by the prefect of Soochow, who in turn had received a note from the *taotai* of Shanghai, that the five vessels of the foreign fleet would pass the port of Fuh-shan on April 2. While translating this document, the sensitive British "Interpreter" noted that this would be: "The day on which the *Susquehanna* left Shanghai, and on which, if she had gone on, she would have been seen at Fuh Shan."[30] This British suspicion was apparently groundless.[31]

Other British writers even claimed that Commissioner Marshall had sailed as far as Chinkiang, halfway between Nanking and Shanghai. Here "the unlucky *Susquehanna* had struck upon the rocks . . . and that the crew had abandoned her."[32] This mistaken statement had led another writer to state: "What damage the *Susquehanna* received in this exploit is not mentioned in either Perry's or Marshall's letters. However, since it was shortly thereafter taken by Perry as his flagship to Japan, the damage could not have been serious."[33] Actually this accident did not occur to the *Susquehanna* at all but to an "old American receiving ship," the *Science,* which Russell and Company had leased to the *taotai* of Shanghai, "at the monstrous rate of 50,000 piasters per month." It later ran aground off Chinkiang and was abandoned by its crew.[34] No American source ever indicated that the *Susquehanna* had really sailed up the Yangtze with Commissioner Marshall on board. Commissioner McLane, Marshall's successor, mentioned it briefly in one of his dispatches to the Department of State, but McLane's information was based upon the *North China Herald,* which obviously had used the same source as had the other contemporary British writers.[35]

As in the case of British suspicions regarding himself, Commissioner

---

[30] *British and Foreign State Papers,* XLIV, 500-501.

[31] Cf. above, footnote 8.

[32] Charles MacFarlane, *The Chinese Revolution* (London: G. Routledge and Co., 1853), pp. 111-12.

[33] Chester A. Bain, "Commodore Matthew Perry, Humphrey Marshall, and the Taiping Rebellion," *Far Eastern Quarterly,* X, No. 3 (May, 1951), 262.

[34] Joseph M. Callery and Melchior Yvan, *History of the Insurrection in China* (New York: Harper and Brothers, 1853), pp. 239-40.

[35] *Sen. Exec. Doc.,* No. 22, 35 Cong., 2 sess. p. 64.

Marshall's suspicions of his British colleagues were also aroused by the constant British secret activities in the Yangtze. In fact, he thought that the British were attempting to establish a protectorate in China by extending assistance to the rebels. Although these mutual suspicions exceeded the facts, they did help to widen the Anglo-American gap, which eventually was to become so wide that it could not be closed.

II

Marshall's suspicion that the British were attempting to intervene on behalf of the rebels seems to have originated early in May. The day after Sir George Bonham's return from a visit to Nanking, Marshall met him for the second time, hoping to obtain his firsthand observations of the rebels in Nanking. After their first meeting early in April, however, Bonham had already characterized the American commissioner as "a very coarse headstrong man."[36] At their second meeting, Bonham seemed unwilling to talk frankly and freely with Marshall. Bonham's reluctance evidently made Marshall suspicious. In a confidential report to the State Department, Marshall said that he had ascertained from unimpeachable sources that Sir George Bonham had received a letter from ministers close to the Taiping emperor assuring him of commercial concessions to the Western powers. "Sir George Bonham never dropped even a hint to me of any such transaction," Marshall stressed, "and doubtlessly has communicated it only to Her Majesty's government."[37]

By the end of May, Marshall's fears were further aggravated by reports of intensive British secret activities in the Yangtze. After the Manchu Imperialists had suffered a new defeat in the vicinity of Nanking, the American commissioner became increasingly aware of the chance to gain major concessions for the Western countries from the rebels. The Taiping Court, Marshall later wrote,[38]

may be solicitous to form treaties of amity and commerce with Western powers; to invite foreign ministers to reside near his court; to proclaim religious toleration within his realm, and certain securities to personal rights; to open additional ports of entry, and to throw open the navigation of the Yangtze Kiang.

[36] Bonham to Hammond, April 13, 1853, *F.O.*, 17/200, in Costin, *Great Britain and China*, p. 181.

[37] Marshall to the Department of State, No. 19, Shanghai, June 8, 1853, *Marshall's Correspondence*, p. 177. Bonham did receive a letter from the Eastern Prince, the premier of the Taiping court, but he did not make it known to Marshall.

[38] Marshall to the Department of State, No. 17, May 30, 1853, *ibid.*, p. 168.

Thus, recent British gestures toward the rebels at Nanking might very well have given Great Britain an "opportunity of assuming the *protectorate of the young power* . . . at least so far as to mould its first steps to suit the policy of that government." In his report to Washington, Marshall continued:[39]

Great Britain may obtain the opening of a western Chinese port (inland) from the new Emperor at Nankin [*sic*], and the right to navigate the Yangtze Kiang closed from *foreign* commerce beyond the existing port of entry. I do not doubt that with that view her war with Burmahhas [Burma] has been waged and her Indian empire extended. The portage from the Ihrawaddy to the Yangtze Kiang is very short. . . .

The British plot, as he saw it, might lead eventually to the dismemberment of the Chinese Empire.[40]

Refuting Marshall's contention, one modern British historian argues that there is no trace of such a suggestion in the records of the British Foreign Office, and that it was not likely that a trade route between Burma and the Yangtze River, which would be comparable in value to that of the Pacific Ocean, could be dreamed of. He claims that "only a backwoodsman, suspicious and jealous, could have expressed such thoughts."[41]

There is, in the United States National Archives, however, a record of the British request for the opening of a direct route from West China to Burma. Early in 1847, Sir John F. Davis, British plenipotentiary, superintendent of trade, and governor of Hong Kong, had presented such a request to Imperial Commissioner Ch'i-ying.[42] An accurate assessment of the distance between Burma and the Yangtze, and of the feasibility of establishing a trade route, was almost impossible in the middle of the last century because of the limited geographical data. It was not until 1861, when an armed expedition led by the British Admiral Hope returned from southwest China, that the British realized that the inland water route was not only longer and more difficult than they had imagined, but actually did not run into the rivers of Burma and India.[43] Thus Marshall's suspicion did not derive from the imagination of a suspicious and jealous backwoodsman; it really had some basis.

---

[39] *Ibid.*, p. 169.

[40] *Ibid.*

[41] Costin, *Great Britain and China*, p. 182.

[42] Alexander H. Everett to James Buchanan, No. 26, Macao, February 28, 1847, *DD-USNA*, 92:4.

[43] Earl Cranston, "Shanghai in the Taiping Period," *The Pacific Historical Review*, V, No. 2 (1936), 158-59.

Failing to obtain any cooperation from the British, Marshall proceeded on his own and did what he could to get in touch with the local Manchu authorities. He was able to arrange a meeting with Manchu Governor-General I-liang on July 4 at K'un-shan, a city near Shanghai. At this meeting, Marshall brought up the old question of being received at Peking rather than at Shanghai. He also suggested that the Chinese "liberalize" their commercial regulations and open China at large to foreigners. "I understood," said Marshall, "all these points to be promised by the rebels at Nanking." I-liang confided that he could not speak freely, since he feared that his remarks might get back to Peking. He promised, however, that he would memorialize clearly on these subjects to the Emperor. Meanwhile, he and Marshall agreed to write directly to each other whenever the occasion warranted it.[44]

About a week after this meeting, Marshall wrote a long report to the State Department in which he proposed a "sound policy" in sustaining China. Marshall reported that the Chinese civil war was essentially a struggle for power. Regardless of which side won, it "would neither change the substantial exercise of power as it is now wielded, nor essentially the forms of etiquette and ceremony now practiced at court."[45] Though the rebels exceeded the Imperialists in energy and courage, both armies were hardly more than "burlesques on the military." A protracted civil war, Marshall reasoned, would only drain China's resources and make her easy prey for British and Russian imperialistic expansionism.[46]

Thus, in the summer of 1853, following his interview with I-liang, Marshall began to modify his previous program of intervention in the Chinese civil war. In addition to his original conviction that the civil war must be brought to an early end, Marshall was now also concerned with strengthening China's outer defenses in the face of a growing threat of invasion by Great Britain and Russia. Moreover, there was no other Western power whose cooperation the United States could hope to enlist in this situation. Marshall was now certain that the United States would have to act unilaterally.

Britain, in Marshall's view, was taking advantage of the crisis to break up the treaty system. She had already successfully extended

---

[44] Marshall to Marcy, No. 21, Shanghai, July 6, 1853, *Marshall's Correspondence*, p. 195.

[45] Marshall to Marcy, no number, Shanghai, July 10, 1853, *ibid.*, p. 204.

[46] *Ibid.*, pp. 203-4.

· her opium smuggling, the major factor that enabled the British to out-distance the Americans in the China trade. Marshall estimated that the importation of opium into China in 1852 alone amounted to more than $30,000,000; the Chinese paid for it in specie, in addition to the tea and silk that found their way into the British market and yielded 5,000,000 to 6,000,000 pounds sterling to the annual revenue of the United Kingdom.[47] Thus, opium was at the base of the vast system of trade between London, Calcutta, Bombay, and Canton—employing British carriers, sailors, merchants, manufacturers, and planters. As a result of this vicious circle, China was drained of precious metals as well as other valuable resources. "If China could put a stop to the importation of British opium into her ports," said Marshall, "the revenues of Great Britain would be sensibly affected by the result, and her superiority in the commerce of the East would very soon vanish."[48] Therefore, Marshall was convinced that China's stability was necessary not only to preserve the balance of world power, but also to promote American trade in the Far East.[49]

Marshall also viewed Russia as a growing menace from the north to the Chinese Empire. In fact, he thought that Russia might ultimately threaten even the security of the United States by acquiring a power in the Pacific, "which would not only nullify the prosperity of the United States for the future, but materially annoy us in the present, by disturbing the fisheries." The American commissioner, therefore, urged the United States to use every possible means to prevent Russia from extending her Pacific boundaries and to restrain her from interfering in Chinese domestic affairs. "China," wrote Marshall, "is like a lamb before the shearers, as easy a conquest as were the provinces of India."[50] He warned that unless the United States adopted a sound policy, the fate of Asia would be sealed by Russia and Great

---

[47] Ibid.

[48] Ibid., p. 204.

[49] In the same report, Marshall also gave special attention to the interest of southern cotton planters and northern textile manufacturers in the United States. He predicted that if Shanghai continued to be kept open for foreign trade, the United States could successfully compete with Great Britain and France for the supply of such American cotton goods as drills, sheetings, and the like, to China: ". . . until the Manchester brands will not be known in this part of Asia. The Southern planting states must find their interest in China through this medium. The valley of the Mississippi and the valley of Yangtze have such various products as to sustain a profitable commerce with each other, both in raw staples and in manufactures." Marshall to Marcy (Confidential), no number, Shanghai, July 10, 1853, ibid., p. 209.

[50] Ibid., pp. 204-5. Marshall's concern over Russia was to prove itself not without foundation. The Russians were already exploring areas along the Amur River, and only seven years after Marshall's warning, Russia acquired an important tract of

Britain and that "future Chinese relations with the United States of America may be considered as closed for ages."[51] He made his view known to the State Department:

... that the highest interests of the United States are involved in sustaining China—maintaining order here, and gradually engrafting on this worn-out stock the healthy principles which give life and health to government, rather than to see China become the theatre of widespread anarchy, and ultimately the prey of European ambition.

Marshall's plan of 1853 was not entirely new. It was in fact like the one proposed in 1847 by Commissioner Alexander H. Everett.[52] But whereas Everett had sought the cooperation of Russia, France, and the United States against Great Britain, Marshall thought the United States should stand alone, if necessary, in carrying out this mission, since both Russia and France had also turned to colonial expansionism.

When Marshall spoke of upholding China, he was not referring to upholding the imperial government alone. The Manchu regime, Marshall thought, might be sustained,[53]

... when the Emperor of China shall proclaim an amnesty for past political offenses to all the rebels who shall at once return to their homes and avocations, freedom of religious opinion, and religious worship throughout the realm, freedom to citizens of nations having treaties of amity and commerce with China to pass and repass through his dominions at will, without distinction of place; when the Emperor shall install a department of foreign affairs, the Emperor shall open the Yangtze and its affluents to steam navigation, and shall devise some just mode of regulating the same by registry or license; and finally, when he *shall become a subscriber to the law of nations.* . . .

If all these conditions were fulfilled by the Chinese Emperor, the Western powers, or at least the United States, should interfere in the Chinese civil war on the side of the imperial government. In doing so the United States would act with the cooperation of other Western powers to compel the rebel chief to yield to such a "platform"; if refused, the Western powers would force their way into the Yangtze with their own guns, which would deprive the rebel government of "even the shadow of power, and his rebellion will fade away as a dream."

---

land between the Ussuri and the sea (including the city of Hai-ts'an-wei, later changed to Vladivostok) as a reward for her good offices during the Anglo-French Chinese war of 1858-60.

[51] *Ibid.,* p. 204.   [52] See chap. 6.

[53] Marshall to the Secretary of State (Confidential), no number, Shanghai, July 10, 1853, *Marshall's Correspondence,* p. 206.

But if the imperial government could not put the aforesaid conditions into practice, although the rebels were willing to do so, Marshall would not hesitate to persuade all the Western treaty powers to send their ministers to Nanking, and to compel the imperial government to yield its ground.[54] Thus he preferred to negotiate with the Manchus first; but by no means did he neglect the rebels. As a matter of fact, during the last days of his stay in China, Marshall still intended to make known to the "Christian Emperor" his "readiness to recognize a new government."[55]

Thus, the essential feature of his policy was really the security of "the nationality of China" against the aggressive designs of European powers.[56] Such an objective was to bring Marshall gradually into sharp conflict with the British. Unable to coerce the American commissioner, however, the British authorities began to concentrate their efforts on maneuvering the State Department into a position of closer cooperation.

III

As previously explained, the authorities in Washington still had no elaborate China policy. It was only during very critical periods that the Secretary of State would occasionally canvass the China merchants in Boston and elsewhere and request suggestions that might be forwarded to the United States commissioner in China. In the first decade after the Opium War, American merchants gradually became convinced that their best interests were being served when China was least disturbed either internally or by pressure from outside. They had less to gain and more to fear from the use of high-handed methods in China.[57] If Great Britain or other Western countries should obtain new concessions from the Celestial Empire, they would be supported by

---

[54] In a previous dispatch to Washington, Marshall had clearly suggested that the Western powers send their representatives either to Peking or Nanking in order to bring the chaos in China to an end. See Marshall to Marcy, No. 20, June 21, 1853, *ibid.*, p. 182.

[55] Marshall to Perry (Confidential), December 26, 1853, *ibid.*, p. 351. Although Marshall continued to recognize the Manchu imperial government, he seemed also to plan on recognizing the rebel government *de facto*, provided the latter was willing to negotiate with him concerning the aforesaid "conditions." In all instructions to Marshall's successor, Secretary of State Marcy also expressed the opinion that the United States might recognize the rebel government *de facto* while he still continued to negotiate with the imperial government. See following chapter.

[56] *Marshall's Correspondence,* p. 205.

[57] Earl Swisher, "The Character of American Trade with China, 1844-1860," *University of Colorado Studies,* Series C (Studies in the Social Sciences), I, No. 2 (1941), 179-80.

American commercial interests in China. R. B. Forbes, a leading China merchant at Boston, who had been consulted on the United States policy toward China even before Cushing was sent to China, once wrote: "I have always, heretofore, thought it expedient to get all the good we could out of China and let our outlaw John Bull to find the saltpeter. . . ."[58] However, if any nation should really seek to dominate or to disrupt the Chinese Empire, it would be opposed by the United States. In other words, merchants generally were in favor of an open door in China, namely, equal commercial privilege in China for all Western nations.

Since the origin of United States relations with China was clearly a commercial one, the State Department could hardly ignore the views of the merchants. "It was only with an increase in the demands of these engaged in commerce for more official attention to their interests," observed Eldon Griffin, "that official policy took on positive and tangible form."[59] Thus, as long as the *status quo* in China was not seriously disturbed, authorities in Washington apparently were not too concerned about the American commissioner's activities.[60]

After the outbreak of the Taiping Rebellion, and particularly after the capture of Nanking in March, 1853, however, Washington could no longer ignore the fact that China was rapidly undergoing a change. Moreover, the feeling became widespread among Westerners that the Chinese civil war offered a good opportunity to force China to open its doors wide to foreign trade. By 1853 both Americans and English were agreed that the treaties of 1842-44 must be revised. In carrying out the task of treaty revision, however, Washington was entirely lacking in the concrete data necessary to enable it to issue effective instructions to its commissioner in China.[61]

Marshall thought that the United States should play an independent role in the negotiation of a new treaty. Like his predecessors, he insisted that China's sovereign and territorial integrity must be preserved and that the United States must play a leading role in guarding China from being partitioned by foreign powers or dominated by one or two of them. There was another school of thought, however, opposed to this view. The secretary of the American legation in China

    [58] R. B. Forbes to Caleb Cushing, Boston, February 11, 1857, Cushing MSS, Manuscript Division, Library of Congress.
    [59] Griffin, *Clippers and Consuls,* p. 33.
    [60] Cf. chap. 13.
    [61] Tyler Dennett, *Americans in Eastern Asia* (New York: The Macmillan Co., 1922), p. 211.

had been insisting for many years that the United States should cooperate more closely with the British in order to open China to commercial as well as missionary penetration.

In spite of the urgency of Chinese affairs, the State Department was
unable to formulate a clear-cut line of action. Unfamiliar with the
actual situation in China and perplexed by the conflicting reports from
United States diplomats and merchants on the scene, neither the Secretary of State nor the President could make a final decision. During
this period of uncertainty, the British Foreign Office made a timely
overture directly to Washington. First of all it provided Washington
with much needed information on the progress of the revolutionary
movement in China. Previously the United States government's information was limited to a series of contradictory reports from its
representatives in China.

The British thus succeeded in persuading the State Department that
Great Britain was interested in obtaining greater access to China "not
exclusively for its own subjects but for all nations." Urging American
cooperation in this common task, the British asked Washington to
instruct its commissioner in China[62]

... to take such a course in conjunction with Her Majesty's Plenipotentiary
as will be calculated to turn to the best account the opportunity offered by
the present crisis to open the Chinese empire generally to the commercial
enterprise of all the civilized nations in the world.

This proposal seemed reasonable and attractive to the American
authorities at Washington. Consequently, on June 7, 1853, Marcy instructed Marshall:

The end proposed commends itself to the approval of the President and he
directs you to do what you can within your proper sphere of action, towards
its accomplishment. Our treaty stipulations with China must be respected
and our settled policy of non-interference in the contests which arise between the people and their rulers must be observed.

Without a departure from these rules, stressed Marcy, Marshall might
do what he could to influence China to abandon commercial restrictions. Since they did not know what the British would actually do in
China, Marcy cautioned the American commissioner not to join the
British in any enterprise but to keep "only cordial relations and free
conference with them."[63] Thus no specific instructions were given, and

---

[62] Marcy to Marshall, No. 8, Washington, D.C., June 7, 1853, *DI-USNA*, 17:38,
84.

[63] *Ibid.*, pp. 84-85.

Marshall was permitted to use his "own judgment to accomplish the desired object."[64]

This directive was, for all practical purposes, the first explicit statement of the United States policy toward China since the Treaty of Wanghia was signed. In particular, it spelled out the United States position in the Sino-British dispute. It was not, however, in any sense a response to Everett's proposal of 1847, in which he advocated concerted action by the Western powers against Great Britain; nor was it an outgrowth of Parker's recommendation in 1851 that the United States take united action with Great Britain. The directive was rather the consequence of the direct request by the British for American cooperation. Washington, being for the first time forced by diplomatic necessity to take a stand, acceded to the British request.

Marcy's directive of June 7, 1853, did not reach Marshall until September, when the American commissioner's relations with the British had just reached a new low as a result of the Triad Rebellion at Shanghai on September 7, 1853. *"China,"* Marshall wrote in response to this instruction from Washington, *"gives to England no privilege that is not extorted by fear."*[65] China's reluctance to give England privileges was the major reason for its refusal to concede more to the United States. Thus Marshall decided to exercise the prerogative given him: he used his "own judgment" by ignoring the directive altogether and proceeded on his own way. This almost led him into an open clash with the British after the outbreak of the Triad Rebellion.

IV

The Triad Society was originally an underground revolutionary society, independent of the Taiping Rebellion, and organized by natives from Fukien and Kwangtung. After having seized the walled city of Shanghai on September 7, 1853, through a sudden uprising, both the Fukien and the Kwangtung chiefs proclaimed that they were related to the Taiping chiefs at Nanking. Unlike the Taipings, however, most of the Triad chiefs had often dealt with foreigners in the various ports; and one of them was a British subject from Singapore who had worked as a servant in a British firm for years. Since they were aware of the superior military strength of the Western powers, they had no desire

---

[64] *Ibid.,* p. 85.
[65] Marshall to Marcy, No. 31, Shanghai, September 21, 1853, *Marshall's Correspondence,* p. 269.

to provoke clashes with them.[66] As soon as they occupied Shanghai, the top rebel chief, Liu Li-chuan, paid his respects to Commissioner Marshall and the other foreign envoys there, and assured them that he would respect and cooperate with foreign interests. Although they took over the entire area previously occupied by the imperial government in the walled city of Shanghai, the rebels announced that the foreign settlement along the bund would not be invaded and that the imperial institutions within the foreign settlement would be allowed to continue operation.[67] In these circumstances, Marshall urged that the *status quo* within the foreign settlement be preserved. "Certainly," he reported to Washington, "I could not recognize the capture of Shanghai as sufficient to induce the acknowledgement of another government *de facto* within the limits of China."[68] In other words, Marshall thought that the political administration of the foreign settlement should remain unchanged.

The British, however, held a contrary view. On the very eve of the Triad uprising, British marines began to take up the defense of the foreign settlement. No Chinese troops were allowed to remain or to pass through the area. In the meantime, the Committee of Cooperation, which was originally organized by the British resident merchants and later joined by all Western residents in Shanghai, was given the authority to take over political administration in the foreign settlement. Thus they began to exercise rights of sovereignty on Chinese territory and to organize an autonomous settlement within the Chinese Empire.[69]

In the meantime, the British seem purposely to have put the Chinese customhouse at Shanghai out of operation. Previously, during the uprising at Shanghai, the rebels had not intended to occupy the customhouse, which was located inside the foreign section. The rebel leaders, immediately after their successful uprising, not only assured the American commissioner that they would "abstain from any attempt to collect duties on imports,"[70] but also indicated their willingness to permit the collector, Wu Chien-chang, to resume operations at the customhouse.[71]

---

[66] For a general account of the Triad Rebellion at Shanghai consult Hsu Wei-nan, "Shang-hai Hsiao-tao-hui luan-shih ti shih-mo," *I-ching*, XXVI (March 20, 1937), 28-31.

[67] *Marshall's Correspondence*, pp. 315 ff.

[68] *Ibid.*, p. 316.

[69] See following chapter.

[70] Marshall to Marcy, No. 29, Shanghai, September 7, 1853, *Marshall's Correspondence*, p. 254.   [71] *Ibid.*, No. 34, Macao, November 26, 1853, p. 316.

Nevertheless, on September 7, 1853, the Chinese customhouse at Shanghai was demolished and put out of operation. The account of its demolition, which was first reported by the English newspaper, the *North China Herald*, has been repeated by almost all writers since that time. According to this version, the Chinese authorities in charge of the customhouse fled for their lives after the capture of the city of Shanghai. Unruly mobs broke into the structure and ransacked and looted everything that could be carried off. On September 8, after British marines had succeeded in protecting the foreign settlement at Shanghai, a guard was placed around the building to prevent it from being utterly demolished.[72] Because the customhouse was now a shambles, foreign consuls had to set up a "Provisional System" to help the Chinese collect custom duties.

The reliability of this account apparently was never seriously questioned by anyone. But the American commissioner, who had walked unmolested through the city in the midst of the rebellion[73] and had entered the building of the Chinese customhouse just before the "rabble,"[74] presented a different version. In his confidential dispatches to Washington, Marshall said, "the first breach of the new Chinese customhouse was effected by the entry of an employee of a British mercantile firm of this city. . . ." In fact, Marshall entered the building at the very moment that this person was directing his coolies in the hasty removal of certain merchandise kept in storage in the customhouse. The Chinese clerks helplessly stood by, since they were powerless to do otherwise. This pillage was followed by the action of "other British subjects . . . upon the plea that the Chinese superintendent of customs owed them money for the victualing of public ships in the service of the government, and they thought that an opportune moment to *provide collateral security*." Many merchants and citizens witnessed the entire incident, said Marshall, but no resistance was offered. It was only after the British looting of the Chinese customhouse that the Chinese rabble entered. And, significantly, it was after the pillage that the

---

[72] *North China Herald*, September 10, 1853; Hosea Ballou Morse, *The International Relations of the Chinese Empire* (New York: Longmans, Green and Co., 1920), I, 458; Fairbank, "The Provisional System at Shanghai in 1853-54," p. 482; Fairbank, *Trade and Diplomacy on the China Coast*, I, 410 ff.; Stanley F. Wright, *Hart and the Chinese Customs* (Belfast: Wm. Mullan and Son, 1950), pp. 91-92; Kuo Ping-chia, "Hsien-feng ch'ao Chung-kuo wai-chiao kai kuan," *Kuo-li Wu-han-ta-hsueh, She-hui k'o-hsueh chi-k'an*, V (1935), 115.

[73] *North China Herald*, September 10, 1853; Marshall to Marcy, No. 29, Shanghai, September 7, 1853, *Marshall's Correspondence*, p. 254.

[74] Marshall to Marcy, No. 34, Shanghai, October 30, 1853, *ibid.*, p. 286.

British posted their guard "to *protect* the Chinese custom-house within the foreign settlement. . . ."[75] In a report to Washington, Marshall stated:[76]

I have heretofore informed you that the first violence offered at the Chinese custom house within the foreign settlement, and the lawless acts which made the precedents for an entry of the establishment by the populace, *did not proceed from the Chinese insurgents.*

Marshall's version has been completely ignored for more than a century. He was, however, one of the eyewitnesses, and his report cannot be lightly dismissed. In many respects Marshall's account seems more plausible than the one offered by Sir George Bonham, which is often self-contradictory.[77]

V

The day after the customhouse at Shanghai ceased operation, Rutherford Alcock, the British consul, and Edward Cunningham, the American vice-consul at Shanghai, held a conference in which they agreed to issue orders to their respective nationals stating that during the absence of the Chinese customs officers, they, the consuls, would collect the duties for the imperial government according to the treaties. There was, however, a difference between the American and British method for carrying out this policy. The British consul required only that the merchants deposit at the consulate promissory notes which were to be held in abeyance until the Foreign Office at London decided whether they would be honored or not. It was freely predicted that the British Foreign Office would decide against the Chinese government and that the notes would be returned as in fact they were, a year later.[78]

The Americans, on the other hand, were ordered to pay their duties at the American consulate in specie. This measure, of course, put the American merchants at a serious disadvantage in their competition with the British. On September 9, two days after the Chinese custom-

---

[75] *Ibid.*, pp. 286-87.

[76] Marshall to Marcy, No. 36, Macao, November 26, 1853, *ibid.*, p. 315.

[77] For an excellent treatment of the Bonham literature consult John K. Fairbank, "The Creation of the Foreign Inspectorate of Customs at Shanghai," *CSPSR*, XIX (1935-36), 510 ff.

[78] The British Foreign Office later ordered all the promissory notes to be returned to the merchants. In doing so the Foreign Office was acting contrary to Consul Alcock's previous promise to the Chinese for the establishment of the Provisional System. Thus, according to Professor Fairbank, the Chinese government could bring legal claims against England. For further information consult *ibid.*, pp. 513 ff. For general information see Dennett, *Americans in Eastern Asia*, p. 217; and Fairbank, *Trade and Diplomacy*, I, 420 ff. and II, 39, footnote 31.

house was destroyed, Vice-Consul Cunningham, acting under orders from the American commissioner, informed the American merchants in that port that they were required to pay their customs duties in accordance with the second article of the Treaty of Wanghia, and "Provisional Rules" for the clearing of ships, in the absence of a customhouse.[79]

The policy drawn up by the two consuls came to be known as the Provisional System. However, within a fortnight after the destruction of the customhouse, the Chinese customs superintendent, Wu Chien-chang, returned to Shanghai with a new seal and sought to reopen the customhouse for official business. This attempt was blocked by the British. Wu then set up customs operations in two Western-style vessels in the Huang-p'u River, and, on October 10, notified both the British and American consuls that the collection of Chinese customs would now be officially resumed and that the Provisional System had ceased to function.[80] This directive was accepted by the American commissioner but was rejected by the British Consul Alcock. Claiming that their presence *"endangered the foreign shipping,* or that they *were too close to her Majesty's vessels,"* the two customs ships were "twice driven from their anchorage in front of the Chinese customhouse by a British man-of-war."[81]

Moreover, the British consul at Shanghai denounced the Chinese government as having no legal right to collect duties until it recaptured Shanghai and recovered the seal of the *taotai,* which was lost when the city fell in September, 1853. This decision was later fully supported by the British Foreign Office at London.[82] But the Imperialists were powerless to recapture the city early in October, although the Chinese imperial troops succeeded in consolidating their control over the outskirts of Shanghai and in laying siege to the walled city. They were now at a stalemate because one side of the city was connected to the foreign settlement, from which the rebels could obtain valuable supplies, such as Western firearms and food, as well as the services of

---

[79] Cunningham's *Notice* to the American merchants, Shanghai, September 9, 1853, *Marshall's Correspondence,* p. 271. For general reference on this particular problem see Dennett, *Americans in Eastern Asia,* pp. 217 ff.

[80] Eleang [I-liang] to Marshall, October 30, 1853, *Marshall's Correspondence,* pp. 300 ff.

[81] Marshall to the Secretary of State, No. 33, Shanghai, October 30, 1853, *ibid.,* p. 289.

[82] Bonham's dispatch of October 10, 1853, *F.O.,* 17/205; Clarendon's dispatch of November 24, 1853, *F.O.,* 17/198, quoted in Fairbank, *Trade and Diplomacy,* I, 420.

Western technicians and volunteers. The result was, as Professor Fairbank has pointed out,[83]

> ... that, as long as the *taotai* did not control the customs and the settlement boundaries sufficiently to prevent foreign goods from reaching the Triads, he could not re-establish his political authority at Shanghai; but so long as he could not re-establish his authority, Alcock would not allow him to resume control of the customs. This circle was none the less vicious because the *taotai* helped to preserve it.

On the whole, this interpretation is amply substantiated by Professor Fairbank's remarkable documentation and research, although his accusation against the *taotai* is not sufficiently proved.[84]

Since the British had thwarted their attempt to maintain a "floating custom house," the local Chinese authorities now sought to devise new methods. They would either levy duties at some interior point or move the Shanghai customhouse to Wusung at the mouth of the Huang-p'u River. These plans were promptly denounced by the British consul, who branded them as acts of hostility and aggression against Great Britain. Consul Alcock even called upon the Chinese authorities to consider, as Marshall observed, "how far the Emperor can find his interest in the provocation of a great power like Great Britain under existing circumstances."[85] Thus, although the Chinese were trying to rebuild their customs service, Shanghai became a *de facto* free port under British control. Watching helplessly as the British demolished the treaty-system at Shanghai, Marshall, in a report to Washington, wrote: "Great Britain has exhibited in her Eastern conquests neither fear of Heaven nor love of justice among man."[86] Since the American commissioner had considerably less power and influence than the British consul, Marshall could do nothing to bring the British action to a halt. All that he could do was to compel American merchants to pay their customs duties and comply with treaty obligations. This action, of course, aroused considerable opposition to Marshall from within the American community. In order to embarrass him and to force him to rescind his orders, the leading American firms dispatched identical letters to the Shanghai representatives of Great Britain,

---

83 Fairbank, *Trade and Diplomacy*, I, 432.

84 Professor Fairbank suspects that the *taotai*, Wu Chien-chang, was a partner of Russell and Company, which was blamed by the British for trading ammunition with the rebels, but his research on this aspect is not sufficient to prove his hypothesis. *Ibid.*, pp. 430-36.

85 *Marshall's Correspondence*, p. 269.

86 *Ibid.*, p. 286.

France, Portugal, Holland, Prussia, and Hamburg asking "whether, in case we desired to ship in vessels under any of [their] flags, [they] recognized any Custom House establishment; and if so, where situated?"[87] They all replied, of course, that they recognized no customhouse whatever.[88] The Commissioner, however, stubbornly held his ground and insisted that the treaty was still in force.

In order to implement the treaty even further, Marshall sought a meeting with Imperial Commissioner Yeh Ming-ch'en. Marshall's intention was to suggest some means by which the Chinese could put an end to British encroachment on China's sovereign rights. Early in November, Marshall left Shanghai for the South in a vain effort to see Yeh, to whom he wrote on December 11, 1853, that the United States alone was willing "to resume the payment of duties upon the usual terms at Shanghai."[89] Unfortunately, his assurances were completely ignored and his request for an interview was spurned by the inept Imperial Commissioner.

Yeh's refusal to grant even an audience to Marshall, however, was not merely the result of the ignorance of an individual. As explained previously, in the early 1850's, China's foreign affairs had begun a new phase. The newly recruited "barbarian experts" had adopted a general "barbarian" exclusion policy. Thus from the very beginning of his mission, Marshall had been treated as an unwelcome guest in China. When the news of Marshall's arrival at Shanghai reached Peking on June 16, Emperor Hsien-feng promptly instructed I-liang to send the American commissioner back to Canton, where Yeh Ming-ch'en, the Imperial Commissioner, was authorized to deal with him.[90] On September 1, 1853, Yeh complained that the Chinese officials at Shanghai had mistakenly offered to hire steamers through Marshall and that Marshall had assumed thereby that China was seeking foreign support to suppress the rebellion.[91] This memorial tended to increase the young

---

[87] *Ibid.*, p. 313; see also Fairbank, *Trade and Diplomacy*, p. 425.

[88] The representatives of Portugal, Holland, and Hamburg were all British merchants, who were appointed by the governments of the respective countries and served as their consuls. The appointment of American or British merchants as representatives of other European countries was a common practice at that time. In 1860 one American by the name of Albert F. Heard was appointed by the Russian government and served as the Russian consul at Shanghai. See John E. Ward to Lewis Cass, No. 15, Shanghai, June 29, 1860, *DD-USNA*, 92:20. For general information see Fairbank, *Trade and Diplomacy*, p. 425; Griffin, *Clippers and Consuls*, pp. 304 ff.; *Chinese Repository*, XVIII (1849), 11-12, and XX (1851), 16-17.

[89] Marshall to Yee [Yeh] Macao, December 11, 1853, *Marshall's Correspondence*, p. 343.

[90] *IWSM-HF*, VI, 15.

[91] *Ibid.*, VI, 29b-30a.

Emperor's suspicion of Marshall's mission in Shanghai. Thus, while Marshall was working at Shanghai for the sovereign and territorial integrity of China, the Emperor issued another confidential edict to I-liang, the governor-general of Liang-Kiang, to send Marshall back to Canton immediately.[92]

Since Marshall failed to convince the Chinese, who were, after all, the ones presumably to benefit from his policy, it was unlikely that he could obtain any support from his own countrymen. As a matter of fact, he had already had a serious rift with Parker, the secretary of the legation, who refused to stay with him at Shanghai.[93] Marshall was on equally bad terms with the American missionaries, merchants, and navy commanders. The former two groups were anxious to break away from Marshall's policy of "neutrality in good faith," while the latter were indifferent to Chinese affairs. In a word, in the middle of the last century, American missionaries and merchants in China were unable to appreciate the so-called open door principle which had been promoted by Caleb Cushing and Alexander H. Everett and which Marshall was seeking to preserve.

Hence, Marshall's policy was completely rejected, not only by the British and the Chinese, but also by his own countrymen, who furnished the public and press at home with a flood of anti-Marshall correspondence. Marshall himself made no attempt to counteract these attacks; he wrote to the State Department: "I have nothing to do with the press or with the effect produced upon private circles by letters written from China."[94] Nevertheless, it was on the basis of these private sources that Washington officialdom, as well as later historians, judged the achievement and practicability of his efforts. Since the Commissioner was too stubborn to change his course of action, and continued to ignore the directives from the State Department, he had to be removed. Consequently, he was dismissed by Washington on

---

[92] *Ibid.*, VI, 31.

[93] In the summer of 1853, Marshall and Parker had a serious quarrel. It was started by Marshall's opening an official letter addressed to Parker from the State Department. Parker complained in a long letter to the Commissioner that the latter had no right to open dispatches not addressed directly to the Commissioner. Marshall was irritated by Parker's discourteous letter and wrote a stormy letter in reply to Parker. Besides defending his right to open an official dispatch belonging to his secretary, Marshall also complained: "You are drawing $2,500 per year for the performance of duties and you remain eight hundred miles from the chief of the legation, pursuing another profession. . . . Whenever my course does not please you, *resign,* or ask the department, through me, officially, to correct my decisions." See *Marshall's Correspondence,* pp. 233-37.

[94] Humphrey Marshall to the Secretary of State, Macao, November 21, 1853, *Marshall's Correspondence,* p. 307.

October 21, 1853, when his successor, Robert M. McLane, was appointed.[95]

Being unaware of his removal, however, Marshall continued to vigorously defend his policy. Staying in Macao for the winter, Marshall still attempted to persuade the authorities in Washington that his aim was to keep the government of the United States advised correctly and to prevent its action from being based on information that was *not sound or true.*" "Hence," stressed the stubborn Commissioner, "I guard you against the acceptance of miscellaneous authority for your ideas of events or the tendency of events in this country."[96]

At this time, however, Marshall's efforts in China had collapsed completely. In Shanghai, his order to pay customs duties in specie had already been ignored by the American vice-consul, who instead authorized payment by promissory notes as the British had been doing. Gradually, Marshall himself realized that his bold policy would not work. It had not brought the other foreign nations into line, and, moreover, the American merchants had suffered seriously. Therefore, on January 4, 1854, he directed Vice-Consul Cunningham at Shanghai to change his policy immediately and "to clear American ships without taking any note of the duties whatever, without requiring any port clearance, and in all respects treating Shanghai as a free port."[97]

This action was primarily designed to remedy the plight of the American merchants and at the same time to embarrass Great Britain. Since he had failed in his effort to defend the treaty-system at Shanghai, he now sought to take advantage of the most-favored-nation clause to declare Shanghai a free port. The issuance of promissory notes by the British was merely a sham, since it was obvious to all that the promissory notes were mere scraps of paper. In fact, the British Foreign Office had, by November, 1853, ordered the British consul at Shanghai to return the notes to the British merchants, although Marshall did not know it at the time. Many foreign vessels had already left Shanghai duty free. Since Shanghai had been recognized *de facto* as a free port by the British and other European powers, Marshall was merely acknowledging an established fact when he declared Shanghai a free port. He preferred this forthright position to misleading and hypocritical expressions of idealism. In this respect, Marshall re-

---

[95] *DI-USNA*, 77:38, p. 86.

[96] Marshall to Marcy, No. 35, Macao, November 21, 1853, *Marshall's Correspondence*, p. 307.

[97] *Marshall's Correspondence*, pp 366-67; for general information consult Dennett, *Americans in Eastern Asia*, pp. 221-22.

flected the difference between an honest amateur and the shrewd and highly experienced professional colonizers from the banks of the Thames.

Tyler Dennett feels that Marshall's anti-British action in China was a struggle "in defense of the Imperial revenues."[98] Professor Fairbank rejects this conclusion. Instead he develops the thesis that Marshall's declaration that Shanghai was a free port was made merely to provide an excuse for American merchants not to make good to China on the promissory notes already issued.[99] Actually, Marshall's anti-British efforts in Shanghai could not have been aimed merely at protecting revenue for the imperial government, which he had repeatedly condemned as the worst government that ever existed. His action was in defense of a principle, namely, the inviolability of the treaty-system and the territorial integrity of China—the foundation of the famous Open Door doctrine. Unfortunately, no one, not even the Chinese, ever appreciated Marshall's untiring effort. "The Superior Man," as an ancient Confucian sage once remarked in the *Great Learning*, "believes that he must be alert even when he is alone." But when a moral man lives in an immoral community, he is bound to fail, regardless of how alert he is. Marshall's declaration of Shanghai as a free port was a frank recognition of his failure in carrying out a remarkable policy. Outmaneuvered by the British, neglected by his own people, ignored by the Chinese, and finally distrusted by his government at home, Marshall's efforts in sustaining China were bound to have a tragic ending. Informed of his removal through a newspaper item, Marshall left China for home on January 27, 1854.[100]

---

[98] Dennett, *Americans in Eastern Asia,* p. 221.
[99] Fairbank, *Trade and Diplomacy,* I, 434; II, 42n.
[100] *Marshall's Correspondence,* p. 333.

10

COMMISSIONER McLANE AND THE

RESULTS OF A "COOPERATION"

I

MARSHALL was the first United States commissioner to China to be officially recalled by the State Department. All of his predecessors, except Alexander H. Everett, who died in office, had resigned their positions voluntarily. In fact, the post was not one eagerly sought after by those aspiring to public life. A number of prominent persons had previously declined the appointment because of the poor compensation.[1] It was therefore quite unusual to find a man like Humphrey Marshall, a well-known attorney with a good record of public service, to fill the post. It was even more surprising that he should have been recalled so abruptly.

Actually, the recall of Marshall and the appointment of McLane only reflected a change in United States policy toward the British in China. Marshall was removed because of his anti-British action in China; McLane was sent there to reverse it. The new commissioner, Robert M. McLane, was the son of a former Secretary of State, Louis McLane. Like his predecessor, he was a graduate of the United States Military Academy and a lawyer by profession. He had also served for two terms in Congress as representative from Maryland.[2] For his

---

[1] On the difficulty of finding appointees to the China post consult President Fillmore's Annual Message delivered on December 2, 1851. James Daniel Richardson, comp., *A Compilation of the Messages and Papers of the President, 1789-1897* (Washington, D.C.: Government Printing Office, 1896-1900), V, 122. In fact three persons had declined appointments to China; two (Thomas A. R. Nelson and Joseph Blung) immediately preceding Marshall, and one (Robert J. Walker) just after him. See *DI-USNA*, 7:38, pp. 71-72; also consult Tyler Dennett, *Americans in Eastern Asia* (New York: The Macmillian Co., 1922), Appendix, p. 705.

[2] William L. Marcy to Robert M. McLane, Washington, D.C., October 21, 1853, *DI-USNA*, 77:38; for good biographical sketches of McLane consult Allen Johnson, ed., *Dictionary of American Biography* (New York: Charles Scribner's Sons, 1943), XII, 115; Ben Poore, comp., *The Political Register and Congressional Directory* (Boston: Houghton, Osgood and Company, 1878), p. 516; Dennett, *Americans in Eastern Asia*, p. 191; John K. Fairbank, *Trade and Diplomacy on the China Coast, the Opening of the Treaty Ports, 1842-1854* (Cambridge, Mass.: Harvard University Press, 1953), I, 446.

important mission to China, McLane possessed many more advantages than his predecessors had. First of all, his salary was raised from six thousand to nine thousand dollars, with some additional allowance. He was given the power to choose the permanent location of the legation and to remove or to appoint the Chinese secretary or interpreter. In addition to these privileges vested in him by the State Department, he was also provided with a "small naval force" by the Secretary of Navy.[3]

Most important of all was the fact that McLane was the first American commissioner to China under the Treaty of Wanghia to receive comparatively specific instructions from the State Department, which somewhat clarified his position in different diplomatic activities.

In addition to the routine instructions common to all his predecessors, McLane was specifically instructed to negotiate a new treaty with China, so that unrestricted commercial intercourse between the two countries might be established. In this treaty the right to fish along the coasts of China and the free use of Chinese harbors and rivers by United States citizens were also to be included. On these specific points, McLane was told that he might even assent to a reciprocal stipulation, because "there might not be much cause to apprehend that the Chinese subjects would avail themselves of it."[4]

Regarding the United States policy toward the rebels, he was instructed that he might, at his own discretion, recognize the rebels' government *de facto* if he saw fit. If China should be divided and several governments promising stability be organized within its limits, the Commissioner was to present himself to each as the diplomatic representative of the United States and to enter into such treaties with them as he might deem advisable.

Concerning the relations between the United States and Great Britain in China, McLane was instructed to aid the British "in a

---

[3] *DI-USNA*, 77:38, pp. 87, 90, 99-100. The privilege of appointing the Chinese secretary and interpreter given to McLane seems to have been inspired by Marshall's disputes with Parker. McLane's privilege of obtaining a special ship for his service was the result of negotiations between the State and Navy departments. Professor Fairbank stated that McLane made friends with the U.S. Navy, and received the use of a ship (*Trade and Diplomacy*, I, 446). Actually, the ship was assigned to him through a formal request from the State Department to the Navy Department, not merely through private friendship. In fact, Commodore Perry was reluctant to carry out this instruction. See Edward M. Barrows, *The Great Commodore, the Exploits of Matthew Calbraith Perry* (New York: The Bobbs-Merrill Co., 1935), p. 298.

[4] Marcy to McLane, No. 2, Washington, D.C., November 9, 1853, *DI-USNA* 77:38, p. 93.

proper way to get liberal concessions to commerce for whatever Great
Britain may obtain on the renewal of her treaty. . . ."[5]

With these specific instructions for his important mission to China,
McLane sailed from New York at the end of 1853, and arrived at
Hong Kong on March 13, 1854. Soon after, Commodore M. C. Perry
assigned him a big steamship, the *Susquehanna,* under the command
of Commander Franklin Buchanan "for an indefinite time."[6] In the
meantime, Peter Parker, the secretary of the legation, announced
McLane's arrival to Governor-General Yeh and requested an interview. As usual, Yeh refused this request on the pretext that he was
"superintending the affairs of the army in several provinces," with no
leisure to meet the American commissioner. Because of this discour-
tesy to McLane, Parker tried to influence the Commissioner to take
some action against the Chinese. "If the British plenipotentiary, soon
to arrive, asks for an interview," Parker wrote to McLane on April 6,
"he will obtain it; and, as an American, I should be very sorry to
see your Excellency outdone in this or any other matter of public
moment."[8] McLane, however, was not moved by Parker's rhetoric.
He had his own strategy to meet the new circumstances.

Generally speaking, McLane's policy toward China was no different
from that of his immediate predecessor, Humphrey Marshall.[9] First
of all, McLane felt he should get well acquainted with the real situation of the imperial government and with "the actual condition of the
revolutionary army." Then he would take advantage of all the con-
tingencies that might arise out of the extraordinary state of things
then existing in China to achieve his desired objective.[10]

In the meantime, he was invited for an interview with the new
British envoy, Sir John Bowring, who had replaced Bonham and
reached Hong Kong on April 13. The meeting took place on April 15.
During this interview, Bowring told McLane that he was instructed

---

[5] Marcy to McLane, No. 7, Washington, D.C., May 8, 1854, *ibid.,* pp. 99-100.

[6] McLane to Marcy, No. 1, Hong Kong, March 20, 1854, printed in *Senate Ex.
Doc.,* No. 22, 35 Cong., 2 sess., pp. 2 ff. The *Sen. Ex. Doc.,* No. 22 contains all the
official dispatches delivered by Commissioners Robert M. McLane and Peter Parker
(when the latter was promoted to commissionership) from March, 1854, to August,
1857, in 2 volumes. The first volume will be hereafter cited as *McLane Correspondence,* the second *Parker Correspondence.*

[7] Yeh to Parker, Canton, April 6, 1854, *McLane Correspondence,* p. 19.

[8] Parker to McLane, Macao, April 6, 1854, *ibid.,* p. 20.

[9] Dr. Dennet also remarked: "On the basis of his [McLane's] observations he
formulated a policy not very dissimilar from that of Marshall's the preceding year."
Americans in Eastern Asia, p. 234.

[10] McLane to Marcy, Macao, April 8, 1854, *McLane Correspondence,* p. 8.

by his government to enlarge commercial relations with China, to secure access to the interior of that country, and especially to establish direct diplomatic relations with the government at Peking. He proposed to the American commissioner a "combined action" by the two countries.[11] McLane, however, was not moved by this British proposal. First, he had decided it was too early for him to take any definite action; secondly McLane thought that Great Britain, then handicapped by the Crimean War in Europe, was incapable of taking any aggressive action in China at the moment.[12]

McLane, therefore, decided to search for firsthand information before taking any action. In a report to Washington, he mentioned that he would not precipitate any negotiation with the imperial government or the revolutionists until, by his personal observation, he should have formed a "mature judgment" of their relations to each other and to foreign nations. When he reached this point, he would act without delay.[13]

Without further intercourse with the Chinese or the British, he sailed for Shanghai, arriving on April 29, 1854.[14] From Shanghai, McLane, after a brief meeting with local Chinese officials, made an inspection tour around the other ports, Ningpo and Foochow, where he found very little American commerce. Even in Shanghai, the American import trade had been almost destroyed by the Chinese civil war, although the export trade was carried on as usual. Returning from the southern ports, McLane sailed up the Yangtze River on May 22, to make a firsthand investigation of the civil war in that area. With him on board the *Susquehanna*, McLane had scores of aides, sailors, and staff members of the legation, giving a remarkable demonstration of power on the Yangtze that his predecessor could only dream of. Passing the Silver Island where the Imperialist fleet had formed a blockade against the Taipings, Captain Buchanan sent an announcement to the Chinese governor-general of Liang-Kiang and asked for an interview. Without waiting for an answer, which would take at least a few days, McLane sailed up the river and entered the area controlled by the rebels.[15] Five days later, the *Susquehanna* dropped her anchor outside the city wall of Nanking, the capital of the Taipings. There the Commissioner immediately sent an official

11 McLane to Marcy, No. 3, Hong Kong, April 20, 1854, *ibid.,* pp. 23-24.
12 *Ibid.*
13 *Ibid.,* p. 24.
14 McLane to Marcy, No. 5, Shanghai, May 21, 1854, *ibid.,* pp. 40-44.
15 McLane to Marcy, No. 6, Shanghai, June 14, 1854, *ibid.,* pp. 47 ff.

dispatch to the chief of the Taipings. Several of his assistants also went ashore and entered the city of Nanking for firsthand observation. In the meantime, the *Susquehanna* was opened to visitors. "During the two or three days the ship remained at Nanking," wrote one of the ship's crew, "she was crowded with thousands of visitors, from princes and generals down to coolies all of whom appeared filled with amazement at her immense size and elegance."[16]

On the third day, an official reply was received from the Taiping authority. This official reply as well as some of the dispatches that he received from the local Taiping officers while on his way to Nanking had really incensed McLane, for they had been couched in the language of a "heavenly empire" treating with tribute bearers.[17] Failing to obtain a satisfactory official interview with the rebels, McLane ordered the ship to proceed up the Yangtze for a brief visit to Wuhu and then returned without further connection with the Taipings. This trip to Nanking was very disappointing to Commissioner McLane. In a subsequent report to Washington, he denounced the Taipings as incompetent to govern the people, and too ignorant and peculiar to be recognized even "as a *de facto* government over a portion of the Chinese empire."[18]

After the trip to Nanking, McLane became very hostile toward the rebels. However, like Marshall, McLane recognized that, regardless of the Taiping incompetency in state administration, the Imperialists were unable to suppress them. He was also pondering another problem: "What shall be the policy of foreign nations having treaty stipulations with China?" If a strict and impartial neutrality were to be maintained until one or the other of the contending parties should obtain ascendancy, it would have to be a long term commitment, for, according to McLane's observation, prediction as to eventual victory was impossible. In the meantime, the American import trade in Shanghai had already been jeopardized, and the causes which induced that result in Shanghai might extend to the other ports.[19]

Upon his return from Nanking, McLane's judgment of the situation in China had "matured." McLane suggested to Washington that foreigners should "enforce their treaty rights" in China. By doing so they would at least maintain their presence in that country, and

---

[16] *Ibid.*, p. 67.
[17] *Ibid.*, p. 41.
[18] *Ibid.*, p. 53.
[19] *Ibid.*

whether the one power or the other should prevail, they could not fail to greatly extend their relations with the Chinese people. McLane believed that the foreigners would have no practical difficulty in enforcing their treaty rights—even if the imperial authorities and the revolutionary chiefs would both oppose them—for either faction was equally incapable of offering effective resistance. Besides, once additional privileges were obtained by the foreigners from the present dynasty, the rebels would never be able to reverse them, even if they should succeed in overthrowing the Manchu dynasty in China.[20]

Relying on this "matured judgment," which was similar to Marshall's observation a year before, McLane decided to negotiate with the Manchu authorities for the extension of treaty privileges and other problems. An interview with him was granted by Governor-General I-liang. It was scheduled on June 21, 1854, at the same place where Marshall had been given his interview. A few days before the interview took place, however, McLane held a meeting with Sir John Bowring, the British plenipotentiary to China, who had just arrived in Shanghai,[21] and the two ministers reached an agreement on what requests the American envoy should present to I-liang during the coming interview. They included a proposal for treaty revision and programs concerning "local problems" at Shanghai. An example of the full cooperation between these two ministers may be seen in the American commissioner's decision to let the British envoy read extracts from his latest dispatch to Washington, delivered on June 14, 1854. In the meantime, the British consul, Alcock, was also busily drafting practical programs for solving the local problems, particularly the customs service at Shanghai.[22] These British proposals were apparently accepted by the American commissioner, who was to present them to the Chinese at his meeting with I-liang.

At the time appointed, McLane went to K'un-shan where he was

---

[20] McLane to Marcy, No. 6, Shanghai, June 14, 1854, *McLane Correspondence,* p. 55.

[21] Sir John Bowring had been granted an interview by Yeh Ming-ch'en, the Imperial Commissioner, on May 22, 1854, at a packing house outside the city of Canton. Bowring, however, insisted on meeting Yeh only in a public office inside the city. This Yeh declined, and the scheduled interview was cancelled. The British envoy then proceeded to Shanghai. See Bowring to Clarendon, May 15, 1854, *F.O.,* 17/213, quoted in W. C. Costin, *Great Britain and China 1833-1860* (Oxford: The Clarendon Press, 1937), p. 187. "Packing house" is apparently a direct translation from the Chinese term "chanfang" used in Yeh's official letter to the British envoy. Actually, it was not a "packing house" but "a fine suburban residence." See chap. 7, footnote 3.

[22] Bowring's dispatches, No. 61, June 17, *F.O.,* 17/214, quoted in Fairbank, *Trade and Diplomacy,* I, 456.

greeted by the Manchu governor-general. The interview was conducted in a very pleasant atmosphere. McLane, like Marshall, was "pleasantly surprised" by I-liang's attractive personality and enlightened statesmanship. "Nothing could have been more satisfactory than his friendly disposition and demeanor," said McLane.[23] "The general deportment of the viceroy was all that refined courtesy and good breeding could have desired," McLane continued, "perfect simplicity of manners and a generous hospitality attended the reception, and everything was done by the subordinate authorities at Shanghai and on the route to render the journey agreeable."[24]

In this interview, the discussion was concentrated on two major topics: the American request for more treaty privileges from China; and determining a proper solution for the local problems at Shanghai. McLane's request for the extension of treaty privileges was based on four major demands: free navigation of the Yangtze River for American vessels; privileges for American citizens to move freely in any portion of the Chinese Empire for reasons of commerce or otherwise; absolute freedom of religious opinion and worship; and permanent residence for the American commissioner at the capital of China.[25]

I-liang firmly stated that he was not empowered to discuss the extension of treaty privileges in China with a foreign commissioner. All he could do was to forward them to Yeh Ming-ch'en, the governor-general of Liang-Kuang, who, according to I-liang, was the only Imperial Commissioner with the power to discuss such problems with foreigners.[26]

With regard to the local problems, however, I-liang freely and frankly conceded that the imperial authorities had failed to protect the foreigners at Shanghai during the uprising of the Triad Society, and professed an earnest desire to exert all his authority to protect the rights and privileges given in those treaties.[27] Thus he agreed to empower the *taotai* at Shanghai with full authority to make plans for a solution of these problems with foreign consuls. "As far as the local difficulties at Shanghai were concerned," reported McLane to Washington, "the result of that interview was in all respects satisfactory."[28]

---

[23] *McLane's Correspondence*, p. 112.

[24] *Ibid.*, p. 119.

[25] McLane to Marcy, No. 8, Shanghai, July 27, 1854, *ibid.*, pp. 118-24.

[26] *IWSM-HF*, VIII, 18f-21b; or Earl Swisher, *China's Management of the American Barbarians* (New Haven, Conn.: Yale University, Far Eastern Publications, 1951), pp. 215-18.

[27] *McLane Correspondence*, pp. 123-24.

[28] McLane to Marcy, No. 7, Shanghai, July 7, 1854, *ibid.*, p. 112.

II

The "local problems" that the American commissioner discussed in the interview were actually Anglo-Chinese problems which originally had little to do with the Americans. These "local problems" may be divided into two categories: problems concerning the political status and civil administration of the foreign settlements in Shanghai; and problems concerning the re-establishment of the Chinese customs service in that port.

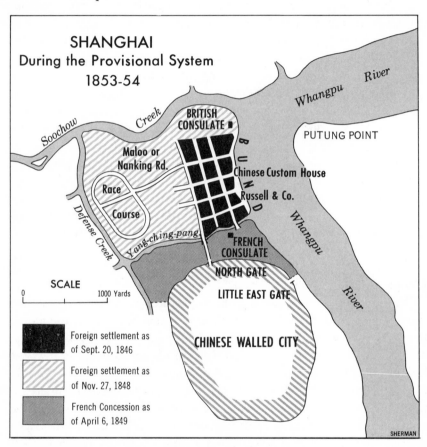

The first presented a strange and interesting question. As already mentioned, the foreign settlement was first established in 1843, when Shanghai was opened for foreign trade. With the consent of the local Chinese authorities, the first British consul at Shanghai, Major Balfour, circumscribed a large piece of land along the bank of the Huangp'u River as the area for the British settlement. Consequently a land-renting regulation covering that territory was issued by the British consul, and the Chinese government entered into an agreement with the British consul whereby all land within certain boundaries was to be leased exclusively through the agency of the British consul. When the first Americans moved to Shanghai they had to lease land for a residence through the British rather than the Chinese. The first American consul was even forbidden by the British to raise an American flag in the "British settlement." This restriction was maintained until 1848, when the regularly appointed American consul, J. Alsop Griswold, refused the British demand and raised the American flag over his consulate.[29]

Early in 1849 the French secured land from the Chinese government for a French settlement. The area lay between the English settlement and the city wall. The French arrangements with the local Chinese authorities were similar to those in the British settlement, namely, that the person desiring to lease land therein should first apply to the French consul. When a Chinese proclamation was issued giving this authority to the French, the American consul, J. Alsop Griswold, immediately lodged a protest against the Chinese *taotai* at Shanghai. After he had failed to reverse the *taotai*'s decision, Mr. John W. Davis, the American commissioner to China, took over the negotiations and presented a protest to the Imperial Commissioner Hsü Kuang-chin of the Chinese government at Canton.[30] Hsü, however, intimated that he saw no good reason to repudiate the conditions established by the grants to the English and French, and hoped the Americans would be content to have a distinct quarter set apart for them elsewhere.[31] Although Davis was dissatisfied, he did not pursue the issue again during his term in China. Thus it was left unsolved.

Despite the attitude shown toward the American protest by the Chinese, British, and French, the American residents at Shanghai refused to bow to reality. On March 16, 1852, Edward Cunningham, vice-consul of the United States at Shanghai, issued a proclamation to the American residents in the city drawing their attention to the the fact that according to the terms of the treaty, purchases of land

---

[29] See chap. 4.

[30] Davis to Seu [Hsu Kuang-chin], Macao, April 25, 1849, *DD-USNA*, 92:6. In *Marshall's Correspondence,* the word Seu was misprinted as Sen (see p. 216). It was quoted by Dennett in the same way. See Dennett, *Americans in Eastern Asia,* p. 199.

[31] Commissioner Marshall made a very brilliant review of this case in one of his official dispatches to the State Department. See Marshall to Marcy, No. 23, Shanghai, July 26, 1853, pp. 210-15.

within Shanghai or its neighborhood could be negotiated with the Chinese officers through the American consulate, without the intervention in any manner of any other foreign consul. This had since become a deadlock between the American and British consuls.[32]

During this period and until September, 1853, however, the foreign settlement was still subject to Chinese jurisdiction and under the protection of the Chinese police.[33] When the Taiping rebels were approaching Shanghai early in 1853, the foreign residents, particularly the British, began to feel that the Chinese protection was inadequate. In early April of that year, Rutherford Alcock, the British consul at Shanghai, convened a series of emergency meetings among the British subjects residing in Shanghai. They decided to organize a Committee of Cooperation and an armed Volunteer Corps to meet the oncoming crisis. Under British initiation, a public meeting of all foreign residents at Shanghai (about 250 male adults) was subsequently convened on April 12. At this time the British organizations were extended to and approved by all foreign residents at Shanghai.[34]

Probably because of the approach of the Taipings, as well as the increase of tension between Great Britain and Russia over the Turkish problem, which later developed into the Crimean War, Consul Alcock intended to enlist American support in Shanghai. He wrote to Edward Cunningham, the United States vice-consul at Shanghai, that Her Majesty's government had no desire whatsoever to assert either exclusive right or jurisdiction over the unappropriated land at Shanghai. He thereupon submitted a draft code of municipal and land regula-

---

[32] For a detailed contemporary account on the evolution of the British and American settlements at Shanghai and the Anglo-American disputes therein see *Marshall's Correspondence,* pp. 210-15. There is also a brilliant summary in Dennett, *Americans in Eastern Asia,* pp. 194-205; and in Morse, *The International Relations of the Chinese Empire* (New York: Longmans, Green and Co., 1910-18), I, 349 ff. For a general survey of the growth of the foreign concessions at Shanghai see G. Lanning and S. Couling, *The History of Shanghai* (Shanghai: Kelley and Walsh, 1921), pp. 304 ff.

[33] Commissioner McLane reported to Washington on July 27, 1854, saying: "Since the 7th September, 1853, these functions of the local authorities of China have been generally suspended, and the consuls themselves, being no longer in the presence of a civil authority that could act in behalf of the imperial government when it was proper to recognize it, practically surrendered to the naval authorities of the three treaty powers the defense of the foreign settlement." See *McLane Correspondence,* p. 123. Actually, in September, 1853, there was not a single American warship at Shanghai. The foreign settlement was then completely under British domination.

[34] See preceding chapter. These organizations were first initiated by the British subjects, who later invited other Westerners to cooperate. The Minutes of the original meetings are preserved in *British and Foreign State Papers* (London: James Ridgway and Sons, 1842-60), XLIV, 487 ff.

tions which, if accepted jointly by the consuls and the *taotai* and then approved by the home governments of the treaty powers, would have the effect of converting the grant originally made to Consul Balfour into a grant for the use of all foreigners under the joint control and supervision of the consuls and the *taotai*.[35] This draft code was subsequently submitted to Commissioner Marshall. Regardless of his hostility toward the British, the American commissioner supported this program, with minor revisions, and it was later put into practice.[36]

After the British forces took over the foreign settlement following the Triad Rebellion on September 7, 1853, the Committee of Cooperation was given the power to carry on the civil administration under British protection. They formed an autonomous British protectorate. Consequently, Chinese troops were forbidden to enter or pass through the foreign settlement. Thus, when the Chinese imperial troops besieged the walled city of Shanghai, the northern part of the city was left undefended by the rebels because it bordered the foreign settlement. This opening naturally provided an opportunity for the rebels to obtain support from the foreigners. In November, 1853, a battalion of imperial troops, three to four hundred men strong, rushed into the foreign settlement. Their object was to seize three cannons destined for the rebels from a foreign firm. British marines were called to expel the intruders, who left six or seven of their number dead. The *North China Herald* reported that only "a few foreigners received some slight flesh wounds."[37] After this incident, the imperial troops never entered the foreign settlement again, but set up a camp west of the foreign settlement near the race course. The appearance of these troops near the foreign section made many of the foreign residents feel unsafe. On April 3, 1854, a column of British marines and the Vounteer Corps consisting of four hundred American citizens and British subjects, under the command of a British captain, routed the imperial camp by a surprise attack.[38] The clash known as the "Battle of the Muddy

---

[35] Alcock to Cunningham, May 23, 1853, included in *Marshall's Correspondence*, pp. 215-22. A full text of the draft of the new "Land Regulations" is also included.

[36] For a good survey of Marshall's reaction see Dennett, *Americans in Eastern Asia*, pp. 202-3.

[37] *North China Herald*, Nov. 19, 1853; for a Chinese account see *Tung-hua hsu-lu (Hsieng-feng)*, XXIV, 6b.

[38] Concerning the clash the *NCH* (April 8, 1854) reported that action of the foreigners might have been unprecedented, violent, or illegal, but it was necessary for the salvation of a community. This clash occurred outside the foreign section. See *IWSM-HF*, VII, 19 ff. See also W. S. Wetmore, *Recollections of Life in the Far East*, quoted in Fairbank, *Trade and Diplomacy*, I, 445-46.

Flat" marked the end of Chinese jurisdiction over the "foreign settlement" at Shanghai. The legal status of the foreign section, however, was yet to be settled with the Chinese authorities.

In his interview with I-liang on June 21, 1854, therefore, McLane brought up this question and the Manchu governor-general promised a readjustment. The same topic was apparently presented by the British envoy in his meetings on June 27 and July 3 with Hsü Nai-chao, governor of Kiangsu, and Chi-erh-hang-a, Hsü's successor, who seemed also to have agreed to make some readjustments, although he dared not report them to Peking.[39] Consequently, a public meeting of foreign renters of land at Shanghai was held on July 11, 1854. In this meeting, the organization of an autonomous foreign municipality was formally proposed. The introduction to the Minutes of the said meeting stated: "The question for the meeting to decide seemed, therefore, not so much whether a municipal government was necessary, or whether there should be one, but what form it should take?" But the introduction further stated that "there was no international law that could lead its sanction." The committee, however, justified its action under the pretext that "it was based on an obvious necessity under the law of self-preservation."[40]

As a result of this meeting, a "Municipal Council" was organized, and the former Committee of Cooperation was disbanded.[41] Shortly after, a police squad was organized, civil and penal codes were issued, and a local taxation system was established. Hence the foreign settlement at Shanghai took the form of an autonomous state within the Chinese Empire, in which the Chinese government lost its jurisdiction even over its own citizens.[42] This organization of the foreign settlements, therefore, became one of the strangest institutions in the political history of modern times.[43]

The problem of the customs service was again an Anglo-Chinese dispute. After the trading season of 1853-54 was over, the British consul at Shanghai, Alcock, thought it was time to close the "Provisional

---

[39] IWSM-HF, VIII, 30-36; Costin, Great Britain and China, p. 188. In Chi-erh-hang-a's memorial to Peking, the settlements of local problems were not mentioned.

[40] McLane Correspondence, p. 130.

[41] Ibid., pp. 135, 137.

[42] Ibid., p. 123.

[43] Even more interesting was the situation of the Chinese residents in the "foreign settlements" who were under the jurisdiction of the Municipal Council and gradually became a group of isolated colonists within the boundaries of their own country. They had to pay tax, but they had no voice in the colonial administration: a strange Oriental equivalent of "taxation without representation." This unorthodox system was gradually introduced to other treaty ports.

System." Consequently, the Chinese *taotai* was allowed to establish a customhouse on the northern bank of Suchow Creek on February 9, 1854; on the same day, the so-called Provisional System ceased functioning. The custom duties in the form of "promissory notes" which the British consulate had collected for the Chinese government from September 7, 1853, to February 6, 1854, were not handed over to the Chinese, but later returned instead to the British merchants.[44]

Even after the re-establishment of the customhouse at Shanghai, however, the Chinese were still unable to collect custom duties, for they lacked the coercive power to carry on the collection. Ships continued sailing from the harbor, free. Failing to make the customhouse at Shanghai work, the Chinese local authorities tried all other means of customs collection, such as collecting export duties in the inland customhouses, or preventing Chinese products, particularly tea and silk, from coming to Shanghai.[45] This Chinese effort as well as the increase of smuggling, which could jeopardize the foreign trade at Shanghai, alarmed the honest merchants. Two days after McLane's arrival at Shanghai, British Consul Alcock drafted a program for the so-called Inspectorate System to substitute for the old service at Shanghai.[46] This British proposal was apparently accepted by the American commissioner. Thus in the I-liang–McLane interview at K'un-shan and the Sino-British conferences at Shanghai, Alcock's proposal was brought up, and the Chinese authorities promised to reconstruct the customs service as proposed by the Western envoys. The Chinese *taotai* was given full power to carry out the plan.

Consequently, on June 29, 1854, an international conference for the readjustment of the Chinese customs service was held at Shanghai. Participants included Rutherford Alcock, the British consul at Shanghai, B. Edan, the French consul *ad interim*, R. C. Murphy, the newly appointed full-time service consul from the United States who had arrived in Shanghai in April, and Wu Chien-chang, the Chinese *taotai* at Shanghai.[47]

---

[44] Clarendon to Bowring, January 24, 1855, *F.O.*, 17/224; Costin, *Great Britain and China*, p. 163.

[45] *IWSM-HF*, VII, 12a. During this period the import trade almost ceased. The duties of a small quantity of imported goods were paid by promissory notes.

[46] Alcock's proposal was brought out on May 1, 1854. A detailed program for the organization of the Inspectorate System was submitted by Alcock to the British minister on June 15, a week before McLane's interview with I-liang at K'un-shan. For the original program see Bowring's dispatch No. 77, July 7, 1854, *F.O.*, 97/100, quoted in Fairbank, *Trade and Diplomacy*, I, 456.

[47] *McLane Correspondence*, pp. 154 ff.

Through this conference, the new system proposed by the British for the operation of the Chinese custom service was adopted. Under the new system—the so-called Inspectorate System—several foreigners were to be selected and nominated by the respective consuls of the three Western powers. They were to be appointed by the *taotai* to serve in the Chinese customhouse, "under his order as *inspectors of customs,* with a mixed establishment of Chinese and foreign subordinates, to consist of linguists, writers and tide-waiters, together with a revenue cutter well manned by foreign sailors, and under the command of a trustworthy and intelligent master."[48] The whole expense of the establishment was to be paid out of the proceeds of the revenue. Each of the three countries was to select and nominate one inspector; these three inspectors were to form a "Board of Inspectors," who would select the various subordinates, foreign and Chinese. If any dispute occurred in the service, a decision would be reached by majority vote. Each inspector had one vote, but the *taotai* had two.[49]

The inspectors, however, were not to be liable to dismissal or removal by the Chinese government unless a total change of system was effected with the concurrence of the consuls. The administration of this new system formally began on July 12, 1854. Three foreigners, M. Smith from France, Thomas Francis Wade from England, and Lewis Carr from the United States, were appointed inspectors.[50] From then on the Chinese gradually lost the right to manage their own customs service. This peculiar system at Shanghai was later extended to other trading ports and led to the establishment of the Chinese Maritime Customs Service which controlled the Chinese customs service for nearly a century.

It is worth noting that negotiations for solving the so-called local

---

[48] The minutes of the customs conference have been preserved in *McLane Correspondence,* pp. 152-54, and in the *North China Herald,* July 8, 1854.

[49] For a survey of the operation of this system consult Fairbank, "The Creation of the Foreign Inspectorate of Customs at Shanghai," *Chinese Social and Political Science Review,* XIX (January, 1963), 470-514; XX (April, 1936), 42-100.

[50] The British inspector, Wade, was later replaced by Horatio Nelson Lay, who became the first inspector general. For general reference see Stanley F. Wright, *Hart and the Chinese Customs* (Belfast: Wm. Mullan and Son, 1950), pp. 111 ff. One source refers to Lewis Carr as having been connected with the United States legation in China. The story of his life and work is not clear. See Eldon Griffin, *Clippers and Consuls, American Consular and Commercial Relations with Eastern Asia, 1845-1860* (Ann Arbor, Mich.: Edwards Brothers, 1938), p. 429. Lewis Carr had accompanied Commissioner McLane to Nanking in May, 1854, and participated in many interviews with the rebel agents. He later also wrote a lengthy report on the Nanking expedition. McLane to Marcy, No. 6, Shanghai, June 14, 1854, and "Trip of the 'Susquehanna' to Nanking and Wu-hu," *McLane Correspondence,* pp. 47-55, 64-76.

problems had been carried out very smoothly. All the participating parties had been satisfied. As the primary designer, the British had directed these arrangements, along with their commercial interests in China, and had later supervised the Chinese customs service for nearly a century. The Chinese were equally satisfied. Although these arrangements had done great harm to Chinese sovereignty, the Chinese authorities were not aware of it. To Governor-General I-liang and Governor Chi-erh-hang-a, these arrangements were a "local" settlement of long-disputed problems in Shanghai. The new arrangements were under their discretionary power and they did not bother even to report them to the Imperial Court at Peking. The Court did not know that the Chinese customs service had been placed under the joint control of the Chinese and foreigners. Wu Chien-chang, the *taotai* and superintendent of customs at Shanghai, seemed to have been well satisfied with the new arrangements, which had settled the problems facing him. Under the new system the Americans soon paid him over 40,000 taels of back duties, which was a move he could hardly have imagined before. Since the foreign settlement at Shanghai now took care of itself, it had definitely lightened the responsibilities of the local Chinese government.[51]

The Americans were satisfied in a different way. The foreign settlement previously had been dominated by the British. Under the new system, the American commissioner, who had been supervising the negotiations with close attention, was given new importance in both the municipal government and the new inspectorate system. In a report to the State Department, Commissioner McLane wrote proudly:[52]

You will be gratified to find that the arrangements are of a very comprehensive character, and have been adopted with the full cooperation and assent of the imperial authorities, and without any dissent on the part of the insurgents, who are still in possession of the city. But what is of paramount importance, these arrangements are of a character that makes it impossible that any one nation, whether Great Britain or Russia, should exercise any jurisdiction whatever at this port without the concurrence of the authorities of the United States; and thus the apprehension that some have entertained of a design on the part of England to assume exclusive dominion or ascendancy here is effectually disposed of.

In a subsequent report, McLane stated:[53]

---

[51] *IWSM:HF*, VIII, 34a; Swisher, *China's Management*, p. 224.
[52] McLane to Marcy, No. 7, Shanghai, July 7, 1854, *McLane Correspondence*, p. 113.
[53] *Ibid.*, No. 8, Shanghai, July 27, 1854, p. 124.

The land regulations signed by the ministers of the three treaty powers, renounce the pretensions heretofore set up by Great Britain and France to the exclusive enjoyment of certain concessions made to them respectively by the local authorities of China, and all foreigners under the jurisdiction of their respective consuls enjoy the same privileges; the concurrent and joint action of the consuls and local authorities of China having established a fundamental basis on which the rights and privileges of all are firmly planted.

McLane's expectations of equal commercial rights for all Western powers trading in China, however, soon proved to be merely wishful thinking. Shortly after, the Chinese customs service fell completely under the control of the British. This led Commissioner Ward to complain that the Chinese customs service was "under the control of an Englishman," and that the regulations he issued were "odious and oppressive to all merchants."[54]

---

[54] See chap. 17, sec. 3.

11

THE PEI-HO EXPEDITIONS—

AN IMPERIAL GAME

I

ALTHOUGH the "local problems" at Shanghai were gradually settled, the American and British envoys were far from satisfied. On the contrary, they were seriously pondering another important problem: the extension of treaty privileges. Soon after his interview with I-liang on June 21, McLane contacted the British minister. The two held constant consultations. ". . . we entered into a cordial cooperation," McLane reported to Washington, "as to the general and local matters which had been in discussion."[1] Since their demand for the extension of treaty privileges was completely ignored by the Chinese authorities, they decided to make a joint expedition to Tientsin at the mouth of the Pei-ho in order to approach the central authority at Peking directly.[2]

On July 25, 1854, the two envoys held a joint interview with Chi-erh-hang-a, the newly appointed Manchu governor of Kiangsu, and notified him of the projected Anglo-American expedition to the Pei-ho. This decision seems to have been initiated by the British. In the meeting between McLane and I-liang at K'un-shan on June 21, McLane had said that he would not go to Tientsin. When I-liang was informed about the new American decision, he reported to Peking: "How is it that within barely twenty days he talks about accompanying the English chief to Tientsin? Not only is this contrary to his previous statement; it is also a treaty violation."[3]

---

[1] McLane to Marcy, No. 8, Shanghai, July 27, 1854, *McLane Correspondence*, pp. 212-22.

[2] *Ibid.;* W. C. Costin, *Great Britain and China 1833-1860* (Oxford: The Clarendon Press, 1937), p. 188.

[3] *Ibid.; IWSM-HF*, VIII, 27. English translation quoted from Earl Swisher, *China's Management of the American Barbarians, A Study of Sino-American Relations, 1841-1861, with Documents* (New Haven: Yale University Far Eastern Publications, 1951), p. 220.

In dealing with this new action of the foreign envoys, Chi-erh-hang-a on the one hand tried to persuade the envoys to abandon their projected trip to Tientsin, while on the other hand he advised the "Son-of-Heaven" to appoint an Imperial Commissioner for negotiation with them at Shanghai. In a lengthy memorial to the Court, the Manchu Governor said that the American Commissioner insisted on the promise of treaty revision after twelve years, and desired to establish ports along the Yangtze up to Hankow. Since the Chinese government was unable to stop him, it would be better to take advantage of the present circumstances to "perfect a plan" for a long range settlement. "Besides," he emphasized, "the English and American barbarians being outwardly friendly and inwardly jealous, we can temporarily use the Americans to oppose the English." In this memorial, Chi-erh-hang-a also reminded Peking that in case of a sudden rupture of diplomatic relations, the British and Americans would take advantage of the Chinese civil war and force their way into the Yangtze. It would certainly create "an additional sorrow."[4]

Despite the Governor's advice, the two ministers decided to launch a joint expedition to Tientsin. To prepare for the expedition, McLane left Shanghai for South China at the end of July. After visiting both Foochow and Amoy, he reached Hong Kong on August 10. Two days later he proceeded to Canton to hold a conference with Commodore M. C. Perry, the commanding officer of the United States Navy in the East, after which he returned to Hong Kong. McLane's departure from Shanghai for a trip south was followed by that of Sir John Bowring, who on August 19 arrived at Hong Kong, where he and McLane were joined by the French minister.[5]

In the meantime, a new instruction issued by the State Department ordering McLane to aid the British treaty revision movement "in a proper way" to get liberal commercial concessions from the Chinese, had also reached Hong Kong.[6] This timely instruction from the State Department, which McLane said he had "fully anticipated," gave fresh impetus to his cooperative policy with the British. With the full

---

[4] *IWSM-HF,* VIII, 35a. The memorial submitted by Chi-erh-hang-a was received by the Imperial Court on August 30, 1854. A full English translation is included in Swisher, *China's Management,* pp. 223-26.

[5] *McLane Correspondence,* p. 169.

[6] Marcy to McLane, No. 7, Washington, D.C., May 8, 1854, *DI-USNA,* 7:38, p. 99. This directive was written under the influence of R. B. Forbes, a leading merchant of Boston. At the request of Secretary of State Marcy, Forbes expressed his opinion on the China policy of the United States, which was enclosed in this directive and sent to McLane.

support of the American and French ministers, the British envoy began to demand a revision of the Treaty of Nanking, which had been signed twelve years earlier, stating that according to the Treaty of Wanghia, it was now time for the British to revise their treaty with China.[7] Completely ignoring the local Chinese authorities, the three envoys decided to undertake a united expedition to Tientsin. "In a few days," wrote McLane to the Secretary of State on September 10, 1854, "we will proceed to Shanghai, and thence to the mouth of the Pei-ho, from which point it is proposed to communicate directly with the minister of state or the Emperor himself."[8] The British and French ministers left Hong Kong on September 16; McLane followed three days later.

At the end of the month the three ministers held a conference at Shanghai and respectively notified the Chinese authorities of their intention to go north. The French minister, however, was suddenly handicapped because the French frigate *Jeanne d'Arc*, on entering the port of Shanghai, had grounded on the bar at the mouth of the Yangtze River. Using this accident as a pretext, the French minister suddenly reversed his decision, but he sent an aide to accompany the Anglo-American team.[9]

The five ships of the expedition, with several hundred sailors and marines on board, reached the mouth of Pei-ho on October 16, 1854. Almost immediately after their ships dropped anchors, Dr. Peter Parker, on behalf of McLane, and Dr. W. H. Medhurst, Chinese secretary of the British legation, on behalf of Bowring, were sent ashore to meet the Chinese officers who had been notified of their coming by the Chinese authorities at Shanghai. On the shore at Ta-ku (on the northern coast of the mouth of the Pei-ho) they were received by Brigadier General Shuang-jui of the Tientsin garrison, and Wen-ch'ien, Ch'ang-lu salt controller.[10]

The Ta-ku negotiation between the Chinese and the two ministers was dramatic. Before the joint expedition reached Pei-ho, the Court

---

[7] *McLane Correspondence*, p. 169. For general reference see Hosea Ballou Morse, *The International Relations of the Chinese Empire* (New York: Longmans, Green and Co., 1910), I, 412 ff.; Costin, *Great Britain and China*, pp. 186 ff.; Tyler Dennett, *Americans in Eastern Asia* (New York: The Macmillan Co., 1922), pp. 238 ff.

[8] *McLane Correspondence*, pp. 199-200.

[9] Morse, *The International Relations of the Chinese Empire*, p. 191.

[10] For a detailed account of these interviews see *McLane Correspondence*, pp. 295-348. For the Chinese side of the story see *IWSM-HF*, IX; for the initial interviews see the memorial submitted by Wen-ch'ien and Shuang-jui (10a-11b), or Swisher, *China's Management*, pp. 233-37.

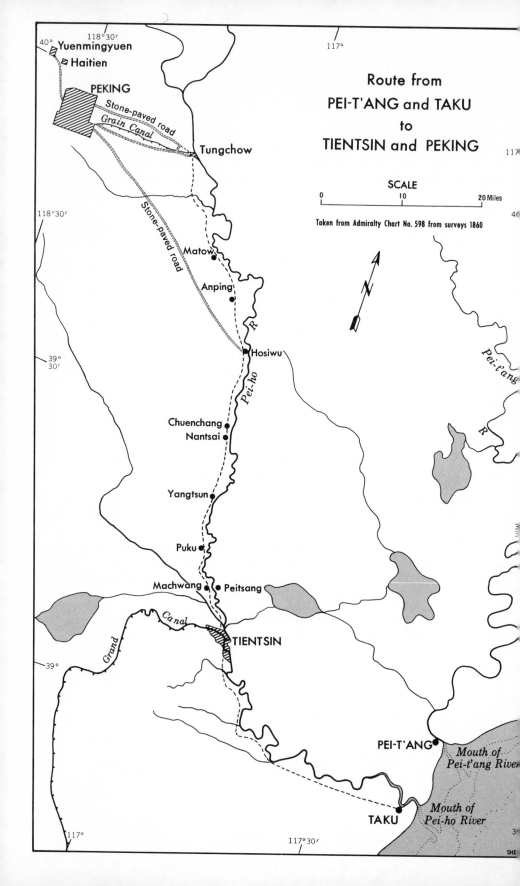

Route from
PEI-T'ANG and TAKU
to
TIENTSIN and PEKING

SCALE

0   10   20 Miles

Taken from Admiralty Chart No. 598 from surveys 1860

118°30'

40° Yuenmingyuen
Haitien

PEKING

Stone-paved road
Grain Canal

Tungchow

117°

118°30'

Stone-paved road

Matow

Anping

Pei-ho R.

39°
30'

Hosiwu

Chuenchang

Nantsai

Yangtsun

Puku

Machwang   Peitsang

Canal

Grand

TIENTSIN

39°

117°

Pei-t'ang R.

PEI-T'ANG

Mouth of
Pei-t'ang River

TAKU

Mouth of
Pei-ho River

117°30'

SHE

at Peking was already on the alert. This time, contrary to all precedents, the Chinese stage was set directly by the young Emperor himself. In a series of edicts, the Emperor ordered the Chinese local authorities in the Tientsin area to prepare to meet the "barbarians." From the time prior to the arrival of the foreign vessels at the mouth of the Pei-ho until their departure, the Court at Peking kept in daily contact with the local authorities at Tientsin. It was informed with remarkable precision as to what was going on in that area.[11] Every minor decision was made by the Emperor himself; each mandarin there appeared no more than a puppet whose every gesture was subject to the pulling of a string from behind the scene.

When the foreign envoys reached Pei-ho, Kuei-liang, the governor-general of Chih-li province, in which Tientsin was located, considered it his duty to deal with the "barbarians" and offered to go to Tientsin to meet them. But he was immediately ordered to stay back. Instead, Ch'ung-lun, former Ch'ang-lu salt controller, was appointed to this duty. When Kuei-liang again offered to go, the Emperor became irritated. In a Vermilion Endorsement, he noted:[12]

You do not need to be so disturbed. When Ch'ung-lun arrives he will manage suitably as a matter of course. You must not allow it to leak out whether or not you are going to leave the provincial capital [Pao-ting]. If you do leave the capital and still do not have an interview with the barbarian chiefs, it is better not to let them know you are in Tientsin.

When the foreign vessels reached the mouth of the Pei-ho, Ch'ung-lun was ordered by the Emperor to proceed to Ta-ku to meet the foreign envoys as a commissioner directly appointed by the Emperor. Actually he held a very inferior position in the Ch'ing officialdom; he did not have the title of an Imperial Commissioner, for which he was not qualified.[13] After Ch'ung-lun reached Tientsin, a formal interview between the two ministers and himself took place at noon on November 3, 1854, in a tent erected particularly for that purpose on the shore in front of the Haikow fort. In this protracted interview, the two ministers each submitted a précis to the "high" Chinese

---

[11] From October 15, 1854, the day before the arrival of the envoys at the Pei-ho, to December 8, the day they left, scarcely a day passed without an edict to or memorial from Tientsin. See *IWSM-HF*, IX, *passim*. For an English translation of most of the important edicts and memorials see Swisher, *China's Management*, pp. 231-85.

[12] Swisher, *China's Management*, p. 255; *IWSM-HF*, IX, 28b-29a.

[13] For a brief biographic sketch of Ch'ung-lun see Arthur William Hummel, *Eminent Chinese of the Ch'ing Period (1644-1912)* (Washington, D.C.: Government Printing Office), I, 379; or Swisher, *China's Management*, p. 715.

negotiator. The British précis contained eighteen items and the American twelve. The most important demands of both nations were:[14] the free navigation of the Yangtze River, the right to trade and reside in any part of China, the right to fish in the Chinese coastal waters, gold payment of custom duties, and permission for foreign ministers to reside at the capital.

During this tiring and unpleasant meeting, Ch'ung-lun stated that he had not "the slightest full powers" as demanded by the foreign ministers.[15] He promised, however, that he would examine the papers submitted by the honorable foreign commissioners, and then he would point out what facts therein he could present in a memorial, and what he could not. "I must look out for the interest of the emperor," said Ch'ung-lun; "that which is exclusively advantageous to the foreigners cannot be granted. For example, should you wish to come and work our mines, this could not be granted." By the end of the meeting, Ch'ung-lun said that he was aware of the lateness of the season, the approach of cold weather, and the inconvenience of delay. "I will memorialize the throne for the power to do whatever is reasonable," he remarked voluntarily, "and be as expeditious as possible."[16] The two ministers then asked how soon they could get an answer. Ch'ung-lun said that the proposals would have to be deliberated in detail and an answer would be returned to them on November 8. "The barbarians immediately agreed," Ch'ung-lun reported to the Emperor, "and, leading the barbarians who came with them, boarded the small boats, left the harbor, and returned to their ships."[17] Returning to their ships, the two envoys waited five days for a reply from Peking.

On the Chinese side, the two documents submitted by the foreign envoys were copied in full and sent to Peking just as the Emperor had ordered. Consequently, an imperial edict was promptly issued on November 5. It rejected all the major demands submitted by the two ministers. However, there were three minor points that the Emperor

---

[14] For the Chinese versions of these two documents see *IWSM-HF*, IX, 4-47; for the English draft of the American document and the translation of the Chinese version see *McLane Correspondence*, pp. 343-46, and Swisher, *China's Management*, pp. 269-73.

[15] *McLane Correspondence*, p. 341.

[16] *Ibid.*, p. 342.

[17] The last part of the conversation was not included in the minutes preserved by the American legation, but it was reported in detail to Peking by Ch'ung-lun, see *IWSM-HF*, IX, 34 ff; for English translations of some essential parts of the documents see Swisher, *China's Management*, p. 267.

promised to take up for further adjudication by local officials at the Five Ports. These were: foreigners who suffered in controversies with the Chinese would be allowed to ascertain whether the local authorities had judged unjustly; the back duties requested from the foreign merchants might be reduced; and the Chinese government might consider reducing the duty on tea in Canton.[18] Ch'ung-lun was instructed to present this reply to the two envoys as if it were his own idea.

On November 8, Ch'ung-lun, therefore, sent a lengthy reply to the two ministers, together with the two original précis. In this reply, Ch'ung-lun rejected all the foreign demands and promised only "three points" for future adjudication in the Five Ports, precisely in accord with the imperial edict. Since there were no records at Tientsin that he could examine in reference to these three points, Ch'ung-lun, ostensibly on his own initiative, advised the envoys to return to Canton and to wait. If the foreign ministers neglected his advise, he would not, he warned the two ministers, meet them again in a personal interview.[19]

To this dispatch, both the American and the British ministers protested vigorously. In the American dispatch, McLane complained: "This communication affords the undersigned no evidence whatever that the views of the government of the United States, as submitted in writing to your excellency by the undersigned, have been or will be communicated to his Imperial Majesty."[20] Actually the "three minor points," which the two ministers thought had been decided by Ch'ung-lun, were drafted on the Emperor's desk by the vermilion brush. For years the foreign ministers had complained that they had no way to communicate directly with the authority at Peking. But this time they were unaware of the fact that they were bargaining with the Emperor personally, even if ostensibly through his agents. Since winter was approaching and ice would soon render the harbor of Tientsin unnavigable, the two envoys, after sending their protest to Ch'ung-lun, had no choice but to return to Shanghai.[21]

---

[18] *IWSM-HF*, IX, 41; Swisher, *China's Management*, pp. 267-69. Between September 7, 1853, and July 12, 1854, the British merchants had owed the Chinese custom duties (on promissory notes) of about tls. 1,000,000 (about £400,000), the Americans about tls. 350,000; the British notes were never paid; the Americans paid about one-tenth of the total amount. See Fairbank, *Trade and Diplomacy on the China Coast* (Cambridge, Mass.: Harvard University Press, 1953), I, 460-61.

[19] *McLane Correspondence*, pp. 346-48.

[20] McLane to Tsung-lung [Ch'ung-lun], on board the *Powhatan*, November 8, 1854, *ibid.*, p. 348.

[21] Costin, *Great Britain and China*, p. 194; *McLane Correspondence*, pp. 349 ff.

The joint expedition to Pei-ho was an unprecedented peak of Anglo-American cooperation in intercourse with China, but it produced no results. On the contrary, the failure of the Anglo-American expedition to Pei-ho unexpectedly encouraged the stubborn and ignorant mandarins (such as Yeh Ming-ch'en) and their young militant master, Emperor Hsien-feng, to continue their nonintercourse policy, and at the same time it degraded the more enlightened Chinese diplomats, such as I-liang and Chi-erh-hang-a.

It was very natural that when the envoys at last departed from Pei-ho, the Emperor considered it a personal victory. In an edict issued on November 8 in reply to the memorial submitted by Chi-erh-hang-a suggesting the appointment of an Imperial Commissioner to settle the demands, the Emperor wrote in a rather proud and sarcastic tone and blamed the governor for being unable to stop the Western envoys from going north. He boasted of his "victory" in Tientsin and declared:[22]

On this occasion have not Ch'ung-lun, Wen-ch'ien and others on the one hand flung back the barbarian document and on the other hand managed to memorialize it? But their reasoned explanations and conflicts were all done as on their own initiative, making the barbarians realize that inordinate requests cannot be presented with impunity. And even the above-mentioned three items were not immediately accepted. Besides, ordering them back to Kwangtung or Shanghai to await settlement is the way to effect revision. What need is there to appoint Imperial Commissioners?

The Emperor obviously believed that the "barbarian" envoys were outmaneuvered by him and that they had withdrawn from Tientsin simply because the three granted points could only be adjudicated through negotiation at the place of business. Subsequently, in a series of edicts, he ordered I-liang and Chi-erh-hang-a to negotiate with the "barbarians" in accord with these three points. Thus the Pei-ho expedition produced results contrary to what the foreign ministers had expected.

II

Disappointed and humiliated at the unsuccessful expedition to Pei-ho, the two ministers reached Shanghai by the middle of November. In Shanghai, they held another interview with the Manchu Governor, Chi-erh-hang-a, who was anxiously seeking to collect the "back duties" from the foreign merchants in order to pursue his military campaign against the rebels in the city of Shanghai. At the same time,

---

[22] Swisher, *China's Management,* p. 276; *IWSM-HF,* IX, 50a.

the Governor was also seeking the cooperation of the foreigners to build a wall cutting off the roads that connected the foreign settlement with the entrances of the walled city, which was held by the rebels. The wall would prevent the rebels from taking shelter in the foreign settlement.[23] This conference was held at the British consulate at 4:00 P.M., November 18, 1854.[24] In this meeting, Chi-erh-hang-a informed the two ministers that Ch'ung-lun held a much inferior position than himself. "I could have managed the business better," said the Governor rather proudly. "I wish to take your excellency up at this point," said McLane. "Both Eleang [I-liang] and your excellency wished to act, but inasmuch as you had no power, therefore, I went to Teen-tsin." "Remember," said Chi-erh-hang-a, "that at my camp on the 9th of October, I offered to memorialize in behalf of your government, but you would not wait, and last July I memorialized to obtain the imperial will, and did it although it might cost me my button."[25]

At that very moment, however, the edict reprimanding Chi-erh-hang-a for his failure to stop the envoys from going north as well as for his undesirable suggestion of appointing an Imperial Commissioner to negotiate with the foreigners was on its way to Shanghai.[26] Chi-erh-hang-a's memorial presenting such suggestions had reached the Court by August 30, and had then been endorsed by the imperial hand only as *Chih-tao-la,* i.e., "noted."[27] He was not reprimanded until after the conclusion of the Ta-ku negotiation and the Emperor's diplomatic "victory."[28]

Two days after this Shanghai conference, McLane held another interview with the Governor, obviously at the request of the latter. In this meeting McLane further complained that the "three points" promised by Ch'ung-lun at Ta-ku were "too unimportant." Chi replied with a smile: "It is of no consequence; [viz., the implication that he had been overreached by the foreign ministers] give me copies of all your correspondence." McLane then handed to him a three-piece document: a list of grievances that the Americans wanted re-

---

[23] *IWSM-HF,* X, 3-7; Swisher, *China's Management,* p. 289.

[24] A detailed *Minutes* for this conference was preserved in *McLane Correspondence,* pp. 409-10.

[25] *Ibid.,* p. 409. The rank of a Ch'ing official was shown by the color of the button on his official hat. Thus the loss of the button meant the loss of his official position.

[26] *IWSM-HF,* IX, 49-50; Swisher, *China's Management,* pp. 275-76.

[27] *IWSM-HF,* VIII, 36a; Swisher, p. 226.

[28] The edict that reprimanded Chi was issued on November 8, 1854, *ibid.,* IX, 49b-50a; Swisher, pp. 275-76.

dressed; a draft of proposed modifications of the treaty; and his correspondence with Ch'ung-lun.[29] After further discussion of the local problems, Chi-erh-hang-a said: "If all foreign officers were like you and Dr. Parker, and all Chinese like me, there never would be any difficulty." Thus ended an amiable interview.

In this conference, however, Chi-erh-hang-a's main purpose was not to discuss foreign demands with the American commissioner. He had previously been disregarded by the foreigners, who insisted on going north. The Governor obviously had no intention now to renew his previous promise. He was seeking American cooperation to build a wall to cut off the rebels from the foreign settlement in Shanghai. As soon as the conference was over, he addressed a memorandum to McLane stating that the conditions presented by the foreign ministers were "difficult in ten thousand ways to condescend to grant."[30]

Obviously thinking that negotiation for a new treaty was hopeless, Commissioner McLane sent a long dispatch on November 19, 1854, to the State Department. "As far as the revision of the British treaty is concerned," he said, "the prospect of such a result, by any means now at the command of the British minister, is absolutely hopeless." In these circumstances, he asked the authorities at Washington what next step he should take. To him, there were three alternatives: to maintain the neutrality he now professed between the imperial government and the insurgent forces and to await the restoration of order and tranquillity; to enter upon "a new line of policy" by a positive demonstration of the power of Western nations to enforce existing rights and, by extending them, to obtain their security in the future by commanding the respect and obedience of both parties; to revise the American policy of neutrality in response to the desire of the imperial government for the aid and assistance of Western nations in suppressing the revolution.[31]

McLane preferred the second choice. He recommended that the President address a letter to the Emperor of China requesting treaty revision. This letter should be confided to the commissioner of the United States in China, for delivery to his Imperial Majesty, and should be supported by the presence of the United States naval forces in the China seas "precisely as the letter of the President was delivered

---

[29] *McLane Correspondence*, p. 411.

[30] *Ibid.*, p. 413.

[31] McLane to Marcy, No. 20, Shanghai, November 19, 1854, *McLane Correspondence*, pp. 285-93. In the spring of 1853, the Chinese local authorities at Kiangsu had appealed to foreign consuls at Shanghai for military assistance. See chap. 9.

to the Emperor of Japan."[32] Should the Emperor of China, when thus addressed by the President, refuse to enter upon negotiations for the adjustment of grievances, decline all propositions, and persist in a refusal to provide for the full enjoyment of the rights and privileges of commerce, he proposed that the United States should adopt some "measures more positive than a simple demonstration of naval power." Then he suggested a program of *"quasi* hostility."[33]

. . . I would recommend in such a contingency, that the *Peiho* and the *Yang-tsze-kiang* as well as the river *Min* and the *Whampoa* river be placed under blockade by the united forces of the three treaty powers—Great Britain, France, and the United States—and so held until the commercial privileges of buying from and selling to all persons in China, without limitation or restraint, is [are] respected, and all the other treaty stipulations recognized and enforced, where the authority of the imperial government is paramount.

McLane, in making these suggestions, said that he was much influenced by the conviction—derived from his own personal experience and observation—that much time would elapse before the revolutionary Taiping movements in progress in different parts of China would consolidate political power or form a political organization that the Western powers would recognize. He was of the opinion that new commercial relations as satisfactory as those maintained with the Manchu government could not be effected. In adopting these measures of *"quasi* hostility," the cooperation that had been "cordially and promptly executed" by the three treaty powers must be maintained. Moreover, the "protectorate" created by the presence of the naval forces of the three powers in Shanghai and Canton must be continued.[34] Furthermore, a more perfect cooperation between the American commissioner and the United States navy commanders in the Chinese waters should be established through orders from the State and Navy Departments in Washington.

McLane's proposal was impractical during this period. The Crimean War was still in progress; it handicapped both the British and French diplomatic activities in the Far East. In the United States, the Kansas-Nebraska issue continued to be a vital question, and the problems aroused by so-called squatter sovereignty had split the country. The Far East was still too far away to attract much attention

---

[32] *Ibid.,* p. 288.
[33] *Ibid.,* pp. 290-91.
[34] *Ibid.*

on Capitol Hill, and the ambitious program proposed by McLane was more than the federal government could accept at the time. Moreover, McLane's dispatch of November 19, 1854, did not reach Washington until February, 1855. It was promptly rejected by Secretary of State Marcy. In a reply to McLane issued on February 26, 1855, Marcy said that he had submitted McLane's dispatch to President Pierce. Then the Secretary continued:[35]

I think, however, I can anticipate that he will have serious objections to uniting with Great Britain and France in what you call the aggressive policy, that is the bringing together a united naval force of the three powers in order to obtain the revision of the Treaties with China, securing larger commercial privileges by intimidation, or possibly by force. The powers, with which we should cooperate in that case, not to call them allies, would probably have less reluctance to that mode of negotiation than this Government. Such an association would not at all suit the present feelings of this country.

McLane did not really have any intention of carrying out this program himself. Within a week after sending his dispatch, suffering from poor health and intending to resign, he decided to leave Shanghai on November 26, 1854, for Hong Kong, where he would take a ship for Europe and from there return home.[36]

To see him off, the Manchu governor, Chi-erh-hang-a, went aboard the U.S.S. *Powhatan* at 11:00 A.M., November 26, 1854, three hours before her scheduled departure. The Governor and the Commissioner held a final brief meeting. "Now, as my parting words, I say to you," remarked McLane, "if something is not done our relations will become bad—our amity be disturbed. I believe but for the officers of both governments there might have been a state of things that might have led to a war; but we have exerted ourselves to prevent it." "If the Emperor does not listen and appoint a commissioner to adjust the foreign relations," further warned McLane, "so sure as there is a God in the heavens, amity cannot be preserved." The Governor bowed, and the Commissioner ordered the ship to sail.[37]

---

[35] Marcy to McLane, No. 14, Washington, D.C., February 26, 1855, *DI-USNA*, 77:38, p. 105.

[36] McLane left Hong Kong for France by the end of 1854. On April 29, 1855, he sent his resignation to Washington, while he was visiting Paris. See McLane to Marcy, No. 28, Paris, April 29, 1855, *McLane Correspondence*, p. 490.

[37] *Ibid.*, p. 417.

12

PARKER'S TREATY-REVISION EFFORT

AND THE "ARROW WAR"

I

AFTER Commissioner McLane's departure from China, Dr. Peter Parker was, for the sixth time, appointed chargé d'affaires ad interim.[1] In this official capacity, Parker began to communicate with the British and French envoys. Thus the "cordial cooperation" among the three powers in China promoted by McLane was continued. On March 13, 1855, when Canton was again endangered by a new rebellion, the envoys of the three treaty powers, on the initiative of Sir John Bowring, held a conference at Hong Kong and the cooperation was further consolidated.[2]

On May 10, Parker also left China for home on the grounds of a "precarious state" of health. He signed all the archives of the legation over to Robert S. Sturgis, United States vice-consul at Canton, and requested Commodore Joel Abbot, commanding officer of the United States naval forces in the Chinese seas, to meet any emergencies that might arise.[3] While Parker was on his way home, McLane's resignation, submitted from Paris, was formally accepted by President Pierce, who intended to appoint Parker to the position. For the position vacated by Parker, Dr. Samuel Wells Williams was appointed.[4]

Soon after his arrival in the United States, Dr. Parker was summoned to Washington, where on September 5, President Pierce formally appointed him commissioner to China.[5] Parker was a capable and energetic man. He was the first United States diplomat to the Far East who was trained in the field; he could speak the Cantonese dia-

---

[1] McLane to Parker, Canton, December 9, 1854, *McLane Correspondence*, p. 498.

[2] Peter Parker to W. L. Marcy, No. 3, Canton, March 13, 1855, *ibid.*, p. 471.

[3] Parker to Marcy, No. 6, Canton, May 4, 1855, *ibid.*, p. 609.

[4] Marcy to S. Wells Williams, Washington, D.C., June 28, 1855, *DI-USNA*, 77:38, pp. 113-14.

[5] Marcy to Parker, No. 1, Washington, D.C., September 5, 1855, *ibid.*, pp. 117-19.

lect and read Chinese. He understood the mandarin political situation in China and knew how to deal with it more effectively than any of his fellow countrymen. Despite all these advantages, however, Parker was by no means a suitable man for this post. First of all, when he had been an active missionary, he had become prejudiced by his profession, whose interests in some respects paralleled the British interests. Moreover, as a young graduate from Yale he had been sent to China, where he stayed for more than twenty years. He learned many political tactics in dealing with the politicians of that country, but he was ignorant of the actual interests of the country he was to represent. Nor did he possess adequate knowledge of international affairs among the European powers. Ever since the Opium War, farsighted American diplomats had realized the significance of the territorial integrity of China—a concept that later formed the basic principle of the "Open Door" doctrine. In this respect, however, Parker was the exception among American diplomats in the Far East.

He was without doubt an astute politician,[6] but he was a man lacking democratic idealism, a United States tradition that was admired throughout the world. Regardless of Parker's shortcomings, he was appointed at a period when the time was ripe, according to Article 34 of the Wanghia Treaty, for a treaty revision. And in addition to the ordinary post of commissioner, he was also appointed plenipotentiary to China, entrusted with power to revise the existing treaty in July, 1856.

To guide Parker on this important mission, Secretary Marcy wrote to him:[7]

The two provisions in the revised treaty which you will regard as important are the residence of the diplomatic representative of the United States at Peking, the seat of the Imperial Court, the unlimited extension of our trade, wherever, within the dominions of China, commerce may be found, and restrictions to the personal liberty of our citizens should be removed.

---

[6] Parker's shrewdness is indicated in a statement he made in September, 1855. Before leaving Washington for his new position in China, Parker tried to please the southern politicians and New England cotton manufacturers by addressing a dispatch to the State Department saying that he would use his "best endeavors" to procure the introduction of cotton, "whether the raw material or in fabrics, free of any duty," in China. This was a very attractive announcement during the period when cotton was "king." Parker knew, however, better than any of his countrymen that this privilege was impossible for him to obtain. And as a matter of fact, he never mentioned it again. For the aforesaid statement see Parker to Marcy, No. 2, Washington, D.C., September 20, 1855, *Parker Correspondence,* p. 612.

[7] Marcy to Parker, No. 2, Washington, D.C., September 27, 1855, *DI-USNA,* 77:38, p. 122.

In addition to these major points for treaty revision, other miscellaneous arrangements were to be added, such as some readjustment of the system of customs and duties, and the acceptance of American coins as currency in Chinese trade. "The President . . . entertains the hope," wrote Marcy, "that, from your long residence in China, your familiarity with the language, and peculiar laws and usages that obtain in that country, and by a *friendly, firm* and *judicious* diplomacy, your negotiations may be crowned with success." Should the Emperor of China refuse to negotiate in a satisfactory manner, the directive went on, the next step would be decided by Congress.[8] Concerning his relations with the agents of other powers in China, Parker was instructed to cooperate with them in any way that might be deemed proper in their attempts to extend their treaty privileges with China by treaty stipulations.[9]

In another instruction, Parker was reminded that his action was not to be controlled by the views of the European powers. But Marcy stressed: "If the three Powers should concur in any line of conduct, it would be much less likely to meet with opposition or resistance from the authorities in China."[10]

Since the time for a treaty revision (which was supposed to be on July 3, 1856, according to Article 34 of the Wanghia Treaty) was approaching, Parker was urged to sail for China as soon as possible. On October 10, 1855, he left Boston on the ship *America* and started the first leg of his return trip as the new United States commissioner to China. On his way to Canton, Parker made stops at London and Paris, where he was to consult the British and French authorities in the hope of agreeing upon joint action in revising the treaties with China. For this purpose he had obtained two letters of introduction from James Buchanan to Lord Clarendon, the British foreign minister, and Count Walewski, the French minister for foreign affairs.[11]

In London he remarked to Lord Clarendon that it was the desire of

---

[8] *Ibid.*, pp. 125-26.

[9] *Ibid.*, p. 126. Concerning Parker's new commission to China, W. C. Costin remarks that Parker had "won the approval of the American government for a policy of diplomatic activity, backed by a demonstration of force, to be pursued in cooperation with the other two Treaty Powers." See Costin, *Great Britain and China 1833-1860* (Oxford: The Clarendon Press, 1937), p. 195. As Marcy's instructions show, however, the United States government seemed to have no intention to back Parker's activity with a "demonstration of force"; nor had the United States Navy Department issued any order to American navy commanders in the Far East for that purpose.

[10] Marcy to Parker, No. 3, Washington, D.C., October 5, *DI-USNA*, 77:38, p. 131.

[11] Parker to Marcy, Boston, October 8, 1855, *Parker Correspondence*, pp. 615 ff.

the United States government that the same concurrent policy and action which hitherto had characterized the three powers in China should be continued and that the naval forces of the three powers should anchor at the mouth of the Pei-ho River while their negotiations with the Chinese government were in progress.[12] "...were I a Chinese, and the greatest patriot of the empire," Parker said, "I could desire nothing better than is contemplated by our governments." "Yes," was the answer, "not only do our consciences approve, but the whole world must commend the policy." Clarendon therefore promised "to speak of the *triple alliance*"[13] to Parliament as the American commissioner proposed. The British statesman also seems to have been pleased by Parker's visit.[14]

In Paris he was even more favorably received. In an interview with Count Walewski, Parker stated that he bore to the Emperor of China a letter from the President of the United States, addressed in a frank and friendly spirit, in which allusion was made to the reception of the representative of the United States at Peking. He suggested that a similar letter be addressed in the name of His Majesty the Emperor of France. "The suggestion was received most cordially," Parker wrote to Washington, "and the Count proposed at once to correspond with Lord Clarendon upon the subject, that the Queen of England might be induced to concur in the measure."[15] Parker then further proposed to the French that a joint naval force might be present during the projected negotiation and "that the English and French naval forces might anchor as well for a fortnight in the Gulf of Pechele [at the mouth of the Pei-ho], whilst negotiations are pending, as in the harbor of Hong Kong." This idea also seemed unobjectionable to the French. Parker seems to have been confident of Anglo-French support in the oncoming treaty revision movement; he proceeded to Hong Kong, where he arrived on December 31, 1855.

II

Upon his arrival at Hong Kong, Parker was welcomed by the British with unusual ceremonies. Sir John Bowring, the British governor of Hong Kong, invited him to live in the Government House, where

---

[12]Minutes of an interview with the Earl of Clarendon, Fenton's Hotel, St. James Street, London, October 26, 1855, *ibid.*, p. 620.

[13] *Ibid.*

[14] Clarendon to Bowring, November 8, 1855, *F.O.*, 17/225 in Costin, *Great Britain and China*, p. 195.

[15] Parker to Marcy, Paris, November 8, 1855, *Parker Correspondence*, pp. 621-22.

remarkable banquets were given in his honor. During a long discussion about an Anglo-American collaboration in the treaty revision movement, Bowring was in full agreement with his guest in desiring an extension of trade. There was, however, a difference in opinion between these two ministers. Parker intended to secure from the Chinese government the privileges of unlimited trade and a universal grant of freedom of opinion. Bowring did not want to go so far. In Bowring's opinion it would be safer to confine trade to specified ports on the Yangtze and on the coast; and he did not think it practical to insist, as Parker desired, on the universal grant of freedom of opinion. Thus no definite agreement between these two envoys was concluded.[16]

On January 24, 1856, Parker proceeded to Macao, where he "temporarily" established his legation. At Macao the same ceremonies in honor of the American commissioner were repeated by the Portuguese. He was also welcomed by his own countrymen with an enthusiasm that the eye doctor had never before experienced. "Nothing could be more gratifying than the civilities I have received at the hands of the British, Portuguese, and the United States officials civil and naval," Parker reported to Washington in a particularly confidential dispatch. The British were extremely friendly to him. Before Parker left for Macao, Rear Admiral Sir James Stirling of the British Navy even made a special call upon him, offering to place at his convenience one of the steamers under his command, should the American commissioner require her services to communicate with Canton, Hong Kong, and Macao in the absence of the United States vessels-of-war.[17]

Upon his arrival at Macao, Parker began to seek an interview with the Chinese authorities. As he had expected, his request was refused by Imperial Commissioner Yeh Ming-ch'en. This refusal, however, did not irritate Parker, who had in view a long-range project. He intended to wait for the arrival from Siam of Commodore James Armstrong, commanding officer of the United States naval forces in the Far East, and his warship *San Jacinto*. As soon as he had obtained naval support, Parker would communicate with the British and French envoys in China in order to organize a joint armed expedition to Pei-ho.

With this program in mind, Parker, therefore, asked the American consul at Shanghai to send a communication to the Chinese governor-general of Liang-Kiang announcing in advance his projected expedi-

---

[16] Bowring to Clarendon, February 6, 1856, *F.O.*, 17/245 in Costin, *Great Britain and China*, p. 197.
[17] *Parker Correspondence*, p. 675.

tion to the north and his intention to seek treaty revision.[18] At Macao, Parker waited patiently until the middle of May without performing any diplomatic function.

On May 15, 1856, when the time for Parker's projected allied expedition to the Pei-ho was approaching, he addressed communications to both the British and the French envoys, inquiring if they had received any instructions from their respective governments, with whom Parker had made arrangements.[19]

To this request the British governor replied that he had received orders from the British government authorizing him to cooperate cordially with the American envoy. He was therefore sending an official communication to the Chinese Imperial Commissioner Yeh Ming-ch'en at Canton in support of the American request for a treaty revision, but he was doing nothing further. It seemed that there had been no specific instructions from the British government for Sir John Bowring to render practical support to the American course of action.[20] During this period, the British envoy was as anxious as Parker for a joint expedition to the north. His real goal was a joint Anglo-American advance on Peking, where, as the British thought, they could bring the Russian expansion in North China, Korea, and Japan to a halt.[21] But Bowring did not want to repeat the mistake of 1854, when his predecessor, Bonham, had launched a fruitless expedition to Pei-ho with the American commissioner, Robert McLane. The British envoy seems to have doubted Parker's capability to carry on such an extensive program, and he thought it impractical to insist on the universal grant of freedom of opinion. If a large-scale expedition to Peking could not be organized at the moment, he preferred to settle the immediate and specific questions relating to piracy, emigration, cur-

---

[18] On February 3, 1856, Dr. M. W. Fish, the United States acting vice-consul at Shanghai presented, at the direction of Parker, a public notice to the *taotai* of Shanghai announcing Parker's arrival at Canton and his intention to revise the treaty. This communication was forwarded to I-liang, governor-general of Liang-Kiang, who promptly memorialized it to the throne. On March 24, the Emperor isued an edict ordering Yeh Ming-ch'en to receive the American commissioner at Canton and to "make use of both magnanimity and intimidation to frustrate their idea of coming North." If the revision Parker wanted was only of "trifling matters," Yeh Ming-ch'en was directed to negotiate with him and at the same time memorialize it to the Court. See *IWSM-HF,* XII, 29a-30b. In the spring of 1856, however, Parker sent no more communications to the Imperial Commissioner. Thus, the imperial edict of March 24 was neglected by Yeh Ming-ch'en.

[19] *Parker Correspondence,* pp. 813-17.

[20] John Bowring to Peter Parker, Hong Kong, May 16, 1856, *Parker Correspondence,* p. 815.

[21] Bowring to Clarendon, December 10, 1855, *F.O., 17/235,* in Costin, *Great Britain and China,* p. 195.

rency, and custom service, rather than the vague suggestions of Parker.[22] Thus Bowring was rather indifferent toward Parker's hasty program.

A more disappointing answer to Parker came from the French envoy. In reply to Parker's inquiry, the French chargé, Count René de Courcy, wrote that he had not yet received the instruction that Parker had anticipated.[23]

The most disappointing news, however, was yet to come. It was from the navy commanders of his own country. There was no American force that could be assigned to him for his projected Pei-ho expedition. Commodore James Armstrong, commanding officer of the United States naval forces in East India and the China Seas, did arrive in Hong Kong in June, but his instructions from the Navy Department to proceed with his flagship, the San Jacinto, directly to Japan were imperative and no discretion was left him, no matter how urgently required were the services of the flagship in China. Nevertheless, Commodore Armstrong agreed to assign a sloop of war, the Levant, to the American commissioner. Consequently, Parker decided to sail alone from Hong Kong for Shanghai on July 1.[24]

Before leaving Hong Kong, however, Parker still expected that he might be joined by Commodore Armstrong's naval force after the latter's return from Japan. Consequently, Parker sent letters to the British and French envoys stating that from August 20 to September 1 he might proceed to Pei-ho with the United States naval force for the revision of the Treaty of Wanghia and that he hoped the British and the French would be able to join him at that time.[25] "Another failure at Teen-tsin," the British governor wrote in reply, "might greatly add to our future difficulties."[26] The French chargé replied that he was still waiting for instructions from his home government, and he was not able to give any definite answer. Disappointed, Parker proceeded north with the Levant without consulting his European colleagues further.

On his way to Shanghai, Parker visited Amoy, Foochow, and

---

[22] Bowring to Clarendon, February 6, 1856, F.O., 17/245, in Costin, p. 197. Parker's proposal to demand "universal freedom of opinion" from China was not included in any of his dispatches to Washington. Also see Bowring to Parker, Hong Kong, Juy 1, 1856, Parker Correspondence, pp. 925-26.

[23] René de Courcy to Peter Parker, May 18, 1856, Parker Correspondence, pp. 816-17.

[24] Parker to Marcy, No. 15, Hong Kong, June 30, 1856, ibid., p. 846.

[25] Parker to Bowring, Hong Kong, June 30, 1856, ibid., pp. 923-24.

[26] Ibid., pp. 926-27.

Ningpo. In Foochow he was cordially received by Wang I-te, the governor-general of Min-Che. During their friendly interview, Parker asked Wang to forward the President's state letter to Peking. Wang, however, was curious and asked why it had not been delivered to the Imperial Commissioner at Canton. Parker replied that the articles of the treaty of Wanghia designated three channels of communication to Peking of which he personally preferred the channel at Foochow to the ones at Canton and Shanghai.[27] This letter was later returned with its seal broken. The authorities at Peking insisted that it should be handled by the Imperial Commissioner at Canton; the ignorant mandarins at Peking thought that the "barbarians" had purposely avoided the more experienced Imperial Commissioner at Canton and were taking advantage of Wang who was unfamiliar with "barbarian management." Had Parker told Wang the real reason was that he had been refused an interview at Canton by Yeh, this incident might have been avoided.[28]

Arriving in Shanghai on August 1, 1856, Parker still had hopes that the British and the French might join him in an expedition. On August 12, he wrote again to the envoys of these countries saying that he had conclusive evidence that the Chinese were seeking foreign aid against the rebels. If the ministers of the three great Western powers were now in readiness to present themselves at Peking, he was sure the Chinese cabinet would be delighted to receive them.[29] To his surprise, his suggestions met with a negative answer from the British envoy, who charged that it implied an interference with internal questions, which the British government did not want to undertake. Besides, said Bowring, he had discussed the matter with Count de Courcy, the French envoy to China, who had received rather negative instructions from his home government, giving him no immediate hope of having any maritime force at his disposal.[30]

It is interesting as well as surprising to note that Parker had been too optimistic and that mistakenly he still thought that Bowring was in full cooperation with him. Actually, while Parker set out for a lonely operation in a vain effort for treaty revision, Bowring, instead

---

[27] Minutes of an interview between their excellencies Peter Parker, commissioner of the United States of America, and Wang, viceroy of the Min and Cheh [Che] provinces, held at the palace of the viceroy, within the city of Foo-Chow, 8:00 A. M., July 15, 1856, *Parker Correspondence*, p. 863.

[28] *IWSM-HF*, XIII, 16a-18a.

[29] *Parker Correspondence*, p. 928.

[30] John Bowring to Peter Parker, Hong Kong, August 21, 1856, *ibid.*, pp. 957-58.

of offering some assistance, was sabotaging the effort behind his back. He spread the rumor that Parker had already been recalled by Washington and that the State Department had supposedly reappointed Humphrey Marshall as the new commissioner to China to replace him. This rumor, diffused by the highest British authority in China, did great harm to Parker's prestige among the Chinese as well as among his own countrymen.[31] Why Bowring spread the rumor is not clear. Early in September, when he was informed by Caleb Jones, the United States consul at Foochow, about this British sabotage, Parker naturally was very disturbed.

At the same time, he was also informed that the United States warship, the *San Jacinto,* had been disabled by an accident. In such circumstances, Parker decided to suspend the whole plan for sailing to the Pei-ho.[32]

Filled with disappointment, Parker held several interviews with the Chinese *taotai,* Lan Wei-wen, who thought erroneously that Parker was now on his way to Tientsin.[33] The last interviews that Parker held with the *taotai* on September 15 and 23 respectively, took place on board the United States frigate, *San Jacinto,* which arrived from Japan on September 14 in a "crippled condition." In these interviews, Parker stated that he expected to go north "alone." "I do not wait," said Parker to Lan, "as this is the year, according to the treaty of Wang Hia, for its revision." The Chinese then asked when the Commissioner thought of leaving for the capital. Parker replied that it was uncertain, but if an Imperial Commissioner, empowered to form a treaty with an article allowing the residence of an American minister at the Court, was sent to Shanghai, it would not be necessary to go at present; otherwise he would not wish to meet the Imperial Commissioner. At that time, however, Parker had already made up his mind to retire to the south. During another interview with Lan Wei-wen and Wu Chien-chang, the former *taotai* who was now serving as consultant to the Governor-General, Parker was pleased by the promise and prediction that Governor-General I-liang would memorialize in behalf of the American minister, and Ch'i-ying probably would be sent to Shanghai or Ningpo to take up the negotiation. Wu further

[31] Caleb Jones to Peter Parker, No. 19, Foochow, August 27, 1856, *ibid.,* pp. 961-62.

[32] Parker to Marcy, No. 28, Shanghai, November 1, 1856, *Parker Correspondence,* pp. 967-68.

[33] Lan Wei-wen was the former prefect of Sung-chiang under Wu Chien-chang. When Wu was removed in the summer of 1854, Lan was promoted to take his place. See *IWSM-HF,* VIII, 19a, 34a.

proposed that Parker send two communications to Governor-General I-liang: one should be a "public" dispatch to state the request for an Imperial Commissioner to be appointed in order to negotiate with him at Shanghai; the other should be a "private" one to state the "sine qua non" (a residence at Peking), which Wu thought the Emperor might grant since the Russians were now living in the capital. This successful interview with Wu gave Parker new hope.[34]

Further good news reached Parker early in October when he learned from Bowring that the British government was sending a British fleet into Chinese waters for the purpose of obtaining (in cooperation with the other treaty powers) a revision of the existing treaties with China. In his reply to Bowring, Parker stated that he had given up the plan of sailing north but had consented to negotiations at Shanghai. He graciously, though erroneously, informed the British that Ch'i-ying had been named as the personage likely to be entrusted with the power to revise the existing treaty.[35]

Unfortunately, two official instructions issued respectively by Governor-General I-liang and the new governor, Chao Te-ché, to the taotai, Lan Wei-wen, arrived a week later, stating that it was impossible to memorialize for the American commissioner. I-liang stated that "the present request by the Americans to have a commissioner appointed to confer with them would certainly excite suspicions in the Emperor's mind." Hence he could not venture to memorialize to this effect. The Governor's reply was written in the same style.[36]

Without any means to enforce his request, Parker had no choice but to return south and wait for a future chance. He embarked on the San Jacinto on November 3, reached Hong Kong five days later, and retired to Macao on November 11. His effort to revise the treaty had, at long last, reached its end. The triple alliance about which he had dreamt so long never materialized.

The collapse of Parker's mission came as a great surprise. Having resided in China for more than twenty years as an old China hand,

---

[34] Minutes of a conversation held on board the United States steamer San Jacinto on September 23, 1856, between Peter Parker, Lan Wei-wen, the taotai, and Wu Chien-chang. Parker Correspondence, pp. 945-48. This informal "conversation" between Wu, Lan, and Parker's representative, Leang, a Cantonese who had served as Parker's private interpreter, was continued for a month despite a number of interruptions. After reading Leang's reports, Parker was hopeful, though not "over sanguine," that an Imperial Commissioner might be appointed to Shanghai or Canton to conduct negotiations for a treaty revision. See ibid., pp. 968-81.

[35] Sir John Bowring to Peter Parker, Hong Kong, September 29, 1856, and Peter Parker's reply, Shanghai, October 14, 1856, ibid., pp. 978-80.

[36] Ibid., pp. 972-73.

Parker was beyond doubt more familiar with Chinese affairs than were any of his contemporaries in the United States. Throughout his more than a decade of service as Chinese secretary, during which he acted as chargé d'affaires on six occasions, Parker had met all the Chinese Imperial Commissioners in charge of the trade of the Five Ports. He had also helped most of the American commissioners to China present their respective credentials. But when he himself had become the commissioner of the United States, he could not obtain an interview with the Chinese Imperial Commissioner, and was unable even to present his own credentials. At Shanghai, he could achieve only two informal interviews with the *taotai;* he did not even have a chance to see the governor-general of Liang-Kiang, who had received his predecessors with respectful diplomatic ceremonies.

Parker's failure may be attributed to several sources. First of all, he lacked experience in international politics. A triple alliance, or even an international armed cooperation against China, as he had designed, was not an easy undertaking. It required serious planning and could not be achieved by a novice. If successful, his project could have resulted in a general war against China, yet none of the three governments had made any serious plans for such an event. Having misjudged the temper of European governments, Parker's proposal for a combined effort was quite naturally fruitless. Moreover, although Parker singlehandedly set up a timetable for a combined expedition to North China and requested his Western colleagues to line up behind him, he was not even able to bring the navy commanders of his own country into line. The basic reason for Parker's failure, however, was the lack of cooperation of the two governments between which Parker was working. On the one hand, he did not have sufficient support from the State Department for such an enterprise as treaty revision. On the other, his effort was seriously sabotaged by the Imperial Commissioner at Canton.

While Parker was sailing north from Hong Kong, Yeh submitted a long memorial to the Emperor in which he described in great detail Parker's life story and his diplomatic career at Canton. "The chief was originally an American physician, had been in Canton for twenty years," said Yeh, "and was generally regarded as crafty." Two years ago, as Yeh understood, Parker had expected a rebel victory around Canton and had made connections with the rebels. After the Chinese government forces had suppressed the rebellion in that area Parker lost "face" from that event. Thus, even after he was made the United

States commissioner to China, he was still determined to find expression for his personal views and "to silence people's ridicule."[37]

This memorial, which reached the Court on July 23, was accepted and quoted by the Emperor with compliments. Consequently, in his subsequent edicts, the Emperor ordered the local Chinese officials along the coast that regardless where Parker went he must be sent back to Canton, where Yeh Ming-ch'en would deal with him.[38]

Two weeks later on August 6, President Pierce's state letter to the Chinese Emperor, which was forwarded by Governor-General Wang I-te, reached the Court. It was, as the Emperor understood, another evidence that the foreigners attempted to avoid the more experienced Chinese diplomat at Canton. He wrote:[39]

But in Yeh Ming-ch'en's previous memorial there was no mention of these barbarians having any credentials at Kuangtung. It is perfectly apparent that in Kuangtung there was nothing to be gained, so they were unwilling to present them at Kuangtung. And besides, since in previous years at Shanghai and Tientsin there was no chance to try their schemes, they hoped to give Fukien a try. Their inscrutable mentality is apparent without inquiry.

Therefore he ordered Wang to send the original letter back to the American commissioner and to direct Parker to go back to Canton. The state letter was at last returned to Parker by the end of August.[40] Thus while Parker was returning south, he was being humiliated as well as disappointed.

III

Retiring to South China, however, Parker was surprised and delighted by the Arrow Incident, which occurred on October 8, 1856. It gradually developed into a local war between the Chinese and the British; the latter anxiously sought Parker's assistance. The Arrow Incident, which handicapped both belligerent parties, naturally put the Americans in an advantageous position and gave Parker new hopes to revive his ambition for a triple alliance against China.

The Arrow Incident arose over a Chinese raid on a lorcha (a small

---

[37] *IWSM-HF*, XIII, 11a-13b; for a good English translation of this document see Earl Swisher, *China's Management of the American Barbarians* (New Haven, Conn.: Yale University Far Eastern Publications, 1951), pp. 313-16.

[38] *IWSM-HF*, XIII, 13b-14b; 30.

[39] Swisher, *China's Management*, pp. 319-20; *IWSM-HF*, XIII, 18b-19a.

[40] Wang-E-Tih [Wang I-te)] to Parker, August 24, 1856, *Parker Correspondence*, pp. 941-42.

craft with a Chinese hull and a foreign rig), the *Arrow*, which had previously registered at the British Colonial Government of Hong Kong. During this raid, it was said that the British flag on the ship was hauled down. When the Chinese apology failed to satisfy the British, the latter began to take military action; and this small incident at last developed into a local war.[41] "It takes two to make a quarrel," wrote a contemporary American writer, "but no two could be better fitted to produce one and to nurse it into a war than the two who were parties in this subject."[42] Bowring had placed the responsibility for an offensive action against Canton in the hands of Admiral Michael Seymour, who commanded the British naval forces in the Chinese seas. "The brave officer," the American observer continued, "having lost an eye by the explosion of a Russian torpedo in the Baltic during the Crimean War, could see only one way to negotiate."

In the meantime, over the vigorous protest of his subordinates, the Chinese governor-general generated a policy of absolute nonresistance and nonintercourse with the British. He ordered all Chinese troops to retreat wherever they met the enemy, and at the same time he ignored the British communications. By the end of October, nearly all the Chinese forts outside the city of Canton were occupied by British marines, who began to bombard the city; the Imperial Commissioner's office building was directly fired upon on October 28, and one shot struck the desk on which the Imperial Commissioner was writing. The next day the city wall in front of his official building was breached and his office was stormed by British marines.[43]

During this conflict at Canton, the usually tactless Imperial Commissioner treated the Americans and the French with unusual diplomatic skill. When the British bombardment of Canton began, Yeh wrote a very careful and polite note to Oliver H. Perry, the United States consul at Canton, and Captain A. H. Foote, the United States naval officer commanding the United States navy force in that harbor, advising them to withdraw all American personnel from the dangerous area. This appeal received a favorable response. The Americans

---

[41] For general information about the Arrow Incident consult Hosea Ballou Morse, *The International Relations of the Chinese Empire* (New York: Longmans, Green and Co., 1910-18), I, 419-37; Ch'i-hsuan ho-shang tiao-sou, *Ying-chi-li Kuang-tung ju-ch'eng shih-mo chi* (The Story of the English Entry of Canton) (*Ch'ung-shu-chi-ch'eng*, No. 3999, Shanghai: Commercial Press, 1939), pp. 3 ff.

[42] W. A. P. Martin, *A Cycle of Cathay or China, South and North* (New York: Fleming H. Revell Co., 1897), p. 143.

[43] *Ying-chi-li Kuang-tung ju ch'eng shih-mo chi*, pp. 3 ff.

accordingly left Canton on November 15, 1856; five days later they were followed by the French.[44]

American opinion was divided over the British attack on Canton. In the absence of specific instructions from Washington, Consul Oliver H. Perry at Canton seemed quite sympathetic with the Chinese; but the United States consul at Hong Kong, James Keenan, and Commodore James Armstrong, who had just returned with Commissioner Parker from Shanghai, were not. At this moment, Dr. Parker's own feelings were mixed; he was in sympathy with neither side. As usual, he was opposed to the mandarins, but he was equally unsympathetic toward the British, for they had recently refused to cooperate with him in the Pei-ho expedition.[45]

While the British marines were preparing an attack at Canton, Keenan joined them on October 24. When the city of Canton was breached by British fire on October 29, Keenan took an American "volunteer" with him, carried an American flag, and stormed the city with the British invading force. "He went in furthest and came out last," and displayed the Stars and Stripes on the city wall as well as atop the Imperial Commissioner's palace. During the retreat, the American consul "discharged his revolver at a Chinese before he came out."[46] This blind heroism and unauthorized display of the American flag with the British invading force caused much confusion among the Chinese, who mistakenly thought the Americans were helping the British against them.[47]

On November 15, when one of the American warships sailing from Macao to Canton passed the Barrier Forts, which the Chinese had just recaptured from the British, it was fired upon by the Chinese guards in the forts. Feeling the American flag had been insulted, Commodore Armstrong sent his flagship *San Jacinto* there the next day and

---

[44] The Imperial Commissioner to the American Consul, November 10, 1856, *Parker Correspondence*, pp. 1027-28. For general information consult Morse, *The International Relations of the Chinese Empire*, I, 432.

[45] Parker's feeling was well expressed in a letter to Bowring on November 17, 1856, see *Parker Correspondence*, pp. 1038-40.

[46] Peter Parker to Lewis Cass, Macao, May 22, 1857, *Parker Correspondence*, pp. 1385-86.

[47] In his letters to Armstrong on November 20 and 28, Yeh stated very frankly, though very politely, that the people of Canton had watched "men of other countries" as they "scrambled over the walls" with the British. The people had repeatedly reported to the Chinese government that "there were Americans mixed up among their [the British] forces," and that Harry S. Parkes, the British consul at Canton, had spread the report of American support. "If no American had really been in the melee...assisting with the English," said Yeh, "the people of Canton would have had no quarrel with them." *Ibid.*, pp. 1030, 1048-49.

destroyed the forts on both sides of the Pearl River. In the mean-time the Commodore also addressed the Imperial Commissioner and demanded an explanation of this incident within twenty-four hours. Without awaiting an answer from Canton, however, the Commodore renewed his attack on the Barrier Forts. By a series of operations conducted on November 20, 21, and 22, he captured the five forts containing 167 mounted guns and dismantled them.[48] During this small war the casualties on the part of the United States forces were five killed and nine wounded; the Chinese suffered a loss of over 160 killed in action. Watching this unprecedented attack on the Chinese by elements of the American fleet, Parker was deeply pleased, because it was the "first demonstration of our force . . . specifically concerning the naval authority of the United States in China." In his report to Washington, Parker wrote: "This is the first blow that has ever been struck by our navy in China, and it has been done in a manner calculated to secure for it an important prestige in the mind of this haughty government."[49]

This clash between the Chinese and American forces was apparently caused by misunderstanding, for neither party wanted war with the other. The Chinese fired upon American ships that were sounding the river in the vicinity of the forts on November 15 and 16 because Keenan's blind action at Canton had led them to look upon the Americans as aggressors. The Chinese garrison in the forts obviously had no difficulty in recognizing the American flag, which they had seen just a fortnight before displayed in the ranks of the victorious invading British troops, on the city wall, and atop the Governor-General's palace. For them, this was incentive enough to fire.

Commissioner Yeh, although remaining stubborn, feared that the irritated Americans might join the British; he replied to the Commodore in very friendly terms. In his last communication to Armstrong, on December 5, 1856, the Imperial Commissioner stated: "There is no matter of strife between our two nations. Henceforth let the fashion of the flag which American ships employ be clearly defined (or made known) [sic] and inform me what it is beforehand. This will be a verification (or proof) of the friendly relations between our countries."[50] Thus the Sino-American dispute was closed without further

---

48 For general reference see Morse, *The International Relations of the Chinese Empire*, I, 433.

49 Parker to Marcy, No. 31, Whampoa, November 22, 1856, *Parker Correspondence*, p. 1021.

50 Yeh to Armstrong, Canton, December 5, 1856, *Parker Correspondence*, p. 1053.

communication, although it later attracted more attention at Washington than at Peking.[51] Apart from this sole incident, the Americans remained in a state of neutrality during the first stage of the "Arrow War."

IV

Unable to obtain sufficient support from the Americans and French, the British could do nothing more against the tactless but stubborn Imperial Commissioner, because the limited number of British marines, although they had captured the city of Canton, had failed to capture the whole urban area of Canton. Hence Sir John Bowring had to communicate with his home government for further instructions and reinforcements. At the same time he was obliged to seek more support from other Western representatives.

It was, however, not an easy job to enlist the support of the American commissioner at this moment, for Parker had just returned from Shanghai in a state of emotional uncertainty. Arriving in Hong Kong on November 8, while the Arrow War was at its peak, Parker seems to have been very cool to the British minister, whose support for treaty revision had never materialized. Parker's apathy toward the British was understandable. He had believed that a timely cooperation of the three envoys in a joint expedition to Tientsin, combined with a demonstration by a sufficient naval force, would have obtained all the concessions they wanted. Contrary to his advice, however, the British started a meaningless attack on Canton in the winter season, when an expedition to North China was impracticable. Parker saw that the Arrow War could have little effect on the basic problems of a treaty revision.[52] Upon his arrival at Hong Kong, Parker seems to have purposely avoided meeting Bowring, who was obviously eager to see him.

A week later, when Parker had already reached Macao, Bowring

Yeh's letter of December 5 was filled with the statements that he had presented to the Commodore before. Using a different translation of the same letter from the British Navy (Papers relative to proceedings of H. M. naval forces at Canton, Oct.-Dec. 1856, presented to both Houses of Parliament, 1857), H. B. Morse stated that the Imperial Commissioner had tendered "a complete apology." It was accepted by the Commodore; thus the incident was closed. See Morse, The International Relations of the Chinese Empire, I, 433.

[51] Commodore Armstrong's destruction of the forts was not reported to the Court by the officials at Canton. But the news was reported by I-liang, governor-general of Liang-Kiang, who had been informed by his own agents at Canton. The Emperor, however, did not believe that the news was true. He thought it was merely a rumor spread by the British. See IWSM-HF, XIV, 21a.

[52] Peter Parker to John Bowring, U.S. Steam Frigate San Jacinto, Whampoa, November 17, 1856, Parker Correspondence, pp. 1038-40.

suggested that a joint Anglo-American communication be sent to Tien-tsin by a British steamer. Bowring said that he was earnestly desirous of preserving the harmony of purpose and unity of action among the Western powers.[53]

Only two months earlier it had been Parker who had made an appeal to the British for a joint expedition to the north, and he had been refused. Now Bowring appealed to the American minister for a joint, though belated, expedition to the same destination, and it was Parker's turn to give his refusal. In answering Bowring's brief appeal, Parker wrote a lengthy letter refusing to send a joint communication to Tientsin.[54] Sarcastically he noted that he should deem the viceroy of Liang-Kiang a more expeditious and eligible means of communicating with the cabinet. Furthermore, he said, the "ostensible question" of the present dispute—satisfaction for violation of the treaty in the case of a British ship and entrance to the city of Canton—was a trifle compared with all the grievances that he had tried so urgently to redress a few months before. Therefore, he said, the government of the United States "must remain *neutral* in the controversy *solely* initiated by her Britannic Majesty's government, and specifically British in origin," although he was still interested "in the success of the measures adopted to bring to a speedy and satisfactory conclusion the present contest."[55]

Canton now remained partly occupied by the British, who were waiting for reinforcement, while Yeh still indulged in his policy of non-resistance. The Americans and French stayed neutral and watched events. Nearly a month later, however, another incident occurred at Canton, which at last put American and French neutrality to an end. On December 14, 1856, the foreign factories which were located outside the city wall and were then under heavy British guard were burned by a mysterious fire, which destroyed foreign property amounting to millions of dollars. Nobody knows how the fire started.

---

[53] John Bowring to Peter Parker, No. 263, Hong Kong, November 15, 1856, *ibid.*, pp. 1037-38.

[54] In the first part of his reply Parker offered a strong protest against the British abuse of the phrase "all foreign officials." "If I am correctly informed," wrote Parker, "one of the demands of her Britannic Majesty's government made to that of China is the entry of '*all foreign officials to the city of Canton.*'" If such was the case, Parker said, it had been without the knowledge of the representative of the United States; and while appreciating the generous motive that prompted Admiral Sir Michael Seymour to the act, he, however, must disclaim, on behalf of the government of the United States, the right to perform it. See Peter Parker to John Bowring, U.S. Steam Frigate *San Jacinto,* Whampoa, November 17, 1856, *ibid.*, pp. 1038-40.   [55] *Ibid.*

Hosea Ballou Morse, the noted historian in this field, has put the responsibility to the Cantonese people, but the statement Morse made in his invaluable book, *The International Relations of the Chinese Empire,* is self-contradictory. In his description of British actions done for the protection of the "foreign factories" in November, Morse states that "a sufficient number of the Chinese houses at the back [of the foreign factories] were pulled down to make the factories defensible."[56] This "sufficient number" actually involved several blocks of Chinese streets containing thousands of homes of innocent Chinese civilians. After the houses were destroyed, no Chinese could reach the dangerous zone. As a matter of fact, many Chinese civilians lost their lives in vain efforts to save their beloved homes.[57] Then, ignoring his own statement, Morse further states that "the Chinese, unable to make head against the armed forces of the British crown, now proceeded to attack the defenceless factories."[58]

Yeh Ming-ch'en's report on this event, which was quoted by the Emperor in an edict, stated that the burning of the foreign factories was caused by a sudden change of wind at a time when the British were setting fire to the Chinese houses in the neighborhood.[59] The most detailed description of this mysterious fire, however, is found in the United States archives. Immediately after the foreign factories were burnt, the Chinese victims of the fire, consisting of the inhabitants of "twelve streets, outside of Tai-ping gate, in the suburbs of Canton," whose homes were burned along with the foreign factories, or destroyed by the British, issued a *United Manifesto* to the "gentlemen of all nations." This document was dated "Winter of 1856" and was later translated into English by a staff member of the American legation and forwarded to Washington on January 13, 1857. It reads in part as follows:[60]

At the beginning of the present [Arrow] affair with the English, they [the English] issued a general intimation, that if there were actual hostilities it did not concern and did not interfere with us living in those streets, which declaration we firmly believed, and quietly went on with our business as usual. Unexpectedly, about the 1st of November, they destroyed all the

---

[56] Morse, *International Relations of the Chinese Empire,* I, 430.

[57] Ch'i-hsuan ho-shang tiao-sou, *Ying-chi-li Kuang-tung ju ch'eng shih-mo-chi,* p. 4; also consult *Parliamentary Papers,* 1857, No. 2163, 40 ff.

[58] Morse, *The International Relations of the Chinese Empire,* I, 435.

[59] *IWSM-HF,* XV, 18a.

[60] This document was translated from Chinese into English by Thos. J. Reynolds of the American legation in China. See *Parker Correspondence,* p. 1127.

shops in the streets near the factories, on which occasion we lost our property in moving away, and were put to more distress than we can well describe.

Then the English soldiers kept a very strict guard thereabouts, so that no vagrants could lurk and spy the place, and this also made it impossible for the shopmen to return to their shops to take care of them.

How surprising was it then, in the night of the 14th December [1856], while the English troops were guarding the place, to see a furious fire break out in Shih-san-hong (thirteen factories [sic]).

We supposed they would put it out, being skilled in all things requiring strength and bravery, but they could not do so, and thus more than a thousand shops belonging to us were destroyed.

When we sent fire engines from each street to put out the fire, they drove away this assistance, killing several men and wounding over twenty more. Alas! how distressing to see many thousands of human beings so suddenly turned out of their homes, widows and orphans deprived of their support, and all at once thrown upon the world. The previous destruction of the shops and hongs near the Yu-lan and Tsing-hai gates by fire is now increased by this afflictive calamity; indeed, how can we bear these outrageous wrongs? . . .

On January 14, 1857, just two days after the British burned several thousand remaining Chinese houses, the occupants of that area, covering "more than thirty streets," issued another *Joint Manifesto*. They charged that the British had purposely set fire to the foreign factories and by so doing intended to make the Cantonese people appear responsible so that the other Western nations would become involved.[61]

In his letter replying to Parker's demand for indemnity of the American losses during this mysterious fire, Yeh Ming-ch'en wrote: "The goods and property in the houses of American merchants were set on fire and destroyed by Englishmen, and you must look to them for indemnification, and not to the Chinese government."[62]

In their official reports to London, the British officials did not seriously charge the Cantonese with being responsible for the mysterious fire.[63] On the other hand, Chinese writers of a later period, such as Hsieh Fu-ch'eng, who did not have firsthand information about the fire, complimented the Cantonese people on their success in burning the "barbarian" property.[64] Without citing any reliable source at all, a

61 *Parker Correspondence*, pp. 1157-58.

62 Yee [Yeh] to Parker, January 15, 1857, *ibid.*, pp. 1156-57.

63 See *Parliamentary Papers*, 1857, No. 2163, 40-44.

64 Hsieh Fu-ch'eng, "Shu Han-yang Yeh hsiang Kuang-chou chih pien," *Chung-kuo chin-tai shih tzu-liao hsuan chi*, p. 69.

recent historian even went so far as to make such a firm statement as: "There is no doubt that the Cantonese set fire to the factories."[65]

The fact was that when the foreign factories were burned, more than a thousand Chinese houses in the neighborhood were burned along with them. It is hardly believable that the Cantonese would be willing to burn their own homes in order to destroy the foreign factories. Besides, the fire actually started in the American factory at midnight on December 14; it did not reach the English factory until the next afternoon. During this time the English marines shot and killed several Cantonese and injured twenty more, while the latter were trying to put out the fire.

Regardless of its mysterious origin, however, this fire helped the British to draw both the Americans and the French into the controversy, for both envoys sent their claims to the Chinese authorities rather than to the British.[66] On December 24, Parker suggested to Sir John Bowring that the American claim of indemnity for the lost property be included in the British claims for indemnification.[67] The British were, of course, only too glad to accept Parker's suggestion, which clearly released the British from responsibility for the damage to American property, and assured the British of American support for their future claim against China over the incident. Thus the temporarily interrupted Anglo-American collaboration was started anew, and Parker's ambition for a triple alliance was aroused to new heights.

---

[65] Huang Yen-yu, "Viceroy Yeh Ming-ch'en and the Canton Episode (1855-1861)," *Harvard Journal of Asiatic Studies*, VI, No. 1 (March, 1941), 104.

[66] Actually the American and French should have presented their claims to both the British and Chinese authorities for the loss of property at Canton. After the Chinese government paid up the American claims in 1858 at the request of Commissioner William Reed, the latter said: "... the bulk of our claims are of recent occurrence, for loss of property at the factories [at Canton in 1856] when the Chinese were defending their own soil, and for which they are only responsible on the unChristian principle of English and American public law, that the assailed party always pays the damages." See William B. Reed, *Speech of William B. Reed at Philadelphia Board of Trade, May 31, 1859* (Philadelphia: Philadelphia Board of Trade, 1859), p. 5.

[67] *Parker Correspondence*, p. 1098.

13

THE "LAST RESORT"

AND A COMPULSORY DECISION

I

PARKER's sudden return to his old policy of close Anglo-American collaboration following the short period of American neutrality during the early stage of the Arrow War is by no means surprising. Rather, it came as a natural consequence of contemporary international politics regarding China. Ever since the outbreak of the Arrow War British agents in Washington and Paris had been active. While Washington was pondering the British overtures,[1] Paris received them with open arms.

After Napoleon III came to power in 1848, the French had begun to adopt a more aggressive policy in the East. From the very beginning of her relations with China, however, France had very little commercial interest in the trading ports. Thus she found herself to be too insignificant a power to be able to raise her voice in Chinese affairs without the support of the British or the Americans. The Crimean War (1853-56) had led to a period of mutually successful cooperation with England that lasted for three years. France naturally wanted to extend this cooperation to matters in the East after the Crimean War.

A timely pretext for negotiations between England and France presented itself when a French Catholic missionary, Père Chapdelaine, was slain in Kwangsi province, the home of the bloody, Christian, Taiping Rebellion. The French government made his death a major international issue and prepared for armed revenge against the Celestial Empire. By the end of 1856, an Anglo-French negotiation for united action against China was concluded by Lord Clarendon, the British foreign minister, and Count de Persigny, the foreign minister of France. A policy promising concerted action was agreed upon:[2] Can-

---

[1] See section II below.

[2] Henri Cordier, *L'Expédition de Chine de 1857-1858* (Paris: Félix Alcan, 1905), pp. 90-102; also consult Hosea Ballou Morse, *The International Relations of the Chinese Empire* (New York: Longmans, Green and Co., 1910-18), I, 479-85.

ton would be held under joint occupation; the possibility of a naval demonstration on the Yangtze River was also discussed. The two countries further agreed to unite in the demand for reparation for the murder of Père Chapdelaine and to undertake a joint expedition to the mouth of the Pei-ho for the revision of the treaties.

Parker was fully informed of the progress of this Anglo-French negotiation and was on the alert.[3] As a major promoter, if not the original designer, of the idea of a "triple alliance," Parker could not keep himself away from the Anglo-French alliance. His recent rejection of the British appeal for cooperation during the Arrow War had been merely an emotional reaction to the previous British sabotage of his projected expedition to North China. A triple alliance or at least an Anglo-American collaboration had always been the foundation of his project for treaty revision. After his anger toward the British had subsided, he was ready to resume his old position at any opportunity.

In order to meet the new situation, Parker devised a more aggressive plan. On December 12, he summarized all his ideas in a lengthy report to Washington in which he clearly expressed his ambitious policy toward China.[4] To begin with, Parker stated that the failure to revise the existing treaty was not his fault. He had not possessed the necessary means to force such a revision. He thought, however, that the year 1857 would be the decisive year for treaty revision. "The present order of things in China cannot continue in *status quo*," wrote Parker. He was informed by the British envoy that there would be more British warships in the Chinese waters in the coming years. There would also be an increase of the French naval force. What should the United States do under such circumstances? He offered some "confidential" suggestions: the three representatives of England, France, and America should be in close cooperation and should present themselves at the Pei-ho; in case they were not welcomed to Peking, the French flag should be hoisted in Korea (then a Chinese vassal state), the English at Chushan, and the American in Formosa. The flags should continue to fly until compensation for past grievances was made and a satisfactory understanding regarding the future was reached. The American occupation of Formosa, he said, would be used only as a "last resort" and would not be adopted until friendly application had been made at Peking. After all Western demands were

[3] Parker to Marcy, No. 34, Macao, December 12, 1856, *Parker Correspondence*, p. 1082.
[4] *Ibid.*, pp. 1083 ff.

met, the Chinese authority in these areas would be instantly restored. In speaking of the forthcoming Anglo-French negotiations for a new alliance, Parker proposed to the authorities in Washington that if the federal government still wished to pursue a "concurrent policy with England and France in China, not an alliance, but independent and distinct action, yet similar, harmonious, and simultaneous," it should direct its ministers at London and Paris to confer with the foreign ministers of these two powers.[5]

This proposal was written in a comparatively reserved tone. It appears as if Parker wanted to test the reaction at Washington before disclosing his real plan. His ultimate intention, as reflected in the project on which he was working and in the reports he submitted during a later period, far exceeded his written suggestions in this dispatch. After December, 1856, Parker's diplomacy in China was of a double nature. On the one hand he aimed toward a closer cooperation with the British and the French, even to the extent of participating in the British war with China, while on the other hand he worked on an independent project directed at the American colonization of Formosa.[6]

On December 26, 1856, Parker received formal notice from Bowring stating that Great Britain and France had already come to an agreement and would take decisive measures for redressing grievances and for revising the treaties. "We feel all the importance of co-operation and common action," wrote Bowring, "and hope the fleets which will proceed to the north will have the advantage of your presence, and that your flag will accompany ours, as in 1854."[7] This British appeal was what Parker wanted. Subsequently, he was in close touch with both the British and the French envoys planning a joint program of action against the Chinese. " . . . it appears the English and French governments are determined upon their course in China, and will early the ensuing season pursue it in an efficient manner," Parker wrote to Washington on December 27, 1856, "and I entertain the hope that the United States will do the same." Parker, therefore, asked the authorities at Washington for extensive naval support. "A force not less efficient and imposing than the Japan expedition of 1853-'54 is most desirable, not to say indispensable," remarked Parker.[8]

---

[5] *Ibid.*, pp. 1083-84.

[6] See sections IV and V below.

[7] Bowring to Parker, Confidential, Hong Kong, December 26, 1856, *Parker Correspondence,* p. 1099.

[8] Parker to Marcy, No. 36, Macao, December 27, 1856, *ibid.*, pp. 1087-88.

II

Parker's willingness to participate in the new movement was made known quickly to Washington by the French diplomats (who were then trying to persuade the American government to approve it), even before Parker's own dispatch on the same subject reached the State Department.[9] The French overture was later followed by formal appeals from the British government.[10] These successive French and British appeals gave Secretary of State Marcy the impression that there was "an entire unanimity of sentiment and action between Great Britain and France, extending even to armed cooperation."[11] In the meantime, the news of American participation in the Arrow War also reached Washington. [12] Thus, because the situation was urgent, President Pierce and Marcy were compelled to reach a prompt decision. They could not let it be solved by their successors.

During this crucial moment another pressure group favoring a collaboration with the Anglo-French alliance appeared in Washington. These were the China merchants in Boston, whose advice regarding a proper Chinese policy had usually been sought and respected by the Secretary of State. These merchants now also shifted their previous stand of promoting peace in China to one of limited cooperation with the European powers. Accordingly, some of their agents were sent to Washington to influence the President and the Secretary of State on this subject.[13] " . . . if any one of the three nations were to undertake the negotiation alone," wrote one editor of a commercial paper to Marcy, "John Chinaman might be tempted to resist."[14] Their persuasive efforts were concentrated on winning over Attorney General Caleb Cushing, a Massachusetts man and an old China expert, who, as an expert on constitutional law, could help to justify a military cooperation with Great Britain and France for a limited belligerent action against China, without Congressional action.

Early in February 1857, R. B. Forbes, one of the leading members of Russell and Company, an eminent merchant firm in Boston, wrote

---

[9] Marcy to Parker, No. 10, Washington, D.C., February 27, 1857, *DI-USNA,* 77:38, p. 151.

[10] Lewis Cass to William B. Reed, No. 2, Washington, D. C., May 30, 1857, *ibid.,* p. 156.

[11] *Ibid.*

[12] Marcy to Parker, No. 9, Washington, D.C., February 2, 1857, *ibid.,* p. 145.

[13] Pierce to Marcy, Philadelphia, April 5, 1857, Marcy MSS, Library of Congress, LXXV, 49475.

[14] Gerard Hallock to Marcy, April 2, 1857, *ibid.,* LXXV, 49471.

a long letter to Cushing.[15] In it Forbes recalled that early in 1854, while the State Department was pondering over the problems caused by the recall of Commissioner Humphrey Marshall, Secretary Marcy had honored him by asking his view in regard to China. His reply had been later forwarded to the new American commissioner to China.[16] At the present time, said Forbes, when the federal government was on the verge of a change in administration, it was probable that no very decided orders would be given to Dr. Parker and Commodore Armstrong. " ... and yet there never has occurred a time, since I have known China," stressed Forbes, "when it appears to me so necessary to act promptly as at the present moment."[17] Thus he desired to offer his suggestions for the formulation of a new policy. The Americans now had "a just ground for quarrel." Therefore, he thought that it was now time to make a permanent treaty with China. " ... at this time, and if we can act in concert with England and France," said Forbes, "the show of force will bring the Emperor to terms without much bloodshed."

This change of attitude by the leading China merchants in Boston is very interesting but not surprising. During the peaceful early 1840's when the more enlightened Ch'i-ying was in power, trade in the Five Ports had progressed profitably and easily absorbed the capital that Americans could provide for the China trade. They were comparatively satisfied with conditions as they were. Any change of the *status quo* along the Chinese coast could conceivably injure American commercial interests. In practice the American merchants had no objection even to the illegal opium trade so long as they had a profitable share in the carrying trade.[18]

After the outbreak of the Taiping Rebellion, the circumstances regarding trade seem to have changed rapidly. The situation in China

---

[15] R. B. Forbes to Caleb Cushing, Boston, February 11, 1857, Cushing MSS, Library of Congress.

[16] Forbes's recollection is confirmed on Marcy's instruction to McLane, No. 7, Washington, D.C., May 8, 1854, *DI-USNA*, 77:38, p. 94.

[17] See footnote 15. Few writers have believed that the Boston merchants were so strongly in favor of a U. S. collaboration with the Anglo-French alliance in 1857. Some scholars even indulged in the conviction that they were constantly anti-British. See W. C. Costin, *Great Britain and China 1833-1860* (Oxford: The Clarendon Press, 1937), p. 305.

[18] For an exhaustive treatment of Sino-American trade from 1844 to 1860, see the excellent article by Earl Swisher, "The Character of American Trade with China, 1844-1860," *University of Colorado Studies,* Ser. C (Studies in the Social Sciences), I, No. 2 (1941), 156-80. Also consult Eldon Griffin, *Clippers and Consuls, American Consular and Commercial Relations with Eastern Asia, 1845-1860* (Ann Arbor, Mich.: Edwards Brothers, 1938), pp. 17-24.

which had been unsatisfactory to the British also gradually failed to satisfy the Americans, whose commerce in the Far East was expanding. The policy of Yeh Ming-ch'en at Canton and the chaotic situation caused by the Taipings in the Yangtze valley and along the coast hurt the Americans more than the British, who had better protection from their home government. Commissioner Marshall's insistence on neutrality during the Triad Rebellion in Shanghai helped to reinforce the merchants' desire for a change in the traditional policy. Since the new group of "barbarian experts" under Emperor Hsien-feng appeared more ignorant than those under the previous Emperor, and since there was no way to get them to alter their policy, a group of American merchants gradually began to favor a limited collaboration with the British.

III

Under these pressures both at home and from abroad, therefore, both President Pierce and Secretary of State Marcy felt it extremely hard to formulate a China policy. If the United States joined the alliance, she would have to participate in the war with China. However limited the projected war might be, it would still not be approved by Congress, which was already beset by the slavery issue and other internal problems. Thus, even given the prospect of a limited war, to commit the United States to the Anglo-French alliance was out of the question.[19]

Maintaining such a stand at this crucial moment, however, was not easy. The President and the Secretary of State had to restrain Commissioner Parker, order the already involved United States naval officers away from Chinese waters, persuade Attorney General Cushing to oppose a belligerent action in China, and, most important of all, persuade their successors, President-elect Buchanan and Secretary-to-be Lewis Cass, to continue the Pierce-Marcy policy. Though they had only a few weeks left in the White House, Pierce and Marcy set busily to work to put their policy into operation.

In an instruction issued on February 2, 1857, Marcy wrote to Parker: "The British Government evidently have objects beyond those contemplated by the United States and we ought not to be drawn along

---

[19] John W. Foster, *American Diplomacy in the Orient* (New York: Houghton, Mifflin and Co., 1903) pp. 229 ff.; Roy Franklin Nichols, *Franklin Pierce, Young Hickory of the Granite Hills* (Philadelphia: University of Pennsylvania Press, 1958), p. 499; Tyler Dennett, *Americans in Eastern Asia* (New York: The Macmillan Co., 1922), pp. 290, 292-93.

with it however anxious it may be for our cooperation."[20] In the same instruction, the Secretary also lamented that many Americans, in the absence of instructions from Washington, had already erroneously joined the British or adopted their method of dealing with the Chinese. Concerning the assault at the Barrier Forts, Marcy said, "it was not a discreet act to send a boat from the *San Jacinto* to 'sound the River in the vicinity of the Forts.' This act provoked the fire upon the boat." The President, said Marcy, was "inclined to regret that there had not been more caution on the part of our naval force in the beginning and more forebearance in the subsequent steps."

The Secretary of State requested the Commissioner to conduct a thorough investigation of the display of the American flag during the British attack of the city. Should he prove that Consul Keenan had done it, Keenan should be removed from office. Marcy said: "The President is called upon by a high sense of duty to manifest his displeasure at such conduct."[21] These instructions clearly indicate that both President Pierce and Secretary Marcy were opposed to intervention in China and to collaboration with England.

On February 27, nearly four weeks after this instruction had been sent to the Commissioner, Parker's dispatch No. 34, in which he had proposed the "last resort" action, reached Washington. This dispatch further irritated Marcy. In his reply to Parker,[22] Marcy noted that the subject of a collaboration with the two European powers had already been submitted to President Pierce through the French minister in Washington. However, the President did not believe that Sino-American relations warranted the "last resort." Besides, the military and naval forces of the United States could be used only by the authority of Congress. "The 'last resort' means war," said Marcy, "and the Executive branch of this government is not the war-making power." Furthermore, there was no obligation resting upon China to negotiate in regard to the revision of the treaty at Peking or any place in the vicinity of the capital. "For the protection and security of Americans in China, and the protection of their property," concluded Marcy, "it may be expedient to increase our naval force on the China station, but the President will not do it for aggressive purposes."

In the meantime, Pierce and Marcy had to keep the Boston mer-

---

[20] Marcy to Parker, No. 9, Washington, D.C., February 2, 1857, *DI-USNA*, 77:38, p. 147.

[21] *Ibid.*, p. 149.

[22] Marcy to Parker, No. 10, February 27, 1857, *DI-USNA*, 77:38, p. 151.

chant lobby from gaining influence in Washington and had to bring their colleagues and successors in the executive branch of the government into line. This work they did, it seems, very successfully. In a letter to Marcy on April 5, 1857, after he had already left the White House, Pierce wrote:[23]

I was glad to receive your note of the 3rd inst., and to learn that our policy in regard to affairs in China is not to be departed from. You have, of course, seen Mr. [William] Appleton who visited Washington at the request of the merchants of Boston, who are specially interested in China trade. He doubtless found it vain to urge their views in reference to our friend Genl. Cushing alth' the eminent fitness of the selection [of a new commissioner to China (?)] wd not be questioned by any intelligent man. . . .

This is the only instance to be found in the American archives up to that time indicating a president's concern over the continuation of his China policy by his successor.

The Pierce-Marcy China policy was fully continued by President Buchanan and Secretary of State Cass for the next four years. This approach was formulated without regard to the pressure of various vested interest groups. It was not based on the immediate commercial interests of the United States, but upon the interest of the nation in the long run.

After the change of administrations at Washington from Pierce to Buchanan, the British renewed their appeal to the American government for close cooperation in China. The matter was formally taken up by Lord Napier, British minister at Washington, who negotiated with Lewis Cass, Secretary of State of the Buchanan administration. In several meetings starting on March 14, 1857, the British suggested that the United States government grant "concurrent and active cooperation" with the two European powers—Great Britain and France— and authorize the United States naval and diplomatic authorities in China to act in concert with the agents of the two allied powers.[24] At the same time, the British minister explained fully to the United States the intentions of Great Britain in China, transmitting copies of instructions to Sir John Bowring for the revision of the treaties and of the instructions that had been issued to the British naval force. The

---

[23] William L. Marcy MSS, Manuscript Division, Library of Congress, LXXV, 49475.

[24] Napier to Cass, March 14, 30, 1857, Notes from the British Legation, Vol. XXXIV, Department of State Archives; quoted in Dennett, *Americans in Eastern Asia,* p. 300.

plan contemplated the complete destruction of the Barrier Forts, and, if that were not suffcient, a blockade of the Yangtze River as far as the Grand Canal and a further blockade of the mouth of the Pei-ho. The instructions for the revision of the treaty included: residence at Peking for diplomatic representatives of foreign powers; extension of commercial intercourse with the coast and into the interior; abolition of transit taxes in the interior. No exclusive privileges were sought for Great Britain and legalization of the opium trade was not mentioned.[25]

The negotiations at Washington continued intermittently for a month. On March 30, Lord Napier forwarded to Cass a memorandum to be placed in the hands of the President. In this document the British argued that China would not be able to offer greater resistance than she had done in the war of 1842, for since then she had been worn down by internal troubles while the British had been strengthened by a new ally, France. They promised that the new war would be "abridged" as much as possible and that the imperial government of China would not be weakened more than necessary. The allied objects were later summarized by Secretary Cass:[26]

1. To procure from the Chinese Government a recognition of the right of other powers to have accredited Ministers at the Court of Peking, to be received by the Emperor, and to be in communication with the authorities charged with the Foreign Affairs of the Empire.

2. An extension of commercial intercourse with China, which is now restricted to five ports enumerated in the treaty.

3. A reduction of the tariff of duties levied upon domestic produce in transit from the interior to the coast, as the amount now imposed is said to be a violation of the treaty....

4. A stipulation for religious freedom to all foreigners in China.

5. An arrangement for the suppression of piracy.

6. Provision for extending the benefits of the proposed treaty to all the other civilized Powers of the earth.

These "objects," as Cass stated, were recognized by President Buchanan as just and expedient; but the Americans hesitated to agree because these objects would not justify a war with China. Moreover, President Buchanan and Secretary Cass seem to have suspected, as had their predecessors, that the British had "objects beyond those con-

---

[25] *Ibid.*, pp. 301-2.

[26] Lewis Cass to William B. Reed, No. 2, Washington, D.C., May 30, 1857, *DI-USNA*, 77:38.

templated by the United States,"[27] such as the legalization of the opium trade, which, for various reasons, were omitted from the British overture to the United States. The new President and Secretary of State were fully convinced by the reasoning of their predecessors, whose policy was continued unchanged. Since the British war with China had already started and would be extended to other areas in China by the new Anglo-French alliance, the Buchanan administration also felt that it should keep from being involved. Hence, the British appeal for cooperation with the United States was formally rejected on April 10, 1857.[28]

This clear decision made the recall of Parker inevitable, since he favored military action against China and even territorial acquisition. On April 22, 1857, William B. Reed was appointed to replace him, and two days later Parker was formally recalled.[29]

IV

While both the Pierce and Buchanan administrations were formulating an independent policy toward China, Commissioner Parker was working eagerly in the direction of close cooperation with the allies. Parker, of course, was in the dark about what was going on in Washington. Marcy's instruction of February 2, which emphatically disapproved of his previous proposal, did not reach him until May 5. Before that directive reached China, Parker hoped that his policy would have the support of the authorities at Washington, or at least the approval of the new President. Even before Buchanan took office, Parker addressed him a long letter on February 13, 1857, trying to convince the President-elect to back his "last resort" policy.[30]

In that letter Parker first complained of the maltreatment of foreigners in China and argued that only the revision of the treaty could rectify the situation. Great Britain, France, and the United States were very similarly situated in respect to China. *"It is a settled point that the former two governments will apply themselves to the task with vigor,"* said Parker, *"and every sentiment of national respect and interest demand that the United States should do the same."* He requested that a sufficient naval force be sent to China to join the British

---

[27] Marcy to Parker, No. 9, February 2, 1857, Washington, D.C., *ibid.,* 145.

[28] Dennett, *Americans in Eastern Asia,* p. 302.

[29] Cass to Reed, No. 1, Washington, D.C., April 22, 1857, *DI-USNA,* 77:38, pp. 153-55; Cass to Parker, No. 12, Washington, D.C., April 24, *ibid.,* p. 156. For the reason of Parker's recall see also Foster, *American Diplomacy in the Orient,* p. 230.

[30] *Parker Correspondence,* p. 1205.

and the French *"in the campaign already initiated."* Favoring the cooperation of the three powers, Parker said: *"Of the propriety of concurrent yet independent action in relation to China on the part of the treaty powers, the sentiments of the governments at London, Paris, and Washington have been unanimous."*[31] By this time, however, the British and French had already formed a plan for joint action against China. Parker seems to have purposely avoided mentioning the alliance in order to make his proposal more acceptable to Washington.

Without waiting for approval from Washington, Parker went ahead with his own program in China. Early in 1857 he seemed to have given serious consideration to a permanent territorial acquisition from China. Since it was his understanding that Great Britain and France had already begun working in that direction, he felt the United States must not be left behind. The best place for American occupation within the Chinese Empire was Formosa.

Parker was not the first American citizen to show his interest in the island of Formosa. The idea of American occupation of that island had long attracted the attention of ambitious Americans, especially the merchants at Canton who had repeatedly tried to exploit this island for a new fortune. In 1854, Commodore M. C. Perry sent a well-arranged expedition to that island. Although Perry did nothing more than collect information, he did speak of the necessity of extending the "territorial jurisdiction" of the United States to the island of Formosa[32] and encouraged American merchants in China to sponsor other expeditions.

In 1855 two American adventurers, Gideon Nye, Jr., and W. M. Robinet, a Peruvian naval officer who had become an American citizen in a somewhat informal way, sent a well organized, large-scale commercial expedition to Formosa. By the orders of Peter Parker, who was then the chargé d'affaires, and Commodore M. C. Perry, they made a thorough investigation of the political and economic conditions of that island.[33] In the meantime, several American commercial houses were also attracted by the success of the expedition. Rather than create opposition among themselves, they made arrangements to carry

---

[31] Peter Parker to President-elect Buchanan, Macao, February 13, 1857, *Parker Correspondence*, pp. 1025-28.

[32] *Senate Exec. Doc.*, No. 34, 33 Cong., 2 sess., p. 81. For a brief analysis of Perry's expedition to Formosa, consult Dennett, *Americans in Eastern Asia*, pp. 272-73.

[33] Gideon Nye, Jr., to Peter Parker, Macao, February 10, 1857, *Parker Correspondence*, pp. 1203-5.

out their business jointly and bought the *Science,* an American barge.[34]
It was probably the same vessel that Russell and Company had once
leased to the Chinese *taotai* at Shanghai to help fight the rebels in the
Yangtze.[35]

The *Science,* under the command of Captain George A. Potter, was
sent to the port of Taiwan (presently Tainan) in the summer of 1855.
Here they established a firm and raised the American flag. Captain
Potter even signed an agreement with the local Chinese *taotai* who,
by ignoring completely the law of the nation, opened the port of Taiwan to American traders.[36]

On February 10, 1857, Nye wrote a long letter to Parker suggesting
that since China had failed to exercise her sovereignty over the abo-
riginals in Formosa, "Formosa's eastern shore and southern point . . .
should be protected by the United States of America." Nye said that
he and some other persons would be willing to assist in its "colonization" if he received the assurance of the government of the United
States that he should be recognized and protected. " . . . *at this time,*"
Nye stressed, "a commencement might be made without objection
from any power."[37]

This letter impressed Parker deeply. He forwarded it to the State
Department and hoped that "the government of the United States
may not *shrink* from the action."[38] At the same time, he started to
work energetically for a true American colonization of Formosa. On
February 27, Parker held a conference with Commodore Armstrong
at Macao after which he wrote, "the subject of Formosa has been
confidentially considered."[39] Both men agreed that Formosa was "a
most desirable island, and would be particularly valuable to the United
States." They felt an American occupation of it was justifiable in accordance with the principles of international law. But both of them
were afraid that the small United States naval force in the Five Ports
might not be able to protect the American citizens and interests,
"should the Chinese government, on consequence of the adoption of

---

[34] W. M. Robinet to Peter Parker, Hong Kong, March 2, 1857, *ibid.,* pp. 1211-15.

[35] Cf. chap. 9.

[36] *Agreement entered into with the Taoutae, or Intendant of Circuit in the island*
signed between the Intendant of Formosa and George A. Potter, Taiwan, June 27,
1855, *Parker Correspondence,* p. 1218.

[37] Gideon Nye to Peter Parker, Macao, February 10, 1857, *Parker Correspondence,*
pp. 1203-5.

[38] Parker to the Secretary of State, No. 5, Macao, February 12, 1857, *ibid.,* pp.
1183-84.

[39] *Memoranda* of the conference between Parker and Armstrong, Macao, February
27, 1857, *ibid.,* pp. 1210-11.

such a measure [as the United States occupation of Formosa] see fit to initiate hostilities towards them." Then Parker warned the authorities that if Formosa should "unfortunately pass into other hands," it would not be his fault, but due rather to the inadequacy of the naval force in China.[40]

Five days after the Parker-Armstrong conference, W. M. Robinet wrote a long letter to Parker in which Robinet summarized the development of American trade on that island during the last three years and reported in great detail about the economic and political conditions there. He particularly mentioned the poor Chinese defense work. ". . . 250 men well armed could take the island and hold it," said Robinet. Thus, he suggested prompt American action to colonize Formosa. He wrote:[41]

Since it is generally said that it is against the views of the United States to have settlements or colonies far from their own borders, it therefore might not be desirable for the government to take measures to acquire the control of the island, yet it would advance the cause of humanity, religion, and civilization, if they would guaranty protection to Americans who should erect an independent government there. . . .

Robinet further stated that it seemed to him "such a plan would not meet the disapproval of European powers."

Parker seemed to have been convinced by Robinet's argument, which, as Parker saw, was similar to his own "last resort" proposal of the previous December. At the time he forwarded Robinet's letter to Washington, Parker wrote:[42]

That island [Formosa] may not long remain a portion of the empire of China is possible; and in the event of its being severed from the empire politically, as it is geographically, that the United States should possess it is obvious, particularly as respects the great principle of balance of power. Great Britain has her St. Helena in the Atlantic, her Gibraltar and Malta in the Mediterranean, her Aden in the Red sea, Mauritius, Ceylon, Penang, and Singapore in the Indian ocean, and Hong Kong in the China seas. If the United States is so disposed, and can *arrange* for the possession of Formosa, England certainly cannot object.

Parker further stated that had he been given adequate naval force, he might have acted at once, "*pending reference to the government at Washington* for confirmation." This action, adopted by a minister with

---

[40] *Ibid.*, p. 1211.
[41] W. M. Robinet to Peter Parker (Private), Hong Kong, March 2, 1857, *ibid.*, p. 1215.
[42] Parker to the Secretary of State, No. 6, Macao, March 10, 1857, *ibid.*, p. 1208.

"full powers" without previous approval from his home government, would have been permissable under the laws of nations.[43]

In the meantime, however, he received word that Britain might forestall the Americans in the occupation of the island of Formosa.[44] On receiving this report, Parker promptly addressed a solemn protest to Bowring against England's taking possession of that island. In doing so, Parker protested, Britain would violate her previous assurances that the policy of Her Majesty's government did not contemplate the acquisition of any exclusive rights or privileges in China. ". . . it is my full conviction," said Parker, "that the government of the United States is disposed to adopt the same policy in China as is represented by your excellency to be that of Great Britain." "In the event of the island of Formosa being severed politically from the empire of China," Parker thus claimed, "I trust to be able to substantiate a priority of claim to it on the part of the United States."[45]

To this protest, Bowring answered rather humorously that he could assure the American commissioner that the British government would not be jealous of the territorial ambitions of the United States toward China. He further said he would "cordially support your excellency in the attempt to give to it the strength and security of *legality*."[46] This answer was accepted as satisfactory by Parker, who was then awaiting word from Washington with regard to naval reinforcements.

This amusing episode not only indicated, as Dr. Dennett observed, that Parker wholly lacked a "sense of humor,"[47] but also showed Parker's poor observations as to the trend of development of contem-

---

[43] *Ibid.*, p. 1209.

[44] On March 21, 1857, Parker received a report from W. M. Robinet, who stated that Admiral Seymour and two important officers of the British Navy had visited him the previous afternoon. They asked for information about the island of Formosa and requested charts of the different ports. Admiral Seymour is reported to have said: "This island ought not to be allowed to exist in the hands of such a people, which cannot control even the cannibals of the eastern part, who murder our wrecked seamen." The Admiral then asked Robinet's cooperation in allowing a British officer to reside at the American firm to gather information. Seymour also asked Robinet to keep their conversation confidential. Robinet immediately reported the British visit to Commodore Armstrong, who thought it a pity that the Americans could do nothing about Formosa at that moment and asked Robinet to report to Parker about what had taken place. See Robinet to Parker, Hong Kong, March 21, 1857, *Parker Correspondence*, p. 1246.

[45] Parker to Bowring, Macao, March 21, 1857, *ibid.*, pp. 1247-48. Parker's letter from Macao was written on the same day that Robinet wrote his from Hong Kong. It seems that Robinet wrote in the morning, while Parker wrote in the evening immediately after he received Robinet's letter.

[46] Bowring to Parker, No. 10, Hong Kong, March 24, 1857, *ibid.*, pp. 1248-49.

[47] Dennett, *Americans in Eastern Asia*, p. 289.

porary international politics in the world. The British, prior to this incident, seemed to have abandoned their traditional territorial expansion in the Far East. Early in that year, the British Opposition in the Parliament had moved for votes of censure upon Bowring, whose high-handed proceedings had brought about hostilities in China. His position in China was saved by the popularity of Palmerston alone, who dissolved Parliament; Bowring was not in the position to adopt any policy of territorial acquistion in China.[48] The American commissioner had suddenly and belatedly adopted an expansionist policy of action, just as the British were giving it up.

V

In early April, two weeks after his amusing correspondence on Formosa, Parker held two conferences in Macao with Bowring and M. de Bourboulon, minister plenipotentiary of France, at the American legation and the French legation respectively. The three ministers each submitted a memorandum regarding their further cooperation in Chinese affairs. In the British memorandum, Bowring proposed "a common cooperation of the military and naval force of the treaty powers for the reduction of Canton."[49]

With apparently full confidence of support from his home government for close cooperation with the allies, Parker also wrote that the United States government wished to carry out a concurrent policy with the allies in respect to the revision of the treaties. He said that the local problems at Canton at first had concerned the British flag alone,

---

[48] On March 3, 1857, the Canton question was brought up for debate in the British House of Commons, where many eminent statesmen were opposed to Bowring's "attempt by force to increase our commercial relations with the East." In a speech Disraeli said: "Fifty years ago Lord Hastings offered to conquer China with 20,000 men ... but since the time when our Clives and Hastings founded our Indian Empire the position of affairs in the East had greatly changed. Great Powers have been brought into contact with us in the East. We have the Russian Empire and the American Republic there, and a system of political compromise has developed itself like the balance of power in Europe; and, if you are not cautious and careful in your conduct now in dealing with China, you will find that you are likely not to extend commerce, but to excite the jealousy of powerful states, and to involve yourselves in hostilities with nations not inferior to yourselves." For the complete text of the debates on China see *Hansard's Parliamentary Debates,* 3rd Series, CXLIV (March 3, 1857), 1726-1846; for the text of Disraeli's speech consult p. 1836.

In April, Palmerston dissolved Parliament and the Opposition were temporarily removed from their seats; thus Bowring's position in China remained unshaken. See Herbert Maxwell, *The Life and Letters of George William Frederick Fourth Earl of Clarendon* (London: Edward Arnold, 1913), II, 138-40.

[49] Memorandum of agreement submitted by Sir John Bowring, Macao, April 2, 1857, *Parker Correspondence,* p. 1282.

but that now all of the Western treaty powers were affected. Then Parker continued:[50]

> If at *this point* it should please the three powers to regard and treat [British attack on Canton] as affecting the whole of our diplomatic relations with China, the same will receive the cordial approval of the United States plenipotentiary and his aid in carrying it through in the manner contemplated by the propositions above presented and explained by the British plenipotentiary.

But he also stated that this promise would necessitate the sanction of his government. Sufficient time had not yet elapsed for these instructions to reach China, said Parker, but, confident that his project would be approved by the new President, he was sure they might be expected by an early mail.

A week later, on April 10, he sent another report to Washington saying that the cooperation of the United States was desired by the English and French ministers. So far as success was concerned, the advantage of the "triple co-operation" was very obvious. Although the executive branch of the federal government had no power to declare war, he thought the intended action at Canton would be of a local nature, which did not require the previous action of Congress.[51]

On April 30, the instruction no. 9 issued by former Secretary of State Marcy on February 2, 1857, reached Parker.[52] With this instruction, all Parker's previous expectations evaporated. Parker was even blamed for his failure to report the abuse of the American flag by Consul Keenan to Washington.[53] It should have been obvious to him that all his suggestions for a triple cooperation with the Anglo-French alliance (although not yet received in Washington) would be completely rejected. Unaware of his having been removed from office, Parker still hoped to win the support of the new Secretary of State, whose name he did not yet know. In a dispatch sent on May 5, Parker tried to justify his failure to report the abuse of the American flag by saying that it had never been officially presented to his notice. Besides, the Chinese had not protested. Then he stubbornly argued that failure to adopt his suggestion for a concurrent policy with the Anglo-

---

[50] Memorandum by the American Commissioner, Macao, April 2, 1857, *ibid.*, p. 1283.

[51] Parker to the Secretary of State, No. 14, Macao, April 10, 1857, *Parker Correspondence*, pp. 1278-79.

[52] See footnote 21.

[53] Marcy to Parker, No. 9, February 2, 1857, *DI-USNA*, 77:38, p. 145.

French alliance would prove, one day, to be a calamity rather than an advantage.[54]

It was, however, already too late for Parker to argue with his superiors. The instructions that he had received had given a hint of his impending removal. Parker suddenly reversed his previous cooperative attitude toward the British. He pursued thereafter a completely uncooperative policy. In July, Lord Elgin, the special plenipotentiary from the British government, reached Hong Kong. He immediately invited Parker to participate in a joint expedition to the north, but his invitation was discourteously rejected by Parker. This action was later considered by his successor, Commissioner William B. Reed, as one of the "double mischiefs" that Parker had done to jeopardize Anglo-American relations in China.[55]

Early in August, the dispatch for his recall at last reached him.[56] Greatly disappointed, Parker left China on August 21, 1857. This ended his long career in that country.

Thus, Parker was the second United States commissioner to China who was forced against his will to leave his position. Commissioner Humphrey Marshall had been recalled because he was too hostile to the British; Parker, however, was recalled because he had cooperated too closely with them. Both of them had dangerously overdeveloped their own policies in the absence of specific instructions from the State Department.

. [54] Parker to the Secretary of State, No. 19, Macao, May 5, 1857, *Parker Correspondence*, p. 1322. It is interesting to note that at this moment Parker's doggedness in defending his position, and the wording he chose in his dispatch arguing with his superiors in Washington, D. C. were similar to the position taken by Humphrey Marshall when the latter was recalled, although the two men were advocating diametrically opposed policies. See Marshall to the Secretary of State, Macao, November 21, 1853, *Marshall's Correspondence*, p. 307, and Parker to the Secretary of State, Macao, May 5, 1857, *Parker Correspondence*, p. 1322.

[55] William B. Reed to Lewis Cass, On Board the *Minnesota*, in the Harbor of Hong Kong, November 10, 1857, see *Senate Executive Documents*, No. 30, 36 Cong., 1 sess., p. 17. Hereafter to be cited as *Reed Correspondence*.

[56] Parker was recalled on April 24, 1857, but the official dispatch from the State Department did not reach him until nearly four months later.

14

WILLIAM B. REED AND THE SIGNING

OF THE TREATY OF TIENTSIN

I

WHEN the United States replaced Peter Parker, her commissioner to China, with William B. Reed, who later signed the Treaty of Tientsin, United States diplomacy in China made marked progress. The instructions to Reed indicated that the authorities at Washington were now trying to formulate the China policy themselves. Many former practices of policy making, such as consulting the merchants and missionaries or vesting large discretionary power in the United States commissioners in China, had become history.

This trend was readily understandable. First of all, the President himself had served as Secretary of State for a long time. He was comparatively more experienced in Far Eastern affairs than most of his predecessors in the White House—more so, indeed, than his Secretary of State, Lewis Cass, who did not have the experience of William L. Marcy, the former Secretary. Thus, during the four years of the Buchanan administration, the President was the "real Secretary" who took matters of foreign affairs, particularly Far Eastern affairs, in his own hands. Both Cass, the Secretary of State, and Reed, the commissioner to China, served only as his assistants in the making of China policy.[1] Moreover, after six years of civil war in China, the story of the Chinese rebels was well known by the authorities in Washington; this information greatly aided the President in making a proper decision regarding the Taipings. In addition to these advantages, the policies being pursued by the European powers in China were now made comparatively clear to Washington. With the recall of two commissioners from China, the authorities at Washington had passed

---

[1] Excellent reviews of the diplomatic careers of Buchanan, Marcy, and Cass are included in Samuel Flagg Bemis, ed., *The American Secretaries of State and Their Diplomacy* (New York: Pageant Book Co., 1958), V, 237-338; VI, 145-386.

their apprenticeship in Far Eastern diplomacy. Now they knew the China policy that would best serve the interests of the United States. Commissioner Reed was assigned to carry out this new policy, but he was subject to rigid control from the White House.

The new commissioner, William Bradford Reed, was an old-line Whig from Philadelphia. Born in 1806, Reed was graduated from the University of Pennsylvania in 1822. Then he studied law, joined the bar, and became a prominent attorney in his home state. In his thirties, he served in the Pennsylvania General Assembly, both in the House and in the Senate. He was appointed district attorney for Philadelphia for two terms in the early 1850's. Besides his law practice and public service, Reed was a part-time professor, teaching American history at the University of Pennsylvania for six years, until 1856.

With the growth of the Know-Nothing party and the decline of the Whigs, Reed became dissatisfied with his political affiliations. He joined the Democratic party in 1856 and supported Buchanan zealously in his presidential campaign. Because of his usefulness in urging his fellow Whigs to cast their votes for Buchanan, Reed was rewarded for his service by being appointed commissioner to China, a position desperately in need of a change.[2]

Unlike his predecessors under the Treaty of Wanghia, who were given comparatively simple instructions and much discretionary power in conducting their missions to China, Reed received the most detailed instructions since Cushing and was given little discretionary power for policy making. These instructions may be classified into three different fields: United States relations with the Chinese (including both the Imperialists and the rebels); United States relations with the European powers in China; and the readjustment of American diplomatic and consular services in that country.

With regard to the Chinese civil war, the new Secretary's instruction to Reed was more decisive and specific than any issued by his predecessor, Marcy. "We have no other concern in its progress or result than to take care that our rights are preserved inviolate," wrote Cass. "We have no reason to believe that one of the contending parties is more favorably disposed towards foreigners than the other, or more ready to extend commercial intercourse with them."[3] The Manchu re-

---

[2] *Dictionary of American Biography* (New York: Charles Scribner's Sons, 1943), XV, 461-62.

[3] Cass to Reed, No. 2, Washington, D.C., May 30, 1857, *DI-USNA*, 77:38, p. 165.

gime and the Taiping authorities were equally bound to the Western treaty powers by treaty stipulations, the directive continued, and would be held to their faithful observance. Since there was no sign that the government of the rebels would be recognized by the United States *de facto,* United States diplomatic intercourse with the Manchus would be continued and extended under the present circumstances. The former claims and grievances against China must be redressed and the Treaty of Wanghia should also be revised. In all these matters Reed was instructed that he must be guided by his own discretion, but within a specific limit set by the President. " . . . on your side these efforts must be confined to firm representations," the directive stated, "appealing to the justice and policy of the Chinese authorities, and leaving to your own Government to determine upon the course to be adopted, should your representation be fruitless."[4]

In speaking of the American commissioner's relationship with other envoys of the European powers, Cass reminded Reed that Great Britain and France had more extensive objects in China and would use coercive measures to obtain them. There seemed to be an entire unanimity of action between Great Britain and France, said Cass, extending even to armed cooperation. Since most of the American demands against China were included in theirs, Reed should offer "peaceful cooperation" to them and should communicate with them frankly upon all the points of common interest and give them proper aid in their accomplishment.[5] But Reed was further reminded that the United States was not at war with the government of China, nor did it seek to enter that empire for any purposes other than those of lawful commerce and the protection of the lives and property of its citizens. The whole nature of the policy of the United States government necessarily confined its action within these limits and did away with all motives either for territorial aggrandizement or the acquisition of political power in that distant region.[6] Thus, the Commissioner was cautioned not to join the British and the French for military actions against China; nor was he allowed to advocate the legalization of opium in that country. In carrying out his mission, Reed was also directed to cooperate with the Russians, whose envoy was reported on the way to China for a supposedly peaceful mission.[7]

---

[4] *Ibid.,* p. 159.

[5] *Ibid.*

[6] *Ibid.,* p. 161.

[7] *Ibid.,* pp. 159-60. This part of the instruction actually alienated the Americans from the British almost completely. Ever since the outbreak of the Crimean War, the

Buchanan's policy toward China actually contained nothing new. His judgment about both the rebels and the Imperialists in that country and the policy adopted toward them were exactly the same as those of the former commissioners, Marshall and McLane. The difference between the earlier proposals and the new decision, however, was apparent only in attitudes expressed toward the European powers in China. As previously explained, Marshall had preferred to negotiate singlehandedly with the Imperialists, and McLane was in favor of limited armed collaboration with England and France for the same purpose; but the new administration now chose a middle course between them, namely a "peaceful cooperation" with the Western powers.[8]

Reed was given more supervisory power over the American diplomatic and consular institutions in China than any of his predecessors. The State Department addressed a circular to the United States consuls in China requesting them to carry the Commissioner's wishes into effect. Moreover, through an arrangement between the State and Navy Departments, the naval forces in the Eastern seas were placed, as far as possible, within the Commissioner's control, and a magnificent warship, the *Minnesota,* was specially assigned to him not only for his passage to China, but during his residence there. In addition to the warship, the commander of the East India squadron of the United

---

major concern that drove the British to favor a collaboration with other Western powers in China was their fear of the Russian expansion in the East. They were afraid that "the Chinese authorities might make use of Russia to drive the Western Powers out of the five ports." See Bowring to Clarendon, November 27, 1855, *F.O.,* 17/235, in W. C. Costin, *Great Britain and China 1833-1860* (Oxford: The Clarendon Press, 1937), pp. 195-96. The British envoy to China even believed that the Russians might get possession of the island of Chusan, from where the Russian traders were to operate. See "Minutes of a meeting held at the American legation on April 1, 1857, at 4 p.m., by the representatives of the treaty powers," in *Parker Correspondence,* p. 1281. Thus the British anxiety for Western cooperation in an early expedition to the north was based more or less on the conviction that the Russians might be combatted in the north before they had a chance to drive to the south seas. See Costin, p. 196.

[8] In his instruction No. 12 issued on June 20, 1858, Cass directed the Commissioner to obtain from China "a lease, say for a century, of the Island of Kean" twelve miles north of Macao. See *DI-USNA,* 77:38, p. 181. This is probably the first, if not the only, attempt made for territorial acquisition in China ever to be initiated by a Secretary of State of the United States. It seems that the State Department was then under the influence of the U.S. Navy, which desired a coaling station along the China coast. Since Cass had left this directive up to the discretion of the Commissioner, Reed did not take it up with the Chinese authorities, primarily because the center of foreign trade in China had moved from Canton to Shanghai. Besides, Reed argued that a lease for a century was equal to permanent possession, and the United States did not have any desire for territorial acquisition in China. See Reed to Cass, No. 32, on board the *Minnesota* off Woosung, September 15, 1858, *Reed Correspondence,* p. 435.

States was ordered to charter a small steamer for the purpose of ascending rivers or entering ports inaccessible to the other vessels in China.[9]

After accepting this new appointment with its specific instructions for his important mission to China, and even before he sailed from the United States, Reed began to plan a course of action. The only procedure that he felt was necessary to reverse was the method of redressing American claims against China. His predecessor, Peter Parker, had suggested to both the British authorities in China and the authorities at Washington that the American claims be included in those of the British when the British government presented its claims for indemnity to the Chinese. "It is unnecessary for me to say," wrote Reed, "this suggestion impresses me unfavorably." Thus he intended to discard this proposal. Reed's decision on this matter was fully supported by the Secretary of State.[10]

When he arrived at Hong Kong on November 5, 1857, Reed found the port of Canton completely paralyzed by the allied blockade ordered by Lord Elgin and Baron Gros. These two men had just been sent to China by the British and French governments respectively to carry out the new allied policy against China. The suburbs of Canton were completely ruined by the skirmishes that had been occurring intermittently for nearly a year; the Chinese fleet of war junks had been decimated by the British naval attack; all the forts along the Pearl River were in the hands of the British invaders. An all-out allied attack on the city of Canton was imminent. The mandarins, particularly Yeh Ming-ch'en, were as stubborn as usual. They were unaware of the coming danger and no defense work had been undertaken. Had the British forces not been delayed by an uprising in India, the allied attack on the city of Canton might have started before the arrival of Commissioner Reed.[11]

---

[9] *DI-USNA*, 77:38, pp. 166-67.

[10] Reed to the Secretary of State, No. 1, Old Point Comfort, Virginia, June 26, 1857, *Reed Correspondence*, pp. 13-14. The Secretary of State promptly replied to the Commissioner's first dispatch: ". . . to unite our claims with those of other countries would imply a disposition on our part, not only to let them share the fate of their associates, but to participate actively in all the proceedings which might be thought necessary for their advancement. This, you are aware, is not the policy which has been adopted by the United States in respect to the affairs in China. . . ." See Cass to Reed, No. 5, Washington, D.C., June 29, 1857, *ibid.*, p. 14.

[11] For general reference to the situation in Canton see Hosea Ballou Morse, *The International Relations of the Chinese Empire* (New York: Longmans, Green and Co., 1910), I, 489 ff. For a detailed firsthand account of the long-range planning of a British attack against the Chinese see Laurence Oliphant, *Narrative of the Earl of Elgin's Mission to China and Japan in the Years 1857, '58, '59* (London: William

Knowing that the new American commissioner would not cooperate with their projected assault on Canton, Lord Elgin and Baron Gros gave Reed a cold reception at Hong Kong, in sharp contrast to that given to Commissioner Parker by Sir John Bowring nearly two years before. [12]

While the American diplomats were discussing a new method of action in China, Lord Palmerston, obviously aware of the change in United States diplomacy, also delivered an important statement to the House of Commons, on June 19, 1857. Concerning foreign claims in an international war, he said: [13]

Now, it is an undoubted principle of international law, that when one government deems it right to exercise acts of hostility against the territory of another Power, the subjects or citizens of third Powers, who may happen to be resident in the place attacked, have no claim whatever upon the Government which, in the exercise of its national rights, commits these acts of hostility ... if they have any claim at all, it must be upon the Government of the country in which they reside; but they certainly can have no claim whatever upon the Government which thinks right to commit acts of hostility against the State.

Being informed of this declaration upon his arrival in Hong Kong, Reed remarked: "It can hardly be questioned that this view has reference to possible claims on his government, arising out of hostilities last fall against Canton." Thus he found himself in a very embarrassing position with the British at Hong Kong; and any possibility of rapprochement had been made even more difficult by his predecessor, Peter Parker. After a brief conversation with Lord Elgin, Reed reported to Washington about the harm caused by Parker to Anglo-American relations in China. "Down to a certain point the ministers of the treaty powers, and especially Sir John Bowring, were encouraged [by Parker] in the most extravagant expectation of cooperation on our part to the extent even of acquisition of territory," said Reed. "This was the first harm done." Further harm was done when Parker, discouraged by Washington in his extreme policy of cooperation, suddenly repelled all suggestions of friendly concert on points of common interest. This imprudence of Parker, said Reed, was very hard to remedy.[14]

Blackwood and Sons, 1859), I, 15-40. The author of this book was Lord Elgin's private secretary.

[12] Wiliam B. Reed, MS Private Diary of Mission to China, Manuscript Division, Library of Congress, pp. 122-27.

[13] *Hansard's Parliamentary Debates*, 3rd Series, CXLVI (June 19, 1857), p. 41.

[14] Reed to Cass, No. 3, Hong Kong, November 10, 1857, *Reed Correspondence,* pp.

During these lonesome hours, however, Reed was cheered by the sudden arrival of the Russian envoy, Count Evfimii Poutiatin, who reached Hong Kong on November 14, on board the Russian steamer *Amerika*. With instructions for close cooperation between themselves from their respective governments, the two ministers were delighted to greet one another. Count Poutiatin, as Reed saw him, was an "oldish man," who had married twice—both times to English women—and spoke good English.[15]

After a brief meeting, the two envoys journeyed together to Macao on November 16. On the same day, Reed announced his arrival in China to Imperial Commissioner Yeh Ming-ch'en, requesting an official interview so that a negotiation for the revision of the Treaty of Wanghia might be discussed. This request was politely rejected by Yeh on the ground that there was no suitable place to meet the American envoy because the suburbs of Canton had been completely ruined by the British. Furthermore, Yeh said, there was no necessity for a revision of the American treaty. To Reed, Yeh's refusal seemed valid. "Yeh has certainly touched the weak point of our case," Reed wrote in a report to Washington. "No one can read the thirty-fourth article without being struck with its ambiguous terms."[16]

While Reed was pondering his next action, the allied forces, 6,000

17-18. In this dispatch, Reed also quoted from Palmerston's speech of June 19; but he used a different version, which was probably printed in contemporary newspapers. For this criticism of Parker's policy see William B. Reed to Lewis, on board the *Minnesota* in the harbor of Hong Kong, November 10, 1857, *ibid.*, p. 17.

[15] Count Poutiatin was sent by the Russian Court to Japan early in the spring of 1857. On April 22, he reached Kiatchka, on the Chinese frontier, and communicated his arrival to Peking, asking the Manchu authority for access to the Imperial Court. His request was ignored. After staying in Kiatchka for six weeks, he continued eastward until he reached the Amur River, at the mouth of which he embarked on a Russian steamer, the *Amerika*, for the Pei-ho, where his request for access to Peking was again rejected. After visiting that port twice with no results, he went to Japan and succeeded in signing a treaty with her on October 24, 1857; then he returned to Shanghai to await the arrival of the American commissioner. The Count personally related this story to Reed. See Reed to the Secretary of State, No. 35, Macao, November 25, 1857, *Reed Correspondence*, p. 20. Also William B. Reed, MS Diary, pp. 122-27, 138. For a good brief review of Russia's expansion in the Far East and the early period of the Poutiatin mission, see Aitchen K. Wu, *China and the Soviet Union* (New York: The John Day Co., 1950), pp. 47 ff, 64-68.

[16] Reed to Cass, No. 36, On board the *Minnesota* in the Harbor of Hong Kong, December 15, 1857, *Reed Correspondence*, p. 49. Although Article 34 of the Treaty of Wanghia gives the United States the privilege of treaty revision after twelve years, it also states that "its provisions shall not be altered without grave cause." It was hard, therefore, for the American commissioner to define whether "the grave cause" had existed between the two countries. See *Treaties, Conventions, etc., between China and Foreign States* (Shanghai: Statistical Department of the Inspectoral General of Customs, 1908), I, 486.

strong, launched their attack at Canton on December 15. Twenty days later Chinese resistance at Canton collapsed completely and on January 5, 1858, Yeh and his colleagues were taken prisoner by the allies. The allied authorities, however, soon found it impossible to hold a city of over a million residents with such a tiny force, even though they adopted a brutal rule over the populace.[17] Compelled by necessity, they restored Pei-kuei, the governor of Kuangtung, as the chief magistrate of Canton to maintain order in the city under the direction of the allied authorities. When the news reached Peking, however, the Court does not seem to have comprehended the real situation at Canton. The young Emperor simply ordered Yeh to be removed from his official position and appointed Huang Tsung-han, a member of the Grand Council, to succeed him.[18] Besides, the loss of Canton in 1857 was completely different from the loss of that same city in 1840; this time it created no serious alarm elsewhere. In Shanghai and other treaty ports along the coast, the Chinese people and the mandarins were peacefully mingling with the foreigners and business was going on as usual. This seeming indifference of the Chinese to the allied capture of Canton nullified the possibility of any gains that the allies had expected in a localized war with China. Thus they were obliged to take more decisive action in the north.

On February 6, 1858, the two allied ministers issued invitations to both Commissioner Reed and Count Poutiatin suggesting that the four treaty powers immediately demand that the Manchu government send an Imperial Commissioner to Shanghai to negotiate simultaneously with the four ministers. Should this demand be rejected, the four powers would launch a combined expedition to Tientsin.[19] After a brief meeting among themselves, both the American and the Russian ministers decided to accept the Anglo-French invitation and to sail north. Late in February, the communications, drafted by the four ministers,

---

[17] In one of his dispatches, Commissioner Reed reported to Washington: "A few weeks ago, in consequence of a murderous attack made on a party of camp stragglers, the French commanding officers took possession of a street or neighborhood, marked off by measurement and carefully guarded a number of houses, and then sent in armed parties with orders (executed with characteristic fidelity) to butcher every male inhabitant found within. A large number perished." See Reed to Cass, No. 29, On board the *Minnesota*, off Shanghai, July 29, 1858, *ibid.*, p. 387.

[18] *IWSM-HF*, XVII, 41a. For a brief biographic sketch of Huang see Arthur W. Hummel, ed., *Eminent Chinese of the Ch'ing Period* (Washington, D.C.: Government Printing Office, 1943-44), I, 283; *Ch'ing-shih lieh-chuan* (Shanghai: Chung Hua Book Co., 1928), XVIII, la.

[19] *Reed Correspondence*, p. 125. Reed obviously believed that this could be done peacefully.

were formally presented by the consuls of Great Britain, France, and the United States, to the office of the governor-general of Liang-Kiang, which was then temporarily located at Soochow. The American and the Russian letters were enclosed in one envelope.[20]

Late in March, the four ministers arrived in Shanghai, where they received official replies from Ho Kuei-ch'ing, the new governor-general of Liang-Kiang. In reply to the ministers' requests, Ho advised them to go back to Canton and to negotiate with the new Imperial Commissioner, Huang Tsung-han, who was on his way to that city. This suggestion was rejected by all four ministers. Thus, another joint expedition to the Pei-ho became inevitable.[21]

Reed explained his position on the forthcoming expedition to the Pei-ho in a dispatch to Washington dated April 3. He said that should the action of Great Britain and France be peaceful, though decisive and urgent, he would join with it thoroughly and completely. If, however, hostilities should recommence, he would obey the spirit and letter of his instructions, either continuing as a passive spectator of the war or retiring to await a chance for peaceful interposition or further instructions from home. He also said that he had the support of the Russian minister, who had recently received new and decisive instructions to abstain strictly from any measures of hostility except in the event of extreme difficulty, in which case he would be given sufficient support by the Russian navy.[22]

After the four ministers had agreed to make a simultaneous expedition to the Pei-ho, Count Poutiatin sailed north from Shanghai on April 9; Lord Elgin followed him on the next day. Reed departed on April 11 on the United States frigate *Mississippi*, which was accompanied by a chartered steamer *Antelope*. In addition to Dr. Samuel Wells Williams, the official Chinese interpreter and secretary of the American legation, Reed enlisted another Chinese interpreter, W. A. P. Martin, a Presbyterian missionary from Ningpo, who could speak Mandarin. Four days after the departure of Reed, Baron Gros sailed from Shanghai. An unprecedented large-scale Western expedition therefore was on the way to the Pei-ho.[23]

---

[20] *IWSM-HF*, XVIII, 18a; Oliphant, *Elgin's Mission to China and Japan*, I, 195-204; *Reed Correspondence*, p. 220.

[21] Elgin to Clarendon, April 3, 1858, *F.O.*, 17/287, in Costin, *Great Britain and China*, p. 251; Reed to Cass, No. 11, Shanghai, April 3, 1858, *Reed Correspondence*, p. 220.

[22] *Ibid.*

[23] Morse, *The International Relations of the Chinese Empire*, p. 511; Costin, *Great Britain and China*, pp. 251 ff.; Henri Cordier, *L'Expédition de chine de 1857-58*,

II

When the news of a possible united expedition to the Pei-ho with a remarkable naval force from four Western powers reached Peking late in March, the Chinese authorities were understandably alarmed. Consequently, Chinese troops were sent to various strategic points in readiness for a possible Western attack. At the same time, the Emperor began, as he had done in 1854, to direct the negotiations personally and to follow his own policy—namely, to satisfy the Western envoys with limited concessions and to send them back south for further negotiations. In 1854, however, there had been only two envoys escorted by a small fleet at a time of unfavorable weather. Now there were four envoys with a much larger escorting fleet, which, as it was spring, could remain at the mouth of the Pei-ho for at least five or six months. Hence, the Emperor understood that the negotiation must be conducted more skillfully. In 1854, the Emperor had prevented Kuei-liang, the governor-general of Chihli (Tientsin was under his jurisdiction), from going to Tientsin. Now he directed T'an T'ing-hsiang, the new governor-general, to proceed to Tientsin to supervise the negotiations in person.[24]

On March 21, the Emperor issued an edict giving precise instructions as to what preliminary steps the Chinese negotiators should take. First he ordered T'an to direct his subordinates to strengthen the defenses in the Ta-ku area without making obvious show. Also, the coastal inhabitants were to be prevented from supplying food to, or trading with, the Western ships; thus, the foreigners would not be able to remain in the area for long. At the same time, T'an was ordered to

---

histoire diplomatique notes et documents (London: G. Routledge and Co., 1858), pp. 333 ff; *Reed Correspondence*, pp. 220-24; Reed MS Diary, April 1858; Frederick Wells Williams, ed., *The Life and Letters of Samuel Wells Williams, LL.D., Missionary, Diplomatic Sinologue* (New York: G. P. Putnam's Sons, 1889), pp. 254 ff. The *Mississippi* was temporarily assigned to Reed for his conveyance to the Pei-ho. On April 28, 1858, however, when the *Minnesota* also reached the same destination, the legation was moved back to it. See Reed to Cass, No. 15, On board the *Minnesota*, Gulf of Pechele, April 28, 1858, *Reed Correspondence*, pp. 256-57.

[24] For a general account of the Chinese preparation for the meeting of the four foreign ministers at Ta-ku see Ch'en Kung-lu "Ssu kuo T'ien-ching t'iao-yueh chih ching kuo," *Chin-ling hsueh-pao*, I (1931), 407-22. Regardless of the shortcomings of this article, the author does provide a brief but adequate survey of the total picture. For a good biographic sketch of T'an T'ing-hsiang consult *Ch'ing-shih lieh-chuan*, XLVII, 18a-22a. Also consult Hummel, *Eminent Chinese of the Ch'ing Period*, I, 428, and Earl Swisher, *China's Management of the American Barbarians, A Study of Sino-American Relations, 1841-1861, with Documents* (New Haven, Conn.: Yale University Far Eastern Publications, 1951), p. 745.

delegate a suitable official to persuade the Westerners to return to Kwangtung and to await a settlement.[25]

Meanwhile, Ch'ung-lun, a veteran of the 1854 negotiation, was also called into service under the general supervision of T'an. He was to go to Tientsin to work with Wu-lo-hung-e, the Ch'ang-lu salt controller at Ta-ku, and Ch'ien Hsin-ho, the provincial treasurer of Chihli. But Ch'ung-lun was to remain in the background. Should Wu-lo-hung-e and Ch'ien fail to persuade the "barbarians" to leave Ta-ku, Ch'ung-lun was then to step forward; he might use his old trick of four years ago. Behind Ch'ung-lun, still further in the rear, was T'an T'ing-hsiang, the governor-general of Chihli. Should Ch'ung-lun fail in dealing with them, T'an might be able to do it.[26]

The Emperor also believed that Tientsin could be more readily defended than Canton. The Chinese, Manchu, and Mongolian troops stationed there were better trained and equipped. Moreover, the Emperor believed, as the Chinese traditionally did, that the "barbarians" feared the people more than the soldiers. Since the people in North China were more militant than the southerners, it was felt that the invaders would withdraw in the face of the hostile and militant populace, who would help defend the strongholds of Ta-ku and Tientsin.[27]

As for the technique of conducting the oncoming foreign negotiations with the four foreign ministers, the Emperor ordered the Chinese negotiators to offer special treatment to the Russian and the American envoys as distinguished from the British and French. If they could do it skillfully and successfully as instructed, the English and French would be isolated.[28] Well prepared, the Chinese now awaited the arrival of the Western vessels.

On April 13, two foreign ships appeared at the mouth of the Pei-ho. Their number soon increased to six, of which four were British and

[25] Imperial Edict, March 21, 1858, *IWSM-HF*, XIX, 3a.

[26] Imperial Edict, April 8, 1858, *ibid.*, XIX, 23a. For Ch'ung-lun's method of action during the previous negotiations consult chap. 11. For brief biographical sketches of T'an T'ing-hsiang, Ch'ung-lun, Wu-lo-hung-e, and Ch'ien Hsin-ho see Swisher, *China's Management of the American Barbarians,* pp. 705 ff.

[27] Ch'en Kung-lu, 414 ff. The foreigners also had the impression that the northern Chinese were stronger than the people in South China. Having seen the northern troops for the first time on May 3, at Ta-ku, Dr. Martin wrote: "They were finer looking fellows than any I had seen in the southern provinces—as tall and heavy as the average of our [American] rank and file...." W. A. P. Martin, *A Cycle of Cathay or China, South and North, with Personal Reminiscences* (New York: Fleming H. Revell Company, 1897), p. 151. Lord Elgin's secretary also remarked: "They were fine looking men...." Oliphant, *Elgin's Mission to China and Japan,* p. 270.

[28] *IWSM-HF*, XIX, 23b. This imperial instruction was issued under the suggestion of Ho Kuei-ch'ing, governor-general of Liang-Kiang.

Chinese drawing of forts at Ta-ku

two were Russian, including the *Amerika* with Poutiatin on board. Immediately, a team of Chinese deputies, headed by Pien Pao-shu, the prefect of Ts'ang-chou, was sent by the local authorities to meet the Russians on board the *Amerika,* while other Chinese officials set up their headquarters at the Ta-ku forts and waited for their return.[29]

On board the Russian ship, the Chinese deputies were told the whole story of the large scale expedition and the intention of the four ministers to proceed to Peking. After an interview of three hours, the deputies were fully convinced that this time these "barbarians" had really serious intentions and were "not making empty threats."[30] Two days later, Pien was sent to Peking where he was given a special audience by the Emperor, who inquired about all details.[31] After Pien's report, the Emperor began to realize that the first bastion of his diplomatic mission had fallen. Immediately he sent word to Ch'ung-lun to step forward. Ch'ung was given the most detailed orders, so precise that even the wording of Ch'ung's statement to the foreigners was drafted by the vermilion brush. First, the Emperor said, after Ch'ung-lun's arrival at Tientsin he must not see the foreign commissioners at once. After a minimum of five or six days he might send an officer to tell them that a certain high official, who was now examining and receiving the ocean transport of rice from South China, was currently in Tientsin. Since this man was an imperially commissioned official, important matters, which the Western envoys were supposed to have, could be discussed with him. And the said minister would memorialize on this matter fully.[32]

Next, the Emperor ordered Ch'ung to deal with the four ministers in three different ways. They should tell the Russian minister that the Russian communication could only be referred, as usual, to the Court of Colonial Affairs. The Kwangtung incidents had nothing to do with Russia. Hence the Russians must keep away from the British and the French and wait for a separate settlement.[33]

As to the other three nations, the Emperor ordered Ch'ung to deal with them in two groups. The English and French were to compose one group and the Americans the second. Both groups should be informed that owing to their neglect of Ho Kuei-ch'ing's advice at Shanghai, their communications delivered at Tientsin were unaccept-

---

[29] *IWSM-HF*, XX, 11a-13b.
[30] *Ibid.*, XX, 13b-14a.
[31] *Ibid.*, XX, 19b-20a.
[32] *Ibid.*, XX, 14a-15a.
[33] *Ibid.*

able. The Americans, however, should be told that since they had not helped the evil-doers at Canton during the previous winter, they might be treated with some special imperial favor. The English and the French must be ordered back to Kwangtung to await the equitable settlement of the Imperial Commissioner Huang Tsung-han. But Ch'ung-lun and other negotiators were also ordered to give the allied ministers "face" by agreeing to memorialize for them, provided the Americans acting on their behalf explained with regret about the previous evils the British had done at Canton.[34] While this edict was being issued, the Emperor had apparently realized that his program could not be put into practice; he seemed to have purposely made the wording of the edict ambiguous and flexible. It could be interpreted in a number of different ways so as to open the way for future revision.

III

While the Emperor was revising his program and arranging the reception of the foreign ministers, Lord Elgin reached the Pei-ho on April 15 with the British fleet. He was followed by the Americans and the French. The large naval force consisted of over thirty Western warships which, lined up at the mouth of Pei-ho, provided the curious and frightened Chinese with an awe-inspiring sight. [35] Soon after their arrival, and at the initiative of the French and the British, the four ministers again addressed identical letters on April 23 to the Court at Peking. They demanded that within six days the Court should send an Imperial Commissioner with "full powers" to negotiate with them. The receipt of this communication was immediately acknowledged by Ch'ung-lun and Wu-lo-hung-e and dates were set for official interviews. The foreign ministers, however, refused to see the two Chinese because they lacked "full powers."[36]

The failure of Ch'ung and Wu-lo-hung-e to negotiate with the ministers made the appearance of T'an T'ing-hsiang inevitable. When T'an's arrival was made known to the foreign ministers on April 28, both the American and Russian ministers expressed their willingness

---

[34] *Ibid.* This was apparently a face-saving statement. The Emperor seemed very reluctant to allow the British to communicate with the Court directly, but he said that if the Americans wished to make some apologetic statement for them, the British communication would also be received.

[35] *IWSM-HF*, XXI, 3b-4a; Oliphant, *Elgin's Mission to China and Japan*, I, 265, 287-88.

[36] Costin, *Great Britain and China*, pp. 253-54; Cordier, *L'Expédition de chine de 1860*, pp. 338-44.

to meet with him for peaceful negotiations at Ta-ku, although the allied ministers still refused to accept his communication.[37]

At this point, the four Western ministers divided themselves clearly into two groups, one friendly to the Chinese and one hostile. The allied envoys then adopted a completely noncooperative policy toward both the Americans and the Russians. After sending identical letters to the Chinese authorities on April 23, said Reed, not one word passed between the English and French plenipotentiaries and himself for a full week, and the time passed without a conference of any kind.[38]

Feeling rather curious about the secret activities of the allies, Reed wrote to the State Department that until the morning of April 30 he still received no indication of the intentions of the English and French.[39] Regardless of the opposition from the allies, however, Reed proceeded with his preparations to meet T'an. "It seemed to me," he wrote to Washington, "that when an officer of high rank announced himself as specially deputed by his sovereign 'to deliberate seriously concerning the affairs' at issue, it would have been a mischievous punctilio that prevented me from meeting him, and ascertaining the precise extent of his functions."[40] On this occasion, he also commented that the two allied ministers' refusal to meet T'an was not justified. Lord Elgin, said Reed, had adopted the doctrines of European public law, which made the "full powers" of a minister evidence of "an ability to bind the sovereign." This request, he said, was entirely distinct from his own American training, for the power he himself exercised was subject to ratification by the President and the Senate.[41]

Actually, the British demand for "full powers" was merely a pretext for a projected invasion of Tientsin. This allied program, of which Reed was entirely unaware, had been designed even before the allied fleet sailed from Shanghai. "On the second day after our arrival [at the mouth of the Pei-ho]," wrote Laurence Oliphant, Lord Elgin's private secretary, " . . . Lord Elgin had not abandoned his intention of pushing up to Tientsin with as little delay as possible."[42] But he

---

[37] Reed to Cass, No. 16, On board the *Minnesota,* Gulf of Pechele [i.e. the mouth of the Pei-ho], May 6, 1858, *Reed Correspondence,* p. 260. Also see Costin, *Great Britain and China,* pp. 255-56.

[38] *Reed Correspondence,* p. 260.

[39] *Ibid.*

[40] Reed to Cass, No. 16, On board the *Minnesota,* Gulf of Pechele, May 6, 1858, *Reed Correspondence,* p. 260.

[41] Reed to Cass, No. 17, Off the Pei-ho river, May 15, 1858, *ibid.,* p. 298.

[42] Oliphant, *Elgin's Mission to China and Japan,* I, 264. According to Oliphant, the British plenipotentiary had even intended to push toward Peking, but the lack of sufficient troops finally forced him to limit his projected expedition to Tientsin.

soon found that the allied fleet possessed only a few light gunboats that were capable of ascending the Pei-ho, and he had to wait for more reinforcements. On April 24 a part of the reinforcements arrived with the two allied admirals on board. Lord Elgin lost no time in telling the British admiral, Sir Michael Seymour, how important he considered a movement on Tientsin. On April 28, 29, and May 1, repeated attempts were made by the allied navy to carry out an assault against the forts. On the last attempt "excited midshipmen, staggering under blankets, canteens, and havresacks, rushed frantically about the deck. . . ."[43] But in the afternoon the naval commander in chief again called off the action for strategic reasons. Regardless of the impatience of Lord Elgin, the allied naval commanders decided to wait for more gunboats before they would agree to launch an attack against the Chinese batteries. Lord Elgin had to wait.[44] On May 6, however, the allied plenipotentiaries found themselves compelled "to seek a new pretext for correspondence, in order to gain time, and for that purpose reopened negotiations with Tan and Tsung [T'an T'ing-hsiang and Ch'ung-lun]."[45] The negotiation was, of course, fruitless. But it was during this period, when the allies were waiting for naval reinforcements, that the Americans and Russians were given the chance to begin their negotiations with the Chinese at Ta-ku.

The first interview between Governor-General T'an T'ing-hsiang and Commissioner Reed was held on May 3, 1858, at Ta-ku, in a specially erected tent.[46] The initial meeting was a dramatic one. Commissioner Reed arrived at 4:00 P.M., saluted by three guns and a flourish of music. The scene, a curious one to both sides, was accompanied by amusing conversation. "At the opening of the interview," noted the American interpreter, "the viceroy spoke of our President as *Kuo Wang* [vassal prince]." At the suggestion of the interpreters, Commissioner Reed demanded that the Chinese negotiators either pronounce the word "President" or give the President the same title as the Chinese Emperor. T'an stammered out *Po-le-si-tien-teh* a time or two, and then accepted the alternative, pronouncing *Ni-men-ti ta*

---

[43] *Ibid.*, I, 272, 273-74.

[44] Elgin to Malmesbury, May 9, 1858, *F.O.*, 17/288; in Costin, *Great Britain and China*, p. 253. It was not until May 11 that all available reinforcements had arrived.

[45] Oliphant, *Elgin's Mission to China and Japan*, I, 278-79.

[46] For detailed records of the Sino-American conference at Ta-ku see W. A. P. Martin, *A Cycle of Cathay*, pp. 152-64; Frederick Wells Williams, ed., *The Life and Letters of Samuel Wells Williams*, pp. 254 ff; William B. Reed, MS Diary, May, 1858; *Reed Correspondence*, pp. 282 ff; *IWSM-HF*, XXI, 14a-16b.

Hwangti, i. e. "Your Great Emperor," in a derisive tone.[47] President
Buchanan was referred to as the "Great Emperor of the United States"
for the duration of the negotiations. In comparing credentials, another
question naturally came up. "Have you powers to enable you to negotiate and sign a treaty?" asked Reed. "I am an officer of the highest
grade," replied T'an, "and have equal powers with Kiying [Ch'i-ying]
who negotiated your treaty at Canton; and I and my colleagues are
deputed by the Emperor to meet you for this purpose."

"Will it be necessary to refer each article to Peking, or only the
treaty as a whole?" This question was promptly replied to by T'an
and his colleagues: "Only the whole, for too much time would be con-
sumed by separate reference." However, T'an said he would not sign
the treaty unless it were approved by the Emperor. In this respect,
T'an explained, the rules of China differed from those of the Western
powers, whose ministers were sent abroad to great distances and for a
long time and were, therefore, allowed greater discretion. "We are
within the limits of our own country, and near the court," stressed
T'an, "to which we can speedily refer any important questions for his
Majesty's decision."[48] This approval of the Emperor involved little
or no delay, Dr. Martin, the official interpreter, recalled in 1897, "and,
as it made him [T'an] the mouthpiece of the throne, the negotiations
were really conducted with the emperor and his cabinet, which, in
these days of telegraphs, has come to be the universal practice."[49]

The second interview between T'an and Reed was held on May 10.
Notwithstanding an unpleasant beginning, the conference was amicable, and the discussions free and easy. All the proposed articles
were passed in review. The meeting was continued late into the evening.[50] After that meeting, the two commissioners did not meet again,
and the discussions were carried on through deputies. Chien Hsin-ho,
provincial treasurer of Chihli province, was deputed by T'an, and Dr.
Williams by Reed. They held the last meeting at 11:00 A.M., May 19,
1858. The discussion lasted for four hours, during which time an
American program of thirty-three articles was the subject of study.
"Many of them were agreed to, subject to the approval of the minis-

[47] Martin, *A Cycle of Cathay*, p. 153.

[48] "Notes of an interview held at the Takoo forts, May 3, 1858, between his Excellency Mr. Reed, United States Plenipotentiary, and the Imperial Chinese Commissioner, Tan Tingsiang [T'an T'ing-hsiang] with his colleagues, Tsung [Ch'ung-lun]
and Wu [-lo-heng-e]," included in Reed to Cass, No. 16, On board the *Minnesota*,
Gulf of Pechele, May 6, 1858, *DD-USNA*, 92:17.

[49] Martin, *A Cycle of Cathay*, pp. 152-53.

[50] *Ibid.*, p. 155.

ters," wrote Dr. Martin, who was the official interpreter for these discussions. This meeting, however, was interrupted when the Americans obtained secret information that the allies intended to storm the forts at Ta-ku the next day. When the American negotiators asked to retire from the meeting, using as an excuse the lateness of the hour, the Chinese negotiators, unaware of the oncoming attack, asked them when they would meet again. "Poor fellows!" wrote Martin, "it would have taken more than human ken to answer that question."[51]

At ten o'clock on the morning of May 20, the allied force bombarded the fort suddenly, using the pretext that the Chinese Imperial Commissioner had lacked the "full powers" that the British demanded. While the bombardment was in progress, the Chinese authorities sent special messengers both to the American and to the Russian ministers, begging them to continue the conferences and to offer their good offices to procure a suspension of offensive operations for three days. This Chinese move failed. Hostilities continued and all negotiations ceased.[52] The forts of Ta-ku were destroyed by the allied forces, who proceeded to Tientsin with little resistance. Tientsin fell to the allies by the end of the month. As victors in a captured city, the allied forces seized a great quantity of rice that was being shipped from South China to Peking, and without which Peking would starve. Setting up their headquarters in a Chinese temple, the victorious ministers continued their demand for the appointment of an envoy with "full powers" to negotiate with them.

The American legation was also moved from Ta-ku to Tientsin. Taking passage with Count Poutiatin on the Russian steamer, the *Amerika*, Reed reached Tientsin on May 30, where he continued the negotiation with the Chinese on June 7.[53]

---

[51] *Ibid.*, p. 162.

[52] Reed to Cass, No. 18, On board the *Minnesota*, Gulf of Pechele, May 21, 1858, *Reed Correspondence*, p. 319. W. C. Costin gives the impression that the final British decision to attack Ta-ku and Tientsin was made only after May 11, when Elgin received an evasive refusal from the Court of Peking to give full powers to T'an. Costin states: "Elgin's analysis of the situation proved quite correct, for an interview which Reed had on the 10th May was far from satisfactory" *(Great Britain and China, 1833-1860*, pp. 256-57). This statement is contrary to historical facts. The allied invasion of Tientsin, as told by Laurence Oliphant, was a predetermined project. In writing the story of this event, Mr. Costin seems to have relied entirely upon the official dispatches preserved in the British Foreign Office and neglected all other primary sources. Such insufficient use of source materials has even led him to misspell T'an's name as Tau.

[53] Reed to Cass, No. 20, Tientsin, June 2; No. 21, June 15, 1858, *Reed Correspondence*, pp. 329, 335.

IV

After the loss of Tientsin, the Emperor realized that to continue
fighting only meant to suffer further defeat. In the face of opposition
from many of his close advisers, including his younger brother, Prince
Kung, the Emperor made a determined effort to bring the calamity to
a quick and peaceful settlement. On May 28, at the suggestions of
Governor-General T'an T'ing-hsiang, the Emperor appointed Kuei-
liang, a member of the Grand Council, and Hua-sha-na, president of
the Board of Civil Appointments, Imperial Commissioners to proceed
posthaste to the port of Tientsin.[54]

Kuei-liang, the elder brother of I-liang, was a seventy-four-year-old
Manchu noble. He was a veteran of domestic politics in the Ch'ing
Court, but he was new in "barbarian affairs." Hua-sha-na, a Mongolian, was fifty-two. Like his colleague, he had never seen a Westerner before, though he himself was an intelligent and capable statesman.
Under further threats and demands from the allied powers, both were
given "full powers" as demanded by the allied ministers.[55]

The Emperor feared that these two officials would not be able to
stop the foreigners, and clearly realized that to fight was out of the
question, but he could not accept all the unreasonable terms at once.
As he always did in his personally directed negotiations, he set up a
second front. Five days after the appointment of Kuei-liang and Hua-
sha-na, the Emperor restored Ch'i-ying to the brevet rank of Board
vice-president and sent him to Tientsin as the third Imperial Commissioner. The Emperor also called into service two of his former
aides, Huang En-t'ung and Chao Ch'ang-ling. But Ch'i-ying's appointment was only to prepare for the "second step."[56] Kuei-liang and
Hua-sha-na were assigned to the first front in an effort to reject as
many of the foreign demands as they could. Should they fail as T'an
had, Ch'i-ying, a "barbarian" favorite, might step forward to offer
some concessions so that further hostilities could be avoided. Consequently, Ch'i-ying was given all facilities and discretionary power

---

[54] *IWSM-HF*, XXIII, 7a.

[55] The two Imperial Commissioners arrived in Tientsin on June 2, 1858, but were
still rebuffed by the allied ministers for failure to provide themselves with seals. See
Oliphant, *Elgin's Mission to China and Japan*, I, 342-43. According to old practice in
the Ch'ing officialdom, an Imperial Commissioner sent from the capital on short
errands was not provided with a seal. At the demand of the allies, however, a special
seal was made for this particular occasion. For brief biographic sketches of these
two Imperial Commissioners consult Hummel, *Eminent Chinese of the Ch'ing Period*,
I, 428-30.

[56] *IWSM-HF*, XXVII, 29a.

and was ordered to act independently of Kuei-liang and Hua-sha-na. "On any matters requiring discretion in handling," an edict issued for Ch'i-ying on June 10 stated, "Ch'i-ying does not necessarily have to consult with Kuei-liang and the other [Hua-sha-na] but can explain to the barbarian personally."[57]

Kuei-liang and Hua-sha-na arrived at Tientsin on June 2. After a short conference with the British interpreters, Horatio Nelson Lay and Thomas Francis Wade, they immediately realized that there was no way out but to sign a dictated truce.[58] In a report to the throne, they wrote: "The difficult position of your slaves can not be fully appreciated excepting by an eyewitness. . . ." They reported that the British interpreter, H. N. Lay, who still held the position as British inspector in the Chinese customhouse at Shanghai, had given them a "self-made treaty of 56 articles," and pressed them to agree to it. "His pride and anger everyone with eyes could see," said the Imperial Commissioners. "Not only could there be no discussion but not even one word could be altered."[59] Unless they acceded to these terms, they felt that the "barbarians" would proceed to invade the capital.

In the meantime, Ch'i-ying suffered even more at the hands of Lay, who produced some captured documents to embarrass the elderly statesman.[60] The allied envoys refused even to accept Ch'i-ying's courtesy call, although he was well received by the American and Russian envoys. Considering his stay useless, Ch'i-ying left Tientsin ex-

---

[57] Swisher, *China's Management*, p. 483; *IWSM-HF*, XXIV, 38b.

[58] Both Wade and Lay had been hired by the Chinese customhouse at Shanghai as British inspectors. Wade resigned in 1855; he was succeeded by Lay, who later became inspector general of the Chinese Customs Service. See above, Chapter 10. Also consult Stanley F. Wright, *Hart and the Chinese Customs* (Belfast: Wm. Mullan and Son Ltd., 1950), pp. 111 ff.

[59] *IWSM-HF*, XXVI, 28a-29b. The scene of the outrageous meeting of Lay and the Imperial Commissioners was also told by a Russian admiral, whose story led Dr. Williams to write as follows on June 10: "The Russian Admiral went today to the temple where the Commissioners lodged, to see them concerning an article of his treaty, when he found them in a state of high excitement and disgust at the conduct and threats of H. N. Lay, one of the British interpreters. He had forced himself upon the high commissioners, threatening them with a bombardment of the city unless they signed the treaty soon, or unless they allowed the Allies entrance up all the rivers in the country as well as liberty to appoint consuls wherever they pleased. Lay was using extremely harsh language to these high functionaries, who were so alarmed by his threats that the Count [Poutiatin] found it useless to attempt any negotiation, and retired chagrined and surprised at such conduct. Soon after he reached his rooms, the Chinese officers sent to inquire whether it was true that the town was to be bombarded tonight." See Williams, ed., *Life and Letters of Samuel Wells Williams*, p. 267.

[60] Many of Ch'ing's previous confidential memorials had been captured by the allies at Canton. Oliphant, *Elgin's Mission to China and Japan*, I, 357-59; *IWSM-HF*, XXV, 19a.

pecting to secure an audience with the Emperor at the capital. On his
way to Peking, he was arrested by imperial order. Ostensibly, he
was charged with an unauthorized return from duty; actually the
Emperor thought that the present "barbarian uprising" was a result
of Ch'i-ying's earlier appeasement policy. This charge was based upon
a belief popular among the dignitaries at Peking at the time,[61] and
the Emperor agreed with it. His appointment of Ch'i-ying had been
only as a last resort. Since Ch'i-ying, a "barbarian" favorite, also
failed to stave off the calamity, he was bound to die. Consequently,
Prince Kung was assigned to preside at the trial of the aged statesman,
and on June 29, Ch'i-ying was ordered by the Emperor to commit sui-
cide. Thus ended the difficult career of the first modern diplomat of
the Ta-Ch'ing Empire.[62]

V

After the arrest of Ch'i-ying, the negotiations at Tientsin were continued by two inexperienced negotiators, Kuei-liang and Hua-sha-na.
They had little chance of seeing either Lord Elgin or Baron Gros, but
heard from the two British interpreters what they had better do. In
these circumstances, the Sino-American negotiation, which was still
in progress, turned out to be entirely unimportant. The American
demands submitted by Reed, as compared with the allied terms, were
so moderate that little bargaining was needed. The first interview
between Reed and the two Imperial Commissioners took place on June
7 in a Buddhist temple. For a week after this interview, the
Sino-American negotiations were conducted with comparatively little
discussion on either side.[63] The only difficulties occurring in the negotiations were over the question of a permanent residence for foreign
ministers at Peking and the free navigation of the interior rivers.
Reed did not insist even on these two subjects, nor did the Chinese
give them much attention, for both sides knew that the British would
bring them up for discussion. The Chinese realized clearly that even

---

[61] Among those who bitterly opposed the recall of Ch'i-ying to service was Prince
Kung, whose memorial can be cited as a typical anti-Ch'i-ying statement: "Your
official is of the opinion, however, that in Ch'i-ying's previous handling of barbarian
affairs, if he did not humble himself to give in to them, he mumbled what was taken
for consent, feared barbarians like tigers and treated the people like grass, and
brought about a great disaster with evil consequences to the present." See Swisher,
China's Management, p. 478. Also see chap. 8 in this book for the edict of Ch'i-ying's
dismissal in 1850.

[62] *IWSM-HF,* XXVII, 27b-30a.

[63] *IWSM-HF,* XXVI, 28a-29b; Martin, *A Cycle of Cathay,* pp. 171 ff.

if they succeeded in refusing the American demands, the refusal would be useless. The British would make the same demands anyway, and the Americans would obtain them automatically through the most-favored-nation clause. Consequently, the Sino-American negotiation progressed smoothly. Within a week, on June 18, 1858,[64] the new treaty was signed.

The Treaty of Tientsin was a new treaty entirely. For years the Chinese had considered the "revision" referred to in Article 34 of the Wanghia Treaty to mean merely an "inconsiderable modification." On this point Reed himself had found that the American demand for a completely new treaty was weak on legal grounds. During the negotiations at Tientsin, however, the Imperial Commissioners never voiced this objection, but "went to work earnestly, and apparently in good faith, to make a new and revised treaty, exactly as if no such difficulty had been suggested."[65]

In this new treaty, with the exception of the "two great points of difficulty" (i.e., the permanent residence of foreign ministers at Peking and the free navigation of the interior rivers), which Commissioner Reed did not insist upon, the Americans obtained almost everything they expected.[66] They were given the privilege of direct correspondence, in sealed envelopes, with the Grand Council at Peking (Article 4). The American envoy was also permitted an annual visit and sojourn at the capital (Article 5). The obstacles in the way of American citizens obtaining leaseholds in the trading ports, set by the former treaty, were removed (Article 12). Wrecked American ships were now provided with more ports, open or not, in which to drop anchor for repair, for the former treaty had limited them to the "nearest of the Five Open Ports" (Article 13). In addition to the previous five ports, the new treaty also opened two more ports, Taiwan (present Tainan) and Swatow (i.e., Ch'ao-chou), for the American traders (Article 14). The Imperial Commissioners and the American minister also reached

---

[64] *IWSM-HF*, XXVI, 29a; Martin, *A Cycle of Cathay*, p. 183. Being without a private seal to make the impression as the Chinese had done, Reed made good use of his finger ring, which was engraved with his family crest. The seal was stamped with the pelican and the letters "W. B. R." Reed MS Diary, June 18, 1858. For the official report see Reed to Cass, No. 22, Tientsin, June 18, 1858, *Reed Correspondence*, p. 350.

[65] Reed to Cass, No. 23, Tientsin, June 30, 1858, *Reed Correspondence*, p. 352.

[66] For the whole text of the treaty see *Treaties, Conventions, etc., between Chinese and foreign states*, I, 509-24; also consult William M. Malloy, ed., *Treaties, Conventions, International Acts, Protocols, and Agreements between the United States of America and Other Powers, 1776-1909* (Washington, D.C.: Government Printing Office, 1910) I, 211-21.

an understanding that tariff reductions and Chinese payments on American claims should be discussed in a supplementary conference to be held at Shanghai, so that a fair settlement could be worked out on the spot.

There are several articles worth particular mention. One is the opium clause. In the Treaty of Wanghia (Article 33), dealing in opium was prohibited to American citizens. In the new treaty, the word "opium" was purposely omitted. In his report to Washington, Reed said: "I have omitted the word 'opium' and left the trade to be dealt with as with that of any other article declared by law to be contraband." This omission was the result of British influence. In the same report, Reed said:[67]

In one of the few interviews I have had with Lord Elgin, he expressed a strong wish that the word "opium" should be omitted in the American and Russian treaties. He seemed to think, and I thought with some reason, that it was a reflection on England, who derived a large revenue from the trade, and he assured me that if I would accede to this he would not attempt to legalize the trade by treaty, as he was instructed to do [Dispatch of the Earl of Clarendon to Lord Elgin, April 20, 1857].

This episode is yet another instance demonstrating how the inexperienced American diplomats were constantly outmaneuvered by the politicians from London. Had the opium trade been formally outlawed in the new American treaty as it was in the Treaty of Wanghia, it would have been embarrassing for the British to move for its legalization. Without the British promise that they would not press the Chinese for legalization of the opium trade, the Americans would never have removed this clause from their new treaty with China. After the Americans had done as the British requested, however, the British argued that any system governing the opium trade would be better than the present smuggling system. Thus the opium trade was at last legalized without changing a single article of any Western treaty with China.[68]

Article 29 of the new treaty provided for the toleration of Protestantism and the protection of its Chinese converts. This article exceeded the original instructions issued from Washington. From the very beginning of the international relations between the two countries, the United States government had given no particular privileges to Ameri-

---

[67] Reed to Cass, No. 23, Tientsin, June 23, 1858, *Reed Correspondence,* p. 357.
[68] For further information see following chapter.

can missionaries in China.[69] They were merely protected by the treaty provisions as any other private American citizen. In the negotiations at Tientsin, Reed added this article to the new treaty simply as a reward to the missionaries, particularly W. A. P. Martin and Samuel Wells Williams, for their indispensable services to the American legation.[70]

In addition to these privileges, the new treaty guaranteed all the old rights obtained in the Treaty of Wanghia. Among them the most important one was the "most favored nation" clause (Article 30). It was through this article that the treaty privileges enjoyed by the allied powers, who succeeded in signing treaties with China on June 26 (the Chinese-British treaty) and on June 27 (the Chinese-French treaty), were soon extended to the Americans. In these treaties, signed after the American treaty, the "two great points of difficulty" that had worried Commissioner Reed were settled. The permanent residence at Peking and the access to the interior of China were permitted both allies by the Chinese government and were extended to the Americans. Moreover, the number of new trading ports was increased from two to six by the British and French treaties. Additional ports along the Yangtze River were to be opened provided the Taiping Rebellion was terminated. American citizens, like the British subjects, might go anywhere in China "for pleasure or for purposes of trade." They might hire vessels for the carriage of baggage or merchandise. The internal transit duties that the Chinese had established to provide for military expenditure were also removed.[71] Thus by the signing of these treaties at Tientsin, the Celestial Empire at last was completely opened up for free trade to all Western nations.

---

[69] The Wanghia Treaty did not give special protection to the American missionaries. They obtained the privileges to reside and preach in the Five Ports only through the Sino-French Treaty of 1844, which extended the privileges to the American missionaries automatically through the most-favored-nation clause. See chap. 5. For a good review on this aspect of the Wanghia Treaty see Frank E. Hinkley, *American Consular Jurisdiction in the Orient* (Washington, D.C.: W. H. Lowdermilk and Co., 1906), pp. 108 ff.

[70] Reed to Cass, No. 23, Tientsin, June 30, 1858, *Reed Correspondence,* p. 361; Martin, *A Cycle of Cathay,* pp. 181 ff. This missionary clause became a serious subject which the Emperor intended to rescind. Reading over a memorial sent by his commissioners from Shanghai, the Emperor made some comment about the missionary activities in China by saying: "At first they propagate gospel; later their motives become inscrutable." See Swisher, *China's Management,* p. 540.

[71] The six new ports were: Neuchuang, Tengchow, Taiwan (now Tainan), Swatow, Kiungchow, and Tamsui. For the texts of the Russian, British, and French treaties consult *Treaties, Conventions, etc., between China and Foreign States,* I, 29-35, 212-29, 602-23.

Satisfied by the achievement of the "greatest act" of his life, Commissioner Reed prepared to leave Tientsin for Shanghai. In a farewell interview with Kuei-liang and Hua-sha-na, he was assured by the two Imperial Commissioners of supplementary negotiations at Shanghai to settle the miscellaneous and less important problems between China and the United States. On July 4, 1858, the eighty-second anniversary of the independence of the United States, the Chinese Imperial Commissioners forwarded a formal imperial rescript to Commissioner Reed, announcing their Emperor's ratification of the American Treaty with China.[72] Honored and deeply pleased, Reed retired to Shanghai on July 11, where he was to wait for the Imperial Commissioners to negotiate the supplementary clauses of the new treaty—specifically the intended reduction of the tariff duties and the settlement of American claims against the Chinese government.

---

[72] Kweiliang [Kuei-liang] and Hwashana [Hua-sha-na] to Reed, June 25, 1858; for the imperial rescript ratifying the Treaty of Tientsin, July 3, 1858, see *Reed Correspondence*, pp. 375, 379-80.

15

A COUNTER

TREATY-REVISION MOVEMENT AND

THE NEGOTIATIONS AT SHANGHAI

I

THE signing of the treaties at Tientsin brought the treaty-revision movement, initiated by the Western powers in 1854, to its end. From the Chinese point of view, however, the treaties had been signed under duress. Many influential princes and mandarins at Peking raised strong objections. The Emperor himself was deeply grieved by the dictated truce. Thus, after the Western envoys left Tientsin, the Chinese immediately started a counter movement for treaty revision. It was their intention even to repudiate the treaties just signed at Tientsin.

Superficially, it would seem that this movement was started at the suggestion of the original Chinese negotiators, Kuei-liang and Hua-sha-na. Even before the treaties were signed, they had said to their young master: "If in the future we want to repudiate the agreement and give up friendly relations, it will require only the punishment of your slaves for the crime of mismanagement to make waste paper out of them."[1]

This suggestion, however, was no more than a face-saving device to persuade the Emperor to accept the Western terms. The two diplomats did not intend to repudiate the treaties they had negotiated. Soon after the Western forces had withdrawn from Tientsin, the two statesmen jointly memorialized the Emperor to appoint "a high official" from the Board of Revenue and to send him to Shanghai for supplementary negotiations with the Western envoys in order to settle the tariff question as well as the foreign claims. They also recommended that Chao Te-ch'e, the new governor of Kiangsu, and Hsueh Huan, the provincial judge, who was now also in charge of the office of the circuit Su-

---

[1] Records of the Hsien-feng period (1851-61), *Ta-Ch'ing li ch'ao shih-lu* (Photo-lithographic edition by the Council of State Affairs of the "Manchoukuo," 1937), *chüan* 256, pp. 11b-12a. This citation will be hereafter abbreviated as *Shih-lu:HF*.

Sung-T'ai (i.e., the *taotai* of Shanghai), should be appointed to participate in the supplementary negotiations on tariff.[2] It was apparent that
both Kuei-liang and Hua-sha-na had thought that the supplementary
negotiations to be held at Shanghai would only consider the settling of
the custom duties and foreign claims. For these matters no special
Imperial Commissioner was needed.

The Emperor, however, held otherwise. He thought that the supplementary negotiations would be a "turning point" of China's *yang-wu*
(oceanic affairs);[3] they would give the imperial government a good
chance to repudiate or at least to revise the Tientsin treaties. Consequently, both Kuei-liang and Hua-sha-na were ordered to remain in
their former positions as Imperial Commissioners in order to renew the
negotiation. For their assistance, two Imperial Commissioners of
inferior rank—Ming-shan, director of the Imperial Armory, and Tuan
Ch'eng-shih, second secretary of the Board of Punishments—were
appointed at the end of July, 1858. In addition to the four Imperial
Commissioners, Ho Kuei-ch'ing, governor-general of Liang-Kiang, was
also ordered to take part in the coming supplementary negotiations.
This made a Chinese staff of five to conduct the negotiations at Shanghai, negotiations that were ostensibly for the settlement of tariff rates
and other miscellaneous and trifling matters. In the meantime, many

---

[2] Hsueh Huan was appointed *taotai* of Su-Sung-T'ai (also in charge of the customhouse at Shanghai) in 1857. Early in 1858 he was promoted to provincial judge of
Kiangsu. A certain Shih I-chiu was appointed to his former position. Shih, however, was soon charged with incompetency and a bad record in the military service
and was discharged in April, 1858. Since the office of the *taotai* of Shanghai was so
important and no competent person had been found to fill it, Hsueh was again ordered
to take charge as acting *taotai* of Su-Sung-T'ai, while he still held the office of provincial judge of Kiangsu. It was a temporary arrangement because in the political
system of the Ch'ing dynasty a higher official would seldom take charge of a lower
office. See *Shih-lu: HF, chüan* 258, p. 1b; *chüan* 256, pp. 11b-12a; *chüan* 257, p. 24a.
Professor Swisher seems not to have understood this queer arrangement. In his
translation of Hsueh's titles, such as ". . . Judicial Commissioner, Acting *Tao-t'ai* of
Shanghai, Hsueh Huan," Mr. Swisher cautiously put a "[sic]" before "Hsueh Huan"
to indicate his doubt. See Earl Swisher, *China's Management of the American Barbarians: A Study of Sino-American Relations, 1841-1861, with Documents* (New
Haven, Conn.: Yale University Far Eastern Publications, 1951), p. 526. For a brief
biography of Hsueh Huan consult *Ch'ing shih lieh-chuan* (Shanghai: Chung Hua
Book Co., 1928), LIII, 22a-25a. Hsueh was an important figure during the Anglo-
French war (1858-1860) and during the first years under the *Tsungli yamen* (1861-
1863). In Arthur William Hummel's *Eminent Chinese of the Ch'ing Period* (Washington, D.C.: Government Printing Office, 1943), however, he is described only
briefly.

[3] After the Tientsin negotiations, the traditional term *i-wu* (barbarian affairs) was
replaced by the term *yang-wu* (oceanic affairs), because on several occasions the
careless use of the term "barbarian" by some of the Chinese negotiators was resented
by angry "barbarian chiefs," and in Article 51 of the Sino-British treaty the usage
of the term "*i*" was formally outlawed.

of the old-school "barbarian experts," such as P'an Shih-ch'eng, Wu Ch'ung-yao (Howqua), and others, who had played eminent roles in foreign negotiations during the Tao-kuang period, but who had been humiliated and dismissed by the young Emperor, were now recalled to service. They were restored to their former ranks and ordered to Shanghai to participate in the coming negotiation.[4] Moreover, some comparatively unknown figures who were reportedly familiar with foreign affairs were also urgently ordered to come to Peking for imperial consultation.[5] Only a few years had passed since the young Emperor had forced many of these outstanding "barbarian experts," trained in his father's time, to retire. History repeated itself. The young Emperor followed step by step what his father had done in the early 1840's.

Before the Imperial Commissioners left Peking for the south, the Emperor gave them a "farewell audience," which was actually a secret conference with the Emperor in the chair.[6] During this audience, which was held in absolute secrecy, the Emperor projected a "secret plan."[7] No written records of this meeting were kept. Even the Court diary, the *Shih-lu*, fails to give any report of it. The entire plan may be reconstructed, however, from the imperial edicts and memorials submitted by those who had participated in this conference.

Generally speaking, the main task of the "secret plan" was to revise or even to repudiate the previous treaties signed at Tientsin. If a complete repudiation could not be worked out, at least the "four important provisions" that were "most injurious" to China were to be rescinded. These were: sending officials to reside at Peking; trading in inland waters; traveling in the interior; and indemnification for the allied military expenses before evacuation of the city of Canton.[8] "The Emperor did not mean to break faith," remarked Dr. T. F. Tsiang. "He hoped he could achieve the nullification or revision of the treaties by a fair bargain, in other words, by paying what he considered to be a fair price."[9]

---

[4] *Shih-lu:HF, chüan* 256, p. 14b.

[5] *Ibid., chüan* 261, p. 20b.

[6] *Ibid., chüan* 263, p. 25; *chüan* 262, p. 19.

[7] Dr. Ting-fu Tsiang is the first scholar to detect the "secret plan." See T. F. Tsiang, "The Secret Plan of 1858," *CSPSR*, XV (1931), 291-99. Owing to the lack of sufficient materials at the time of writing, Dr. Tsiang's thesis, only eight pages long, was not fully developed.

[8] *Shih-lu:HF, chüan* 264, pp. 5, 10; *IWSM-HF*, XXXI, 31b. The so-called trading in inland waters, pointed out by the Emperor, included the free navigation of the Yangtze and other interior waters.

[9] Tsiang, "The Secret Plan of 1858," p. 291.

The "fair price" that Emperor Hsien-feng wanted to pay was to declare China free from customs duties for all foreign trade. This imperial offer was made with the conviction that the Westerners only wanted profits in China. Their demand for a permanent residence at Peking, which obviously had no economic value, was, he thought, merely the result of a Russian plot.[10] Once the Westerners were given greater profits through the abolition of tariff duties and the legalization of the opium trade, the Emperor was sure they would agree to repudiate the treaties signed at Tientsin and continue to trade only in the Five Ports. In line with this reasoning, the Emperor ordered the Chinese negotiators to meet the foreigners as soon as they arrived in Shanghai, and to announce voluntarily the abolition of China's tariff and the legalization of the opium trade. At the same time, they would also declare that all foreign treaties signed at Tientsin were invalid. The Chinese negotiators were directed not to bargain with the foreign ministers on individual items. Instead, all the problems were to be settled simultaneously and permanently.[11]

While this secret plan was being formulated, many reports reached the Grand Council from Ho Kuei-Ch'ing, governor-general of Liang-Kiang, saying that foreign envoys were tired of waiting for the projected supplementary negotiations at Shanghai. In an attempt to placate the impatient foreigners, the Emperor ordered Ho to send Hsueh Huan to Shanghai to calculate the back duties with them. This move would also give the Chinese negotiators more time to work on the secret plan."[12] At the same time, he directed the two Imperial Commissioners of inferior rank to go to Kiangsu province immediately to confer with Ho Kuei-ch'ing and then to proceed to Shanghai for immediate announcement of the Emperor's decision.[13] In an edict issued to Ho on September 14, the Emperor told the Governor-General that he would be informed of a new plan by the coming Imperial Commissioners. Ho was reminded not to be "overcautious" about the results but to carry out the imperial order faithfully.[14]

---

[10] *Shih-lu:HF, chüan* 250, p. 20b.

[11] *Ibid., chüan* 262, pp. 6a, 19, 28a.

[12] *Shih-lu:HF, chüan* 260, p. 19b.

[13] *Ibid., chüan* 257, p. 24a. Hsueh Huan went to Shanghai early in September. Unaware of the Emperor's secret plan, he immediately started his negotiations with the American deputies and other foreign representatives concerning a new tariff schedule and other miscellaneous matters. Thus, when the Imperial Commissioners arrived in Shanghai a month later, Hsueh's pleasant negotiations with the Americans were almost finished.

[14] *Shih-lu:HF, chüan* 260, p. 19b; *IWSM-HF*, XXX, 31a.

The two Imperial Commissioners, Ming-shan and Tuan Ch'eng-shih, reached Ch'ang-chou on September 20. Immediately they forwarded an imperial message closed and stamped with "vermilion seals" to Ho. After consulting with the Governor-General about the content of the imperial message, however, the two began to doubt its wisdom. Although they continued their trip to Shanghai, they decided to postpone the announcement of the Emperor's decision to the foreigners at Shanghai.[15]

On September 25, Kuei-liang and Hua-sha-na reached Ch'ang-chou. They too held a conference with Ho. During this conference, Ho voiced strong objections to the imperial plan for abolition of China's tariff duties to all Western nations. The two high-ranking Imperial Commissioners were obviously convinced by Ho's eloquence. The very day after the conference the three high officials jointly submitted a memorial to Peking proposing that the announcement of tariff abolition be postponed and the Emperor's intention of a treaty revision not be made known to foreign envoys.[16] Then they sent out an urgent call to Tuan Ch'eng-shih and Ming-shan, who were traveling ahead of them toward Shanghai, and asked them to stop at Soochow for an emergency conference. With their obvious encouragement, Governor-General Ho Kuei-ch'ing hurriedly submitted two long memorials to Peking within three days.[17]

In these two memorials, Ho argued that the secret plan would not work. The abolition of the tariff would not offset the four injurious provisions. "The barbarian chiefs and the barbarian merchants were in two separate categories . . . ," said Ho. "If we were to abolish import and export duties, the barbarian chiefs would still not be grateful." Moreover, custom duties were indispensable for the national revenue, particularly during wartime. Even in time of peace, from a purely economic point of view, tariff duties could not be abolished, because the abolition of the tariff would mean the complete loss of control over foreign merchants in China. It would turn over the economic lever of the Empire to foreigners, while the Chinese people would perish with their capital depleted.[18]

---

[15] *Shih-lu:HF, chüan* 262, p. 5b; *IWSM-HF,* XXX, 38.

[16] *IWSM-HF,* XXX, 42a-43b. This memorial reached the Grand Council at Peking on October 3. It is probably the first memorial during the whole period of "barbarian affairs" ever submitted by Imperial Commissioners who exercised their own judgment in rejecting an imperial order.

[17] These two memorials, which reached the Grand Council on October 5 and 9 respectively, are fully translated in Swisher, *China's Management,* pp. 520-24.

[18] *IWSM-HF,* XXX, 45a; XXXI, 18; Swisher, *China's Management,* pp. 520-24.

Neither Ho's eloquent argument, nor the proposal submitted by the four Imperial Commissioners, convinced the Emperor of the need for reconsideration. He assumed that their unanimous rejection of the imperial plan was inspired by personal motives. The four Imperial Commissioners were under the influence of the Governor-General, while the Governor-General was influenced by his corrupt subordinates, who in turn were afraid that there would be no means of lining their pockets after the duties were abolished.[19] ". . . if it benefits barbarian merchants," the Emperor argued confidently, "why shouldn't the barbarian chiefs be pleased." In a series of confidential edicts, he ordered the four Imperial Commissioners and the Governor-General to adhere scrupulously to the program originally determined. No alternatives would be allowed.

On the diplomatic front, however, the five high negotiators seem to have neglected completely the original imperial plan and to have worked earnestly on their own, even while they continued to submit memorials repeating the same arguments and asking for new instructions. After an emergency conference of the five dignitaries at Soochow, the four Imperial Commissioners arrived at Shanghai on October 4. Ho followed them the next day. At Shanghai further conferences were held between the five high negotiators and Hsueh Huan, the acting *taotai* of Shanghai, who had been negotiating with the American and British representatives for nearly a month.

In the middle of October, preliminary negotiations with the foreign delegates under the direct supervision of the five high negotiators began formally. Unaware of the Chinese intention to revise the treaty, both the American[20] and British delegates concentrated on the tariff schedule and other less important problems. The Chinese nego-

---

[19] Imperial Edict, October 5, 1858, *IWSM-HF*, XXX, 46. Among Ho's "corrupt" aides, the Emperor particularly mentioned Wu Chien-Chang, whom he charged as being equally as treacherous as the late Ch'i-ying. The notorious Samqua (Wu's business name by which he was known to the American merchants) had many foes in Peking, who impeached him constantly in the Court. In July, 1854, as previously explained, he was removed from the office of the *taotai* at Shanghai. But the energetic Samqua, the only one of the mandarins at the time who could speak a "barbarian language," proved indispensable to the foreign service at Shanghai. Regardless of the imperial orders that had put Wu under arrest and trial, the high officials at Shanghai enlisted him as private consultant during the foreign negotiations.

[20] The American delegates to these negotiations were headed by Samuel Wells Williams, secretary and interpreter of the legation. See *Reed Correspondence*, p. 493. British sources, however, indicate that the Americans and Chinese never held any formal meetings on tariff revision. Instead, Dr. Williams had only informal discussions with the British delegates. See *British Parliamentary Papers*, XXXIII, No. 2571 (1859), pp. 303, 400, 437-38.

tiators seemed not to bother themselves with the secret plan, but to negotiate on the subjects the foreigners wanted to settle. Thus the negotiations went smoothly

On the domestic front, however, the five high negotiators found it difficult to convince their master, a man more stubborn and ignorant than the "barbarians." They needed an endless amount of diplomatic skill and patience to deal with him. In a series of joint memorials, the Chinese high commissioners formally and sternly warned the Emperor that they had reversed his original plan.[21] They told the young master that the foreign envoys were not on a mission to China merely for profits. The Chinese government could never move them to revise the treaties by using customs as bait. In their preliminary meetings with the foreign envoys, they said they had skillfully recommended the Chinese proposal for a treaty revision, but the foreign envoys definitely refused to consider any change in the treaties, even if China should abolish all her customs duties. They said they were deeply concerned about the Emperor's plan, which they sincerely hoped to put into practice. They were now mentally tortured and physically exhausted, but the "barbarians" were so stubborn that not a single provision of the treaties could be revised.[22]

Obviously fearing that their stubborn master still would not concede, the five high negotiators showered the Emperor with a series of groundless but threatening statements. They said that with their arrival at Shanghai—four Imperial Commissioners and one governor-general at one time—the foreigners had become suspicious that the Chinese might attempt to repudiate the treaties. Some irresponsible Chinese mandarins in Canton had leaked inside information of the secret plan to them. There was constant talk among the foreigners in

---

[21] *IWSM-HF*, XXX, 44a-46a; XXXI, 18a-19b, 29b-31a; XXXII, 3a-4a, 5a-8b, 15a-18a, 22b-24b, etc.

[22] The British source indicates that the Chinese negotiators did bring up the subject of a foreign residence at Peking "like the postscript in a lady's letter" during one of the more friendly social meetings, which took place after the Chinese had conceded everything in these negotiations. In a letter to Lord Elgin on Ocotber 22, 1858, referring to a foreign residence at Peking, the Chinese high commissioner wrote: ". . . we beg your Excellency to consider what compromise may be effected. . . . In making this request we have not the smallest intention of violating the Treaty." See Kuei-liang and others to Elgin, Shanghai, October 22, 1858, collected in Laurence Oliphant, *Narrative of the Earl of Elgin's Mission to China and Japan in the Years 1857, '58, '59* (London: William Blackwood and Sons, 1859), I, 478; also II, 285. No source confirms that they ever mentioned any of the other three provisions to the foreign envoys. Even the letter above was written after the tariff negotiations were nearly completed. It was apparently used as a shield to meet the Emperor's further inspection.

China of a new northern expedition to Tientsin. If the Emperor should
not grant what the foreign envoys asked for, not only would it be impossible to arrange other matters, but there would be danger of immediate rupture, and war would be the only alternative. "In case they
really sail to Tientsin again," the commissioners warned the Emperor,
"what would be the results upon the general state of affairs of the
whole nation?"[23] Thus they said that the original secret plan was
entirely unworkable. All that they could do at the moment was to
continue negotiations on tariff duties.

After reading all these threatening memorials, the Emperor was not
so much angered as grieved. In an edict issued on November 3, 1858,
the Emperor lamented that his original plan had been completely set
aside by his officials at Shanghai. In a tone of agrievement he asked
his subjects: "Were my sending Kuei-liang and others to Shanghai
and also ordering Ho Kuei-ch'ing to cooperate in negotiations really
for the mere purpose of settling the tariff schedules? [Of course,
not!]"[24] In this edict, however, the Emperor seemed to have been
sympathetic toward the Chinese negotiators. Although he still ordered
the Imperial Commissioners to continue their untiring efforts on behalf
of the revision program, his language was more moderate than it had
been.

The Emperor's confidence in a treaty revision was further shaken
by Ho Kuei-ch'ing's lengthy memorial, which reached the Grand
Council on November 14.[25] In this document, the Governor-General
not only warned the Emperor that a repudiation of the treaties would
mean war, but also gave a most critical review of the numerous
blunders made by the Chinese diplomats during the past ten years.
If there had been suitable administration since the opening of the
Five Ports, said Ho, friendly relations without trouble would have
been possible. Owing to the incompetent management of the Chinese
officials, however, the foreigners were particularly irritated when the
Chinese banned their entry into the city of Canton and the Imperial

---

[23] *IWSM-HF*, XXXI, 36b.

[24] Imperial Edict, November 3, 1858, *IWSM-HF*, XXXII, 3a. This edict was a
most elaborate document showing the Emperor's real intention in sending the five
high negotiators to Shanghai. The above statement was also quoted in the memorial
of the four Imperial Commissioners received by the Grand Council on November 27.
This memorial was fully translated into English and included in Mr. Swisher's
selection. The edict itself was not included in his selection. See Swisher, *China's
Management*, p. 544.

[25] *IWSM-HF*, XXXII, 5a-8b. For a good English translation of the whole memorial consult Swisher, *China's Management*, pp. 532-36.

Commissioner refused to receive them. These situations were really the origin of the recent hostilities. Since the foreigners had been badly treated for nearly ten years, they began to take advantage of the Taiping Rebellion to retaliate.

Ho further reminded the Emperor that in the spring of 1858, when the four envoys asked that an Imperial Commissioner be sent to Shanghai for negotiation before March 31, their requests were still not extravagant. Ho said he had wept bitterly and pleaded with Imperial Commissioner Huang Tsung-han to stop at Shanghai in order to settle the matter with the foreign envoys there. But Huang refused his suggestion. So it was that while Huang was on the way south to Canton, the foreign envoys were on their way north to Tientsin.

In speaking of the foreign demands for a treaty revision, the Governor-General said that they were more or less justifiable. He separated the foreign treaties into two categories: one was never to be changed; but the other, which he called trade convention, should be subject to revision after twelve years. All previous officials in charge of foreign affairs since the change of regimes had neglected the foreign demands entirely. They never fully memorialized to the Emperor about what the foreigners actually demanded, nor had they made the Imperial will known to the foreign envoys. Thus they aroused the suspicions of the foreigners, who mistakenly thought that the Chinese officials did not forward their communications to the Court at all. It was this suspicion that engendered the foreigners' desire to reside in Peking so that they could settle all the problems with the Emperor personally. All these "barbarian troubles" were really initiated more by Chinese mismanagement than by the foreigners, he said. The treaties of Tientsin were certainly injurious. But they were signed under duress. The inexperienced Chinese negotiators were by no means responsible for them. They merely signed as dictated, lest the war be extended to the capital. Since the treaties had already been signed, repudiating them was no easy job. It could not be accomplished with words, nor could it be effected by promise of petty gains. It was only possible by use of force, but China was now unable to do this.

Having read Ho's long review of foreign policy for the last eight years, the Emperor seems to have been deeply touched. Apparently convinced by Ho's logic and informative arguments, the Emperor endorsed this memorial with the vermilion brush saying that it had "considerable significance." He turned this memorial over to the Grand

Council for "thorough deliberation."[26] He seems to have awakened from an eight-year dream. After reading more memorials from Shanghai, the unbending young sovereign at last bowed to reality. In an edict issued on November 24, 1858, the Emperor reluctantly accepted all the proposals submitted by his officials from Shanghai. The approval of all the foreign demands, he said in an edict, was the "worst tactic" that he had adopted. "I do not wish at this time to find further fault and to reject any more lest Kuei-liang and others, through want of ability, would bring about a rupture." The Emperor stressed that he had merely tried to prevent a rupture from occurring. It did not mean that he reluctantly approved of all that the commissioners had done at Shanghai.[27] And so the inept treaty-revision movement on the part of the Chinese was ended.

This episode, which lasted a few months, clearly shows how the Emperor and his "barbarian experts" learned their trade by following the same route, step by step, that their predecessors had pursued in the early 1840's. Ho's long memorial reviewing the blunders made in the past ten years was testimony in defense of the policy of Ch'i-ying in the early 1840's. The old statesman had been executed just a few months before, but his policies were now highly praised and copied. These events also show that the Emperor had really no intention of fighting a war with foreigners; on the contrary, he was forced to accept treaty revisions, not by threats from his enemy but by warnings from his own trusted officials. Many historians have treated him as a warmonger; rather, he was a coward.

II

The most interesting aspect of the supplementary negotiations at Shanghai was that the real situation was not known to the Emperor. He was under the impression that, as in Tientsin a few months before, there were serious talks going on at Shanghai in the very face of foreign cannon, with the likelihood of war breaking out at any moment should the negotiators fail to reach an agreement. Actually, the supplementary negotiations at Shanghai were one of the few friendly negotiations ever conducted between the Chinese mandarins and the Western envoys during the entire period of "barbarian affairs." Unaware of the secret plan of the Chinese, the Western delegates con-

---

[26] *Ibid.*
[27] *Shih-lu:HF, chüan* 267, p. 19a; *IWSM-HF, XXXII,* 18a-19a; Swisher, *China's Management,* pp. 542-43.

centrated only on bargaining for new tariff rates. On the Chinese side, matters were even simpler. The Chinese negotiators neither mentioned the projected treaty revision to the foreign representatives, nor did they pay much attention to tariff rates. Since the Emperor already intended to abolish the tariff completely, they had no difficulty in settling the tariff problem with the foreign delegates. They merely waited to sign whenever the foreigners reached an agreement among themselves on tariff rates.

Thus the tariff talks between the Chinese and the foreign delegates went on smoothly. The Chinese high negotiators and the foreign commissioners met only for courtesy's sake. The negotiations were conducted by subordinates on both sides. "The meetings between the subordinates began on 12th October," wrote Mr. Costin, "and although it was not until 8th November that the treaty was ready for signature, there was no sign of serious conflict between the British and Chinese negotiators."[28]

The Sino-American tariff negotiations started early in September and were carried on in an even smoother manner. As previously explained, Hsueh Huan had been sent to Shanghai earlier to keep the foreigners occupied so that they would not sail to Tientsin again. Unaware of the secret plan, Hsueh started negotiating in good faith with the Americans and other delegates as soon as he reached Shanghai. At Hsueh's initiation, Reed sent Secretary Williams to meet him in order to make new arrangements on tariff rates. In the meantime, he also issued circulars to the American mercantile houses in China asking for information and suggestions on both tariff rates and the opium trade. The answers he received generally concurred that "the tariff of 1844 was a fair one, and that little modification was needed," although there was general objection to the illegal opium trade, which had to be settled with the British rather than with the Chinese.[29] Thus the Hsueh-Wil-

---

[28] Costin, *Great Britain and China 1833-1860* (Oxford: The Clarendon Press, 1937), p. 273. The Anglo-Chinese negotiations were finished on October 30. "It only remained to obtain the concurrence of Baron Gros and Mr. Reed to the tariff and trade regulations," wrote one of the British negotiators, "as agreed upon between the British and Chinese governments, preparatory to their being formally signed." The Anglo-Chinese supplementary negotiations were carried on in the most amicable atmosphere. Both the high commissioners and the lesser negotiators had wonderful times together. They greeted one another as "old friends." Very few foreign warships were then in Shanghai, and no harsh words were exchanged. At a luncheon party given by Lord Elgin, Governor-General Ho even became drunk. See Oliphant, *Elgin's Mission to China and Japan*, II, 266-88. Oliphant was one of the two British representatives who negotiated with the Chinese.

[29] Reed to Cass, No. 32, On board the *Minnesota*, off Wusung, September 15, 1858, *Reed Correspondence*, p. 436.

liams talks at Shanghai went on without even a hint of bargaining on either side. "In these preliminary conferences," reported Reed to the State Department, ". . . negotiations are advancing happily."[30]

Even before the arrival of the four Imperial Commissioners in Ch'ang-chou late in September (when Ho Kuei-ch'ing and Hsueh Huan were for the first time informed about the secret plan), the Sino-American tariff talks at Shanghai had almost been concluded. In a dispatch written on September 15, 1858,[31] Reed reported to the State Department:[32] "The arrangement of the details of the new tariff, to be determined on so soon as the imperial commissioners arrive, has been delegated to gentlemen familiar with commercial relations, and have been nearly completed." For this reason there was no important business for him to conduct in Shanghai until the arrival of the Imperial Commissioners, who were merely to sign these new agreements on tariff.[33] Reed took the leisure time for a visit to Japan on September 16. Returning to Shanghai three weeks later, he found that the four high Imperial Commissioners had already arrived at that port and formal negotiations had begun.[34] In these negotiations, the Americans did not even want to change the rates, although they could have done so.[35]

The English, however, insisted on a tariff revision. They declared that the price of various articles of merchandise had fallen since the treaties of 1842 and 1844. Thus the fixed rate of the Chinese tariff duties had been more than 5 per cent, which was supposedly agreed upon by the Chinese when they signed their first treaties with Western countries.[36] The Americans would be adversely affected by such a re-

---

[30] *Ibid.*, p. 493.

[31] The Chinese Imperial Commissioners, Tuan and Ming reached Ch'ang-chou on September 20, 1858; they were followed by Kuei-liang and Hua-sha-na five days later.

[32] Reed to Cass, No. 32, On board the *Minnesota,* off Wusung September 15, 1858, *Reed Correspondence,* p. 436.

[33] "The current business of the legation is not important," Reed wrote to the State Department on October 22, after a short visit to Japan. See *Reed Correspondence,* p. 488.

[34] Reed to Cass, No. 33, Shanghai, October 21, 1858, *ibid.,* p. 438.

[35] The Chinese-American Treaty signed at Tientsin did not indicate that the Chinese tariff rates had to be revised. It did state that the rates might be modified at such time as the other nations might reach an agreement with China. Thus, during the negotiations at Shanghai, the Americans had more to discuss with the British than with the Chinese. See above, footnote 20.

[36] The traditional assumption that the Chinese tariff rates were fixed on 5 per cent ad valorem did not appear in any agreement signed in the 1840's. It came as a result of the first agreements between the Chinese government and the foreign envoys at Canton, because the rates they fixed then were about 5 per cent ad valorem. Thus

vision. For the last fifteen years, the price of the main article of American manufactured goods used in China—cotton fabrics—had constantly gone up rather than down; hence a revision of the fixed rate of tariff according to an ad valorem rate of 5 per cent would be an increase rather than a reduction of tariff duties to the Americans. Consequently the rate fixed by the former treaty was more favorable to the Americans than a new ad valorem duty.[37]

The opinion of the three treaty powers was also divided on export duties. If the ad valorem rate of 5 per cent were applied, the export duties on tea would be reduced, while those on silk would be increased. Although the English and the Americans favored a new reduction on tea, the French, who had a sizable silk trade with China, were strongly opposed to any increases on silk duties and insisted on maintaining the old duty.[38] Since China was then bound by the most-favored-nation clause, a uniform tariff for the treaty powers was a necessity. In a letter to Commissioner Reed, Lord Elgin wrote:[39]

I fear, therefore, that even if I could persuade the Chinese commissioners to carry out inflexibly the principle of a five per cent duty in the amended British tariff, the result would be that under the most-favored-nation clause the tea merchants would look to the English treaty, the silk merchants to the French, for the duty which they were to pay on their respective exports; a system which would give rise to much confusion, and which would probably be regarded by the Chinese authorities as characterized by sharp practice, if not indifferent faith. . . .

Thus the Western representatives had only to reach an agreement among themselves before presenting their respective terms to the Chinese. In the Shanghai negotiations, therefore, the Western delegates like their Chinese colleagues spent more energy and time in settling differences among themselves than with their common opponent.

The Western representatives at last reached an agreement among themselves and then signed their agreements with China on November 8, 1858.[40] As was usual in Chinese diplomacy of the last century, the

it became a tradition. During the negotiations at Shanghai in 1858 and thereafter, however, the supposed 5 per cent agreement was only binding to the Chinese. Once the fixed rate was above that level because of a fall in prices, Western envoys would request the Chinese to reduce the rate. But when the fixed rate was below it because of a rise in prices, this rule was usually ignored.

[37] Reed to Cass, No. 36, Shanghai, November 9, 1858, *Reed Correspondence*, p. 497.
[38] Oliphant, *Elgin's Mission to China and Japan*, II, 275.
[39] Elgin to Reed, Shanghai, October 19, 1858, *Reed Correspondence*, p. 513.
[40] Frederick Wells Williams, ed., *The Life and Letters of Samuel Wells Williams, LL.D. Missionary, Diplomatist Sinologue* (New York: G. P. Putnam's Sons, 1889) p. 291.

Western parties obtained what they wanted and were satisfied with the new concessions from the Celestial Empire.

The agreements signed between China and the United States at Shanghai on November 8 were twofold—one purely commercial, embodying a revised tariff and new regulations of trade and transit; the other finally adjusting the indemnities claimed by American citizens. The revised tariff rates were agreeable to the three treaty powers. The export duty on tea was reduced from the previous rate of 7-10 taels per picul (in Chinese currency) or 7-11 cents a pound (in American currency) to 2 taels 5 mace per picul, or about 2½ cents per pound. The import duties on the most popular American product, cotton fabrics, were also slightly reduced. This arrangement was much lower than the traditional 5 per cent. ". . . had a general five per cent *ad valorem* been insisted on by the Chinese," commented Reed, "owing to the rise of value in our manufactures, the duty would have been increased."[41]

The newly agreed upon regulations of trade in the different trading ports, old or new, were also common to all three treaty powers. Reed, however, broke away from the so-called custom inspectorate system. Because of the many complaints submitted by American merchants, Commissioner Reed had, from the very moment of his arrival in China, refused to recognize the legal position of the "American Foreign Inspector" in the Chinese custom service. "For a long time," said Reed, "the oath of the 'American inspector' was taken before the United States consul and filed among his archives as if he were an American officer."[42] With strong objection to this queer system, he advised the Chinese to abolish the system completely. Since the Chinese had no power to do so, Reed struck out the provision from the American trade regulations. In his dispatch to Washington on November 9, 1858, Reed said that the American withdrawal from this peculiar system was inevitable and the result would be either solely English, or English and French, but that in either case the Americans would be excluded.[43] Reed seems to have used his decision as a sign of protest against this illegal system.

Actually, the American withdrawal from the inspectorate system had long been desired by the British. From the very beginning of its establishment, the British seemed to have favored sole control of the customs service without the participation of the Americans and the French.

[41] Reed to Cass, No. 36, Shanghai, November 9, 1858, *Reed Correspondence,* pp. 493-99. For complete texts of the conventions signed at Shanghai consult *Treaties Conventions etc.,* I, 524 ff.

[42] *Reed Correspondence,* p. 497.

[43] *Ibid.,* p. 498. Cf. chap. 10 for more information about the inspectorate system.

As the British, who were old hands in China, understood, the Chinese officials, corrupt as they were, were easier to deal with than their Western colleagues. If some talented American or French personnel were really appointed as custom inspectors and set to work seriously, British commerce, particularly the opium trade, would be seriously handicapped. "It would seem impossible to deny their authority altogether to put a stop to the trade in opium," wrote the British foreign minister to the British envoy, Bowring, in 1856; and if such were to be the result, the efforts of Her Majesty's government to obtain the Chinese consent to the legalization of the opium trade would be rendered useless.[44] Thus Commissioner Reed's decision to withdraw the "American Inspector" from the Chinese customhouse was exactly what the British wanted. When the inspectorate system was formally extended to other treaty ports, H. N. Lay, the first inspector general, formally requested the American inspector to resign. This action led to a vigorous protest from John E. Ward, Commissioner Reed's successor.[45]

The second part of the agreements signed at Shanghai dealt with American claims against China. These claims, as previously explained, were initiated by the Roberts case, which, with ten years' interest, now amounted to $2,800. In addition to the Roberts claim, miscellaneous American claims against China had accumulated as time passed. Among them, the largest was for American losses in the mysterious fire in the foreign factories during the Arrow War at Canton. The total amount of all American claims against China, as Reed estimated in January, 1858, was $1,286,841.88.[46]

At his farewell interview with the Chinese Imperial Commissioners at Tientsin on June 26, 1858, however, Commissioner Reed reduced the amount to $800,000.[47] Since the Chinese were severely troubled by British and French claims that amounted to millions of dollars, the claim of this relatively small amount by a "friendly country" met with the ready acceptance of the Emperor, who ordered Kuei-liang and his colleagues to give the grant through the deduction of tariff "in accordance with former precedents."[48]

Thus the American claims were formally settled by a Chinese payment of 500,000 taels (or $735,288)—300,000 taels for the damages

---

[44] Clarendon to Bowring, January 2, 1856, *F.O.*, 17/242, quoted and paraphrased in Costin, *Great Britain and China,* p. 164.
[45] See following chapter.
[46] *Reed Correspondence,* p. 118.
[47] *Ibid.,* p. 371.
[48] *Shih-lu:HF, chüan* 253, p. 5b.

at Canton, and 100,000 taels each for Foochow and Shanghai. They were to be deducted from the tariff and tonnage dues paid by American vessels. This practice would begin on the following lunar New Year (February 3, 1859).[49] Further calculations made after the Chinese had already paid show that this total exceeded by about one-fourth the amount actually claimed by American citizens. In 1885 the surplus, with interest, amounting to $453,400, was returned to the Chinese government.[50]

The opium trade was another of the problems in China that seriously involved American interests which Commissioner Reed tried to settle. As previously explained, after the Taiping Rebellion extended to southeast China, all important trade in that part of the country suffered serious setbacks. The opium trade, however, flourished, and Shanghai became the largest port for opium smuggling, which was carried on by vessels of every nation trading with China. In the late 1850's opium smuggled to Shanghai accounted for about one-half of the total commodities imported in that port.

The opium imported to China in the 1850's was mostly from Bengal and Malwa. The figures provided by Russell and Company show the amount of the opium trade in China for the years 1854, 1855, 1856, and 1857 to be as follows:[51]

| | BENGAL OPIUM | | MALWA OPIUM | |
Years	Number of Chests	Price of Each Chest	Number of Chests	Price of Each Chest
1854	55,000	$375 (Mexican)	....	....
1855	45,000	450	29,000	$600
1856	40,000	500	33,000	600
1857	36,000	600	34,000	600

Each chest contains 105-60 catties of opium.
One catty is equal to 1⅓ pounds.

According to Lord Elgin's estimate, the average price of opium in 1858 was $1,000 per chest.[52] The total amount of China's foreign trade (including both import and export) as estimated by Russell and Company

---

[49] For a brief summary of this settlement see Tyler Dennett, *Americans in Eastern Asia* (New York: The Macmillan Co., 1922), pp. 326-31; for detailed documents on this subject see *Reed Correspondence*, pp. 520-24, and Williams, *Life and Letters*, p. 292.

[50] Dennett, *Americans in Eastern Asia*, p. 330n; John Watson Foster, *American Diplomacy in the Orient* (New York: Houghton Mifflin and Co., 1903), pp. 243-44.

[51] See Thos. Walsh to Wm. B. Reed, Shanghai, August 28, 1858, *Reed Correspondence*, p. 511.

[52] Elgin to Reed, Shanghai, October 19, 1858, *ibid.*, p. 512.

in 1857 was about 70,000,000 taels. In 1857, opium imported into Shanghai was worth 14,333,000 taels (altogether 32,246 chests); total imported legal commodities were 14,549,000 taels (one tael was equal to $1.48).[53] The opium smuggling, therefore, seriously jeopardized all the legal trade, for it had absorbed the Chinese capital and handicapped all honest merchants.

At the beginning of Reed's mission to China, Secretary Cass instructed him to assist the Chinese government in preventing the importation and consumption of that drug.[54] In the Sino-American negotiations at Tientsin, Reed had spoken to the Chinese Imperial Commissioners of his intention to help the Chinese suppress the opium trade, but the Chinese were obviously too frightened then to talk about opium with the Americans. Returning to Shanghai, Reed began to realize the seriousness of opium smuggling, in which respectable American citizens also participated. The most active opium-carrying ship was reported to be an American steamer, the *Yangtze,* built in New York, owned by an American citizen, and flying the American flag. In addition to the *Yangtze,* other respectable American ships, such as the *Antelope,* a ship owned by the eminent Bostonian, R. B. Forbes, which the Com-missioner had enlisted for service in Tientsin, were also active opium smugglers.[55] These disgraceful reports puzzled the righteous former professor of American history, who tried to seek the means for a proper settlement of the opium problem.

He was, however, surprised by the British indifference to this matter. In the negotiations at Tientsin, the British did not seek a settlement of the opium problem with the Chinese. As with their negotiations in Nanking in 1842, the British negotiations with the Chinese in 1858 completely neglected the opium question. After the foreign ministers returned to Shanghai, Commissioner Reed gradually realized that none of the British were really anxious for a prompt settlement of the opium question. The British diplomats, though indifferent, might still be willing to talk about the legalization of the opium trade; the British opium dealers, however, were opposed even to the legalization movement. The reason for their opposition, as Reed saw it, was very simple.

---

[53] For further information see Walsh to Reed, Shanghai, August 28, 1858, *ibid.,* pp. 507-11.

[54] Cass to Reed, No. 2, Washington, D.C., May 30, 1857, *DI-USNA,* 77:38, 162. *Reed Correspondence,* p. 8.

[55] George B. Glover to William B. Reed, Shanghai, August 31, 1858, *ibid.,* pp. 501-2. Glover was the United States vice-consul at Shanghai. For Robert B. Forbes's influence on American diplomacy in China, see chap. 13.

Ever since the outbreak of the Chinese civil war, the effectiveness of China's attempt to prohibit opium had been diminished. The Chinese prohibition law was practically a dead letter. Thus the British opium traders found it more profitable to smuggle opium than to import it legally. If legalized, they would have to pay at least 5 per cent ad valorem custom duty, which, to them, was an unnecessary burden. In reporting this strange situation at Shanghai, the American commissioner wrote to Washington:[56]

When I say no dissent I perhaps ought to be understood as saying no audible dissent, for it is perfectly well known here that those, especially among the English and Parsees, whose machinery of smuggling is elaborate and complete, wish no change, being content with their monopoly of profitable and indecent violation of law. To defy or corrupt the Chinese officials is with them a normal state and the transition of obedience to law is a painful process.

Since the opium smuggling was "most mischievous in its relation to trade, and most discreditable to all parties, political and individual,"[57] Commissioner Reed decided to do something about it regardless of British indifference or opposition.

On September 13, 1858, Reed wrote a long letter to Lord Elgin. First of all he pointed out the damage resulting to legal trade because of opium smuggling. Then he complained about the British neglect of this problem. Reed suggested to the British envoy two alternatives:[58] either help the Chinese authorities in active and thorough suppression of the opium trade, or persuade the Chinese to legalize it. Reed's letter was not answered until October 19, when Elgin wrote that he would instruct the British negotiator to consider the problem. But he stressed: "I have little doubt but that it will be found that legalization is the only available remedy for evils which attracted your excellency's notice."[59] Thus, with American support, the British now pressed the Chinese to legalize the opium trade. It was finally written into the Sino-British trade agreement and signed on November 8, 1858. Only four months before, the Commissioner had agreed to strike out the "opium clause" from the Sino-American Treaty of Tientsin, supposedly with the British

[56] Reed to Cass, No. 36, November 9, 1858, Shanghai, *Reed Correspondence*, p. 494. The Parsees were the Indian people of a particular clan who lived in India and the Middle East.

[57] Reed to Elgin, Shanghai, September 13, 1858, *ibid.*, p. 506.

[58] *Ibid.*, pp. 505-8.

[59] Elgin to Reed, Shanghai, October 19, 1858, *Reed Correspondence*, p. 512; Oliphant, *Elgin's Mission to China and Japan*, II, 278-81.

guarantee that the latter would not "legalize the trade by treaty."[60] Now the American commissioner became the chief promoter of the legalization of the opium trade in China, and the British appeared to be rather reluctant to accept the American proposal, although they had been working ardently for it for years.

Unaware that he had been outmaneuvered, Reed wrote rather proudly to the State Department the day after the legalization of the opium trade, that legalization was the best solution for the settlement of the opium problem. "On one point there was no dissent," said the honest Commissioner, "that any system would be better than that which now exists." "When I say no dissent," he explained to the State Department, "I perhaps ought to be understood as saying no audible dissent." According to Reed's personal observation there was serious inaudible dissent among the English and the Parsees, but they could not protest openly. Reed seemed to have been proud of his role in being the major promoter of the legalization of the opium trade.[61] For years the British diplomats had been complaining that the American diplomats in China were unprofessional.[62] As far as the legalization of the opium trade in China was concerned, however, Lord Elgin, at least, might have been pleased about this nonprofessionalism.

Along with the opium trade, the immoral coolie trade also attracted the attention of the American commissioner. Although unauthorized, Reed voluntarily looked into the coolie trade and tried to prevent it from developing. "In its ultimate results," he wrote, "I believe this Asiatic slave trade is as bad, if not worse, than the African slave trade ever was."[63] Therefore he urged his government to take some measures to prevent American ships from being used in this traffic. Unfortunately, he could do nothing more than offer some general suggestions.

During Reed's successful stay in China, one amusing incident may be worth brief mention. When the supplementary negotiations at Shanghai were almost concluded, the British suddenly sent a bundle of Chinese documents seized at Canton during the Arrow War to the American legation. The documents were secret Chinese memorials and

---

[60] Reed to Cass, No. 23, Tientsin, June 30, 1858, *Reed Correspondence*, p. 357. Cf. preceding chapter.

[61] Reed to Cass, No. 36, Shanghai, November 9, 1858, *Reed Correspondence*, p. 497.

[62] Frederick W. A. Bruce to Lord Russell (Confidential), November 22, 1859, *F.O.* 17/315, in Costin, *Great Britain and China*, p. 305.

[63] Reed to Cass, No. 30, Shanghai, September 1, 1858, *Reed Correspondence*, p. 425. These seized "Chinese documents," totaling twelve pieces, were translated into English by Thomas Wade, Chinese secretary of the British legation, and printed in full; see *ibid.*, pp. 477-89.

edicts exchanged between the Chinese emperors and their subjects with regard to the Sino-American affairs of the past years. They were full of derogatory terms such as "barbarian," "dogs and sheep," and so forth. Reed was sorely irritated when he read these rather insulting documents. He felt the English and French ministers had made a mistake by withholding these Chinese-American documents until the end of the negotiations. Otherwise, the Americans under his direction might have given full support to the allied course against the Chinese at Tientsin and elsewhere, and the history of Sino-American diplomatic relations during this period might have been entirely different.[64]

Having concluded a remarkably successful mission in China, Commissioner Reed departed from Shanghai aboard his special ship, the *Minnesota,* for Hong Kong on November 11, 1858, three days after the signing of the supplementary agreements. From Hong Kong he sailed on December 8 for Bombay, where he took the mail steamer for home.[65]

---

[64] Reed to Cass, No. 33, Shanghai, October 21, 1858, *ibid.,* p. 439.

[65] Reed to Cass, No. 39, Hong Kong, November 25, 1858, *Reed Correspondence,* p. 540.

16

COMMISSIONER WARD

AND THE WAR AT TA-KU

I

JOHN E. WARD, a capable lawyer from Georgia, was appointed on January 18, 1859, to succeed Commissioner Reed as envoy extraordinary and minister plenipotentiary of the United States to China. Ward was born in Sanbury, Georgia, in 1814. In his teens he went north to study, and graduated from Amherst College in 1832. Then he returned to the South to study law in Savannah, Georgia. Later he enrolled at Harvard Law School and married the daughter of William Sullivan, an eminent lawyer in Boston. In the 1840's he served as a member of the legislature of his home state for three terms and became the mayor of Savannah in 1854.[1]

In 1856 he was elected president of the Democratic National Convention at Cincinnati, Ohio. This was the convention that nominated Buchanan and considered Ward for the nomination of Vice President. After the convention, he was elected president of the state Senate and acting lieutenant-governor of Georgia. He held this position until his appointment as United States commissioner to China. By birth and public service Ward was a southerner; but by education and marriage, he had stronger ties to the North than most of the southern statesmen.

Despite Ward's brilliant career in public service and his obvious qualifications to work for a compromise between the North and the South, he does not seem to have been the most suitable person for the China post, particularly on the eve of the American Civil War. He was

---

[1] Allen Johnson, ed., *Dictionary of American Biography* (New York: Charles Scribner's Sons, 1943), XIX, 426-27; also consult *The National Cyclopedia of American Biography,* (New York: James T. White and Co., 1892), I, 373, and John Howard Brown, ed., *Lamb's Biographical Dictionary of the United States* (Boston: James H. Lamb Company, 1900-3), VII, 489.

more interested in domestic political affairs during this crucial period than in foreign relations with China, of which he was comparatively ignorant. For his coming mission to China, moreover, when the Anglo-French war against China was not yet fully ended, he had not only to deal with the Chinese but also with the British and the French. Ward obviously was not the person to give serious attention to this job while a split within his own country was becoming more serious each day.

Since Ward's chief mission in China was supposed to be conducted in peaceful circumstances after the signing of a new treaty, the Secretary of State gave him no specific instructions except on routine business. In general terms he was ordered to carry on as his predecessors had done, pressing American claims against China or redressing grievances of American citizens resident in China should that be necessary during his stay there.[2]

His principal mission was, of course, to exchange the ratifications of the Treaty of Tientsin. The Secretary desired that this be done at Peking.[3] To facilitate the Commissioner's trip to Peking via the Pei-ho, the State Department had obtained the cooperation of the Navy Department, which was to give Ward the necessary vessels and naval force. He was also authorized to charter a small steamer to ascend the Pei-ho.[4]

Ward was also instructed to continue negotiations for new commercial regulations with the Chinese and to put them into effect as soon as possible. In addition, he was to superintend the payment of the Chinese indemnities, which were to be deducted at the rate of one-fifth of all the tonnage, import, and export duties paid by American ships at Canton, Foochow, and Shanghai.[5]

Ward was further reminded that during his stay in China he was to work in close cooperation with the Russian diplomatic agents there. Through official consultation with the Russian government at St. Petersburg, the State Department had secured the Russians' promise to render their assistance to the American commissioner in China.[6]

For his new mission to China, Ward was given a compensation of $12,000 per annum. Moreover, at his request, his brother, W. Wallace Ward, was appointed secretary of the American legation in China.

---

2 Cass to Ward, No. 1, Washington, D.C., January 18, 1859, *DI-USNA*, 77:38, p. 195.

3 *Ibid.*

4 Case to Ward, No. 2, Washington, January 22, 1859, *ibid.*, p. 197.

5 *Ibid.*

6 Cass to Ward, No. 4, Washington, D.C., February 21, 1859, *ibid.*, p. 200.

Dr. S. Wells Williams, discharged from the secretaryship, was to work only as the interpreter of the legation.[7]

Ward reached Hong Kong on May 18, 1859, where he was greeted by Commodore Josiah Tatnall, commanding officer of the United States naval forces in the Far East, who provided the Commissioner with a small steamer under his command.[8] After announcing his arrival to both the British and the French ministers at Hong Kong and Macao, Ward left South China immediately for the North in order to avoid complications with the allied envoys.[9] Ward reached Shanghai on May 28, 1859. Once there he learned that the Chinese Imperial Commissioners were waiting for the foreign envoys to arrive for the exchange of ratifications of the treaties signed at Tientsin.[10]

For his projected trip to Peking, the American commissioner promptly addressed a letter to the Chinese Imperial Commissioners announcing that he was on his way to the Chinese capital to present his credentials personally to the Chinese Emperor and to exchange the ratifications of the Treaty of Tientsin. This communication was soon answered by the four Chinese Imperial Commissioners,[11] who replied that they could not reach Tientsin by land within two months. "Your excellency must, therefore, see very clearly," the reply went on, "that if you arrive at that city so early, while we are unable to hasten our departure, not only will no officer be there to receive you, but the duty of making the exchange of ratifications will still devolve on us."[12] Thus they advised Ward "to delay a while in Shanghai, before fixing the time to start."

[7] Lewis Cass to Samuel W. Williams, Washington, D.C., January 24, 1859; Lewis Cass to W. Wallace Ward, Washington, D.C., January 25, 1859, *ibid.*, pp. 197-99.

[8] Ward to Cass, No. 14, Shanghai, June 13, 1859, *DD-USNA*, 92:19. A part of John E. Ward's dispatches was also included in *Senate Exec. Doc.*, No. 30, 36 Cong., 1 sess., pp. 569-624. This will be cited hereafter as the *Ward Correspondence*.

[9] The new British minister was Frederick W. A. Bruce, brother of Lord Elgin; the new French minister was A. de Bourboulon. Both had arrived in China before Ward. The American commissioner's avoidance of a meeting with them was obviously under the advice of his predecessor, William B. Reed. On his way to China, Ward met Reed in Lyons, where Reed's advice to him was, "avoiding Hongkong, go as quickly as possible to Shanghai." See Hon. Wm. B. Reed to Dr. Williams, Lyons, March 26, 1859, in Frederick Wells Williams, ed., *The Life and Letters of Samuel Wells Williams, LL.D. Missionary, Diplomatist Sinologue* (New York: C. P. Putnam's Sons, 1889), p. 295. Ward seems to have taken this advice seriously. Also consult Ward to Cass, No. 4, Lyons, March 26, 1859, *DD-USNA*, 92:19.

[10] The four Imperial Commissioners included Ho Kuei-ch'ing, who had been appointed Imperial Commissioner in charge of the trade in the trading ports, but excluded Ming-shan, who had been transferred to another post.

[11] The Imperial Commissioners' reply to Commissioner Ward, May 30, 1859, *Ward Correspondence*, pp. 575-76.

[12] *Ibid.*

In order to arrange for the exchange of ratifications in Peking, the four Chinese Imperial Commissioners also asked for a meeting with the American commissioner. This meeting took place on June 2, 1859 at the Imperial Commissioners' office in the city of Shanghai.[13] At this time they informed Ward that the exchange of ratifications had to be effected in Peking, for the original copy of the treaty was preserved there. Since the deadline of the exchange was June 18, 1859, they further assured the American commissioner in a written statement: "Whenever this does take place it will be equally valid as if it had been done within the prescribed year."[14] Since Ward was not responsible for the delay, he protested that the Chinese must agree that ratifications had been exchanged *de jure* within the specific time and that only the ceremony of exchange had to take place at Peking.[15]

In the meantime, however, Frederick W. A. Bruce and A. de Bourboulon, the English and French ministers, also arrived in Shanghai and communicated with the Chinese Imperial Commissioners. They intended to sail for Tientsin immediately, without seeing the Chinese Imperial Commissioners at Shanghai. The four Chinese Imperial Commissioners, however, repeatedly appealed to the allied envoys for a meeting and tried to keep them from immediate departure to Tientsin by using the same arguments that had worked on Ward. The British and the French ignored the Chinese logic and charged the Imperial Commissioners with acting in bad faith. In the meantime, Bruce notified the Imperial Commissioners that Admiral Hope, commander-in-chief of the British forces, had already started for the mouth of the Pei-ho and warned them that the entire responsibility for any trouble that might arise must rest on the Chinese government.[16] "This firmness", writes Mr. Costin, "brought about the immediate departure on the 13th of the imperial Commissioners."[17] Two days before their

---

[13] The city of Shanghai was recaptured by the Imperialists late in 1855.

[14] The Imperial Commissioners to Ward, June 3, 1859, *Ward Correspondence,* p. 578. On this occasion the Chinese Imperial Commissioners apparently misunderstood that Commissioner Ward had been willing to exchange the ratifications at Shanghai. See *IWSM-HF,* XXXVIII, 15b.

[15] Ward to Cass, No. 14, Shanghai, June 13, 1859, *Reed Correspondence,* pp. 569-71.

[16] For general reference see Tyler Dennett, *Americans in Eastern Asia* (New York: The Macmillan Co., 1922), p. 336.

[17] William Conrad Costin, *Great Britain and China 1833-1860* (Oxford: The Clarendon Press, 1937), p. 291. Actually this "firmness" was the natural result of the determined allied policy of carrying out the exchange of ratifications. Upon their arrival in China, Bruce and de Bourboulon had reached an agreement that they should be forceful in Tientsin as well as in Peking. In a report to Paris in the middle of May, 1859, the French envoy wrote: "Je suis donc d'avis que s'il doit y avoir des difficultés,—et nous devons nous y attendre—il vaut mieux les aborder et même en quelque

departure, the frightened Chinese advised the American commissioner to sail north with the allied envoys.[18]

After receiving this Chinese communication and exchanging brief notes with the British and French ministers, Ward left Shanghai on June 16, 1859, on board the *Powhatan* with the *Toeywan*, a chartered steamer, in tow for the Pei-ho. After five days, on June 21, the *Powhatan* arrived off the mouth of the river.[19]

II

Some historians have doubted the sincerity of the Chinese promise to accept the foreign ministers at Peking. "The question of fact is," said Dennett, "whether the Chinese government was actually sincere in its promise that the British and French ministers would be received in Peking according to the provisions of the treaty."[20] Dr. Williams, however, wrote: "I am convinced that the intention of the Emperor and his cabinet has been all along in favor of permitting the envoys of the three powers to go to his capital to exchange their treaties. . . ."[21] The Russian diplomatic agents who were then staying at Peking also supplied the information that "lodgings had been arranged, by order of the Emperor, for the three embassies."[22] The published Chinese documents also show that the Chinese authorities had prepared to receive the foreign ministers at Peking and due arrangements and preparations had been made even before the allied ministers' arrival in China. These arrangements were made through imperial orders, for ever since the allied capture of Tientsin and the failure of his campaign against treaty revision, the unbending young Emperor at last bowed to facts. He, too, was now in favor of an appeasement policy.

---

sorte les provoquer a l'avance, parce qu'ainsi avant d'être engagés dans l'exécution même de ce que nous nous proposons, nous serons dans une position beaucoup plus avantageuse pour les resoudre." Henri Cordier, *L'Expédition de chine de 1860, histoire diplomatique, notes et documents* (Paris: Felix Alcan, Editeur, 1906), p. 50. Their joint decision was further strengthened by an intelligence report early in June, stating that the Chinese had been reconstructing the forts at Ta-ku. Consequently the allied forces were rushed north, and the allied envoys completely neglected the Chinese appeal as well as the arrangements made by their predecessors. *Ibid.*, pp. 50 ff.; see also Costin, *Great Britain and China*, pp. 289 ff.

[18] The four Chinese Imperial Commissioners to Commissioner Ward, June 11, 1859, *Ward Correspondence*, p. 579.

[19] For a detailed description of the American party and its trip to the Pei-ho consult Williams, *Life and Letters*, pp. 297 ff.

[20] Dennett, *Americans in Eastern Asia*, p. 337.

[21] Williams, *Life and Letters*, pp. 143 ff.

[22] Nicolas Ignatieff to John E. Ward, Peking, July 7, 1859, *Ward Correspondence*, p. 611.

In an edict issued on March 29, 1859, the Emperor set up certain rules to govern the foreign commissioners in Peking. The attendants of each foreign envoy, for instance, would not be more than ten; they could not bear arms, and upon arrival at the capital, in conformity with the regulations for foreigners coming to the capital, they should not ride in sedan chairs.[23] The same edict ordered Ho Kuei-ch'ing, governor-general of Liang-Kiang, and Imperial Commissioner in charge of the trade of the trading ports, to send two or three foreign affairs experts to Peking "post-haste to take charge, so as not to afford the barbarians any excuse for lingering."

On the same day another edict was sent to Prince Seng-ko-lin-ch'in to strengthen the Ta-ku defenses to meet any possible future foreign attack.[24] Seng-ko-lin-ch'in, a Mongol, was an outstanding military leader who had repelled a Taiping expedition in 1853 and saved the capital. But he was ordered to deal with the foreigners peacefully. Should the foreign ships come to request an entrance to the Pei-ho, he was ordered to tell them to wait outside the bar and to say: ". . . at this juncture they are only waiting for word from Shanghai and if Imperial Commissioners Kuei-liang and others did give notice to allow them to enter port, they would certainly not be prevented." Thus they must wait for news from Shanghai. The General was also ordered not to open fire on the foreign ships unless he was attacked by them.

The Prince took the Emperor's order seriously. In a memorial submitted early in April, he suggested that the Pei-ho should be closed to foreign traffic for strategic reasons. Once the foreign envoys arrived at the mouth of the Pei-ho, they should be advised to take another water route to Pei-t'ang, twenty miles north of Ta-ku. From there they might be led to Tientsin by land and then by boat to the vicinity of T'ung-chou from where they could reach Peking by cart.[25]

Since the treaties had not specified by which route the foreign ministers were to proceed to Peking, Seng's suggestion for a landing point at Pei-t'ang was accepted by the Emperor, who issued an edict on the same day that the memorial was received by the Court. It ordered the Grand Council and the local officials to arrange matters as Seng-ko-lin-ch'in had advised.

This plan was formulated two months before the arrival of foreign ships at the mouth of Pei-ho. Since they expected no opposition from

---

[23] *IWSM-HF*, XXXV, 40b.
[24] *Ibid.*, pp. 41b-42a.
[25] *IWSM-HF*, XXXVI, 17b-18a.

the foreigners, who were supposed to be coming on a peaceful mission to Peking, the Chinese Imperial Commissioners at Shanghai were ordered to advise the foreign ministers of this program before their departure for the north.[26]

III

Admiral Hope of the British navy was the first to arrive at the mouth of the Pei-ho. With him was as large a naval force as Lord Elgin had the year before. He was followed, on June 20, 1859, by the two allied envoys, Bruce and de Bourboulon. They found that the mouth of the Pei-ho had been obstructed with barriers. Immediately the allied authorities wrote to the local Chinese officials asking for an unobstructed passage to be made ready within three days. This request was politely rejected by the Chinese ashore, who said that these barriers had been reconstructed by the people as a protection against rebels, not by order of the government for the purpose of keeping the allied forces out of the river. Since the Chinese Imperial Commissioners were still on their way to Peking, there were no competent officials at Ta-ku who could either read or write any Western language or receive the foreign ministers. The local officers sent a great quantity of gifts to the allied forces and informed the foreign messengers that the foreign ministers were invited to Pei-t'ang where Heng-fu, the new governor-general of Chihli province, was waiting for them. But this reply was returned to the Chinese together with the gifts. The allied ministers would not accept any alternative but ascending the Pei-ho to Tientsin.[27]

On June 21, Commissioner Ward arrived at the mouth of the Pei-ho with Commodore Josiah Tattnall on board the *Powhatan*. On the morning of June 24, Ward and Tattnall ordered the *Toeywan*, a chartered steamer, to sail across the bar, but she ran aground one-half mile from the forts. The Commissioner then sent three interpreters, Samuel Wells Williams, W. A. P. Martin, and William Atchison, whose service had been enlisted at Shanghai, ashore. They were likewise advised by the Chinese to sail to Pei-t'ang.[28]

---

[26] *Ibid.*, pp. 18a-19a. The Imperial Commissioners at Shanghai opposed the Emperor's plan for a detour via Pei-t'ang. They thought this arrangement would certainly arouse "barbarian suspicion." Unfortunately when their memorial reached the Grand Council, the battle at Ta-ku was already over. See *IWSM-HF,* XXXIX, 21b-22a.

[27] *IWSM-HF,* XXXVIII, 27a-29a.

[28] Ward to Cass, No. 15, Off Pei-ho River, July 4, 1859, *Ward Correspondence,* p. 586.

In the meantime, the British admiral had already ordered his ships to form a line and stand ready for battle. In order to avoid complications, Commodore Tattnall ordered the *Toeywan*, after she was freed by the evening tide, to drop below the line. About midnight, the British began to blow up the barriers across the river.[29]

According to the Chinese source, the British began to destroy barriers on the evening of June 24. Three iron chains and many wooden and metal booms were removed, but the Chinese guards on the forts were forbidden to fire under strict imperial orders. After midnight, when the British ships withdrew, the Chinese sent workers down the river and repaired the booms. Next morning when the British went to remove the booms again, all the warships were lined up with "red pennants" flying indicating that they were ready for battle. The *taotai* of Tientsin then sent an emergency appeal to the British, hoping to stop the warships from firing at the forts. Admiral Hope, however, refused to accept the messenger. At 3:00 P.M. on June 25, the British warships began to bombard the forts.[30]

In speaking of this Chinese messenger, an American observer, who had witnessed the incident, wrote:[31]

On the morning of the 25th, the gun-boats were arranged in order of battle, preparatory to attacking the forts; and just as the Admiral had completed his preparations, a boat was seen coming from the shore containing a Chinese official, who held in his hand a large document, which he displayed in such a manner as to attract the Admiral's attention, but he directed the bearer to be warned off, saying that it was too late for negotiation.

This time, however, the battle turned against the British. The Chinese were well prepared, while the British admiral was overconfident and his forces poorly disposed. After a few hours of gunfire, the British suffered an unprecedented defeat in the Orient. The flagship of the British fleet was almost sunk, and the Admiral himself was dangerously wounded. "Out of the Admiral's steamer, the *Plover*,"

---

[29] For a firsthand report on the battle at Ta-ku on June 25, consult James D. Johnston, *China and Japan: Being a Narrative of the Cruise of the U.S. Steam-Frigate Powhatan, in the Years 1857, '58, '59, and '60* (Philadelphia: Charles Desilver, 1861), pp. 230-40; or see Williams, *Life and Letters*, pp. 302-13. According to Johnston the allied force in the Pei-ho consisted of 1,350 men, of whom only about 60 were French, and 13 gunboats of which one belonged to France.

[30] *IWSM-HF*, XXXVIII, 40b-41a.

[31] Johnston, pp. 231-32. Both Dr. Williams and Mr. Costin confirmed Johnston's story. See Williams, *Life and Letters*, p. 302, and Costin, *Great Britain and China*, p. 292.

wrote Dr. Williams, who was watching nearby, "only one man escaped unharmed from a crew of forty."[32] Hope then sent small boats to the rear for more reinforcements, but the tide and wind were too strong, and the boats were unable to sail. The situation was desperate; without these reinforcements, he might not be able to return alive.

Throughout the action, Commodore Tattnall showed himself a stanch British partisan. When he heard Admiral Hope was wounded, he sailed under Chinese fire from one British ship to another seeking the injured British commander. While looking for Admiral Hope, Tattnall's own barge was hit and sunk; the coxswain, John Hart, was killed. The shot missed the Commodore by a few inches. The American sailors then joined the British in loading the guns.[33] "Beyond this plucky display," wrote Dr. Martin who was watching the operation with Dr. Williams, Tattnall, who had Ward's prior approval, "gave a substantial proof of sympathy by towing up a flotilla of launches containing a storming-party of five hundred men, exclaiming, as he threw diplomacy overboard, that 'blood is thicker than water.' "[34]

At that moment Commodore Tattnall seems to have seriously thought of sending a landing party to join the British in their attack on the forts. The executive officer, James D. Johnston, of the *Powhatan* was directed "to have 200 men prepared to land at a moment's notice." Johnston recalled that he had ordered the heavy launches to be got ready for hoisting out for that purpose. "The work was performed in less time than it ever had been before," said Johnston, "though it proved to be unnecessary."[35]

In speaking of Tattnall's decision to participate in the war, Tyler Dennett wrote:[36]

The most reasonable explanation of this episode is to be found in the fact that the struggle of the allied forces with the Chinese had assumed in the eyes of both Tattnall and Ward, who were Southerners, the aspect of a conflict of color. An eye-witness of the episode recorded in his diary that Commodore Tattnall finally explained: "Blood is thicker than water" and that he'd "be damned if he'd stand by and see white men butchered before his eyes. No, sir; old Tattnall isn't that kind, sir. This is the cause of humanity. Is that boat ready? Tell the men there is no need of side-arms."

---

[32] Williams, *Life and Letters,* p. 301.

[33] Johnston, *China and Japan,* p. 235.

[34] W. A. P. Martin, *A Cycle of Cathay or China, South and North with Personal Reminiscences* (New York: Fleming H. Revell Company, 1897), p. 192.

[35] Johnston, *China and Japan,* p. 240.

[36] See Private Papers of Rear Admiral Stephen Decatur Trenschard, *U.S. Naval Institute Proceedings,* LX, 1085 ff. in Dennett, *Americans in Eastern Asia,* p. 340n.

After dark, the American commodore withdrew from the battle while the defeated British admiral made another attempt to reverse the situation. Taking advantage of darkness, he landed six hundred British marines at Ta-ku in an attempt to capture the forts, but he met only a bloody defeat. The marines were mowed down like grass in front of the forts. "A single discharge knocked over forty men," wrote Dr. Williams; "out of the six hundred who landed, we hear that two hundred at least were killed or disabled within a few moments." When the marines had at last withdrawn, 452 men were counted as killed, disabled, or missing, with the loss of some 450 rifles.[37]

The Chinese source reports that about "one hundred and several tens" of bodies of British marines were discovered on shore together with forty-one "foreign rifles" and other weapons and one French flag. Four British gunboats were sunk; two prisioners-of-war, one English and one "American," were captured. The English prisoner-of-war had been badly wounded, the "American" was in good health. Chinese casualties showed thirty-two killed in action, including the provincial commander-in-chief of Chihli province. The rest of the Chinese war report is similar to Dr. Williams' account.[38] According to Johnston the English losses amounted to 450 killed and wounded, twenty-nine of the number being officers; the French had four killed and twelve wounded.[39] "It was a disastrous repulse indeed," noted Dr. Williams, "but none of them cursed the Chinese nor seemed to be at all angry with them; all was fair fight, and they had been beaten."[40]

After the battle was over, in spite of their unprecedented victory over the Western "barbarians," the Chinese mandarins were frightened, for they realized that this battle could only be the beginning of a larger war. On the morning following the incident, the mandarins immediately sent agents to try to conciliate the invaders, but the British and the French refused to communicate with them, broke off negotiations completely, and began to pull away from the Pei-ho.

The allied defeat at Ta-ku was, in fact, a real surprise to both sides. The British had never expected an effective resistance from the Chinese. On the other hand, the Chinese never thought that they would fight a battle against the Western invaders at the mouth of the Pei-ho. The skirmish broke out as an accident. In speaking of the

---

[37] Williams, *Life and Letters,* pp. 309, 311.
[38] *Ibid.,* p. 311; *IWSM-HF,* XXXVIII, 43a-44b.
[39] Johnston, *China and Japan,* p. 240.
[40] Williams, *Life and Letters,* p. 311.

responsibility of the clash, Dr. Martin, a witness of the entire course of action, wrote:[41]

The war was rekindled, and the Chinese were accused of bringing it about by treachery. But were they wrong in barring the way to a city that was not opened by treaty? Had the allied ministers a right to expect to reach Tientsin in their steamers when they had neglected to secure it by stipulation? Not only were they aggressors in firing the first shot, they were clearly wrong in the whole issue.

When the news of a surprise British defeat at Ta-ku reached London, many of the British statesmen thought likewise that Bruce and Hope were in the wrong, for there was not a legitimate ground for a new war against China.[42] As a result of this war, however, the treaties previously signed at Tientsin were set aside. Regardless of which side was in the wrong, all diplomatic relations between China and the allies were ended. The allies charged the Chinese government with treachery; it seemed inevitable that a large-scale Anglo-French revenge against the Chinese would ensue.

IV

When the news of a big victory at Ta-ku reached Peking on June 27, the Emperor was not so much pleased as he was deeply worried. He seems to have realized that a temporary victory over the foreigners at Ta-ku would not aid China's foreign relations with the Western powers in the long run. He was thinking of the inevitable results that would follow. Immediately he made a determined effort to maintain the appeasement policy, seeking a peaceful settlement with the three Western powers, and particularly a reconciliation with the British.

He was afraid, however, that the victory at Ta-ku might cause his army to think once more of suppressing the "barbarians" by force, and he took prompt steps to curb his officers. Beginning on June 27, the Emperor issued a series of strict orders to the Chinese officers at various strategic points, forbidding them to take the present victory as a chance to irritate the foreigners. He ordered all the fortifications in the different ports along the coast from Chihli and Shantung down to Canton not to fire on the foreign warships or to provoke any foreign

---

[41] Martin, *A Cycle of Cathay*, p. 193.

[42] For texts of debates in the British Parliament concerning the responsibility for the war at Ta-ku on June 25, 1859, see *Hansard's Parliamentary Debates*, 3rd Series, CLVII (March 16, 1860), 766-814. Also consult Costin, *Great Britain and China*, pp. 293-301.

hostilities so that the government could maintain its appeasement policy.[43]

In order to remain in a safe position with the military men, the Emperor ordered Heng-fu, governor-general of Chihli province, to move out of Prince Seng-ko-lin-ch'in's headquarters so that he could take charge of the appeasement program without outside influence, while the Prince was to take charge of the coastal defense only. They should no longer submit "joint memorials."[44] In the meantime he ordered Heng-fu to set up an office at Pei-t'ang and to send reliable representatives to conciliate the foreign envoys, if they were still in the vicinity. He directed all the Chinese officials in that area to take advantage of the present victory to formulate a plan of control-through-appeasement. "Traditionally control of outer barbarians always eventuated in conciliation," said the Emperor. "If we appeal exclusively to force, how can the matter be brought to a settlement?"[45]

In speaking of the British the Emperor wrote: "It is most important, if there is a chance for reconciliation with them, Heng-fu and others must not miss it."[46] If the English had already returned south and were preparing another expedition to Pei-ho for revenge, Ho Kuei-ch'ing should, as the Emperor wrote in a separate edict, ask the merchants at Shanghai to enlist the American or French good offices to persuade the British to refrain from military acts, but to go to Tientsin for a peaceful settlement.[47]

Although he knew of the American participation in the war, the Emperor still thought that the American envoy deserved even more friendly treatment. Heng-fu should placate him with kind words and conduct him to Tientsin, if he wished, to wait for the arrival of Kuei-liang from Shanghai so that the exchange of ratifications could be arranged at Peking. The local officials were directed to return the "American prisoner-of-war" and to make use of him as a messenger of friendship, so that the Americans might agree upon a peaceful settlement.[48]

---

[43] *IWSM-HF*, XXXVIII, 46a-56b; XXXIX, 6a. The Emperor had paid special attention to Canton, where the local populace was most militant. At the request of the allies, Governor-General Huang Tsung-han was removed. And Lao Ch'ung-kuang, a supposedly moderate figure, was appointed to succeed him.

[44] Order repeated twice in two edicts issued on June 29, 1859, *ibid.*, XXXVIII, 55a, 56b.

[45] This statement was repeated in three different edicts issued within two days. See Imperial Edicts, June 29, 30, 1859, *ibid.*, XXXVIII, 54b, 56; XXXIX, 1b.

[46] Imperial Edict, June 27, *ibid.*, XXXVIII, 46a.

[47] Imperial Edict, June 30, *ibid.*, XXXIX, 2a.

[48] Imperial Edict, June 29, *ibid.*, XXXVIII, 55.

The French, as the Emperor understood, were definitely accomplices of the British invaders; during the fight at Ta-ku the Chinese had captured a French flag. If the French still wished to come to Peking for the exchange of the ratifications, however, the Chinese local authorities were ordered to pretend not to be aware of their "previous crimes" and to treat them as they did the Americans.[49]

After all the orders were issued, the Emperor was pleased to find that even Prince Seng-ko-lin-ch'in would support the imperial appeasement policy. "Although they report a victory of arms," wrote the Emperor, "the said officials are still trying to conciliate, which is eminently suitable. We are deeply relieved." When all these arrangements were made, the Emperor said:[50]

See how the barbarians reply and if they show any inclination to swing around. If they do not reply at all, it may mean that all three countries are equally arrogant. Order them [the officials at Pei-t'ang] by all means to weigh the situation carefully and then determine what action should be taken.

While the Emperor was pondering the future actions of the Western envoys, he was pleased to receive a report on July 2, stating that the American commissioner, John E. Ward had reached Pei-t'ang and had asked that proper arrangements be made so that he might proceed to Peking.

---

[49] *Ibid.;* see also Imperial Edict, July 6, 1859, *ibid.,* XXXIX, 24a.

[50] Earl Swisher, *China's Management of the American Barbarians: A Study of Sino-American Relations, 1841-1861, with Documents* (New Haven, Conn.: Yale University Far Eastern Publications, 1951), p. 571.

17

MARCH TO PEKING:

THE END OF THE PRE-MODERN ERA

I

WHEN the battle at Ta-ku was over, the allied naval forces began to withdraw from the battle area. Their ministers were "exceedingly anxious" to have the American commissioner do the same, but their request was rejected by Ward, who decided to continue his peaceful mission to the Chinese capital as instructed.[1]

On June 29, the American commissioner ordered the *Toeywan* to sail north, seeking the position of Pei-t'ang. Subsequently, his deputies got in touch with the Chinese local authorities and formal communications were exchanged.[2] Although portions of the American communication had aroused Chinese suspicions,[3] Heng-fu, the Manchu governor-general of Chihli received Ward with the utmost civility. Great quantities of gifts were sent to the American visitors, who in turn shared them with the "wounded sufferers on board the English men-of-war."[4]

On July 8 Commissioner Ward went ashore at Pei-t'ang as planned. Here he was greeted by Heng-fu, governor-general of Chihli. The

---

[1] Ward to Cass, No. 15, Off Pei-ho River, July 4, 1859, *Ward Correspondence*, p. 586.

[2] For details concerning the first American landing at Pei-t'ang consult Frederick Wells Williams, ed., *The Life and Letters of Samuel Wells Williams, LL.D., Missionary, Diplomatist Sinologue* (New York: G. P. Putnam's Sons, 1889), p. 313; W. A. P. Martin, *A Cycle of Cathay or China, South and North, with Personal Reminiscences* (New York: Fleming H. Revell Company, 1897), pp. 194-95; *IWSM-HF*, XXXIX, 6a-7a. The stories told in the three different sources are similar.

[3] The first American communication signed by Commissioner Ward and delivered at Pei-t'ang bears the date of June 24, 1859 (i.e., the day before the battle of Ta-ku). It was addressed to Governor-General Ch'ing (or Governor-General King in the original English version). See *IWSM-HF*, XXXIX, 6b, 8, 25a; Ward to King, U.S.F. *Powhatan*, Mouth of the Pei-ho River, June 24, 1859, *Ward Correspondence*, p. 590. There was no such person as Governor-General King. Both these points aroused the Chinese suspicions.

[4] The Chinese gifts consisted of 20 sheep, 20 hogs, 23 bags of flour, 20 bags of rice, 189 chickens and ducks, besides numerous baskets of peaches and apricots and a quantity of vegetables. See James D. Johnston, *China and Japan: Being a Narrative of the Cruise of the U.S. Steam-Frigate Powhatan, in the Years 1857, '58, '59, and '60* (Philadelphia: Charles Desilver, 1861), p. 243.

Commissioner was treated with unusual respect by the Chinese mandarins. During a pleasant interview, proper arrangements were made for the American commissioner to go to Peking for the exchange of ratifications. The only problem to arise during the meeting was the question of how he was to proceed to the Chinese capital. According to both Chinese tradition and a previous edict, the Emperor had ordered that no foreign envoys could ride in sedan chairs on their way to Peking. The Russians had agreed to this practice for years; Heng-fu, therefore, brought up this point to Ward. After protracted negotiations, the American commissioner at last agreed to proceed to Peking partly by boat and partly by cart. This agreement was quickly acted upon. Elegant boats were made ready for the trip and the date of departure was set for July 20.[5]

A week before the scheduled departure, the Russian steamer *Amerika* arrived from the Amur River and anchored near the *Powhatan*. The governor-general of Eastern Siberia, General Muravieff, was on board. He exchanged greetings with the Americans and informed them that he was also on his way to Peking to meet the Russian minister, General Ignatieff. Because he was unfamiliar with the situation at Peking, Ward decided to keep in contact with the Russians at Peking and asked the Chinese to forward a communication to the Russian diplomatic agents at Peking before he started from Pei-t'ang.[6]

On the appointed date, July 20, the American party, consisting of twenty American civil and military personnel and ten native Chinese, who had served as Chinese writers and servants, left the coast.[7] From

---

[5] For a detailed account of Commissioner Ward's visit to Peking, consult Samuel Wells Williams, "Narrative of the American Embassy to Peking," *Journal of the North-China Branch of the Royal Asiatic Society*, III (December, 1859), 315-49. Since the Chinese definitely believed that the Americans had participated in the battle at Ta-ku, Prince Seng vigorously protested against allowing Americans to go to Peking. In a memorial submitted to the Grand Council on July 14, 1859, the Prince stated: "Since the three barbarian countries combined for the intrigue, it is impossible that two of them should withdraw in defeat and allow America alone to proceed with exchange of ratifications. There must be some design. When the Americans were interviewed, they did not admit fighting us. Not only this, but in his note to us the dates and names contain many ambiguities. It must be that he, after consultation and agreement with the English and French, is to stay in Tientsin to keep diplomatic contact." *See IWSM-HF*, XXXIX, 39b. It was the imperial will alone that set this memorial aside. For English translations see Earl Swisher, *China's Management of the American Barbarians* (New Haven, Conn.: Yale University Far Eastern Publications, 1951), pp. 590-93; or T. F. Tsiang, "China After the Victory of Taku, June 25, 1859," *American Historical Review*, XXXV (1929), 80-82.

[6] *IWSM-HF*, XXXIX, 41b; Johnston, *China and Japan*, p. 249.

[7] The names of the twenty Americans are given in Williams, *Life and Letters*, pp. 323-24. Also consult Johnston, *China and Japan*, p. 252.

Pei-t'ang the party traveled by carriage for two days, covering a distance of fifty miles to Pei-tsang, ten miles above Tientsin, where they transferred to boats elegantly decorated for the occasion. After the hundred-mile voyage to T'ung-chou, they proceeded by cart to Peking.

Describing Commissioner Ward's trip to Peking, a later historian wrote: "Over the carts and boats floated an ominous little yellow pennant with the words 'Tribute bearers from the United States.'"[8] It is unlikely that this statement is true. Among Ward's staff members both Williams and Martin were longtime residents in China and knew the Chinese language, politics, history, and custom well. Williams was the leading Sinologist at the time. His famous work, the *Middle Kingdom*, has not yet been completely superseded. Martin's spoken Chinese even enabled him to interpret for Chinese who spoke different dialects during this trip to Peking. In his later service at Peking, Martin's command of Chinese classics even surprised many Chinese scholars and officials working with him. As long as they were with Commissioner Ward, the supposed "little yellow pennant" could never have appeared. Besides, to judge from the attitude of the Chinese officials who escorted the "high American Imperial Commissioner" to Peking, this event could never have happened, nor would the Chinese high officials, say Heng-fu, have dared to think of it. The writer of the above statement was obviously misled by the stories reported in the contemporary Western newspapers in Shanghai, Hong Kong, London, and Paris. During their missions to China the two American commissioners, William B. Reed and John E. Ward, were constantly assailed by the British and French press, which had done all it could to discredit the American missions.[9]

In a speech in the House of Commons, Viscount Palmerston, Prime Minister of the British government, continued this ridicule of American diplomacy in China and also "joked about the American Minister, Mr. Ward." Palmerston said:[10]

The American Minister did accept the invitation [to go to Peking], and we know how he was carried through the country in a wooden box on two wheels, without light or air; how between Tientsin and Pekin he was obliged to get out and walk because the jolting was so intolerable, and it was impossible to submit any longer to the torture of remaining in his "carriage of honor."

---

[8] William Woodville Rockhill, "Diplomatic Missions to the Court of China; the Kotow Question," *American Historical Review*, II (1897), 638.

[9] See *Ward Correspondence*, p. 587; also see John E. Ward to Admiral Sir Michael Seymour, Hong Kong, May 15, 1860, *DD-USNA*, 92:20.

[10] *Hansard's Parliamentary Debates*, 3rd Series, CLVII (March 16, 1860), 806.

Contrary to what the British had imagined, the American party led by Commissioner Ward arrived safely and comfortably in the Chinese capital on July 28. Here they were entertained in a big house formerly belonging to the convicted grand councillor, Sai-shang-a. They were informed that the Chinese Imperial Commissioners Kuei-liang and Hua-sha-na and the provincial judge, Hsueh Huan, had arrived in the city a week before them. The following morning the Imperial Commissioners sent Hsueh to the American residence to make preliminary arrangements for a formal interview. Hsueh informed the American commissioner that because of the part taken by the *Toeywan* and by the American soldiers (one of whom had been taken prisoner) during the battle at Ta-ku, the Emperor was in some doubt as to the sincerity and the peaceful intentions of the Americans. But he assured them that the Emperor would still grant special favors to the Americans by giving their envoy a special audience, which was "absolutely necessary before any other business could be transacted in the capital." Therefore it would be important for the American commissioner to practice the rites and ceremonies to be observed for several days before the audience could take place. This meant that the American commissioner had to practice the kowtow.[11]

This Chinese proposal was brought out formally in the official interview between the American envoy and the two Imperial Commissioners held the following morning at Chia-hsing-szu, a large Buddhist temple near the Forbidden City. The American commissioner, however, refused to bend his knees. After protracted discussions the Chinese yielded so far as to waive the kowtow and offer to accept kneeling instead. Commissioner Ward replied: "I kneel only to God and woman!"

Ward further explained that no Americans had landed at Ta-ku during the Battle on June 25; so there could never have been an "American prisoner." As to the towing conducted by the *Toeywan*, the Commissioner instructed the interpreters to explain it was merely a return of British courtesies.[12]

Since the Chinese failed to persuade the stubborn American commissioner to kneel before the Emperor, they tried to work out a face-saving compromise with Ward. At last they succeeded in persuading

[11] For a detailed account of the kowtow argument see Williams, *Life and Letters*, pp. 334 ff.; Ward to Cass, No. 17, On board the *Powhatan*, August 20, 1859, *Ward Correspondence*, p. 595.

[12] *Ibid.*, p. 596; Martin, *A Cycle of Cathay*, pp. 199-200.

Ward to accept their proposals. It was to work this way: during the audience, the American commissioner was to present President Buchanan's letter to the Emperor. It was to be laid on a big table before the throne in such a manner that its embroidered cover would conceal most of the person of the Commissioner. As he approached it, he should then bow as low as he had already agreed to, and a chamberlain would approach on either side as if to raise him up, crying out:"Don't kneel!"[13]

Although this compromise seemed to have been acceptable to the unbending Commissioner, it was at last turned down by the Emperor, who would not admit the American commissioner to his Court unless "Mr. Ward would either actually touch one knee, or the end of his fingers, on the ground." Commissioner Ward refused this request and an audience was finally refused.[14]

The failure of this possible compromise grieved the Chinese even more deeply than Commissioner Ward, who had not sought an audience. "The Chinese were now apprehensive," wrote Dr. Williams, "that the President would be displeased at the non-reception of his Minister."[15] The Americans were inconvenienced by this incident. First, without an audience with the Emperor they would not be allowed to have even a sight-seeing tour of the ancient capital, which was supposed to be the most beautiful city in the Far East. Second, they were not allowed to meet the Russians in Peking, although they were allowed to communicate with them.[16] Finally, they were worried as to how and

---

[13] Williams, *Life and Letters,* pp. 334-35; Martin, *A Cycle of Cathay,* p. 200.

[14] *Ibid.* During their attempt to persuade the American commissioner to kneel, the Chinese diplomats had exhausted both their sophistry and their modern learning. They cited rather extensively the ceremonies practiced in the European courts. Kneeling was practiced at least at the English Court and at Rome in audience with the Pope. Although they failed in their diplomatic debate, they did give some sign of the rise of a modern diplomacy in China. They were now "experts" in a sense.

[15] Williams, *Life and Letters,* p. 337.

[16] Ever since the Anglo-French capture of Tientsin in 1858, the Chinese had suspected that the Russians were the chief plotters. That year when Commissioner Reed was being invited to Peking, the Russians showed up at Pei-t'ang again. Their appearance raised Chinese suspicions to new heights, because they were reported to have "borrowed" the warships from the Americans. Prince Seng-ko-lin-ch'in was the first to remind the Emperor of a possible Russo-American collaboration. He suggested that the American letter to the Russian minister at Peking be delivered by themselves. *IWSM-HF,* XXXIX, 41b. Seng's proposal was modified by the Emperor, who ordered that the Russo-American communication should be forwarded by the Chinese government in order to prevent them from dealing with each other "privately." The Emperor, however, further ordered that the Russians must be separated from the Americans to prevent further plotting. *Ibid.,* XXXIX, 42a; XL, 2b-3a. During this period, Russian activities in Manchuria alarmed the Court at Peking. Reports constantly came from Manchuria stating that more than eighty

where the ratifications of the treaty could be exchanged and the President's letter presented.

The Chinese were equally anxious to have these problems solved. After further negotiation an agreement was eventually reached specifying that the President's letter be presented at Peking on August 10. Kuei-liang was to receive it on behalf of the Emperor. The treaties would be exchanged at Pei-t'ang. The day after the President's letter was duly presented at Chia-hsing-szu, the American party left Peking for the coast. They reached Pei-t'ang on August 16, where they were received by Heng-fu, the governor-general of Chihli. The exchange of treaties took place immediately; it formally ended Commissioner Ward's mission to North China.[17]

After the ceremony was over, the Governor-General delivered to the American commissioner "as a peculiar favor" an "American prisoner" by the name of James Powell.[18] Since Ward believed it could not be an American, he insisted that the prisoner should be interrogated by a Chinese mandarin who spoke English. It turned out that the prisoner was a Canadian who had lied. Governor-General Heng-fu claimed to be perfectly satisfied by the explanation; he begged Commissioner Ward to forget all that had occurred at Ta-ku and not to refer to that subject again. The meeting therefore ended pleasantly.

II

Immediately after the interview, Ward left Pei-t'ang. He returned to Shanghai on August 22. Having considerable leisure, Ward visited

---

Russian ships were sailing down the Amur River, then still a part of Chinese territory. In the *IWSM-HF* covering this period, the documents concerning Russia are as voluminous as those concerning the three Western countries put together.

[17] Ward to Cass, No. 17, On board the U.S.F. *Powhatan*, August 20, 1859, *Ward Correspondence*, pp. 594-99.

[18] In Dr. Williams' article the name of the "American prisoner" was mentioned as John Powers. See Williams, *Life and Letters*, p. 34. The same name was adopted in Mr. Swisher's translation of the Chinese documents. See Swisher, *China's Management*, pp. 583, 601, 603, 618, 621. It was also adopted in Mr. Rowe's index to the *IWSM*. See David Nelson Rowe, *Index to Ch'ing tai ch'ou pan i wu shih mo*, (Hamden, Conn.: The Shoe String Press, 1960), p. 101. In the official statement issued by the British Foreign Office to the State Department expressing the British appreciation of Commissioner Ward's help for his release, however, the man was mentioned as James Powell. See Cass to Ward, No. 10, Washington, D.C., November 28, 1859, *DI-USNA*, 77:38, p. 214. In the Chinese documents the "American prisoner" was mentioned as Chiang-shih-p'o. See *IWSM-HF*, XXXIX, 25a; XL, 19a, 20b; XLI, 30a, 40a. This Chinese term was originally translated by a Cantonese linguist, Huang Hui-lien. The Cantonese pronunciation of Chiang-shih-p'o sounds similar to James Powell rather than to John Powers. While giving a speech on October 25, 1859 (the text was later published), Dr. Williams might have given a wrong name, which was also used by Swisher and Rowe.

Japan for nearly two months before he returned to China in the middle of October. At that time he hoped to negotiate with Imperial Commissioner Ho Kuei-ch'ing so that the new treaty and the trade regulations could be put into practice at an early date. On October 14, 1859, the American commissioner sent a dispatch to Ho requesting the Imperial Commissioner to put two provisions of the treaty into practice: to let the American vessels pay tonnage dues according to the new rate, and to open the ports of Swatow and Tai-wan (presently Tainan) to American traders.[19]

In this letter, Ward did not mention the problems of tariff and other kinds of trade regulations. He seemed purposely to have avoided those provisions with the understanding that tariff rates and trade regulations could not be put into practice before the existing difficulties between China and the allied powers were successfully settled.

Five days after Ward's dispatch was delivered, the *taotai* of Shanghai came to call on the American commissioner and delivered the reply from Imperial Commissioner Ho to the American legation in person. In the official letter, the Imperial Commissioner stated that he would like the American government to wait until the Chinese difficulties with the English and the French were settled and then all the new treaties would go into effect at the same time. Therefore, the Imperial Commissioner stated that he could not grant what the Commissioner had requested.[20] While delivering the official reply, however, the *taotai* reminded the American commissioner that this reply was only to be viewed for the official record. Imperial Commissioner Ho Kuei-ch'ing actually had a different plan. He wished Commissioner Ward, on receipt of the official Chinese reply, to insist on his demand that the two ports be opened at once. Imperial Commissioner Ho did not, of course, want it to appear that Ward was writing at the request of the Chinese. If Ward put the case strongly, the Chinese Imperial Commissioner felt almost certain that two ports would be opened very shortly, but Ho begged the American commissioner to delay in carrying out the other articles of the treaty until the English and French difficulties were settled.[21]

After he had been informed by the *taotai*, the American commis-

---

[19] *DD-USNA*, 92:19.

[20] *Ibid.* In making this arrangement Governor-General Ho obviously tried to satisfy the Americans and at the same time create good excuses for himself to memorialize the Emperor for requesting the opening of the new treaty ports.

[21] *Memorandum* of the *taotai's* conversation at the American consulate at Shanghai on October 19, 1859, as noted by the United States interpreters in *DD-USNA*, 92:19.

sioner seemed to be sympathetic to the Chinese difficulties. The day after the interview, Ward sent a long report to Washington saying:[22]

My impression is that the Chinese Government is really desirous of carrying out in good faith all the stipulations of the Treaty, but they are afraid of further embarrassing themselves with the English and French and therefore their reluctance to proclaim the Treaty and to carry out its provisions.

Then he reminded Washington that he very much feared that there was an effort on the part of "other nations" to prevent the American treaty from being put into effect until their own affairs had been arranged.

In speaking of the two new ports promised by the Chinese, Ward said that foreign trade was already carried on there "as if those ports had been formally opened." Consequently, he ordered the American consuls at different ports to notify the American traders there to pay the tonnage dues according to the new rates fixed by the treaty.[23] Thus without going through official channels, the most important aspects of the American treaty were put into effect without difficulty. Commissioner Ward was obviously satisfied with what he had done in China. "The intercourse between the two nations is now as friendly as it has ever been," wrote Ward, "and I see no good reason for disturbing them."[24]

Meanwhile, he appointed a committee to calculate the American claims against China as well as to collect the indemnity that China had promised to deduct from her tariff. The committee worked well; it satisfied all the Americans who had made claims and settled all the American claims against China since 1847. The committee also announced that there was a surplus of $210,000 that the Chinese government had overpaid.[25] Dr. Williams later suggested to the State Department that a high school might be set up for Chinese children with use of the surplus. This suggestion never materialized; the surplus, which amounted to $453,400.00 with interest in 1885, was returned to China after a delay of twenty-five years.

III

After he had successfully settled all the problems with the Chinese, Commissioner Ward, like all of his predecessors, had to deal with the

---

[22] Ward to Cass, No. 20, Shanghai, October 20, 1859, *ibid.*
[23] *Proclamation* issued by Commissioner Ward, November 8, 1859; the two new ports were arranged to be formally opened on January 1, 1860, *ibid.*
[24] Ward to Cass, No. 20, Shanghai, October 20, 1859, *ibid.* Cf. chap. 15, footnote 50.
[25] C. E. Roberts to John E. Ward, Macao, February 16, 1860, *DD-USNA*, 92:20.

British concerning the specific problems in the trading ports. The first problem that came to Ward's attention was the so-called inspectorate system in the Chinese customs service. As previously explained, this system had been initiated in Shanghai during the Triad Rebellion and was later introduced into the other ports. The extension of this system to the other treaty ports was not made the subject of a stipulation in the body of any treaty that China signed with the Western powers at Tientsin. It had been written into the rules of trade during the supplementary negotiations in the fall of 1858. The British explained that the system had to be extended to other treaty ports so that it could not be used to discriminate against the merchants at Shanghai. Moreover, since the previous three-power inspectorate system was too often under the guardianship of foreign consuls and unfair to China, in the trade regulations signed between China and Great Britain the problem was solved by what was called the "tenth rule." Through this, the foreign inspectorate system was extended to other treaty-ports and the Chinese government nominally was at liberty to adopt whatever measures appeared to be best suited for the protection of its own revenue.[26]

The rule, however, further stipulated that the high Chinese official appointed by the Chinese government to superintend foreign trade should have the right to select any superintendent or deputy "he may see fit to aid him in the administration of the Customs revenue." In the selection of this personnel, the Chinese government could act independently of the suggestions or nominations of any British authority, but the appointee had to be a British subject. Under this "tenth rule," Horatio Nelson Lay, the former British inspector in the Chinese customhouse at Shanghai, was made the first inspector-general of customs in the newly established Chinese customs service in September, 1859. At the same time, Bruce, the British envoy who had suffered a defeat at Ta-ku about two months earlier, also addressed a circular to all the British consuls in China informing them of Lay's appointment and the establishment of the new institution. If any Chinese authorities were to approach the consuls on the subject, the British consuls were directed to state that Her Majesty's government considered the system the best means of protecting the Chinese revenue and at the same time the interests of trade.[27]

---

[26] For general reference consult Stanley F. Wright, *The Origin and Development of the Chinese Customs Service, 1843-1911* (Shanghai: Privately printed, 1939), pp. 8-18.

[27] See Bruce to Russell, No. 57, December 5, 1859, *F.O.* 228/262, and Bruce's circular dispatch to British consuls in China, September 28, 1859, *F.O., 228/274,* in

Nominally, the inspector-general of customs, a title invented by Lay himself, was appointed by Imperial Commissioner Ho Kuei-ch'ing, but Ho knew little about what Lay was doing. The Imperial Commissioner was then the major promoter of a reconciliation with the British after the battle at Ta-ku. His consent in promoting Lay to the position of chief commissioner of the customs service was no more than a gesture in an attempt for a reconciliation with Bruce.

Lay formerly had been acting vice-consul and assistant Chinese secretary to the British consulate staff at Shanghai. In the summer of 1855, when Thomas Francis Wade, the British inspector in the Chinese customs service, resigned, Lay was appointed to succeed him by the Chinese authority at Shanghai. While serving in this position as "a Chinese official" rather than "a servant of the British Crown,"[28] he acted as the actual negotiator during the signing of the Sino-British Treaty at Tientsin. On this occasion he frightened the Chinese Imperial Commissioners, Kuei-liang and Hua-sha-na, and astonished a Russian admiral, who witnessed the scene.[29]

Lay, an arrogant man with a horrible temper, was an efficient administrator. No sooner had his self-invented title of inspector-general of the Chinese customs service been approved officially by the Chinese Imperial Commissioner, Ho Kuei-ch'ing, than he paid off his former colleagues, the American and French inspectors, who had worked on an equal footing with him. Lay's next measure was to open new, model customhouses at the other treaty ports, and, having appointed H. Tudor Davies as commissioner at Shanghai, he sailed for Canton, where he opened another new customhouse, appointing Glover as first commissioner and Robert Hart as deputy commissioner.[30]

Thus, even before Commissioner Ward returned from Japan, the so-called inspectorate system had already ceased to function. The Chinese customs service in all the treaty ports was under the solid control of an Englishman.

When Ward returned to Shanghai from Japan, he was irritated by

---

Stanley F. Wright, *Hart and the Chinese Customs* (Belfast: Wm. Mullan and Son, 1950), p. 136; Bruce to Russell, October 26, 1860, *British Parliamentary Papers,* LXVI, 249.

[28] In an official dispatch to the British consul at Shanghai, Sir John Bowring stated in October, 1855, that the British inspector of customs was "not a servant of the British Crown but a Chinese official." I. G. Circular No. 28 of 1870 *postea* quoted in Stanley F. Wright, *The Origin and Development of the Chinese Customs Service,* p. 23.

[29] Consult above, chap. 14, sec. 4.

[30] For general reference see Wright, *The Origin and Development of the Chinese Customs Service,* pp. 22-26.

Lay's domination of the Chinese customs service. In a report to Washington, Ward wrote:[31]

> . . . his first act was to remove the only American and Frenchman employed at Shanghai and place the custom house there under the control of an Englishman. He then proceeded to Canton, where he soon published a series of regulations, odious and oppressive to all merchants, and some of them in my opinion, not in conformity with the Treaty. Englishmen were there appointed, and an American, at first engaged in the customs, was told that he held his position only until a successor arrived from England.

As a result of the British domination in the Chinese customs service, the American merchants, particularly those at Canton, began to have trouble with the British customs officers. In his report to Washington, Ward said that the establishment of a system that placed all the customhouses in China entirely under the control of the English was unacceptable to the Americans.

On November 3, the American commissioner succeeded in having an interview with Ho Kuei-ch'ing, Imperial Commissioner in charge of China's foreign trade in the treaty ports. In this interview, he was astonished by Ho's ignorance of the new developments in the Chinese customs service. "Ho . . . had heard nothing of them," said Ward, "and listened to the particulars with interest."[32] Ward then complained that all Americans had been asked to resign from the Chinese customs service. Ho said that "one third of the foreigners engaged as collectors should be Americans." But this proposal could not be carried out by the Chinese alone; it had to be arranged between the Americans and the British. Nominally, Ho was the supervisory director of the Chinese customs service who appointed Lay to his present position; actually, Ho had no power to reverse Lay's decision. In any case, he was trying desperately to appease the British, who had been disgruntled since their defeat at Ta-ku. The Americans had to appeal directly to the British for any reversal.

The British did not dare practice a policy of nonintercourse. The American complaints were soon overheard by the British inspector-general, who immediately corrected this "mistake" and some Americans received their appointments in the Chinese customhouse at Canton. This prompt British reaction to Ward's complaint led the latter to

---

[31] Ward to Cass, No. 21, On board U.S.S. *Germantown*, November 18, 1859, *DD-USNA*, 92:19.

[32] Minutes of the interview between Commissioner Ward and Imperial Commissioner Ho held at K'un-shan, November 3, 1859, *ibid.*

write to Washington rather apologetically:[33] "Coming to China with strong prejudices against the English, it was natural that I should sometimes have imagined that an effort existed to thwart our views, and reluctance on their part to concede to us that to which we were justly entitled."

The next problem that confronted Ward was the increasing coolie trade. Ever since the allied capture of Canton, the coolie trade which, like the opium trade, was mostly operated by influential British subjects, had become a serious calamity in South China. Some American commercial firms and ships also were engaged in it. When Ward arrived at Hong Kong late in October, 1859, the Chinese governor-general in the allied-occupied city of Canton appealed to him for help, for one American ship, the *Messenger,* was about to leave Canton with a cargo of 500 Chinese coolies, most of whom, if not all, had been kidnapped in the coastal regions. With great patience and detective skill, Ward at last succeeded in enforcing the law to control his countrymen in China. Manton, captain of the ship, and its contractors, Vargas and Company, were forced to deliver the Chinese coolies to Canton for reexamination. ". . . yet in doing this I was unwilling to place them under the jurisdiction of the Allied Commissioners who now hold possession of Canton," Ward wrote to Washington. If they were brought up, they were to be examined only by the American and Chinese officials without the slightest interference from the allied powers.[34]

The allied authorities at Canton at last agreed to the American commissioner's request, and 500 Chinese "willing emigrants" were brought to Canton for re-examination, to which Dr. Williams was sent by Ward as a witness. The 250 Chinese whose examination was witnessed by Dr. Williams, all claimed to have been forced onto the ship. Therefore, the American commissioner, who had power to prevent American ships sailing from Chinese waters without the clearance issued by the Chinese authorities, ordered the *Messenger* to release all the Chinese passengers aboard. The Commissioner's order was obeyed. The *Messenger* then sailed to Macao, where the American commissioner held no extraterritorial power. Thus, under the nose of the Commissioner,

---

[33] Ward to Cass, Macao, November 23, December 10, 1859, *ibid.* It is even more interesting to note that four days before Ward mailed this dispatch to Washington, it had already been cited by Bruce, the British envoy to China, in his "Secret and Confidential" report to London on December 6, 1859. See Bruce to Russell (Secret and Confidential), December 6, 1859, *F.O.,* 17/315 in W. C. Costin, *Great Britain and China 1833-1860* (Oxford: The Clarendon Press, 1937), p. 306. How this statement was detected by the British is unknown.

[34] Ward to Cass, Official No. 4, Macao, February 24, 1860, *DD-USNA,* 20:20.

the same American ship again took three to four hundred kidnapped Chinese coolies and sailed for Cuba. It was followed by another American ship, the *Norway,* which took another thousand under the watchful eyes of the Commissioner. American participation in the coolie trade affected Ward deeply, but he could do nothing except write to the State Department suggesting Congressional action on the one hand and on the other hand appealing to the Portuguese governor at Macao for cooperation.[35] The problem, however, remained unsolved long after his departure from China.

IV

With his official business in order, Ward wrote to the State Department asking for permission to return home. President Buchanan, however, felt his service indispensable to the United States diplomacy in China during such a crucial period, when a large-scale Anglo-French Chinese war was pending. The President, therefore, praised the Commissioner's great achievement in China highly in his annual message to Congress. At the same time, through Secretary of State Cass, he asked Ward to stay on in his post until peace had been restored, stating: "As ... this determination has been occasioned by a belief that you might be useful to the belligerents ... as you certainly would be to your own countrymen."[36]

Ward retired to Macao at the end of 1859, where he stayed until May, 1860, while he waited for a decision from Washington. He was then aroused by the overtures of an oncoming Anglo-French–Chinese war. In May, Ward left Macao for Shanghai, where he found the Russian minister, General Ignatieff. The next month the allies began to take military action. The Chusan Islands were attacked and occupied in June. On June 29, 1860, Lord Elgin and Baron Gros, sent respectively from London and Paris to China for the second time to take over the allied command, arrived in Shanghai. Early in July, Elgin and Gros sailed north with their armed forces.

Obeying his instructions from the State Department, Ward sailed north with Commodore C. K. Stribling in an American warship, the *Hartford.* They arrived at the anchorage off the Pei-ho on the morning of July 14, even before the allied forces did.[37] Here they got in

    35 *Ibid.*
    36 Cass to Ward, No. 11, Washington, D.C., December 30, 1859, *DI-USNA,* 77:38, pp. 214-15.
    37 Ward to Cass, No. 16, U.S.S. *Hartford,* Gulf of Pecheli, August 7, 1860, *DD-USNA,* 92:20.

touch with the agents of Chinese Governor-General Heng-fu; communications and gifts were exchanged. During this period, the Chinese were trying to make use of the Americans' good offices, but Ward seemed not to be very enthusiastic about acting as a mediator between the Chinese and the allies, probably because he thought that it was already too late.[38]

The allied forces landed at Pei-t'ang on the morning of August 1. The Chinese garrison, commanded by the Mongol Prince, Seng-ko-lin-ch'in, suffered a bloody defeat. As the fighting moved toward Tient-sin, Ward thought that it would be better to keep himself away from the war zone. In a report to Washington on August 7, 1860, he said that it was not his duty to be a spectator of such a conflict. ". . . nothing now seems to remain for me," said Ward, "but to leave here."[39] After notifying the Russian minister, who had just returned to Peking, Ward retired with Commodore Stribling to Chefoo, a Chinese port in Shantung province. When he heard that Shanghai was again in danger of a Taiping attack, he returned to that port on August 25, but finding the crisis over and "no further business to detain" him, he proceeded to Hong Kong on October 5.

During the time that Commissioner Ward was traveling south from the Pei-ho to Hong Kong, the allied forces were marching victoriously northward toward Peking, and the Ch'ing dynasty was on the brink of destruction. The allied occupation of Peking and the burning of the summer palace, Yuan-ming-yuan, little require description in this study. Later in October a dictated truce was signed by Prince Kung, the younger brother of the Emperor. On the twenty-fourth and twenty-fifth the ratifications of the treaties signed at Tientsin were exchanged at Peking between the Prince and the British and French envoys. On November 14, Prince Kung also signed a treaty with the Russian minister, General Ignatieff, ceding to Russia the entire territory east of the Ussuri, with its capital city, Hai-ts'an-wei, the name of which the Russians later changed to Vladivostok (meaning Dominion of the East). This gave the Russians a naval base in the Pacific.

As a result of the signing of these new conventions, the Chinese Empire was fully opened and formally brought into the family of nations as a much-humiliated member. Thereafter such traditional terms as "barbarians," "barbarian affairs," and the like, were formally wiped

---

[38] *IWSM-HF*, LIV, 32a; LV, 4a-5a.
[39] Ward to Cass, No. 16, U.S.S. *Hartford*, Gulf of Pecheli, August 7, 1860, *DD-USNA*, 92:20.

out of Chinese official documents. Although modern Chinese diplomacy was beginning in the year 1861, the pre-modern period (1842-60) in which Chinese diplomats had twice undergone an apprenticeship in handling modern international affairs and during which the Americans had laid the foundation of the Open Door policy, tragically passed into history.

John E. Ward, the gifted American commissioner, had he remained in China during the crucial period when the allied forces were marching to Peking, could have played an important role as a mediator in the negotiations at the Chinese capital. Unfortunately, during the same period, the United States was undergoing a major political upheaval. While the Anglo-French–Chinese War was in progress, the American people at home were confronted with the most serious Presidential election in the nation's history. Not long after Commissioner Ward arrived in Hong Kong, he seems to have been informed about the exciting news from home, namely the split within the Democratic party and the Republican nomination of Abraham Lincoln for President. The party, as well as the nation, was on the eve of a complete breakdown.

At such a time it was only natural that Ward, a politician with important connections in both the North and the South, was drawn away from his official duties in China by the news from the United States. Although he might have attempted to save the Chinese summer palace and even have tried to dissuade the Russians from taking Vladivostok, Ward remained an inactive minister of the United States during the entire campaign. Later, in October, 1860, when the allied ministers were signing a truce with the Chinese at Peking, Ward decided to sail for home from Hong Kong. The ship was to leave China toward the end of December, 1860.[40] During the period of waiting, news from North China informed him that the truce convention between the Chinese and the allies had been signed.[41] Seeing that the situation in China would soon return to normal, Ward departed for America on December 15.[42]

---

[40] Ward to Cass, No. 24, Hong Kong, October 28, 1860, *DD-USNA*, 92:20. Ward had decided in the summer of 1859 to leave China early in March 1860. See Ward to Cass, No. 15, Off Pei-ho, July 4, 1859, *DD-USNA*, 92:19. His stay in China after that date and his sailing north with the allied envoys was against his will and only under the sincere request of Secretary of State Cass and President Buchanan. See Cass to Ward, No. 11, Washington, D.C., December 30, 1859, *DI-USNA*, 77:38, pp. 214-15; Ward to Cass, No. 15, Shanghai, June 29, 1860, *DD-USNA*, 92:20.

[41] Ward to Cass, No. 25, Hong Kong, November 14, 1860, *DD-USNA*, 92:20.

[42] Ward to Cass, No. 32, Hong Kong, December 14, 1860, *ibid*.

18

TWO CYCLES AND AN OPEN DOOR

DURING the sixteen years after the signing of the Treaty of Wanghia, both the Chinese and the Americans underwent an apprenticeship in diplomacy. Chinese foreign policy during this period passed through two similar cycles. The first cycle began in 1839 with the rigid policy of Lin Tse-hsü and ended with the failure of the appeasement policy of Ch'i-ying, who had signed the first treaty between China and the United States in 1844. Ignorance of the real strength of the Western powers, resistance to the ever-increasing demands of the British, and Chinese popular hostility to the "barbarians," especially in Canton, caused the collapse of Ch'i-ying's plans in 1848. The accession to the throne of the young Emperor Hsien-feng in 1850 marked the commencement of a second cycle of Chinese policy toward the West. Reverting to the intransigence of his ancestors, the new Emperor made stubborn, boastful, and ignorant Yeh Ming-ch'en the guide of China's foreign policy for more than ten years—a period nearly twice as long as that of Ch'i-ying's service.

Though in popular eyes Yeh's long tenure was one of marked success, China's relations with the West were in fact steadily deteriorating during the 1850's. The disastrous consequences of the Arrow War in 1858 finally awakened the young Emperor to his danger, and he reverted to the appeasement policy that had been followed during the last years of his father's regime. China's self-isolation in international affairs disappeared for the second time; like his late subject, Ch'i-ying, the Emperor repeatedly tried to seek American good offices in his difficulties with the Anglo-French alliance. Unfortunately, this shift of policy came too late to produce any effective results; China was again involved in a foreign war, which ended this second cycle and concluded the pre-modern era in the history of Sino-American diplomacy.

The United States during this era was slowly attempting to formulate a proper policy toward China. In the gradual development of this
policy, the successive American commissioners to China took the initiative, for until the recall of Commissioner Humphrey Marshall in the
winter of 1853, the United States had no China policy at all. There
were almost no debates either in Congress or in the cabinet over a
China policy. Prior to the inauguration of President Buchanan in
March, 1857, the United States commissioners to China were given a
comparatively free hand in making their own China policies, with little,
if any, intervention from the Department of State. Even the treaty-
revision movement in 1856 was actually initiated by Commissioner
Parker rather than by the authorities at Washintgon.

Superficially, American policy showed little direction or continuity
during this period. Acting Commissioner Biddle and Commissioners
Everett, Davis, Marshall, McLane, and Parker all had their specific
proposals for a proper policy toward China. With the exception of
Commissioner Everett, however, none of the United States commissioners to China was a professional diplomat. Their policies were based
entirely upon their own private and unprofessional judgments, which
were occasionally self-contradictory. Moreover, with the single exception of Peter Parker, who tried to reverse Commissioner Everett's proposal even when he was only the chargé d'affaires of the legation, none
of the commissioners seemed to care what policy his predecessor pursued.

Throughout the entire period none of the American commissioners
in China waited for the arrival of his successor to transfer his official
duties in person.[1] The American diplomatic service in China was full
of inconsistencies, if not contradictions. The similarity between the
policies adopted by Commissioner Marshall and Commissioner Mc-
Lane toward the Chinese rebels, for instance, was merely accidental.
The contradictory methods of action adopted by Commissioner Reed
and Commissioner Ward toward the inspectorate system in the Chinese customs service were based primarily upon their personal judgments regarding that system rather than upon any fixed policy. Moreover, only one of these commissioners, Peter Parker, lived in China
as much as two years; the others had no personal knowledge of China,
then a very mysterious land, before their appointments. Hence, because of ignorance and transience, they could hardly formulate a work-

---

[1] On his way home in 1859, Commissioner Reed met his successor, John E. Ward,
in France only by chance.

able China policy for the federal government. Consequently none of their suggestions had any definite influence upon Washington; they were usually set aside as soon as the original proposer left China.

Nevertheless, these proposals, once more with the exception of Peter Parker's, were accidentally based upon one common principle. In later years it became known as "the Open Door doctrine"—territorial integrity of China and equal commercial privileges for all Western powers. Thus, any power that aimed to dominate China alone was to be opposed by the United States. This common principle, which was intermittently proposed by different commissioners, formed the general basis of United States policy toward China during the pre-modern period; and President Pierce and Secretary of State Marcy formally recognized it just before they left office in the spring of 1857.

In the process of formation, the open door principle encountered serious resistance from various interest groups and suffered constant setbacks. American missionaries in China, and some American merchants as well, had long been inclined to support British efforts in the Far East. Peter Parker, who was given six interim appointments as American chargé d'affaires, and in 1855 became commissioner to China, actively espoused Anglo-American cooperation. Even after the recall of Parker in April, 1857, his ideas were still supported by the China merchants, who were now in favor of close collaboration with the Anglo-French alliance in China.

Neither merchants nor missionaries, however, were able to change the main trend of United States policy in China. President Buchanan was as firm as his predecessor in guarding it. Thus the history of American diplomacy in China during the pre-modern era was the story of the gradual triumph of the open door principle. When Secretary of State John Hay in September, 1899, officially announced the Open Door doctrine, he was merely continuing the basic American policy that his predecessors had quietly instituted over half a century earlier.

GLOSSARY

Amoy (Hsia-men)	厦門
an-ch'a-shih-ssu	按察使司 (nieh-t'ai 臬台)
Canton (Kuang-chou)	廣州
chan-fang	棧房
Ch'ang-chou	常州
Chang Hsi	張禧
Ch'ang-lu	長蘆
Chao Ch'ang-ling	趙長齡
Ch'ao-chou	潮州
Chao Te-ch'e	趙德轍
Chapu	乍浦
Chefoo	烟臺
Chekiang	浙江
Chen-hai	鎮海
Ch'eng Yü-ts'ai	程矞采
Ch'i Chün-tsao	祁寯藻
Chi-erh-hang-a	吉爾杭阿
Ch'i-Kung	祁墳
Ch'i-shan	琦善
Ch'i-ying (Tsiying, Kiying, Keying)	耆英
Ch'ien-lung	乾隆
chih-chou	知州
chih-fu	知府

chih-tao-la	知道了
ch'in-ch'ai-ta-ch'en	欽差大臣
chin-shih	進士
Chinkiang	鎮江
Chiu-chiang (Kiukiang) Kuan	九江關
Ch'iung-chou	瓊州
ch'üan-ch'üan	全權
chün-chi-ch'u	軍機處
Ch'ung-lun	崇綸
Chungking	重慶
Chusan (Chou-shan) Island	舟山島
co-hong (*kung-hang*)	公行
fan-t'ai	藩臺 (pu-cheng-shih-ssu 布政使司)
Foochow (Fu-chou, Fuhchowfoo)	福州
fu	府
ginseng (*jen-ts'an*)	人參
hai-fang t'ung-chih	海防同知
hai-kuan	海關
Hai-ts'an-wei	海參威
Hakkas	客家
han-chien	漢奸
han-lin	翰林
Hangchow (Hang-chou)	杭州
Hankow	漢口
Heng-ch'ang	恒昌
Heng-fu	恒福
Ho Ju-lin	何汝霖
Ho Kuei-ch'ing	何桂清
Howqua (Hao-kuan) [Wu Ch'ung-yüeh]	浩官 [伍崇曜]
Hsia Hsieh	夏燮
Hsiao I-shan	蕭一山
Hsiao-tao-hui	小刀會
hsien	縣
hsien-chih-shih	縣知事
Hsien-feng	咸豐
Hsien-ling	咸齡
Hsü Chi-yü	徐繼畬

Hsü Kuang-chin 徐廣縉
Hsü Nai-chao 許乃釗
Hsü Ya-man (Sue Aman) 徐亞滿
Hsüeh Fu-ch'eng 薛福成
Hsüeh Huan 薛煥
hsün-fu 巡撫
Hu-men-chai (The Bogue) 虎門寨
Hua-sha-na 花沙納
Huang En-t'ung 黃恩彤
Huang Hui-lien 黃惠廉
Huang-p'u (Whangpu) River 黃浦江
Huang Tsung-han 黃宗漢
Hung Hsiu-ch'üan 洪秀全
i-wu 夷務
I-liang 怡良
Ilipu (Eleepoo) 伊里布
K'ang-hsi 康熙
Kiukiang 九江
kowtow 磕頭
ku 蠱
Kuangsi (Kwangsi) 廣西
Kuangtung (Kwangtung) 廣東
Kuei-liang 桂良
Kulangsu 鼓浪嶼
K'un-shan 崑山
Kung Ch'in-wang
    I-hsin (Prince Kung) 恭親王奕訢
Kung Mu-chiu 宮慕久
Kuo T'ing-i 郭廷以
Lan Wei-wen 藍蔚雯
Lao Ch'ung-kuang 勞崇光
Liang Chia-ping 梁嘉彬
Liang-Kiang 兩江
Liang-Kuang 兩廣
liang-tao 糧道
Liang T'ing-nan 梁廷枏
Lin Tse-hsü 林則徐
Liu-ch'iu 硫球
Liu Li-ch'uan 劉麗川
Liu Yün-k'o 劉韻珂

Macao (Ao-men)	澳門
Min (Fukien)	閩
Ming-shan	明善
Mu-chang-a	穆彰阿
nei-ko	內閣
nieh-t'ai (see an-ch'a-shih-ssu)	臬台
Ningpo	寧波
Niu Chien	牛鑑
Niu-chuang (Newchuang)	柳莊
P'an Ch'i-kuan (Puankhequa)	潘啟官
P'an Chen-ch'eng	潘振承
P'an Shih-ch'eng	潘仕成
[Pan Ting-kwa, Pun Tingqua,	
Pun Ting Kwa, Pwan Tingkwa]	
Pao-ting	保定
Pei-ho	北河
Pei-kuei	柏貴
Pei-t'ang	北塘
pu	部
pu-cheng-shih-ssu (see *fan-t'ai*)	布政使司
Sai-shang-a	賽尚阿
San-ho-hui (the Triad)	三合會
Seng-ko-lin-ch'in	僧格林沁
Shan-hai-kuan	山海關
Sheng-ching	盛京
Shih-p'u	石浦
Shu Kung-shou	舒恭受
Shuang-jui	雙銳
Sinkiang	新疆
Soochow (Su-chou)	蘇州
Su-Sung-T'ai	蘇松太
Sungkiang	松江
ta-hsüeh-shih	大學士
Ta-ku	大沽
T'ai-ts'ang	太倉
Tainan (T'ai-nan)	臺南
Taiping (T'ai-p'ing t'ien-kuo)	太平 (太平天國)
Taiwan (Tainan)	臺灣 (臺南)
Tan-shui	淡水
tao	道

Tao-kuang	道光
taotai (*tao-t'ai*)	道臺
Teng-chou	登州
t'ing	廳
Ting-hai	定海
Ts'ang-chou	倉州
tsung-tu	總督
Tsungli-yamen	總理衙門
Tu Shou-t'ien	杜受田
Tuan Ch'eng-shih	段承實
T'ung-chih	同治
T'ungchow (T'ung-chou)	通州
T'ung-lin	銅麟
T'ung-wen-kuan	同文館
Wang Chi-hsi (Wang Tshih-she)	王繼熙
Wanghai (Wang-hsia)	望廈
Wang I-te	王懿德
Wang Ting	王鼎
Wen-ch'ien	文謙
Wen-ch'ing	文慶
Wen-hsiang	文祥
Whampoa	黃埔
Wu Chien-chang	吳健彰
Wu-lo-hung-e	烏勒洪額
Wuchang (Wu-ch'ang)	武昌
Wuhan	武漢
Wusung	吳淞
Yeh Ming-ch'en	葉名琛
yang-wu	洋務
yen-yün-shih-ssu	鹽運使司
[*yen-yün-tao*]	[鹽運道]
Yüeh-hai-kuan	粵海關
Yung-an	永安
Yung-cheng	雍正

BIBLIOGRAPHY

SOURCE MATERIALS IN WESTERN LANGUAGES

Bibliographies, Guides, and Reference Works

Archives of Government Offices Outside of the City of Washington (*House Doc.*, No. 1443, 62 Cong., 3 sess.). Washington, D.C.: Government Printing Office, 1913.

Bemis, Samuel Flagg, and Grace Gardner Griffin. *Guide to the Diplomatic History of the United States, 1775-1921.* New York: P. Smith, 1951.

Bemis, Samuel Flagg (ed.). *The American Secretaries of State and Their Diplomacy.* 10 vols. New York: Pageant Book Co., 1958.

Born, Lester K. (comp.). *British Manuscripts Project, A Checklist of the Microfilms Prepared in England and Wales for the American Council of Learned Societies, 1941-1945.* Washington, D.C.: Library of Congress, 1955.

Brunnert, H. S., and V. V. Hagelstrom. *Present Day Political Organization of China.* Shanghai: Kelly and Walsh, 1912.

Callahan, Edward W. *List of Officers of the Navy and Marine Corps 1775-1900.* New York: L. R. Hamersly and Co., 1901.

Couling, Samuel. *The Encyclopedia Sinica.* Shanghai: Kelly and Walsh, 1917.

Fairbank, John King. *Bibliographical Guide to Modern China: Works in Western Languages.* Cambridge, Mass.: Harvard University Press, 1948.

Great Britain, House of Commons. *Annual Indexes to Parliamentary Papers, 1852-1861.* Vol. CIV, 1852–1853; Vol. LXXIV, 1854; Vol.

LVII, 1854–1855; Vol. LXIII, 1856; Vol. XLV, 1857; Vol. LXII, 1857–1858; Vol. XXXV, 1859; Vol. LXXIII, 1860. London: By various printers for H. M. Stationery Office.

. *General Alphabetical Index to Bills, Reports, Estimates, Accounts and Papers . . . , 1852–1899.* London: H.M. Stationery Office, 1909.

. *General Index to the Accounts and Papers Reports of Commissioners Estimates etc. Printed by Order of the House of Commons or Presented by Command, 1801–1852.* London: H. M. Stationery Office, 1938.

Gregory, Winifred (ed.). *List of the Serial Publications of Foreign Governments, 1815–1931.* New York: H. W. Wilson Co., 1932.

Guide to the Material in the National Archives. Washington, D.C.: Government Printing Office, 1948.

Hasse, Adelaide Rosalie. *Index to United States Documents Relating to Foreign Affairs 1828–1861.* 3 vols. Washington, D.C.: Carnegie Institution of Washington, 1921.

Hockett, Homer Carey. *Introduction to Research in American History.* New York: The Macmillan Co., 1948.

Hummel, Arthur William (ed.). *Eminent Chinese of the Ch'ing Period (1644–1912).* 2 vols. Washington, D.C.: Government Printing Office, 1943–44.

Johnson, Allen (ed.). *Dictionary of American Biography.* 22 vols. New York: Charles Scribner's Sons, 1943.

List of National Archives Microfilm Publications. Washington, D.C.: National Archives and Records Service, 1953.

Mott, Frank Luther. *A History of American Magazines.* 2 vols. New York: D. Appleton and Co., 1930, 1938.

National Library of Peiping. *Quarterly Bulletin of Chinese Bibliography.* Peiping: National Library, 1934–36.

Poore, Benjamin Perley (comp.). *The Political Register and Congressional Directory.* Boston: Houghton, Osgood and Co., 1878.

(ed.). *A Descriptive Catalogue of the Government Publications of the United States, Sept. 5, 1774–March 4, 1881.* Washington, D. C.: Government Printing Office, 1885; reprinted by Edwards Brothers, Ann Arbor, Mich., 1953.

Schwegmann, George A., Jr. (comp.). *Newspapers on Microfilm.* 3rd ed. Washington, D.C.: Library of Congress, 1957.

Temperley, Harold, and Lillian M. Penson (eds.). *A Century of Diplomatic Blue Books, 1814–1914.* Cambridge, England: Cambridge

University Press, 1938.

Walker, Richard L. *Western Language Periodicals on China.* New Haven, Conn.: Yale University Institute of Far Eastern Languages, 1949.

Yuan, Tung-li (comp.). *China in Western Literature, A Continuation of Cordier's Bibliotheca Sinica.* New Haven, Conn.: Yale University Far Eastern Publications, 1958.

Manuscripts

Cushing, Caleb, Papers. Division of Manuscripts, Library of Congress, Washington, D.C.

East India Squadron Letters, 1845–1847. United States National Archives Service, Washington, D.C.

Everett, Alexander Hill, Papers. Massachusetts Historical Society, Boston. There are also a few letters to and from Everett in the Joseph Blunt Papers in Library of Congress, Washington, D.C.

Foote, Captain Andrew Hull, Papers. Division of Manuscripts, Library of Congress, Washington, D.C.

Marcy, William L., Papers. Division of Manuscripts, Library of Congress, Washington, D.C.

Olyphant, D. W. C., An unpublished letter from China to friends in the United States, August 6, 1827, copied by a Chinese typist under the supervision of D. W. Lyon; Shanghai, 1916. Missionary Research Library, New York.

Pierce, Franklin, Papers. Division of Manuscripts, Library of Congress, Washington, D.C.

Preble, George Henry, Papers and unpublished personal diaries. Massachusetts Historical Society, Boston. Preble was a United States naval officer under Commander Joel Abbot of the East India Squadron in the middle 1850's. He had wide connections with many leading merchants in the China trade and with influential naval officers, including Commodore M. C. Perry, whose letter to him has been preserved with the above papers.

Reed, William B., Private Diary of Mission to China, 1857–1859. 2 vols. Division of Manuscripts, Library of Congress, Washington, D.C. A typewritten sketch of the events of the mission prepared by his son, who accompanied him to China, is included.

Sheppard, E. T., Papers. Division of Manuscripts, Library of Congress, Washington, D.C. Some of S. Wells Williams' papers are also included. Sheppard was the special agent of the United States Treasury Department to China in 1868.

United States Department of State, Consular Dispatches (from United States consuls in China, Hong Kong, and Macao to the Department of State). Microfilmed by the United States National Archives Service, Washington, D.C. These consist of reports to the Department of State from United States consuls in China. The dispatches cover a wide range of subjects dealing with economic, political, and social conditions in contemporary China in addition to routine matters. Many of the dispatches are accompanied by enclosures, such as copies of correspondence between consuls and local government officials, United States diplomatic representatives, other consuls, United States naval officers, and other American citizens and citizens of foreign countries. The sections used in this study consist of several hundred dispatches and the enclosures thereof. They are listed below : (Pages of manuscript are not numbered.)

 Amoy (Oct. 29, 1844—Dec. 31, 1863). 2 rolls. Cited as *CD-USNA*, Amoy, 100 : 1–2.

 Canton (Feb. 21, 1790—Dec. 31, 1867). 5 rolls. Cited as *CD-USNA*, Canton, 101 : 1–5.

 Foochow (July 14, 1849—Dec. 31, 1863). 2 rolls. Cited as *CD-USNA*, Foochow, 105 : 1–2.

 Hong Kong (March 20, 1844—Sept. 20, 1861). 4 rolls. Cited as *CD-USNA*, Hong Kong, 108 : 1–4.

 Macao (1848—Dec. 31, 1863). 1 roll. Cited as *CD-USNA*, Macao, 109 : 1.

 Ningpo (Oct. 1, 1853—July 15, 1863). 1 roll. Cited as *CD-USNA*, Ningpo, 111 : 1.

United States Department of State, Diplomatic Dispatches (from the United States diplomatic representatives in China to the State Department and occasionally to the President or President-elect), June 27, 1843—July 26, 1861, in 20 microfilm rolls. Microfilmed by the United States National Archives Service, Washington, D.C. Checklist number : M 92, Rolls 1–20. Cited as *DD-USNA*, 92 : 1–20. Pages of manuscript are not numbered.

 The present study relies mainly on these papers. The twenty microfilmed rolls contain several hundred handwritten official dispatches with thousands of enclosures in various languages either handwritten or printed. The Chinese versions of many important official and private letters before 1848 are included ; documents in Chinese continue to appear in rolls bearing later dates, though only occasionally. These enclosures cover various subjects in addition to diplomatic relations.

They consist of copies of notes exchanged by ministers of foreign states and American diplomatic representatives, correspondence between American ministers and consular officials, correspondence with private individuals, and pamphlets, issues of newspapers, and other printed materials.

United States Department of State, Diplomatic Instructions (from the State Department to United States diplomatic representatives in China), April 24, 1843—August 23, 1867, in one microfilm roll. Microfilmed by the United States National Archives Service, Washington, D.C. Checklist number M 77, Roll 38. Cited as *DI-USNA, 77 : 38*. This roll contains handwritten instructions issued by various Secretaries of State to the United States diplomatic representatives in China.

Ward, F. T., Papers. Essex Institute, Salem, Mass. Ward was a leading China merchant from Salem. He was in Shanghai during the last years of the Taiping Rebellion. The Essex Institute has also preserved papers of other Salem merchants in the China trade of that period that are worth further exploration.

Printed Government Documents

American State Papers. 38 vols. Washington : Gales and Seaton, 1832–61.

Great Britain, Parliament. *British and Foreign State Papers* (1842–60). London : James Ridgway and Sons, 1842–1860. For specific subjects before 1861 consult indexes printed in Vols. XX, XLIII, and LXIV.

———. *Hansard's Parliamentary Debates* (1830–91). 3rd Series, Vols. XXI–CCCLVI. London : By I. C. Hansard and other printers. In this series the index for each session of the House of Commons is in the last volume for the session.

———. *Parliamentary Papers* (1842–60). (For specific subjects consult *General Indexes* and *Annual Indexes*.)

Clyde, Paul Hibbert (ed.). *United States Policy toward China : Diplomatic and Public Documents, 1838–1839*. Durham, N.C. : Duke University Press, 1940. A source book of poor selections.

Congressional Globe. From 21 Cong., 1 sess., 1834 to 42 Cong., 3rd. sess., 1874. 46 vols. Containing sketches of the debates and proceedings of the United States Congress.

Consular Returns of British Trade with China for the Year 1846 (also 1847 and 1848). Hong Kong : Printed and published at the office of the *China Mail*, 1847 (also 1848 and 1849). Some figures of American trade with China are also included.

Malloy, William M. (ed.). *Treaties, Conventions, International Acts, Protocols and Agreements between the United States of America and other Powers, 1776–1909.* (*Senate Document,* No. 357, 61 Cong., 2 sess.). 2 vols. Washington, D.C.: Government Printing Office, 1910.

Regulations for the Consular Courts of the United States of America in China: Together with the Act of Congress, of August 11th, 1848, and Forms for Blanks in Consular Courts. Canton: Printed by S. Wells Williams, 1849.

Richardson, James Daniel (comp.). *A Compilation of the Messages and Papers of the Presidents.* 20 vols. New York: Bureau of National Literature, 1917.

Statute at Large of the United States, 1789–1873. 17 vols. Boston: Little and Brown, 1845–73.

Swisher, Earl. *China's Management of the American Barbarians, A Study of Sino-American Relations, 1841–1861, with Documents.* New Haven, Conn.: Yale University, Far Eastern Publications, 1951.

Treaties, Conventions, Etc., between China and Foreign States. 3 vols. Shanghai: Published at the Statistical Department of the Inspector General of Customs, 1908.

United States Congressional Documents with special references: (For other specific subjects consult: Hasse, *Index to United States Documents Relating to Foreign Affairs 1828–1861.*)

    Sen. Doc., No. 139, 29 Cong., 1 sess., 1–47. Containing Thomas Kearny's correspondence.

    Sen. Exec. Doc., No. 72, 31 Cong., 1 sess. Containing John W. Davis' correspondence on consular courts in China.

    House Exec. Doc., No. 123, 33 Cong., 1 sess. Cited as *Humphrey Marshall Correspondence.*

    Sen. Exec. Doc., No. 22, 35 Cong., 2 sess. Cited as *Robert McLane Correspondence* (pp. 1–495) and *Peter Parker Correspondence* (pp. 495–1424).

    Sen. Exec. Doc., No. 30, 36 Cong., 1 sess. Cited as *William B. Reed Correspondence* (pp. 1–569) and *John E. Ward Correspondence* (pp. 569–624).

Reports or *Letters* to Congress by the Secretaries of State on the commercial relations of the United States with all foreign nations during the years 1856, 1857, 1858, 1859, and 1860, were published as House or Senate Documents as follows:

    House Exec. Doc., No. 47, 34 Cong., 1 sess. (1856)

    Sen. Exec. Doc., No. 107, 34 Cong., 1 sess. (1857)

House Exec. Doc., No. 60, 34 Cong., 1 sess. (1857)

Sen. Exec. Doc., No. 53, 35 Cong., 1 sess. (1858)

House Exec. Doc., No. 4, 36 Cong., 1 sess. (1859)

Senate Exec. Doc., No. 6, 36 Cong., 2 sess. (1860)

United States Department of State. *The United States Consular System: Manual for Consuls and also for Merchants.* . . . Washington, D.C.: Taylor and Maury, 1856.

Other Primary Sources

Abeel, David. *Journal of a Residence in China.* New York : J. Abeel Williamson, 1836.

Alcock, Rutherford. *The Capital of the Tycoon.* 2 vols. New York : Harper and Brothers, 1863.

Buchanan, James. *The Works of James Buchanan.* Collected and edited by John Bassett Moore. 12 vols. Philadelphia : J. B. Lipincott Co., 1909.

Bush, Charles Peck. *Five Years in China.* Philadelphia : Presbyterian Publication Committee, c. 1865.

Calhoun, John Caldwell. *The Works of John C. Calhoun.* 6 vols. New York : D. Appleton and Co., 1854–60.

China Mail. An English newspaper published in Hong Kong, February 20, 1845—June 21, 1849. The biweekly edition was entitled the *Overland China Mail.*

Chinese Repository (monthly). Edited by Elijah Coleman Bridgman. 20 vols. Canton, May, 1832—December, 1851.

Callery, Joseph Marie. *History of the Insurrection in China ; with Notices of the Christianity, Creed and Proclamations of the Insurgents.* New York : Harper and Brothers, 1853. Translated from French.

Cooke, George Wingrove. *China : being " The Times " special correspondence from China in the years 1857–58.* London : G. Routledge and Co., 1858.

Cordier, Henri. *L'Expédition de chine de 1857–58, histoire diplomatique notes et documents.* Paris : Félix Alcan, Éditeur, 1905.

———. *L'Expédition de chine de 1860, histoire diplomatique notes et documents.* Paris : Félix Alcan, Éditeur, 1906.

Davis, John Francis. *China.* 2 vols. London : J. Murray, 1857.

———. *China during the War and Since the Peace.* 2 vols. London : Longman, Brown, Green and Longman, 1852.

Downing, Charles Toogood. *The Stranger in China, or the Fan Qui's Visit to the Celestial Empire in 1836–7.* 2 vols. Philadelphia : Lea and

Blanchard, 1838.

Forbes, John Murray. *Letters and Recollections of John Murray Forbes.*
2 vols. Boston : Houghton, Mifflin and Co., 1899.

Forbes, Robert Bennet. *Personal Reminiscences.* Boston : Little, Brown
and Company, 1882.

Foster, Lovelace Savidge. *Fifty Years in China; an eventful memoir of
Tarleton Perry Crawford, D.D.* Nashville, Tenn.: Bayless-Pullen Co.,
1909.

Graves, Roswell H. *Forty Years in China.* Baltimore, Md.: R. H. Wood-
ward Co., 1895.

Gros, Baron Jean Baptiste Louis. *Négotiations entre la France et la chine
en 1860.* Paris: J. Dumaine, 1864.

Hawks, Francis L. *Narrative of the Expedition of an American Squadron
to the China Seas and Japan, Performed in the Years 1852, 1853, and
1854, under the Command of Commodore M. C. Perry, United States
Navy, by Order of the Government of the United States.* New York :
D. Appleton and Co., 1856.

Huc, Évariste Régis. *Christianity in China, Tartary and Tibet.* 3 vols.
London : Longman, Brown, Green, Longmans, and Robert, 1857–58.

Hunt, Freeman, *Lives of American Merchants.* 2 vols. New York : Derby
and Jackson, 1858.

Hunter, William C. *Bits of China.* London : Kegan Paul, Trench and
Co., 1885.

　　　　The Fan Kwae in Canton before Treaty Days, 1825–1844. 2nd
ed. Shanghai : Kelly, 1911.

Johnston, James D. *China and Japan : Being A Narrative of the Cruise
of the U. S. Steam Frigate Powhatan, in the Years 1857, '58, '59,
and '60.* Philadelphia : Charles Desilver, 1861.

Lin-Le (Augustus F. Lindley). *Ti-ping-tien-kwoh, the History of the Ti-
ping Revolution.* 2 vols. London : Day and Son, 1866.

MacFarlane, Charles. *The Chinese Revolution.* London : G. Routledge
and Co., 1853.

Martin, W. A. P. *A Cycle of Cathay or China, South and North, with
Personal Reminiscences.* New York : Fleming H. Revell Co., 1897.

Meadows, Thomas Taylor. *The Chinese and Their Rebellions.* London :
Smith, Elder and Co., 1856.

Medhurst, Walter Henry. *General Description of Shanghai and Its En-
virons, Extracted from Native Authorities (Chinese Miscellany, IV).*
Shanghai : Mission Press, 1850.

Nye, Gideon. *The Gage of the Two Civilizations : Shall Christendom*

Waver? Being an Inquiry into the Causes of the Rupture of the English and French Treaties of Tientsin; and Comprising a General View of Our Relations with China: with Notices of Japan, Siam, and Cochin China. Macao: Privately printed, 1860.

————. *Rationale of the China Question.* Macao: Printed at the Friend of China office, 1857.

————. *Tea: and the Tea Trade.* New York: G. W. Wood, 1850.

North China Herald (weekly). Shanghai: August, 1850–61.

Oliphant, Laurence. *Narrative of the Earl of Elgin's Mission to China and Japan in the Years 1857, '58, '59.* 2 vols. London: William Blackwood and Sons, 1859.

Polk, James Knox. *The Diary of James K. Polk during His Presidency, 1845–1849,* ed. Milo Milton Quaife. 4 vols. Chicago: A. C. McClurg and Co., 1910.

Scarth, John. *Twelve Years in China: The People, the Rebels, and the Mandarins.* Edinburgh: T. Constable and Co., 1860.

Seward, George Frederick. *The United States Consulates in China, a Letter with Inclosures of the Consul-General in China to the Secretary of State.* Washington, D.C.: Privately printed, 1867.

Shaw, Samuel. *The Journals of Major Samuel Shaw, the First American Consul at Canton.* Boston: Wm. Crosby and H. P. Nichols, 1847.

Slade, John. *Narrative of the Late Proceedings and Events in China.* Canton: Printed at the *Canton Register* Press, 1839. The author was the editor of the *Canton Register.*

Smith, George. *Narrative of an Explorating Visit to Each of the Consular Cities of China and to the Islands of Hong Kong and Chusan in Behalf of the Church Missionary Society in 1844–46.* 2 vols. London: Seeley, Burnside and Seely, 1847.

Spirit of Missions (monthly). Published by the Board of Missions of the Protestant Episcopal Church in New York, 1836–1939. Thereafter the title was changed to *Forth.*

Webster, Daniel. *The Works of Daniel Webster.* 6 vols. Boston: Little, Brown and Company, 1853–57.

Williams, Frederick Wells (ed.). *The Life and Letters of Samuel Wells Williams, LL. D., Missionary, Diplomatic Sinologue.* New York: G. P. Putnam's Sons, 1889.

————. (ed.). "The Journal of S. Wells Williams, LL. D.," *Journal of the North China Branch of the Royal Asiatic Society,* XLII (1911), 3–232.

Williams, Samuel Wells. *The Middle Kingdom.* 2 vols. New York:

Wiley and Putnam, 1848.

. "Narrative of the American Embassy to Peking," *Journal of the North China Branch of the Royal Asiatic Society*, I (1859), 315–49.

Secondary Accounts

Alden, Carroll Storrs. *Lawrence Kearny, Sailor Diplomat*. Princeton, N. J.: Princeton University Press, 1936.

Angell, J. B. "The Diplomatic Relations between the United States and China," *Journal of Social Science*, XVII (1883), 24–36.

Ashmore, Lida Scott. *The South China Mission of the American Baptist Foreign Mission Society*. Shanghai: Methodist Publishing House, 1920.

Bain, Chester A. "Commodore Matthew Perry, Humphrey Marshall, and the Taiping Rebellion," *Far Eastern Quarterly*, X (May, 1951), No. 3, 258–70.

Barrows, Edward M. *The Great Commodore, the Exploits of Matthew Calbraith Perry*. New York: The Bobbs-Merrill Co., 1935.

Bass, Harold J. "The Policy of the American State Department toward Missionaries in the Far East," *Washington State College Research Studies*, V (1937), 179–90.

Brine, Lindesay. *The Taeping Rebellion in China: a Narrative of its Rise and Progress*. London: J. Murray, 1862.

Callahan, James Morton. *American Relations in the Pacific and Far East 1784–1900*. (Johns Hopkins University Studies in Historical and Political Science, Ser. 19, Nos. 1–3.) Baltimore, Md.: The Johns Hopkins Press, 1901.

Cannon, James. *History of Southern Methodist Missions*. Nashville, Tenn.: Cokesbury Press, 1926.

The China Mission Hand-book. Shanghai: American Presbyterian Mission Press, 1896.

Ch'iu, A. K'aiming. "Chinese Historical Documents of the Ch'ing Dynasty, 1644–1911," *Pacific Historical Review*, I (1932), 324–36.

Chu, Shih-chia. "Chinese Documents in the United States National Archives," *Far Eastern Quarterly*, IX (1950), 377–83.

Clark, Arthur H. *The Clipper Ship Era 1843–1869; an epitome of famous American and British clipper ships, their owners, builders, commanders, and crews, 1843–1869*. New York: G. P. Putnam's Sons, 1910.

Costin, William Conrad. *Great Britain and China 1833–1860*. Oxford: The Clarendon Press, 1937.

Cranston, Earl. "Shanghai in the Taiping Period," *Pacific Historical Review*, V (1936), 146–60.

Cunynghame, Arthur. *The Opium War.* Philadelphia : G. B. Zieber and Co., 1845.

Danton, George Henry. *Cultural Contacts of China and the United States.* New York : Columbia University Press, 1931.

Dennett, Tyler. *Americans in Eastern Asia.* New York : The Macmillan Co., 1922.

. " How Old is American Policy in the Far East," *Pacific Review,* II (1921), 463–74.

Dulles, Foster Rhea. *China and America.* Princeton, N. J.: Princeton University Press, 1946.

. *The Old China Trade.* New York : Houghton Mifflin Co., 1930.

Eames, James Bromley. *The English in China.* London : Sir Isaac Pitman and Sons, 1909.

Eitel, Earnest John. *Europe in China ; the History of Hongkong from the Beginning to the Year 1882.* London : Luzac and Co., 1895.

Fairbank, John King. " The Creation of the Foreign Inspectorate of Customs at Shanghai," *Chinese Social and Political Science Review,* XIX (January, 1936), No. 4, 469–514 ; XX (April, 1936), No. 1, 42–100.

. " The Legalization of the Opium Trade before the Treaties of 1858," *Chinese Social and Political Science Review,* XVII (July, 1933), No. 2, 215–63.

. " The Manchu Appeasement Policy of 1843," *Journal of American Oriental Society,* LIX (December, 1939), No. 4, 469–84.

. " The Manchu-Chinese Dyarchy in the 1840's and 50's," *Far Eastern Quarterly,* XII (May, 1953), No. 3, 265–78.

. " The Provisional System at Shanghai in 1853–54 ; Foreign Consular Administration of the Chinese Customs," *Chinese Social and Political Science Review,* XVIII (January, 1935), No. 4, 455–504 ; XIX (April, 1935), No. 1, 65–124.

. *Trade and Diplomacy on the China Coast, the Opening of the Treaty Ports, 1842–1854.* 2 vols. Cambridge, Mass.: Harvard University Press, 1953.

Foster, John Watson. *American Diplomacy in the Orient.* New York : Houghton, Mifflin and Co., 1903.

Fuess, Claude Moore. *The Life of Caleb Cushing.* 2 vols. New York : Harcourt, Brace and Co., 1923.

Greenberg, Michael. *British Trade and the Opening of China 1800–1842.* London : Cambridge University Press, 1951.

Griffin, Eldon. *Clippers and Consuls : American Consular and Commercial*

Relations with Eastern Asia, 1845–1860. Ann Arbor, Mich.: Edwards Brothers, 1938.

Griggs, David Thurston. *Americans in China—Some Chinese Views.* Washington, D.C.: Foundation for Foreign Affairs, 1948.

Griswold, A. Whitney. *The Far Eastern Policy of the United States.* New York: Harcourt, Brace and Company, c. 1938.

Grosse-Aschhoff, Angelus Francis J. *The Negotiations between Ch'i-ying and Lagrene, 1844–46.* St Bonaventure, N.Y.: Franciscan Institute, 1950.

Hinckley, Frank Erastus. *American Consular Jurisdiction in the Orient.* Washington, D.C.: W.H. Lowdermilk and Co., 1906.

Homans, J. (Isaac) Smith (ed.). *A Cyclopedia of Commerce and Commercial Navigation.* New York: Harper and Brothers, Publishers, 1858.

Homans J. (Isaac) Smith, Jr. *An Historical and Statistical Account of the Foreign Commerce of the United States.* New York: G. P. Putnam and Co., 1857.

Hsieh, Pao Chao. *The Government of China (1644–1911).* Baltimore, Md.: The Johns Hopkins Press, 1925.

Huang Yen-yu. "Viceroy Yeh Ming-ch'en and the Canton Episode (1856–61)," *Harvard Journal of Asiatic Studies,* VI (1941–42), 37–127.

Hughes, Ernest Richard. *The Invasion of China by the Western World.* London: A. and C. Black, 1937.

Johnson, Willis Fletcher. *American Foreign Relations.* 2 vols. New York: The Century Co., 1916.

Jones, Chester Lloyd. *The Consular Service of the United States, Its History and Activities.* Philadelphia: The John C. Winston Co., 1906.

Journal of the North China Branch of the Royal Asiatic Society. Published annually in Shanghai; vols. 1–2, 1858–60.

Journal of the Royal Asiatic Society. Published annually in London; vols. I–XX, 1843–63.

Kearny, Thomas. "Commodore Lawrence Kearny and the Open Door and Most Favored Nation Policy in China in 1842 to 1843," *New Jersey Historical Society Proceedings,* L (1932), 162–90.

"The Tsiang Documents; Elipoo, Ke-ying, Pottinger and Kearny and the Most Favored Nation and Open Door Policy in China in 1842–1844: An American Viewpoint," *The Chinese Social and Political Science Review,* XVI (April, 1932), No. 1, 75–104.

Kuo, Ping-chia. *A Critical Study of the First Anglo-Chinese War, with*

Documents. Shanghai : The Commercial Press, 1935.

. " Caleb Cushing and the Treaty of Wanghia, 1844," *Journal of Modern History*, V (March, 1933), No. 1, 34–54.

Lanning, George and Samuel Couling. *The History of Shanghai.* Shanghai: Kelly and Walsh, 1921.

Latane, John Holladay. *A History of American Foreign Policy.* New York : The Odyssey Press, 1940.

Latourette, Kenneth Scott. *A History of Christian Missions in China.* New York : The Macmillan Co., 1932.

. " The History of Early Relations between the United States and China, 1784–1844," *Transactions of the Connecticut Academy of Arts and Science*, XXII (1917), 1–209.

Littell, John B. " Missionaries and Politics in China— the Taiping Rebellion," *Political Science Quarterly*, XLIII (December, 1928), 566–99.

McCordock, Robert Stanley. British Far Eastern Policy. Unpublished Ph. D. Dissertation, Columbia University, 1931.

MacGillivray, D. (ed.). *A Century of Protestant Missions in China.* Shanghai : The American Presbyterian Mission Press, 1907.

Maxwell, Herbert. *The Life and Letters of George William Frederick, Fourth Earl of Clarendon.* 2 vols. London : Edward Arnold, 1913.

Mayers, William Frederick. *The Chinese Government.* Shanghai : Kelly and Walsh, c. 1877.

Morse, Hosea Ballou. *The Chronicles of the East India Company, Trading to China, 1635–1834.* 5 vols. Oxford : Clarendon Press, 1929.

. *Far Eastern International Relations.* Boston : Houghton Mifflin Co., c. 1931.

. *The Gilds of China, with an account of the gild merchant or Cohong of Canton.* London : Longmans, 1932.

. *The International Relations of the Chinese Empire.* 3 vols. New York : Longmans, Green and Co., 1910–18.

. *The Trade and Administration of the Chinese Empire.* 3rd ed. New York : Longmans, Green and Co., 1920.

Morison, Samuel Eliot. *The Maritime History of Massachusetts 1783–1860.* Boston : Houghton Mifflin Co., 1941.

Niles' National Register, September, 1837—September, 1849. A weekly magazine, first published in 1811 by Hezekiah Niles in Baltimore, continued by his son, William Ogden Niles, 1837–48, in Washington, D. C., and later by George Beatty, again at Baltimore, until September, 1849.

Nolde, John J. The " Canton City Question," 1842–1849 : A Preliminary

Investigation into Chinese Anti-Foreignism and its Effect upon China's Diplomatic Relations with the West. Unpublished Ph. D. dissertation, Cornell University, 1950.

Owen, David Edward. *British Opium Policy in China and India.* New Haven, Conn.: Yale University Press, 1934.

Pan, Stephen C. Y. "The First Treaty Between the United States and China," *Chinese Social and Political Science Review,* XXI (1937), 155–89.

Paullin, Charles Oscar. *Diplomatic Negotiations of American Naval Officers 1778–1883.* Baltimore, Md.: The Johns Hopkins Press, 1912.

Pitkin, Timothy. *A Statistical View of the Commerce of the United States of America.* New Haven, Conn.: Durrie and Peck, 1835.

Pritchard, Earl H. "The Origins of the Most-Favored-Nation and the Open Door Policies in China," *Far Eastern Quarterly,* I (February, 1942), No. 2, 161–72.

Reid, John Morrison. *Missions and Missionary Societies of the Methodist Episcopal Church.* 2 vols. New York: Phillips and Hunt, 1879.

Rockhill, William Woodville. "Diplomatic Missions to the Court of China; the Kotow Question," *American Historical Review,* II (1897), 427–42, 627–43.

Rowat, R. B. *The Diplomatic Relations of Great Britain and the United States.* London: Longmans, Green and Co., 1925.

Scorth, John. *Twelve Years in China, the People, the Rebels, and the Mandarins.* London: Thomas Constable and Co., 1860.

Sheppard, Eli T. *American Consular Service,* in *The University Chronicle,* IV, No. 6, of the University of California. Berkeley: University of California, 1901.

Stelle, Charles C. Americans and the China Opium Trade in the Nineteenth Century. Unpublished Ph. D. dissertation, University of Chicago, 1938.

Stevens, George Barker. *The Life, Letters and Journals of the Rev. and Hon. Peter Parker, M. D.* Boston: Congregational Sunday-School and Publishing Society, c. 1896.

Stuart, Graham H. *American Diplomatic and Consular Practices.* New York: Appleton Century Co., 1936.

———. *The Department of State: A History of its Organization, Procedure, and Personnel.* New York: The Macmillan Co., 1949.

Swisher, Earl. "The Character of American Trade with China, 1844–1860," *University of Colorado Studies,* Ser. C (Studies in the Social Sciences), I, No. 2 (1941), 165–80.

Tai, En-sai. *Treaty Ports in China (a Study in Diplomacy)*. New York: University Printing Office, Columbia University, 1918.

Taylor, Charles E. *The Story of Yates the Missionary*. Nashville, Tenn.: Sunday School Board, Southern Baptist Convention, 1898.

Tsiang, T. F. " China after the Victory of Taku, June 25, 1859," *American Historical Review*, XXXV (1929), 79–84.

    . " Difficulties of Reconstruction after the Treaty of Nanking," *Chinese Social and Political Science Review*, XVI (1932), 317–27.

    . " The Extension of Equal Commercial Privileges to other Nations than the British after the Treaty of Nanking," *Chinese Social and Political Science Review*, XV (October, 1931), 422–44.

    . " New Light on Chinese Diplomacy—1836–1849," *Journal of Modern History*, III (December, 1931), No. 4, 578–91.

    . " The Secret Plan of 1858," *Chinese Social and Political Science Review*, XV (1931), 292–99.

Vinacke, Harold Monk. *A History of the Far East in Modern Times*. New York: F. S. Crofts and Co., 1937.

Williamson, G. R. *Memoir of the Rev. David Abeel, D. P., Late Missionary to China*. New York: R. Carter, 1845.

Wright, Stanley F. *China's Struggle for Tariff Autonomy, 1843–1938*. Shanghai: Kelly and Walsh, 1938.

    . *Hart and the Chinese Customs*. Belfast: Wm. Mullan and Son, 1950.

    . *The Origin and Development of the Chinese Customs Service, 1843–1911*. Shanghai: Privately printed, 1939.

Wu, Chao-kwang. *The International Aspect of the Missionary Movement in China*. (Johns Hopkins University Studies in Historical and Political Science, N.S. No. 11.) Baltimore, Md.: The Johns Hopkins Press, 1930.

CHINESE SOURCE MATERIALS

Primary Accounts

Chang Hsi 張禧. *Fu i jih-chi* 撫夷日記 (A Diary on the Appeasement of Barbarians). Peiping: Wen-hua-k'o, 1935.

Chang Hsing-lang 張星烺 (ed.). *Chung-hsi chiao-t'ung shih-liao* 中西交通史料 (Historical Sources for Sino-Western Communications). 6 vols. Peking: Fu-jen University, 1928.

Chang-ku ts'ung-pien 掌故叢編 (Collected Historical Documents). Published monthly by the Department of Historical Records. 10 vols. Peiping: Palace Museum, 1928–30.

Ch'i Chün-tsao 祁寯藻. *Ch'i kuan-chai hsing nien tzu chi* 祁觀齋行年自記 (An Autobiographic Sketch of Ch'i Chün-tsao). 2 fasc. of 55 pp. N. p., n. d.

Ch'i-hsüan ho-shang tiao-sou 七絃河上釣叟. *Ying-chi-li Kuang-tung ju ch'eng shih-mo-chi* 英吉利廣東入城始末記 (The Story of the English Entry into Canton from Beginning to End). *Ts'ung shu chi ch'eng*, No. 3999. Ch'ang-sha: Commercial Press, 1939.

Chiang T'ing-fu 蔣廷黻 (T. F. Tsiang, comp.). *Chin-tai Chung-kuo wai-chiao shih tzu-liao chi yao* 近代中國外交史資料輯要 (A Source Book of Important Documents in Modern Chinese Diplomatic History). 2 vols. Shanghai: Commerical Press, 1931–34.

Ch'in ting Ta-Ch'ing hui-tien 欽定大清會典 (Collected Statutes of the Great Ch'ing Empire, compiled by Imperial Order). 100 *chüan* in 10 fasc. 2nd printing. Shanghai: Commercial Press, 1909.

Ch'in ting Ta-Ch'ing hui-tien shih li 欽定大清會典事例 (Cases and

308

Precedents of the Collected Statutes of the Great Ch'ing Empire, compiled by Imperial Order). 1220 *chüan*. Shanghai: Commercial Press, 1908.

Ch'ing-tai ch'ou pan i wu shih mo 清代籌辦夷務始末 (The Beginning and End of the Management of Barbarian Affairs under the Ch'ing Dynasty). Photolithograph of the original compilation. 80 *chüan* for the later Tao-kuang period, 1836–50 (cited as *IWSM-TK*), presented to the throne in 1856; 80 *chüan* for the Hsien-feng period, 1851–61 (cited as *IWSM-HF*), presented to the throne in 1867. Peiping: Palace Museum, 1930.

Huang En-t'ung 黃恩彤. *Chih chih t'ang chi* 知止堂集 (Collected Works of Huang En-t'ung). 13 *chüan*. N. p., privately printed, 1871.

———. "Fu yuan chi lioh" 撫遠紀略 (A Brief Record of Pacifying the Men from Afar), *Ya-p'ien chan-cheng* 雅片戰爭 (The Opium War), V, 409–36. Shanghai: Shen-chou-kuo-kuang she, 1954.

"Juan-ch'en szu-i" 軟塵私議 (Private Discussions on the Soft Dust). *Ya-p'ien chan-cheng*, V, 529–44. This article seems to have been written in 1842 or 1843 by an unknown author in Peking.

Liang T'ing-nan 梁廷枏. *I fen chi wen* 夷氛記聞 (Record of the Barbarian Miasma). 5 *chüan*. Preface written in 1874. Shanghai: P'ei-p'ing yen-chiu yüan, 1937.

Liang T'ing-nan (ed.). *Yüeh hai-kuan chih* 粵海關志 (Gazetteer of the Maritime Customs of Kwangtung). 30 *chüan*. Fasc. 1, 7, 8 (*ch.* 1–4, 21–25, 26–30) reprinted in *Kuo-hsüeh wen-k'u* 國學文庫, Nos. 18, 21, and 33. Peiping, 1935.

Shih ch'ao sheng hsün 十朝聖訓 (Sacred Instructions of Ten Reigns [1616–1874]). 922 *chüan* in 286 fasc. Last preface 1880.

Shih-liao hsün-k'an 史料旬刊 (Historical Materials, published three times a month). 40 vols. Peiping: Palace Museum, 1930–31.

Ta-Ch'ing li ch'ao shih-lu 大清歷朝實錄 (The Veritable Records of the Successive Reigns of the Ch'ing Dynasty). Photolithographic edition by the Manchoukuo Kuo Wu Yüan 滿洲國國務院 (Council of State Affairs of the Government of "Manchoukuo"). 4485 *chüan* in 1220 fasc. 1937. Records of the Tao-kuang period cited as *Shih-lu: TK;* those of the Hsien-feng period as *Shih-lu: HF*.

Tso Shun-sheng 左舜生 (comp.). *Chung-kuo chin pai nien shih tzu-liao* 中國近百年史資料 (Material for Chinese History of the Last Hundred Years). 2 vols. Shanghai: Chung-hua shu-chü, 1928.

Wang Hsien-ch'ien 王先謙 and P'an Kung-shou 潘恭壽 (comp.). Tung-hua-lu 東華錄 (Official Records of the Tung-hua Gate). 525 *chüan* in 196 fasc. Ch'ang-sha, 1884–90.

Wang Hsien-ch'ien 王先謙 (comp.). *Tung-hua hsü-lu* 東華續錄 (Continuation of the Records of the Tung-hua Gate). 252 fasc. Editor's preface, 1884.

Wang Yen-hsi 王延熙 (ed.). *Huang-ch'ao Tao Hsien T'ung Kuang tsou-i* 皇朝道咸同光奏議 (Memorials Submitted during the Four Reigns: Tao-kuang, Hsien-feng, T'ung-chih, and Kuang-hsü [1821–1908]). 64 fasc. Shanghai: Chiu-ching-chai, 1902.

Wen-hsien ts'ung pien 文獻叢編 (A Collection of Historical Records). 43 fasc. Published monthly as a continuation of *Chang-ku ts'ung pien* by the Department of Historical Records, Palace Museum, Peiping, March 1930—July 1937.

Yüeh tung sheng li hsin tsuan 粵東省例新纂 (A New Compilation of Provincial Regulations and Precedents of Eastern Kwangtung). 8 fasc. Canton, 1846.

Secondary Accounts

Chang Chung-fu 張忠紱. *Mei-kuo chan-ch'ien ti yüan-tung wai-chiao* 美國戰前的遠東外交 (The Far Eastern Policy of the United States before the War). Chungking: Tu-li Publishing House, 1944.

———. "Tzu ya-p'ien chan-cheng chih Ying-Fa lien-chün ch'i-chung Ch'ing-t'ing pan-li wai-chiao chih chi-kuan yü shou-hsü" 自雅片戰爭至英法聯軍期中清廷辦理外交之機関與手續 (The Organs and Procedures of the Ch'ing Court for Handling Foreign Relations in the Period from the Opium War to the Anglo-French Joint Expedition), *Wai-ch'iao yüeh-pao* II, No. 5 (May 15, 1933), 43–51.

Chang Hsieh 張燮. *Tung hsi yang k'ao* 東西洋考 (A Study of the Nations in the Eastern and Western Oceans). Completed in 1617 in 12 *chüan*. Shanghai: Commercial Press, 1937.

Chang Te-ch'ang 張德昌. "Ch'ing-tai ya-p'ien chan-cheng-ch'ien chih Chung-Hsi yen-hai t'ung-shang" 清代雅片戰爭前之中西沿海通商 (Sino-Western Coastal Trade in the Ch'ing Period before the Opium War), *Ch'ing-hua hsüeh-pao*, X, No. 1 (January 1935), 97–145.

Ch'en Kung-lu 陳恭祿. *Chung-kuo chin-tai shih* 中國近代史 (Modern History of China). Shanghai: Commercial Press, 1935.

———. "Ssu kuo T'ien-chin t'iao-yüeh chih ching-kuo" 四國天津條約之經過 (The Making of the Tientsin Treaties of the Four Powers, 1854–60), *Chin-ling hsüeh-pao* 金陵學報 (Nanking Journal),

I, No. 2 (1931), 407.

Ch'en Shun-nien 陳舜年. " Chung-Mei ch'a-yeh mao-i chien-shih " 中美茶葉貿易簡史 (A Brief History of the Sino-American Tea Trade), *Ch'a-yeh yen-chiu* 茶業研究, I (1944), 129–36.

Ch'en T'i-ch'iang 陳體強. *Chung-kuo wai-chiao hsing-cheng* 中國外交行政 (Administration of China's Foreign Relations). *Kuo-li hsi-nan lien-ho ta-hsüeh hsing-cheng yen-chiu-shih ts'ung-k'an* 國立西南聯合大學行政研究室叢刊 (National Southwest Associated University Administrative Unit Series). Chungking: Commercial Press, 1943.

Chien Yu-wen 簡又文. *T'ai-p'ing chün kuang-hsi shou-i shih* 太平軍廣西首義史 (A History of the Taiping Revolution). Chungking: Commercial Press, 1944.

Chin Chao-feng 金兆豐. *Ch'ing shih ta-kang* 清史大綱 (Outline of Ch'ing History). Shanghai: K'ai-ming Book Co., 1928.

Ch'in-ko chu-jen 琴閣主人 (pseudonym of Hua T'ing-chieh 華廷傑). *Ch'u fan shih-mo chi* 觸藩始末記 (A Complete Account of the Foreign Invasion of Canton). 3 *chüan* in one book.

Ch'in Pen-li 欽本立. *Mei-ti ching-chi ch'in Hua shih* 美帝經濟侵華史 (A History of the Economic Oppression of China by the American Imperialists). Shanghai: Shih chieh chih shih Publishing Co., 1950.

Ch'ing ch'ao wen-hsien t'ung-k'ao 清朝文獻通考 (Encyclopedia of the Ch'ing Dynasty). Completed 1786. Reprinted in 7 vols., including 4 vols. of *hsü-pien* (second series). Shanghai: Commercial Press, 1936.

Ch'ing chün-chi-ch'u tang-an mu-lu 清軍機處檔案目錄 (Checklist of the Palace Museum of the Documents of the Grand Council of the Ch'ing Dynasty). Peking: Palace Museum, 1927.

Ch'ing shih kao 清史稿 (Draft History of the Ch'ing Dynasty). 536 *chüan*. Peking: Ch'ing-shih-kuan, 1928.

Ch'ing shih lieh-chuan 清史列傳 (Biographical Series of the History of the Ch'ing Dynasty). 80 fasc. Shanghai: Chung Hua Book Co., 1928.

Ch'ing yen fa chih 清鹽法志 (Gazetteer of the Ch'ing Salt Administration). 300 *chüan* in 65 fasc. Peking: Yen-fa shu, 1920.

Chu Chieh-ch'in 朱傑勤. " Ou-chou shih-chieh lai Hua k'ao " 歐洲使節來華考 (A Critical Study of the First European Diplomatic Missions to the Court of China), *Shih-hsüeh chuan-k'an* 史學專刊, I, No. 1 (December 1, 1935), 259–96.

Ch'ü Ta-chün 屈大鈞. *Kuang-tung hsin yü* 廣東新語 (New Folklore from Canton). 28 *chüan* in 12 fasc. N. p., 1700.

Fan Tuan-ang 范端昂. *Yüeh chung chien-wen* 粵中見聞 (Seen and Heard in Kwangtung). 30 *chüan* in 6 fasc. N. p., 1801.

Feng Ch'eng-chün 馮承鈞. *Chung-kuo Nan-yang chiao-t'ung shih* 中國南洋交通史 (History of Communication between China and the Southern Ocean). Shanghai: Commercial Press, 1937.

Fu-chien t'ung-chih 福建通志 (Encyclopedia of Fukien Province). 100 fasc. Foochow, 1938.

[Chang] Han-fu [章] 漢夫. *Chung-kuo yü Mei-kuo* 中國與美國 (China and the United States). Shanghai: Ying-ching Publishing House, 1937.

Hou Hou-p'ei 侯厚培. " Wu-k'ou t'ung-shang i-ch'ien wo-kuo kuo-chi mao-i chuang-k'uang " 五口通商以前我國國際貿易狀況 (China's Foreign Trade before the Opening of the Five Trading Ports), *Ch'ing-hua hsüeh-pao*, IV, No. 1 (1927), 1217–64.

Hsi Ti-ch'en 席滌塵. " Hsiao-tao-hui yü T'ai-p'ing t'ien-kuo shih-ch'i ti Shang-hai wai-chiao " 小刀會與太平天國時期的上海外交 (The Small Sword Society and Foreign Relations at Shanghai in the Taiping Period), *Shang-hai shih t'ung-chih-kuan ch'i-k'an* 上海市通志館期刊 (Bulletin of Gazetteer Office of the City of Shanghai), I (1933), 123–46.

Hsia Hsieh 夏燮 (pseud. Chiang-shang-chieh-sou 江上蹇叟, literally " the lame old man on the river "). *Chung-hsi chi-shih* 中西紀事 (A Record of Sino-Western Affairs). 24 *chüan* in 8 fasc. N. p., first preface 1851; second preface to revised edition 1859; last preface 1865; extra title page bears date October 1868.

——. *Yüeh fen chi-shih* 粵氛紀事 (A Record of the Canton Affairs). 6 fasc. N. p., 1869.

Hsia-men chih 廈門志. (Gazetteer of Amoy). 4 fasc. Published in 1839.

Hsia Nai 夏鼐. " Ya-p'ien chan-cheng chung ti T'ien-chin t'an-p'an " 雅片戰爭中的天津談判 (The Tientsin Negotiations during the Opium War), *Wai-chiao yüeh-pao* 外交月報, IV, No. 4 (April 15, 1934), 43–56; IV, No. 5 (May 15, 1934), 95–123.

Hsiao I-shan 蕭一山. *Ch'ing-tai t'ung-shih* 清代通史 (General History of the Ch'ing Period). 3 vols. Vols. I and II, Shanghai: Commercial Press, 1928. Vol. III in two parts, Peiping: Pei-p'ing wen-chih hsüeh-yüan, n. d.

——. " T'ien-ti-hui ch'i-yüan k'ao " 天地會起源攷 (The Origin of the " Heaven and Earth Society "), *Chung-shan wen-hua chiao-yü-kuan chi-k'an* 中山文化教育館季刊, II (Fall, 1935), No. 3, 777–88.

Hsü Chi-yü 徐繼畬. *Ying-huan chih lüeh* 瀛寰志略 (A Brief Description of the Oceans Roundabout). 10 *chüan* in 6 fasc. N. p., 1848.

Hsüeh Fu-ch'eng 薛福成 *Yung-an ch'üan-chi* 庸盦全集 (Collected Works of Hsüeh Fu-ch'eng). 12 vols. N. p., 1897.

   "Shu Han-yang Yeh hsiang Kuang-chou chih pien" 書漢陽葉相廣州之變 (Some Notes on the Canton Crisis That Occurred under Grand Secretary Yeh of Han-yang), *Chung-kuo chin-tai shih tzu-liao hsüan-chi* 中國近代史資料選輯 (Select Source Materials for History of Modern China), pp. 66–75. Peking: San-lien shu-tien, 1953. This article is also included in the author's Collected Works.

Huang Hsü-yüan 黃序鵷. *Hai-kuan t'ung-chih* 海關通志 (Maritime Customs Gazetteer). 2 vols. Peking: Republic Printing Co., 1917.

Huang Ta-shou 黃大受. *Chung-kuo chin-tai shih* 中國近代史 (A History of Modern China). 3 vols. Taipei: Ta-chung kuo t'u-shu kung-ssu, 1953.

Hsü Wei-nan 徐蔚南. "Shang-hai Hsiao-tao-hui luan-shih ti shih-mo" 上海小刀會亂事的始末 (Account of the Small Sword Society Insurrection at Shanghai), *I-ching* 逸經, XXVI (March 20, 1937), 28–31.

Jung Meng-yüan 榮孟源 (ed.). *Chung-kuo chin-tai shih-li piao* 中國近代史曆表 (A Guide to the Use of Chinese and Western Calendars in Modern Times). Peking: San-lien shu-tien, 1953.

Kuang-chou fu chih 廣州府志 (Gazetteer of Kuang-chou Prefecture). 163 *chüan* in 60 fasc. Canton, 1879.

Kuang-tung t'ung-chih 廣東通志 (General Gazetteer of Kuang-tung). First printing of 334 fasc. in 1823. Reprinted in 5 vols. Shanghai: Commercial Press, 1934.

Kuo Ping-chia 郭斌佳. "Hsien-feng ch'ao Chung-kuo wai-chiao kai-kuan" 咸豐朝中國外交概觀 (Survey of China's Foreign Relations during the Reign of Hsien-feng), *Kuo-li Wu-han ta-hsüeh she-hui k'o-hsüeh chi-k'an*, V (1935), 81–126.

Kuo T'ing-i 郭廷以. *Chin-tai Chung-kuo shih* 近代中國史 (Modern History of China). Hong Kong: Commercial Press, 1940.

Li Huan 李桓 (ed.). *Kuo-ch'ao ch'i hsien lei-cheng* 國朝耆獻類徵 (Eminent Persons of the Reigning Dynasty). 732 *chüan* in 300 fasc. Hunan: Hsiang-yin, 1890.

Li Kuei 李圭. *Ya-p'ien shih-lüeh* 雅片事略 (A Brief Account of the Opium Question). 2 *chüan* reprinted from a Kuang-hsü edition.

Peking National Library, 1913.

Liang Chia-pin 梁嘉彬. *Kuang-tung shih-san hang k'ao* 廣東十三行考 (A Study of the Thirteen Hongs at Canton). Shanghai: Commercial Press, 1937.

Liu Ta-nien 劉大年. *Mei-kuo ch'in-Hua chien shih* 美國侵華簡史 (A Short History of the American Invasion of China). Shanghai: Hsin Hua Bookstore, 1950.

Liu Yen 劉彥. *Chung-kuo chin-shih wai-chiao shih* 中國近時外交史 (History of China's Foreign Relations in Modern Times). Shanghai: Commercial Press, 1922.

          Pei ch'in-hai chih Chung-kuo 被侵害之中國 (Oppressed China). Shanghai: T'ai-p'ing-yang Bookstore, 1932.

          Ti-kuo chu-i ya-p'o Chung-kuo shih 帝國主義壓迫中國史 (A History of Imperialist Oppression of China). Shanghai: T'ai-p'ing-yang Bookstore, 1927.

Lo Erh-kang 羅爾綱. *T'ai-p'ing t'ien-kuo shih-kao* 太平天國史稿 (Draft History of the Heavenly Kingdom of Great Peace). 2 vols. Shanghai: Chung-hua shu-chü, 1955.

Lo Yü-tung 羅玉東. *Chung-kuo li-chin-shih* 中國釐金史 (History of Likin in China). Shanghai: Commercial Press, 1936.

Lu Ch'in-ch'ih 陸欽墀. "Ying-Fa lien-chün chan-chü Kuang-chou shih-mo" 英法聯軍佔據廣州始末 (A Complete Account of the Anglo-French Occupation of Canton), *Shih-hsüeh nien-pao*, 史學年報, II, No. 5 (1938), 265–304.

Meng Sen 孟森. "Ch'ing Hsien-feng shih-nien yang ping ju-ching chi chih i-p'ien" 清咸豐十年洋兵入京記之一篇 (Account of the Entry of Foreign Troops into Peking in 1860 during the Ch'ing Period), *Shih-hsüeh chi-k'an* 史學季刊, I, No. 2 (1936), 179–93.

Miao Ch'üan-sun 繆荃孫 (ed.). *Hsü pei-chuan-chi* 續碑傳集 (Continuation of Biographies from Stone Tablets). 86 *chüan* in 24 fasc. N. p., 1908.

Nan-hai-hsien chih 南海縣志 (Gazetteer of Nan-hai District). 26 *chüan* in 15 fasc. N. p., 1910.

P'an-yü-hsien chih 番禺縣志 (Gazetteer of P'an-yü District, second series). 44 *chüan* in 16 fasc. N. p., 1911.

Pei-p'ing t'u shu kuan 北平圖書館 (Library of Peiping). *Ch'ing tai wen chi p'ien mu fen lei so yin* 清代文集篇目分類索引 (Index of Classified Private Works of Ch'ing Authors). Peiping: Library of Peiping, 1935.

Shang-hai t'ung-chih kuan ch'i-k'an 上海通志館期刊 (Transactions

of the Institute of Municipal History of Shanghai). 2 vols. Shanghai: Shang-hai t'ung-chih kuan, 1933–34.

Shang-hai t'ung-she 上海通社. *Shang-hai yen-chiu tzu-liao* 上海研究資料 (Compiled Source Materials for the Study of Shanghai). 2 vols. Shanghai: Chung-hua shu-chü, 1936–37.

Shao Yu-lien 邵友濂. *Yang-wu ching-chi t'ung-k'ao* 洋務經濟通考 (A General Study of Economics and Foreign Affairs). 16 *chüan*. Shanghai: Pao-hung-chai, 1898.

Shih Chao-ying 時昭瀛, "I-pa-ssu-ssu nien Chung-Mei Chung-Fa t'iao-yüeh" 一八四四年中美中法條約 (The Sino-American and Sino-French Treaties of 1844), *She-hui k'o-hsüeh chi-k'an*, IV, No. 2 (December, 1933), 291–308.

T'ai-p'ing t'ien-kuo 太平天國 (Works of Various Authors on the Taiping Rebellion). Chung-kuo shih-hsüeh-hui 中國史學會 (Chinese History Association publication). 13 vols. Shanghai: Shen-chou kuo-kuang she, 1953.

T'ang Ch'ing-tseng 唐慶增. *Chung-Mei wai-chiao shih* 中美外交史 (History of Sino-American Relations). Shanghai: Commercial Press, 1928.

Tao-feng Christian Journal 道風月刊. A monthly magazine published in New York, October, 1953—April, 1954.

T'ien-hsia ti-i-shang-hsin-jen 天下第一傷心人. *P'i-hsieh chih-shih* 辟邪紀實 (Abolition of Heresy with Evidence). N. p., 1861.

Toyama Gunji 外山軍治. "Shanghai dōdai Go Kenshō" 上海道臺吳健彰 (The Shanghai Taotai Wu Chien-chang), *Gakkai*, I, No. 7 (December 10, 1944), 45–54.

Tseng Yu-hao 曾友豪. *Chung-kuo wai-chiao shih* 中國外交史 (Chinese Diplomatic History). Shanghai: Commercial Press, 1926.

Tu Lien-che 杜連喆 and Fang Chao-ying 房兆楹. *San-shih-san chung Ch'ing-tai chuan-chi tsung ho yin te* 三十三種清代傳記綜合引得 (Index of Thirty-three Collections of Ch'ing Dynasty Biographies). Peiping: Harvard-Yenching Institute Sinological Index Series 9, 1932.

Tu Ping-p'o 杜冰坡. *Chung-kuo tsui-chin pa-shih-nien lai ti ko-ming yü wai-chiao* 中國最近八十年來的革命與外交 (Chinese Revolution and Diplomacy of the Last Eighty Years). 2 vols. Shanghai: Shen-chou kuo-kuang she, 1933.

T'ung-chih Shang-hai hsien chih 同治上海縣志 (Shanghai Gazetteer of the T'ung-chih Period). 32 *chüan* in 16 fasc. Published in 1871.

Wang Chih-ch'un 王之春. *Kuo-ch'ao jou-yüan chi* 國朝柔遠記 (Record of the Ruling Dynasty's Graciousness to Strangers). 20 *chüan*.

Hupeh : Hu-pei shu-chü, 1895.

Wang I-t'ang 王揖唐. *Shang-hai tsu-chieh wen-t'i* 上海租界問題 (The Problem of the Shanghai Leased Territory). 3 *p'ien* in 1 fasc. N. p. (dates in text to 1913).

Wei Hsü-chih 魏胥之. *Ying-kuo tsai Chung-kuo ti ching-chi ch'in-lüeh shih* 英國在中國的經濟侵略史 (Historical Survey of England's Economic Aggression in China). Peking : Hsin-min Publishing Co., 1945.

Wei Yüan 魏源. *Hai-kuo t'u-chih* 海國圖志 (An Illustrated Gazetteer of the Maritime Countries). N. p., 50 *chüan*, 1844 ; 60 *chüan*, 1847 ; 100 *chüan*, 1852 ; reprint, 1876.

———. *Sheng-wu chi* 聖武記 (A Record of Imperial Military Exploits). N. p., preface to first edition, 1842.

———. "Tao-kuang yang-sou cheng-fu chi" 道光洋艘征撫記 (Record of the Pacification of the Foreign Ships in the Tao-kuang Period), *Chung-kuo chin-tai shih tzu-liao hsüan chi* 中國近代史資料選輯, pp. 3–33. Also included in *Sheng-wu chi.*

Wu Chao-hsin 吳兆莘. *Chung-kuo shui-chih shih* 中國稅制史 (History of the Chinese Taxation System). 2 vols. Shanghai : Commercial Press, 1937.

Wu Chün-ju 吳君如. *Chin-shih Chung-kuo wai-chiao-shih* 近世中國外交史 (A Diplomatic History of Modern China). Shanghai : Shen-chou kuo-kuang she, 1932.

Ya-p'ien chan-cheng 雅片戰爭 (Works of Various Authors on the Opium War). Chung-kuo Shih-hsüeh-hui 中國史學會 (Chinese History Association publication). 6 vols. Shanghai : Shen-chou kuo-kuang she, 1953.

Yang Ping-nan 楊炳南 (ed.). *Hai lu* 海錄 (Record of the Sea, as told by Hsieh Ch'ing-kao 謝清高, 1765–1821). N. p., privately printed, c. 1800.

Yang Te-sen 楊德森 (ed.). *Chung-kuo hai-kuan chih-tu yen-ko* 中國海関制度沿革 (A History of China's Tariff System). Peking : Commercial Press, 1925.

Yao Pao-yu 姚寶猷. "Chi-tu-chiao shih shu ju hsi-yang wen-hua k'ao" 基督敎士輸入西洋文化考 (A Study of the Introduction of Western Culture into China by Christian Missionaries), *Shih hsüeh chuan-k'an,* I, No. 2 (February 1, 1936), 1–66.

Yeh Meng-chu 葉夢珠 (comp.). *Shang-hai chang-ku ts'ung-shu* 上海掌故叢書 (A Compilation of the Tales of Shanghai, containing fourteen different titles by various authors). 10 fasc. Shanghai :

Shang-hai t'ung-she, 1935.

Yin Kuang-jen 印 光 任 and Chang Ju-lin 張 汝 霖. *Ao-men chi-lüeh*
澳 門 紀 略 (A Brief Gazetteer of Macao). *2 chüan* in 2 fasc. N. p.,
1760.

Yü En-te 于 恩 德. *Chung-kuo chin-yen fa-ling pien-ch'ien shih* 中 國 禁
煙 法 令 變 遷 史 (History of the Changes in Chinese Anti-Opium
Laws). Shanghai : Chung-hua Bookstore, 1934.

INDEX

Abbot, Joel, 173
Abeel, David, 25n, 61, 61n, 71, 74, 75
Adams, John Quincy, 9, 10, 20, 23, 29
Alcock, Rutherford, 123, 138, 138n, 139, 140, 150, 154, 156, 157
American Board of Commissioners for Foreign Missions, 7, 24, 24n, 71, 75, 77, 123n
American missionaries. *See* Missionaries, American
American Revolutionary War, 11
American Sinologists, 27
Amoy: and Sino-American trade, 3, 68, 69, 106n; U.S. consular establishment in, 33, 58n, 60, 61, 61n; local government of, 42; and opium trade, 61, 61n; and Christian missionaries, 74, 75, 76; during Taiping Rebellion, 122; and Robert M. McLane, 162; and Peter Parker, 179. *See also* Five Ports
Amur River, 130n, 216n, 273n
An-ch'a-shih-ssu. See nieh-t'ai
Anglo-French alliance (1856-60): negotiations for, 194-95; U.S. position toward, 196-201, 208-9, 283; armed intervention policy of, 202; 1857 hostilities against China, 214, 217; atrocities in Canton committed by, 217n; and four power expedition to Pei-ho, 217-18; 1858 war preparations of, 224-25; 1858 attack on Tientsin, 227; 1859 Battle of Ta-ku, 261-65; and Peter Parker, 285
Anglo-French Chinese War (1858-60): origins of, 4; and W. A. P. Martin, 76; effect on Chinese diplomacy, 113, 236n; resulting in Russian expansion in Far East, 131n, 281-82; and John E. Ward, 256; and 1859 Battle of Ta-ku, 265; renewal in 1860, 280-82. *See also* Second Anglo-Chinese War

Appleton, William, 200
Armstrong, James, 177, 179, 186, 186n, 187, 188n, 197, 204, 205, 206n
Arrow Incident: and Peter Parker, 37, 194; origins of, 184, 185; U.S. reactions to, 185-89, 196; and Anglo-French alliance in China, 193; and Emperor Hsien-feng, 283
Arrow War. *See* Arrow Incident
Asia, 30, 130n
Assam, 87
Atchison, William, 261
Aulick, J. H., 118, 120n

Balfour, George, 59, 152, 155
Banner Garrisons, 40n, 42
Baptist Church, American, 72; Missionary Union, 24n, 77; Board of Foreign Missions, 75
Barrier Forts, 186, 199, 201
Batavia, 72
Bengal opium, 250
Benton, Thomas H., 29, 30
Biddle, James: trip to China, 10-11; and British occupation of Chusan, 12; as acting commissioner to China, 13, 17; and Wanghia Treaty, 13, 87; and extraterritoriality, 13, 16, 103; departure from China, 16, 16n; and Open Door policy, 36, 284; and U.S. consular establishments in China, 60, 61, 62, 63n; and American missionaries, 73; and Peter Parker, 74
Biddle, Nicholas, 11
Bogue, The, 11, 87
Bogue, Supplementary Treaty of the, 45, 50, 87
Bombay, 130, 254
Bonham, George, 95, 96, 123, 124, 125, 127, 138, 147, 178